To Carmela

Desmond Clarke was born in the parish of St. Ann, Jamaica, on March 1953. He immigrated to England to join his mother and stepfather in October 1967. After leaving school, without any academic qualifications, he worked at a number of odd jobs before joining the British army in March 1971. After leaving the army, he worked as a lorry driver for many years. In 1991, he experienced a very difficult period of his life, including the death of his mother. Since 1992, he has embarked on a number of part-time undergraduate and postgraduate studies, gaining both B.A. and M.A. degrees.

Enjoy 17/07/2021

D.B. Clarke

This book is dedicated to the memory of my dearly departed mother, Iris May Campbell (née Tulloch), and to my beloved son, Benjamin Robert Clarke.

Desmond Clarke

STOLEN INHERITANCE

AUSTIN MACAULEY PUBLISHERS™

LONDON • CAMBRIDGE • NEW YORK • SHARJAH

Ordering Information:
Quantity sales: special discounts are available on quantity purchases by corporations, associations, and others. For details, contact the publisher at the address below.

Publisher's Cataloging-in-Publication data
Clarke, Desmond
Stolen Inheritance

ISBN 9781641827676 (Paperback)
ISBN 9781641827683 (Hardback)
ISBN 9781645364726 (ePub e-book)

Library of Congress Control Number: 2019913429

The main category of the book — HISTORY / Ancient / Egypt

www.austinmacauley.com/us

First Published (2019)
Austin Macauley Publishers LLC
40 Wall Street, 28th Floor
New York, NY 10005
USA

mail-usa@austinmacauley.com
+1 (646) 5125767

A special thanks to my life partner, Sam Bishop, whose love and support has been invaluable, and my precious son, Benjamin Clarke, who is the real inspiration for my writing this book.

I must acknowledge my heavy reliance on the works of many eminent scholars, especially Martin Bernal, Norman Davies, Cheikh Anta Diop, Charles Freeman, George Granville Monah James, Eric Williams, and Chancellor James Williams.

Preface

My perspective of history is that it is the inquiry or study of the past by the living. As such, the questions and research one does reflect more on one's interest and experience. This is true of all historical research, especially in terms of social class, ethnicity, gender, or political perspective. As a black youth, who was born in the parish of Saint Ann, Jamaica, in 1953, I grew up in the post-Windrush era, partly in Jamaica and partly in England. I arrived in England in the autumn of 1967, ill-prepared for the prevailing social and environmental conditions that confronted me. Coming from a rural village of less than four hundred people to a town of some eighty thousand inhabitants, it was indeed a "culture shock." As I later learnt from a government-sponsored Plowden Report of that year, in relation to immigrant children, which stated:

"They [immigrant children] have often been abruptly uprooted, sometimes from rural village community and introduced, maybe after a bewildering air flight, into crowded substandard housing in an industrial borough." (Plowden Report, 1967: 69)

Arriving in England, I was met by my mother and stepfather at Gatwick Airport, some thirty miles south of Central London and driven to a town, some fifty miles north of Central London, called Bedford. This rural town was famous as the home of John Bunyan, author of the *Pilgrim's Progress* and of the London Brick Company, a brick making company that attracted many immigrant workers from the New Commonwealth. Two months after arriving in Bedford, I experienced the trauma of eviction by an unscrupulous landlord. During our search, we came across a number of signs boldly stating: "Rooms to let; no dogs, no Irish or Blacks need apply." That was my first real experience of racism or what was commonly known as "Color Bar!" I was three months away from my fifteenth birthday and for the first time in my short life, I realized that life was not going to be what I had hoped, prior to arriving in England. This made me angry at first, but as time passed, I became fatalistic and wanted to become a "Rude Boy," which was what youth gangs were called at the time in Jamaica.

As I was of school age when I arrived in England, I attended a comprehensive school that was mainly attended by children from the New Commonwealth. I was placed in a classroom with some thirty children of Caribbean, Pakistani, Indian, and Italian backgrounds to learn English. Black youths were not expected to achieve much, in terms of education, so I experienced a very limited curriculum, mainly of basic English, woodwork, metalwork, and sports. After less than a year in school, I left without sitting a single exam. As my mother was a regular Pentecostal churchgoer, I also had to attend church on a regular basis, while attending school. Indeed, most of my mother's generation were ardent churchgoers and over the years, they laid a prosperous Pentecostal Church industry in the black community. The Pentecostal Church was a response to the rejection that was faced by Caribbean people from the English mainstream churches, so even churches practiced the "Color Bar" system. Throughout my school days, I became very involved in the local Pentecostal Church, including being baptized at the age of 16. However, it became clear to me that the church did not have any solution to many of the problems faced by first-generation black youths, especially social, economic, and political challenges. As I had no formal qualification, my job prospect was limited. As a result, a number of menial and low-paid jobs followed, including car cleaning, stocking shelves in a national store, and working in a metalwork factory. The Pentecostal Church movement became dominated by certain charismatic preachers, many of whom were more interested in private gains than in community development. In fact, in the face of mounting discrimination in education, housing, employment, and the criminal justice system, the Pentecostal Church maintained a deafening silence. In these circumstances, just before my eighteenth birthday, I decided to join the British army in the spring of 1971.

I naively thought that the British army offered better prospects but, sadly, this was not the case. In fact, racism in the British army was even more intense, as there was no getting away from it; it was now twenty-four hours of every day. As a black youth in the British army, I was posted to Germany where I had no understanding of the German language or culture, so interaction with the inhabitants was very limited. From Germany, I was posted to Northern Ireland, where there was, to all intent and purpose, a civil war. As a black British soldier in Northern Ireland, there was not much chance of anonymity and, once again, interaction with the inhabitants was strictly restricted. When on patrol, I was often exposed to racial abuse, especially from the Catholic community as, apart from the color of my skin, I was in their enemy's uniform. While in the military, my commanding officer refused to sanction my promotion, as it seemed for him that black soldiers were not suitable material for promotion. In fact, one black lance corporal was posted to his command and was soon stripped of his rank, so that there were no black soldiers under his command above the rank of private. These and other experiences induced a sense of frustration which undermined my ability to motivate myself to achieve promotion, or anything else. It became clear that wherever there was an encounter with white people, racism was never far away. Hence, this constant exposure to social, political, and economic racism became very damaging to my ambitions and my psychological well-being. Alienated from any cultural support, one response was to increase my alcohol intake. I have no doubt that my experience, as a youth in late 1960s and 1970s Britain, was not unique, except that many of my black peer group did not see the British army as a way forward.

By 1974, I had had enough of the British army and took my discharge, as I was no longer prepared to put my life on the line for those who showed me nothing but racial abuse. On my discharge from the British army, I worked for a haulage firm, as I had gained a Heavy Goods Vehicle (HGV) license while being a serving soldier. At the age of 21, I was an angry young man, without a purpose or aim in life, as I had learnt that ambition could be a dangerous thing for a black youth. I soon left one job after another, including five years working in a car factory and various other haulage firms. I also engaged in numerous disastrous relationships which increased my alienation and feeling of failure. In 1991, I was experiencing another failed relationship, when in the summer of that year, my mother died, which was to have an enormous impact on my life. Growing up, my mother had been the greatest influence on my life and would forever be a part of my life, as I am often reminded of her teachings. At the time of my mother's death, I was aimlessly wasting my life away but decided to engage in a few college courses. I achieved a few minor academic successes and decided to pursue further learning and in 1994, I began a three-year university undergraduate course. In 1997, I graduated from university with a 2:1 honors degree, in Community Organization Management, from the then Luton University, now Bedfordshire University. Not content thus far, I further engaged in a part-time university master's degree studies in 1998 and graduated in 2004.

Through these studies, I gained some knowledge and insights about the role of racism, politics, economics, and power. I also learnt the difference between education and domestication. Throughout these studies, my greatest discovery was finding out about people like myself and our role in history. Through this knowledge, I felt confident in my own ability to achieve whatever goals I set for myself and the knowledge that I do not need the affirmation of others to justify my existence. I strongly believe that I have a duty to share what I have learnt with others, especially Africans and those of the African diaspora, who are faced with everyday social, economic, and political exclusion and oppression.

Hence, the aim of this book is to explore how the social, political, and economic contribution of Africans to world development, over the past three to four thousand years, have been appropriated by Asians, including Arabs and Caucasians. My intended audience is the youths of today and the generations to come, especially those who are willing to share the responsibility and rewards of a just and improved co-existence. It is not my desire to induce fear, anger, or hate, which are self-destructive, but to improve our knowledge of our human story and to explore alternative ways of being.

Of course, it is widely agreed that all humans have their roots in Africa but it is equally acknowledged that there are those who have more recent roots in Asia and Europe. There is also an acknowledgment that people from these continents have interbred for millenniums and over time have become various ethnicities, such as Hebrews, Arabs, Moors, Phoenicians, etc., which has re-enforced my belief that there is only one human race, from which various clans, tribes, states, kingdoms, and empires have evolved. As the identifiers "Black" and "White" have been part of racist literature for centuries, it is often difficult to avoid these labels but, where it is possible to do so, I will employ the terms "African," "Asian," or "European/Caucasian" where a distinction is being drawn between "Black," "Brown," or "White." In the era of colonial slavery, the terms "Mulatto" or "half-caste" have been used to signify the progenies of Africans and Asians/Caucasians. Over recent times, numerous labels and statuses have been ascribed to the progenies of mixed parentage. For example, in the United states, whites known to have any amount of "Negro blood" – one-eighth – are classified as Negroes, while in Africa, North Africa in particular, they do the opposite. This scheme was rigorously applied in the history of Egypt, where even mixed black pharaohs became "white" and the original black population was never referred to as Egyptians at all. Blotting Blacks out of history included replacing African names of persons, places, and things with Greek, Arabic, and Caucasian names. Their periodization of African history is carefully arranged in such a way that the history becomes the history of Jews, Greeks, Romans, Arabs, and Caucasians in Africa and not the history of Africans. Whenever it is necessary, I will use the term "mixed heritage," as I do not wish to re-enforce negative racial stereotypes.

Most aspects of this book have been worked over by many able historians, so the originality of this book lies in the selection, rearrangement, and presentation of its contents. The aim is to link causes and effects and to convey a better understanding of those causes which continue to affect our present and future co-existence. The chronological emphasis lies from early Kemet (Egypt), from around 3000 BCE, to the beginning of the 21st century CE. The expanse of this period is truly vast and no single book, no matter how detailed, can capture its social, political, economic, or religious dynamism. The geographical spread from Africa through the Mediterranean region to Northern Europe and extending to the Americas and the Caribbean, with reference to Asia, will, in some way, illustrate certain themes that will illuminate our shared heritage. At every stage of this book, I will endeavor to counteract the prevailing "Eurocentrism" of our diverse, yet shared, heritage by opening up space for these diverse voices to be heard. Too often, the African people are exposed to a narrative of humanity that excludes their contribution to human civilization. European writers have often cited the contribution of Greeks and Romans as the authors of ancient civilization, either by commission or omission, thereby creating the impression that Africans have contributed nothing. Children of African diaspora are, thus, brought up to believe that Africans are inferior and uncivilized.

It is my intention to direct this book at those who may feel marginalized or to be lacking a sense of identity, whilst avoiding over-sentimentality. Historians increasingly applied the social, economic, and cultural concerns of their own day to the analysis of the past. Hence, in this sense, I am guilty as charged, for my own personal experience has influenced my interest and selection of data, on which my analysis is based. According to Jean-Jacques Rousseau (1712–78), "Man is born free, and everywhere he is shackled" (Davies, 1993: 606). The question then is if man is born free, by whom is he shackled? This question is particularly pertinent to me as one who was born in Jamaica, one of the colonies of the British Empire, and who, since the age of fourteen-and-a-half, has resided in England. As a descendent of enslaved Africans, slavery has played a pivotal role in my recent history but in no way has it been my ancestral history. To demonstrate how slavery has interrupted the history of Africans and particularly those in the African diaspora, it would be necessary to start on the continent of Africa. Starting with the eminence of Egypt, before it came under foreign pillages and conquests, first by Asians, including Persians, Greeks, Romans, Arabs, and later Caucasians. No other people on Earth have had so much stolen from them by so many than the African people and, in spite of such treachery, have given so much to mankind.

Africans are from the land of the blacks and were known as such by all people of the world from time immemorial. In ancient times, "African" and "Ethiopian" were used interchangeably because both meant the same thing: a black person. This was before Caucasians began re-ordering the Earth to suit themselves and found it necessary to state their birthright over the land of black people. Hence, in attempting to delete, disguise, or belittle the role of black people in world history, Asians and Caucasian people often reveal the opposite of what was intended. All of Africa is the native homeland of black people and Asiatic peoples who occupy Northern and Eastern Africa are no more native Africans than are Caucasians who populate the Americas. That African people were among the very earliest builders of a great civilization on this planet and how such advanced civilization was lost is one of the greatest and most tragic in the history of mankind. That Africa was the cradle of a religious civilization, based on the conception of one Supreme God, Creator of the Universe, which antedated that of the Jews by several thousand years before Abraham. Moses was born, Joseph lived, and some of the early years of Christ were spent in Africa. It seems, therefore, that Egypt (Northern Ethiopia) and the Sudan (Southern Ethiopia) are ideal places to start to find out the truth of how the great civilization, built by African people, was stolen, concealed, or destroyed. Much of what I will cover has already been explored and trampled over by many eminent scholars. Nonetheless, where I hope to distinguish myself from those before me is the conclusion that I will generally draw from those body of facts.

Williams (1974) highlights a problem with Western scholars who are committed to white supremacy, when he states that they simply ignored and refused to publish any facts about African history that upset or even tend to upset their racial philosophy that rests so solidly on premises sanctified by time that they no longer need to be openly proclaimed. This rests on the phenomenal success in the industrial world, at once, supports and justifies their philosophy, the supremacy of the fittest. Williams went on to say that black people have a thirst for the truth, the whole truth and nothing but the truth, especially as to how Africans lost their rightful place as leaders of the civilized world. How and when did Africans become self-hating and, in contrast, become admirers of their Asian, European, and Arab conquerors and enslavers? For Williams, the black historian, if he is to serve his generation, must not hesitate to declare what he thinks the results of his studies mean. For even when our history shows us where we have been weak, it is also showing us how, through our own efforts, we can become strong again (Williams, 1974: 23).

The relentless searchlights of history were turned on the roles played by the use of both Christianity and Islam in the subjugation of Africans. In their search for racial identity, many people of African descent, especially in the diaspora, are dropping their white Western slave masters' names and adopting – not African – but their Arab and Berber slave masters' names. First came the Crescent flag of the Prophet, which was a three-pronged proselytizing mission claiming one brotherhood, widespread intermarriages, and concubinage with African women based on the Muslim system of polygamy, and forceful conversions at sword's point. The Cross of Jesus Christ followed the Muslim Crescent. The cloak of Christianity was the most convenient hiding place for those who had other designs. Hence, the drive to convert meant far more than conversion to Christianity. As in the case of Muslims, it meant change from African spiritualism into the white man's image, his ideas, and value system. The real object of worship turned out to be neither Jesus Christ nor his Father, God, but Western man and Western civilization. What happened in the process of converting Africans to Islam and Christianity was the supreme triumph of the Caucasian world over the African world. Millions of Africans became non-Africans and Africans who were neither Muslim nor Christians but were classed as "pagan" Africans, in their own right, became non-person members of a race of nobodies.

Ever since, Africans and those in the African diaspora bore the names of their enslavers and oppressors – the ultimate in self-effacement that promotes self-hatred, which makes pride in race difficult. To conceal the Africans' civilization, Asians and their progenies set about destroying everything left by Africans which indicated African superiority. When it was not possible to destroy the evidence, they would claim them as their own. Hence, in history, these great Africans are simply Egyptian but not Kushites, Ethiopians, or Nubians. Indeed, much of the history of Africa has been written by anthropologists, within the theoretical framework of their own ethnology, and others have relied almost entirely on their classification of peoples. The unusual claim that the discipline is a science is made despite the amount of pure guessing that characterizes its conclusions. Racism is obvious in most of the anthropological findings that one may wonder how, if they hope to maintain the fiction of being scientific, it could escape their notice? The main thrust of their findings is to make Africa Caucasian from the beginning of its history and to give Africans a subordinating role. Hence, their great emphasis is on the "Caucasoid" identity of this or that African tribe and failing that in a highly advanced all-African situation where no such classification could be made, to allege Caucasian influence in one way or another. There should be no confusion over "Negroid" or "Caucasoid" types from the earliest times.

In line with their presumption of taking over the continent and reordering its racial composition, the anthropologists and their historian followers have declared that the "time Negroes" are concentrated in West Africa only – the fact that ancient Ethiopia and that of the Kushites were black was simply ignored. The Afro-Asians or Afro-Europeans who were allied with African groups and migrated with them are singled out as the determining elements in whatever the groups achieved. Asiatic Caucasians, who are known to have settled along the northern and eastern coasts of Africa even in prehistoric times, are now being presented as the indigenous inhabitants. For example, George P. Murdock (1959) maintains that black civilization was not, in fact, black civilization. According to Murdock, countless "peoples" thought to be "Negroes" by many, such as the Bushmen, the Masai, Kushites, Pygmies, even Bantu, are of "Caucasoid" origins. The fact that racist writers speak glibly enough about Asian and Western influence on black Africa, but seldom do they write about the influence of black Africa on Asian and Western institutions. However, both Christianity and Islam had to yield to Africanization, and African values did not die, even among the millions of Africans who were enslaved in distant lands. For example, in the United States, Brazil, and the Caribbean, African traditions persisted and influenced not only the Caucasian slave-owning class but also the course of their respective culture and civilization.

Introduction

"History is not everything, but it is a starting point. History is a clock that people use to tell their political and cultural time of day. It is a compass they use to find themselves on the map of human geography. It tells them where they are, but more importantly, what they must be." (J. H. Clarke 1915–1998)

According to John Haywood (2008), since humans first left their evolutionary cradle in Africa (some 100,000 years ago), migrations have been one of the great driving forces of historical change. This has brought about a proliferation of different cultures, as humans entered and adopted, and sometimes, conquered new environments. Separation in time and space led to the development of different languages and genetic drift to the modern (ethnic) racial characteristics. Migrations have often been accompanied by wars and the displacement, or even extermination, of indigenous peoples and cultures, but migration has also strengthened some communities at the expense of others. Hayward has identified four main types of migrations: home-community, colonization, whole-community, and cross-community. Home-community migration is biologically essential for healthy reproduction as it helps maintain a wide gene pool and prevents inbreeding within families. The next form of migration – colonization – occurs when a group of people leave one community to establish a replica of the home-community in another place. The earliest human migrations out of Africa are good examples of colonization of unoccupied territory. In more recent times, successful colonization of territory has occurred where a technologically advanced society has expelled its previous inhabitants, as in the case of the European colonization of the Americas, Australia, and New Zealand. Whole-community involves the displacement of all the members of a community. Hunter-gatherer societies moved camp frequently to exploit seasonally available food sources. Haywood argues that around 70,000 years ago, a group of modern humans left Africa and flourished. Over the next 50,000 years, their descendants would colonize every corner of the world, except for Antarctica, the high Arctic, and some oceanic islands. As generation succeeded generation, the area of the world colonized by humans gradually increased.

As early as 3200 BCE, according to Freeman (1996), Egyptian traders had made contact across the desert with Mesopotamia, the area between the river Tigris and Euphrates, crossing into the area stretching from Turkey, eastwards across the

16

Caspian Sea, and southwards from modern Iran and Iraq. In the southwest, it included modern Syria, Palestine, Jordan, and Lebanon. In the period between 3500–500 BCE, there were major centers of civilization in these areas. To explain the settlement and civilization of Egypt, specialists invoke four hypotheses corresponding to the four points of the compass. The most natural – a local origin – is the one most often challenged, which could be localized in two different places: Upper or Lower Egypt. In the case of the Lower Egypt, it would be a question of what is now called the "preponderance of the Delta." But there is no evidence to support the view that the pioneers of civilization came from abroad. It is Upper Egypt, from the Paleolithic (early phase of the Stone Age) to the present, that material evidence has been found to attest the successive stages of civilization. The Badarian culture provides the earliest direct evidence of agriculture in Upper Egypt, during the Pre-Dynastic Era, which flourished between 4400 and 4000 BCE. This Pre-Dynastic Era is traditionally equivalent to the Neolithic period of the Naqada (3200–3000 BCE) and was characterized by an ongoing process of political unification, culminating in the formation of a single state. Furthermore, it was during this time that the Egyptian language was first recorded in hieroglyphs. According to Diop (1974), from the *Book of the Dead*, whose doctrine is earlier than any written history of Egypt, *Texts of the Pyramids*, temples and obelisks, its abundance of columns at Luxor and Karnak, its avenues of Sphinxes, the colossi of Memnon, its rock carvings, its underground temples with proto-Doric columns (Deir-el-Bahari) at Thebes, are architectural realities still palpable today – historical evidence that no dogma can blow into thin air.

The *Royal Annals* lists the mythical pre-dynastic kings of Egypt, followed by the pharaohs of the first five dynasties. It records information on taxation, religious ceremonies, levels of the Nile, building works, and trade and military expeditions during this early period of Egyptian history, making it the world's oldest history book. One of the largest fragments is housed in the Palermo Archaeological Museum in Sicily. Other fragments can be seen in the Egyptian Museum in Cairo and the Petrie Museum in London. The *Abydos King List* is a list of the names of seventy-six kings of Ancient Egypt, found on a wall of the Temple of Seti I, at Abydos, Egypt. It starts with Menes, founder of the First Dynasty, who is accredited with uniting both Upper and Lower Egypt. The list concludes with Menmaatre Seti I of the Nineteenth Dynasty. The *Royal Papyrus of Turin*, also known as the *Turin Royal Canon*, is an Egyptian hieratic papyrus, thought to date from the reign of Pharaoh Ramesses II (c.1303–11213 BCE, r.1279–1213 BCE), now in the Museo Egizio (Egyptian Museum) in Turin. It is the most extensive list available of kings compiled by the Egyptians and is the basis for most chronology before the reign of Ramesses II. Furthermore, to these authentic documents, we must add the whole body of evidence reported by ancient writers, from Herodotus (484–425 BCE) to Diodorus (died c. 284 BCE), not to mention the *Text of the*

Pyramids, the *Book of the Dead*, and thousands of inscriptions on monuments. The oldest recorded history of human society is to be found on the continent of Africa.

Therefore, it seems to me that a narrative of human society that excludes the people of Africa and the cradle of civilization is at best incomplete and at worse dangerous. The Greek unwittingly applied the second name of the City of Menes (Memphis), "*Aegyptus*" to the whole country. For Memphis was also called Hikuptah, or the "Mansion of Ptah," the god protector of the city. Ptah was known in Egypt as he who existed before all things, he who conceived the world by the thought of his heart and gives life through the magic of his Word. That which Ptah commanded was created. From the Middle Kingdom, onwards, he was one of five major Egyptian gods with Ra, Isis, Osiris, and Amun. Ptah wears many epithets: Ptah the beautiful, Ptah the lord of truth, Ptah the master of justice, Ptah who listens to prayers, Ptah master of ceremonies, and Ptah lord of eternity. From the Greek "*Aegyptus*," Memphis became Egypt and Egypt became the name of the "Two Lands," extending from the Mediterranean Sea to the First Cataract (Cataracts of the Nile are shallow lengths of the Nile River, between Aswan and Khartoum, where the surface of the water is broken by many small boulders and stones jutting out of the river bed, as well as many rocky islets). There was no "Egypt" before the Black Pharaoh, from whose name it was indirectly derived. Before that, the country was called Chem or Chemi – another name indicating its black inhabitants and not the soil, as some have tried to suggest. On several occasions, Herodotus insists on the Negro character of the Egyptians and describes the population of India as having the same tint of skin, which approaches that of the Ethiopians. Diodorus of Sicily writes: "The Ethiopians say that the Egyptians are one of their colonies which was brought into Egypt by Osiris." (Diop, 1974:1)

Authentic tradition, as recorded in the *Texts of the Pyramids* and the *Book of the Dead*, unequivocally informs us that the Egyptian deities belonged to the black race and were born in the south. Furthermore, the myth of Osiris and Isis points out a cultural trait characteristic of Black Africa; the cult of ancestors, the foundation of Negro religious life, and Egyptian religious life. Each dead ancestor becomes the object of a cult and the most remote forebears, whose teachings in the realm of social life have proved effective, gradually become veritable gods. Transformed into gods, they are placed on a plane different from that of the Greek hero, this is what made Herodotus think the Egyptians had no heroes. To assign Egyptian civilization on Asiatic or any foreign origin whatever, it must be possible to demonstrate the prior existence of a cradle of civilization outside of Egypt, but this basic condition has never been met. Apart from some stations of uncertain age in Palestine, no trace of man earlier than 4000 BCE exists in Syria or Mesopotamia. It is in Egypt that we encounter, with mathematical certainty, humanity's most ancient historical date, 4236 BCE.

In contrast, what did Iran (Elam) and Mesopotamia produce prior to the eighth century BCE (the Neo-Assyrian Empire was an Iron Age Mesopotamian empire between 911 and 612 BCE)? Only shapeless clay mounds. In Egypt, the study of history rests largely on such written documents as the *Royal Annals* (Palermo Stone), which is thought to have been created towards the end of the Fifth Dynasty (Old Kingdom), in the twenty-fifth century BCE. The *Pyramid Texts* are a collection of ancient Egyptian religious texts from the time of the Old Kingdom, which were carved on the walls and sarcophagi of the pyramids at Saqqara during the Fifth and Sixth Dynasties of the Old Kingdom. The oldest of the texts have been dated around 2400–2300 BCE. Unlike the later *Coffin Texts* and *Book of the Dead*, the pyramid texts were reserved only for the pharaoh and were not illustrated. The pyramid texts mark the next oldest known mention of Osiris, who would become the most important deity associated with afterlife in Ancient Egyptian religion. The spells, or "utterances," of the pyramid texts are primarily concerned with protecting the pharaoh's remains and helping him ascend to the heavens, which are the emphasis of the afterlife during the Old Kingdom. The *Book of the Dead* is an ancient Egyptian funerary text, used from the beginning of the New Kingdom (c.1550–50 BCE), which consisted of a number of magic spells intended to assist a dead person's journey through the Duat, or underworld, and into the afterlife. It was written by many priests over a period of about a thousand years. The Duat was the region through which the sun god, Ra, traveled from west to east during the night and where he battled Apep – Ancient Egyptian deity who embodied chaos, and was thus, the opponent of light and Ma'at (order/truth). Duat was also the place where people's souls went for judgment after death.

Ethiopian Empire

The land of the blacks was some 12,000,000 square miles, the whole of the second largest continent. The Ethiopian Empire once extended from the Mediterranean north and southward to the source of the Nile in the country (Abyssinia). Even as late as the time of Menes (3,100 BCE), Ethiopia still included three-quarters of Egypt, with the Asian holding the Delta region – hence, "The two Lands." Williams (1974) argues that with both the Saharan transformation and the steady incursion of Asians, blacks were forced back into the interior to face daily struggle for survival. The widespread mixing of Asians and Blacks gave rise to an increased number of Afro-Asians, who viewed themselves as Caucasians or Asians. When these later became known as Egyptians in Egypt, Moors in Morocco, and Mauritanians or Carthaginians in Carthage (Tunisia), great care was taken to distinguish them from Africans in daily intercourse, paintings, and documentary literature. Egypt was the northern region of ancient Ethiopia and had been the object of world attention from the earliest times. This also explains how the Asians came to occupy and control one-quarter of Egypt (Lower Egypt) before the unification of the "Two Lands," in the third millennium BCE. The great agricultural system that was developed along the overflowing Nile was one of the sources of the wealth to support the great cultural advances. The other was gold mines below the First Cataract, which was also the magnet that drew Caucasian peoples from many lands. As these increased in number and variety, the undermining of African civilization was accelerated. The end result was that the Africans were pushed to the bottom of the social, economic, and political ladder, whenever and wherever the Asians and their mixed heritage progenies gained control. Generally, the Asians were very proud of their sons by black women, who remained slaves. As such, they formed a social class that, while never recognized as equal with their Asian fathers, had all the other privileges of free men.

It was the Caucasians, not blacks, who called Africa the "Land of the blacks" until they made it expedient to change this to mean "African countries not yet taken over by Caucasians," and later to the south of the Sahara. In this way, many modern writers are able to blot out, obscure, or reinterpret the earlier writers on Africa that the actual role of blacks in their own land was practically erased from memory. Greek and Arabic names and the accepted "Caucasoid" features in the conventional style of royal portraits all furthered the great deception. There was also the external influence on early African speech and writing in Egypt, as more and more Caucasians moved into Upper Egypt after the unification of the "Two Lands." This mingling of the two peoples not only produced a new breed of Egyptians, but also an increasingly Afro-Asian language and writing system that differed markedly from the original African writing, as it was developed below the First Cataract. Developments in Asia and Europe a few thousand years after the "Golden Age" of black civilization, helped to obscure that civilization or paint it over as an entirely Eurasian achievement. It is worth noting the number of centuries after Thebes's prehistory and Memphis (3100 BCE), that their ancient cities were founded. The Arabs settled in a tiny village called Fostat on the outskirts of the great city of Memphis, pride of the African world, from which now stands the Arab city of Cairo. What great contribution did these roaming nomads make to an already highly developed black civilization? What people in Lower Egypt came from a country with a city as great as Thebes or Memphis? For generations, Memphis was almost entirely an all-African city, with Asian villages slowly growing up around the outskirts.

The Second (2890–2686 BCE) and Third (2686–2613 BCE) Dynasties were also African, although most writers will not flatly state this. They generally designate these dynasties as "Thinite," "Memphite," or "Followers of Seth." One has to know that the First Dynasty (c. 3150–2890 BCE) was African and "Memphite" or "Thinite," so-called after the name of their sacred city Thinis and that the cults of Seth and Amon were African. The Fourth Dynasty (2613–2494 BCE), the chief pyramid builders, was indigenous is equally clear, with the Great

Pyramid being built during the reign of King Knufu (2590–2567 BCE). His nephew, King Khafre, built the second Great Pyramid and the Great Sphinx with his African features boldly and clearly carved into a portrait statue that no one could doubt that this mighty monarch was a "Negro." Having determined that Africans were referred to as "Thinites," "Memphistes," Thebans, Cushites, Libyans, Ethiopians, and Nubians, some of the disguising masks have been removed. But much still remained to be done to restore the role of Africans in world history. The Egyptian language was an African language with later Asiatic influence, similar to that of Arabic on the African language known as Swahili. But, over time, more and more Asian and European conquerors were attracted to the "Bread Basket on the Nile" – Canaanites, Jews, Syrians, Hittites, Persians, Babylonians, Assyrians, Greeks, Romans, Arabs, Turks, and others. Interbreeding between conquerors and conquered continued, which resulted in more and more Egyptians becoming lighter and near white in complexion. But until the Arab Islamic flood which began in the seventh century CE, the vast majority of Egyptians were characterized as "Negroid."

Great Ancient African Kings

The roll call brings forth names that still resound through the corridors of time; Menes, Athothes (who Manetho claimed wrote a treatise on anatomy), and Seth-Peribsen, who ruled during the Second Dynasty (c.2890–c.2686 BCE). Khasekhem (c.2690 BCE) was the last King of the Second Dynasty of Egypt and led several campaigns. He reunited Upper and Lower Egypt after a civil war between the followers of the gods Horus and Set. He was the earliest Egyptian King known to have built statues of himself. Imhotep (c.2650–2600 BCE), meaning "the one who comes in peace," was an Egyptian polymath – a person whose expertise spans a significant number of different subject areas – served under the Third Dynasty King Djoser (the son of King Khasekhem and Queen Nimaathap) as chancellor to the pharaoh and high priest of the sun god Ra at Heliopolis. He is considered to be the earliest known architect, engineer, and physician in history. He was also revered as a poet and philosopher. Zoser, or Djoser, was a pharaoh of the Third Dynasty and his most famous monument was his step pyramid, which entailed the construction of several mastaba, "eternal house" – as the afterlife was a main focus of Egyptian civilization and ruled every aspect of the society. Sneferu (r.c.2613–2589 BCE) was the founder of the Fourth Dynasty, who built a least three pyramids that survived to this day and also introduced major innovations in the design and construction of pyramids. Khufu, originally known as Khnum-Khufu (d.2566 BCE), ruled during the Fourth Dynasty. He is generally accepted as having commissioned the Great Pyramid of Giza, one of the Seven Wonders of the Ancient World.

Khafra (d.2480 BCE), King of the Fourth Dynasty, was the builder of the second largest pyramid of Giza. The view held by the majority of modern Egyptology is that the Great Sphinx was built in approximately 2500 BCE for Khafra. Userkaf (d.2491 BCE) was the founder of the Fifth Dynasty and the first pharaoh to start the tradition of building sun temples at Abusir. He ruled from 2494 to 2487 BCE and constructed the pyramid of Userkaf complex at Saqqara. These pharaohs re-established Ethiopian power and held it without a serious challenge for almost a thousand years. Internal stability was achieved through the process of increased centralization of power at Memphis and the perfection of the bureaucracy of the vast imperial administration. The state became the chief promoter and inspirer of progress on all fronts: agriculture, science, arts, engineering, massive building programs, mining, and shipbuilding. Internal peace and stability provided the opportunity for the outpouring of much hitherto dormant native genius, and religion was the chief motivating source. It was during this time period that stone was first used in building, writing was invented, the great pyramids were built, stone quarrying perfected and expanded, and Imhotep became the world's greatest architect and the "Father of Scientific Medicine." It was seven hundred and fifty years of the most glorious pages in the history of the African world. There was a concentration of some of the greatest leaders in the Fourth Dynasty (c.2613–c.2494 BCE). The Old Kingdom (2686–2134 BCE) – the name given to the period in the third millennium BCE when Egypt attained its first continuous peak of civilization – ended with the Sixth Dynasty (2345–2181 BCE).

Conflicts between the religious cults battling for more and more political power expanded. Rebellions of various chiefdoms, seeking independence from weak rulers at Memphis and decentralization became the order of the day. Asian penetration and expansion in Upper Egypt became normalized. Asian kings were able to hold Lower Egypt again and re-established dynasties under Kheti I (Kheti is a Sanskrit word which means "farming") and his successors. This period is referred to as the First Intermediate (2181–2040 BCE) and further confuses an already confused situation by mixing the Asian rulers of Lower Egypt with the African rulers of Upper Egypt and subsequently listing all the dynasties sequentially, so that it becomes difficult to distinguish the Asian dynasties and kings or pharaohs from the African. So, the eleven kings of Lower Egypt that followed Kheti I appear as "King of Egypt." During the Middle Kingdom (c.2050–c.1800 BCE), also known as the period of "Reunification," and some fifteen hundred years of African-Asian amalgamation (at first largely in Lower Egypt but later in Upper Egypt), and their progenies were called the "New Breed." They had a devotion to Asians and a hatred for Africans, although they were suspended between two worlds and not accepted in either. According to Williams (1974), out of this situation developed a passionate and defiant Egyptian nationalism that restricted the term "Egyptian" to the "New Breed" alone. Thereafter, neither Asians nor Africans were to be called Egyptians.

The New Breed began to treat Asians as strangers and no longer welcomed them *en masse*, even in Lower Egypt. Asians, if unmixed, were now called Asians. Africans, if unmixed, were called Africans or Ethiopians. They alone (the New Breed) were to be called Egyptians and the writers of the world followed this classification, from Homer's (751–651 BCE) time to the present. However, it is interesting to note that unmixed Asians were never called Egyptians, even when they ruled all of Egypt. In the earliest period, "Egyptian" would have meant the Africans. Later, it would have meant Africans and Afro-Asians. The first great southern division of the Ethiopian empire was the kingdom of Wawat, a region that was very rich in gold. Indeed, the south was the real source of Egypt's wealth as it had been of its civilization. The gold mines were there, stone quarries, copper and tin mining and most of the papyrus plants from which Africans had invented paper and boats. There was also ivory and the then only source of highly prized ostrich feathers. In short, Egyptian foreign trade depended almost entirely on Southern Ethiopia. It is worth noting that at various periods in ancient times, the "Land of the Blacks" meant all Ethiopia, all Ethiopia meant all Africa, and all Blacks were Africans or Ethiopians or Thebans.

The Eleventh Dynasty (2134–1991 BCE), starting with Mentuhotep I and end with Nebtawyre Mentuhotep IV (r.1998–1991 BCE), was limited to Upper Egypt, since the Asians had re-established their rule in Lower Egypt during the period of nationwide turmoil and rebellions. There was strong hostility to the Asian invasions in the southern regions and many wanted Lower Egypt conquered and the Asians driven out. The steady movement of Asians from the Delta into Upper Egypt itself was proof enough for Southern Africans that the Asian aim was nothing less than ultimate control of all Ethiopia. The war to bring Nubia under control started near the end of the Eleventh Dynasty, went on for over four hundred years and eventually ended in defeat for the Southern Africans. During the Twelfth Dynasty (1991–1802 BCE), foreign trade expanded (especially with Palestine, Syria, and the land of Punt), there was a "Golden Age" of arts and crafts, land reclamation, and improvement in irrigation. The Thirteenth Dynasty of Ancient Egypt is often combined with the Eleventh, Twelfth, and Fourteenth Dynasties, under the group title of Middle Kingdom. The Thirteenth Dynasty lasted from approximately 1802 until approximately 1649. The Fifteenth, Sixteenth, and Seventeenth Dynasties are often combined under the group title of Second Intermediate Period (c.1802–1650 BCE). The Second Intermediate Period marks a period when Ancient Egypt fell into disarray for a second time and is best known as the period when the Hyksos made their appearance in Egypt and whose reign comprised the Fifteenth Dynasty.

The New Kingdom (1650–1069 BCE) followed the Second Intermediate Period and was succeeded by the Third Intermediate Period (1069–664 BCE) of Ancient Egypt which began with the death of Pharaoh Ramesses XI in 1070 BCE, ending the New Kingdom. The remarkable Eighteenth Dynasty (1550–1292 BCE) had a line of kings and queens who became immortal including Ahmose I (1556–1526 BCE) – meaning "Born of Iah" (Iah means moon) and Nefertari, the wife of Ramesses II. There was also Hatshepsut (1508–1458) the second confirmed female pharaoh, the first being Sobekneferu (d.1802 BCE) whose name means "the beauty of Sobek." Furthermore, Thutmose I (d.1493 BCE), Thutmose III (1481–1425 BCE) who ruled with his stepmother and aunt, Hatshepsut, Amenhotep II (1469–1401 BCE), and Ikhnaton (1391–1336 BCE), the "Great Reformer," is noted for introducing monotheism into Egypt. Lastly, there was Tutankhamun (1341–1325 BCE) which means "Living Image of Amun."

The "Great" Eighteenth Dynasty began under one of the "Great" Queens of Egypt, Nefertari, and her equally great husband Ahmose I. She helped her son, Amenhotep, in the great work of national reconstruction. Sadly, when Tutmose III succeeded Queen Hatshepsut, he set about obliterating her name from all the monuments and temples she had built, destroyed documents bearing her name, smashed all sculptured likenesses, paintings or anything that might indicate that she ever lived. As later Asians and Europeans were to do with all recognized Blacks, in order to take credit for all of the achievements of Black Africans. The New Kingdom (1550–1077) was founded by Vizier Ramesses I (born Paramessu), whom the childless Pharaoh Horemheb chose as his successor to the throne.

The pharaohs of the Nineteenth Dynasty ruled from 1290 to 1189 BCE, which reached its zenith under Seti I (r.1290–1279 BCE) and the Great Ramesses II (r.11279–1213 BCE). Ramesses II campaigned vigorously against the Libyans and Hittites. However, the Nineteenth Dynasty declined as internal fighting between the heirs of Merneptah (r.1213–1203 BCE) for the throne increased. The female Pharaoh Twosret (r.1191–1189 BCE) was the last pharaoh of the Nineteenth Dynasty. The pharaohs of the Twentieth Dynasty ruled for approximately 120 years, from about 1189 to 1064 BCE, starting with Setnakhte (r.1189–1186) and ending with Ramesses XI (r.1107–1077). Pharaoh Setnakhte's son, Ramesses III (r.1186–1155 BCE), ruled at a time when Egypt was threatened by the Sea Peoples but he was able to defeat them. However, as happened under the Nineteenth Dynasty, internal fighting ensued at a time when Egypt was increasingly beset by a series of droughts, below normal flood levels of the Nile, famine, civil unrest, and official corruption. The power of Ramesses XI grew so weak that in the south, the High Priests of Amun at Thebes became the *de facto* rulers of Upper Egypt, while Smendes controlled Lower Egypt, even before the death of Ramesses XI.

Smendes eventually founded the Twenty-first Dynasty at Tanis. The Twenty-first, Twenty-second, Twenty-third, Twenty-fourth, and Twenty-fifth Dynasties of ancient Egypt are often combined under the group title of Third Intermediate Period (1077–664 BCE). This was one of decline and political instability, conquest, and foreign rulers. The pharaohs of the Twenty-First Dynasty (1077–943 BCE) ruled from Tanis, but were mostly active only in Lower Egypt, which they controlled, as the High Priests of Amun at Thebes effectively ruled Middle and Upper Egypt in all but name. Egypt was firmly reunited by the Twenty-Second Dynasty (943–720 BCE), founded by Shoshenq I (r.943–922 BCE) who was descended from Meshwesh-Berber immigrants, originally from Libya. He is referred to in the Hebrew Bible at 1 Kings 11:40, 14:25 and 2 Chronicles 12:2–9. Shoshenq I is generally attributed with the raid on Judah, during the fifth year of King Rehoboam, taking with him most of the treasures of the temple created by Solomon. Shoshenq chose his eldest son, Osorkon I, as his successor and consolidated his authority over Egypt through marriage alliances and appointments. He assigned his second son, Iuput A, the prominent position of High Priest of Amun at Thebes, the title of Governor of Upper Egypt, and commander of the army to consolidate his authority over the Thebaid (Africans). Shoshenq I also designated his third son, Nimlot B, as the "Leader of the Army" at Herakleopolis in Middle Egypt.

The Twenty-Third Dynasty of Ancient Egypt (837–720 BCE) was a separate regime of Meshwesh-Berber Libyan kings, whose rule in ancient Egypt is often considered part of the Third Intermediate Period. There is much debate surrounding this dynasty, which may have been situated at Herakleopolis Magna, Hermopolis magna, and Thebes. There is evidence that they controlled Upper Egypt in parallel with the Twenty-Second Dynasty, shortly before the death of Osorkon II. So now, as the Asians became priests and worshippers of the Supreme God and lesser gods of the Africans in Egypt, the success of erasing every vestige of early African civilization was moving toward the absolute, as they were able to secure control of Thebes, the most powerful stronghold of Africans in Egypt. The Twenty-Fourth Dynasty (732–720 BCE), under Kashta, ruled Nubia from Napata, 400km north of Khartoum, the modern capital of Sudan. Kashta also exercised a strong degree of control over Upper Egypt by installing his daughter, Amenirdis I, as the presumptive God's Wife of Amun in Thebes, in line to succeed the serving Divine Adoratrice of Amun, Shepenupet I. Piye (r.747–722 BCE) established the Twenty-Fifth Dynasty (732–653 BCE) and appointed the defeated rulers as his provincial governors. He was succeeded by his brother, Shabaka, and then by his two sons, Shebitku and Taharqa, respectively. The African victory over the Asians did not lessen the danger from them as new threats came from Asia.

At first, the Assyrian advance seemed to be concerned only with Syria and Palestine, not Egypt. Shabaka, while actively cultivating the friendship of the Assyrian King, Sargon II (r.722–705), was just as active in supporting the armies of the Syrians and Palestinians. In 671 BCE, Esarhaddon (r.681–669) led his

Assyrian forces to victory near the Egyptian border and moved on to capture the city of Memphis. Shabaka's nephew, Taharqa, promptly marched up from the south again and massacred all of the Assyrian garrisons. Esarhaddon died leading a second expedition of vengeance in 669 BCE. His son, Ashurbanipal (685–627 BCE), assumed the leadership invaded Egypt and put Taharqa to flight. Taharqa was succeeded by his nephew, Bakare (Glorious is the Soul of Re). Tanutamun (d.653 BCE) renewed the war against the Assyrians and their Afro-Asian supporters and recaptured Memphis. But in 1661 BCE, the outraged Ashurbanipal returned to Egypt in force, defeated Tanutamun's army in the Delta, and advanced as far south as Thebes, which he sacked. The Assyrians' re-conquest effectively ended Nubian control over Egypt, although Tanutamun's authority was still recognized in Upper Egypt until 656 BCE, when Psamtik I's (r.664–610 BCE) navy peacefully took control of Thebes and effectively re-unified all of Egypt. Psamtik managed to both unite all of Egypt and free her from Assyrian control within the first ten years of his reign and started the Twenty-Sixth Dynasty of Egypt. Africans lost their beloved Memphis, Thebes, and even their Egyptian names now seemed to be final.

The Ancient Egyptian Mystery System

Ancient Egyptian religion was a complex system of polytheistic beliefs and rituals, which were an integral part of ancient Egyptian society. It centered on the Egyptians' interaction with many deities who were believed to be present in, and in control of, the forces and elements of nature. The Egyptians believed in a pantheon of gods, which were involved in all aspects of nature and human society. Amon was a major Egyptian and Berber deity and was attested since the Old Kingdom, together with his spouse, Amaunet. It was believed that the gods' true natures were mysterious, but depictions gave recognizable form to the abstract deities, using symbolic imagery to indicate each god's role in nature. For example, the funerary god Anubis was portrayed as a jackal, a creature whose scavenging habits threatened the preservation of the body. In an effort to counter this threat, the jackal was employed to protect the deceased. At various times, certain gods became preeminent over others, including the sun god Ra, the creator god Amon, the mother goddess Isis, and, for a brief period, the god Aten. Hathor is an Ancient Egyptian goddess who personified the principles of joy, feminine love, and motherhood. She was one of the most important and popular deities throughout the history of Ancient Egypt. In other roles, she was goddess of music, dance, foreign lands, fertility, and also helped women in childbirth and miners.

During the New Kingdom, Akhenaten abolished the official worship of other gods in favor of the sun disk Aten. This is often seen as the first instance of true monotheism in history. Amenhotep IV, the Heretic King Akhenaten, was the Eighteenth Dynasty pharaoh of the fourteenth century BCE, who broke away from his family's and dynasty's worship of Amon and the other gods. He tried to establish a monotheistic religion based on the sun disk Aton. From Aton, he took the new name Akhenaten. He moved from the traditional capital of Thebes to a new one, built at a site now known as El Amarna. Soon after his death, the reform was ended, the worship of Amon was re-established, and the capital returned to Thebes. It is generally and reasonably agreed that members of the royal family of the Eighteenth Dynasty were Nubians. It is equally probable that from their portraits they would seem to have been black. This would suggest that the Jews as a people, or Moses as a man, had learnt their religion from Nubian. By no other religion in the world is Christianity so closely approached as by the faith of Akhenaten.

Formal religious practice centered on the pharaoh, the king of Egypt, who was believed to possess a divine power by virtue of his position. He acted as the intermediary between his people and the gods and was obligated to sustain the gods through rituals and offerings so that they could maintain order in the universe. The state dedicated enormous resources to religious rituals and the construction of temples. Individuals could interact with gods for their own purposes, appealing for their help through prayer or compelling them to act through magic. Another important aspect was the belief in the afterlife and funerary practice, providing tombs, grave goods, and offerings to preserve the bodies and spirits of those who were deceased. Thebes was the holy city of Upper Egypt, from which the Phoenicians took two black women who founded the oracles of Dodona in Greece and Amon in Libya. The ancient name of Thebes was Wase, or Wo'se, and was known to have existed from the Fourth Dynasty (2613 BCE) onward. The earliest monuments that have survived at Thebes date from the Eleventh Dynasty (2081–1939 BCE). Thebes frequently served as the royal capital of Egypt and was called Nowe (City of Amon). During the Twelfth Dynasty (1938–1756 BCE), the royal residence was moved to the area of Memphis, but the kings of Egypt continued to honor Amon, their family god, by building temples at Thebes. The height of Theban prosperity was reached in the fourteenth century BCE, in the reign of Amenhotep III (r. 1390–1353 BCE), much of whose wealth, from foreign tribute, was poured into the temples of Amon. However, for a brief period in the reign of his son, Akhenaten (r.1353–1336 BCE), Thebes was abandoned by the court and the worship of Amon was proscribed. With its restoration by Tutankhamen (r.1333–1323 BCE), Thebes soon regained its revenues and prestige.

Pharaoh was never a formal title for Ancient Egyptian rulers, but its modern use, as a generic name for all Egyptian kings, is based on the usage of the Hebrew Bible. The full title of Egyptian kings consisted of five names, each preceded by one of the following titles: Horus, Two Ladies, Golden Horus, King of Upper and Lower Egypt, and Son of Re (god of the sun and creator god). Egyptians believed their ruler to be the mediator between the gods and the world of men, and after death their rulers became divine. As a divine ruler, the pharaoh was the preserver of the God-given order, called Ma'at, and was responsible for his/her people's economic and spiritual welfare as well as their dispenser of justice. The pharaoh delegated some responsibilities to a chief assistant called a vizier, who was head of the treasury and overseer of all records. From Herodotus of Halicarnassus, Turkey (484–425 BCE) who died at Thurii, Italy, Diodorus of Sicily (c.90–c.30 BCE), and Clement of Alexandria (c.150–c.215 CE) who was a convert to Christianity, we learn that there were six Orders of the Egyptian priests, and each Order had to master a certain number of the books of Hermes.

According to Clement, the procession of the priests started with the Singer Odus, who had to know two books of Hermes. Next came the Horoscopus, who had to know four books of Hermes which deal with Astronomy. The third is the Hierogrammat (a writer of hierograms), with feathers on his head, a book in his hand, and a rectangular case with writing materials, who has to know the hieroglyphics, cosmography, geography, astronomy, the topography of Egypt, the sacred utensils and measures, the temple furniture, and the lands. Next came the Stolistes (purifier of the Temple), carrying the cubit of justice and the libation vessels. He had to know the books of Hermes and deal with the slaughter of animals. The prophets came carrying the vessels of water, followed by those who carry the loaves. The prophets were the residents of the temple and had to know the ten books, which are called hieratic and contain the laws and doctrines concerning the gods (secret theology) and the whole education of the priests. There are forty-two books of Hermes, which contain the whole philosophy of the Egyptians.

In addition to the Hierogrammat and Horoscopus, who were skilled in theology and hieroglyphics, a priest was also a judge and an interpreter of the law. Hence, the Egyptian Mysteries were the center of organized culture and the recognized source of education in the ancient world. Neophytes were graded and had to submit to many years of tests and ordeals, in order that their eligibility for advancement might be determined. Their education included the Seven Liberal Arts and the virtues. Beyond these, the priests entered a course of specialization. According to Herodotus, the Egyptian priests possessed supernatural powers and were experts in magic. They had the power to control the minds of men (hypnosis), the power of predicting the future (prophecy), and the power over nature (i.e., the power of gods) by giving commands in the name of the Divinity and accomplishing great deeds. The curriculum of the Egyptian Mystery System consisted of the Seven Liberal Arts, which formed the foundation training for all Neophytes and included Grammar, Arithmetic, Rhetoric, Dialectic, Geometry, Astronomy, and Music. The Memphite Theology, which is inscribed on a stone (now kept in the British Museum) and contains the theological, cosmological, and philosophical views of the Egyptians, is the basis of all-important doctrines in

Greek philosophy. It is dated to 700 BCE and bears the name of an Egyptian pharaoh who stated that he had copied an inscription of his ancestors.

Ptah is the primate of the gods, the Logos and creative utterance and power, the God of order and form, the Divine Artificer, and Potter. The doctrine of opposites of Memphite Theology, one of the pairs of created gods, Osiris and Isis, was used to represent the male and female principles of nature. In addition to this, Osiris had other qualities attached to him which might be understood from the following derivatives: osh meaning *many* and iri meaning *to do* and *Eye*. Consequently, Osiris came to mean not only many-eyed or omniscient but also omnipotent or all-powerful. It was a habit of the Greeks to Hellenize Egyptian words by transliterating them and adding them to the Greek vocabulary. This practice of borrowing words from nearby nations continued until the New Testament times. For example, in Acts of the Apostles Ch.13: 1, the word Niger (i.e., black man) in the name Simeon the Negro, is a Roman or Latin word (Niger, nigra, nigrum) meaning black. Simeon, of course, was an Egyptian professor attached to the Church of Rome. The atom of science is really the name of the Egyptian Sun God that has come down to modern times and carries identical attributes with the Sun God.

Magic was an important aspect of Ancient Egyptian religious practice. The word "magic" is used to translate the Egyptian term *Heka,* which meant, the ability to make things happen by indirect means. It also means action of Ka or activation of the Ka; the Ka being the ancient Egyptian concept of the vital force. In the Coffin Texts, Heka is created at the beginning of time by the creator Atum. Heka was said to have battled and conquered two serpents and was usually depicted as a man choking two giant entwined serpents. Medicine and doctors were thought to be a form of magic so Heka's priesthood performed these activities. Magical practices were closely intertwined with religion, as even the regular rituals performed in temples were counted as magic. Magic was seen primarily as a way for humans to prevent or overcome negative events. The priesthood and temple libraries contained numerous magical texts. Other professions also commonly employed magic as part of their work, including doctors, scorpion charmers, and makers of magical amulets. Magic frequently involved written or spoken incantations.

The Egyptian Mystery System was the center of organized culture, which had three grades of students: the Mortals, i.e. probationary students who were being instructed, but who had not yet experienced the inner vision, the Intelligences, i.e. those who had attained the inner vision and had received mind or nous, and the Creators or Sons of Light, who had become identified with or united with the Light, i.e. true spiritual consciousness. Walter Marsham Adams (1838–1899) described these grades as the equivalents of Initiation, Illumination, and Perfection. For years, students underwent disciplinary intellectual exercises and bodily asceticism with intervals of tests and ordeals to determine their fitness to proceed to the more serious, solemn, and awful process of actual initiation (G. M. M. James, 1954:33). Students' education consisted of ten virtues, which were made a condition to external happiness, and the seven Liberal Arts, which were intended to liberate the soul. Grammar, rhetoric, and logic were disciplines of moral nature by which the irrational tendencies of a human being were purged away, and he was trained to become a living witness of the Divine Logos. Geometry and Arithmetic were sciences of transcendental space and numerations, the comprehension of which provided the key to the problems of one's being. Astronomy dealt with the knowledge and distribution of latent forces in man and the destiny of individuals and nations. Music, or harmony, meant the living practice of philosophy, i.e., the adjustment of human life into harmony with God, until the personal soul became identified with God, when it would hear and participate in the music of the spheres. Music was used by the Egyptian Priests in the cure of diseases. There was no mediator between man and his salvation, as we find in the Christian theory.

The keepers of the temples of Thebes and elsewhere became a powerful priesthood, thus indirectly reducing the power and influence of chiefs and kings who, in traditional Africa, derived their real powers as the official intermediaries between the gods, sainted ancestors, and the people. Religion, therefore, became the basis of political power in a subtle and much more far-reaching sense. It appears that in almost all societies, religion was recognized as the principal means of social control, economic wealth, and political authority. For who can gainsay one who is in exclusive communication with the almighty? Hence, religion made the people submissive and obedient.

The state's income from religion stemmed from the requirement of sacrificial offerings from the people. The ancient religion that gave birth to science and learning, art, engineering, architecture, the resources for a national economy and political control – that same religion was the mother of history, writing, music, the healing art, the song, and the dance. The ritual of appealing to a power beyond man is called "Magic" by westerners, if they are discussing Africa, but exactly the same belief and practice are called "divine healing" in Christendom. Ancient Greek scholars, through Herodotus, referred to the completion of their education in Ethiopia with pride and, it appears, as a matter of course. The power of the priesthood rose as the kings of Egypt became more preoccupied with secular affairs than their religious role as high priests of the "Most High," the source of the kings' political power.

As custodians of the temples, the priests were promoting and making their own positions more powerful and secure by promoting the divine kingship idea. It meant that each pharaoh would try to outdo his predecessors in building more and more temples, colossal burial structures – the pyramids – for royal saints and the sons and daughters of Amon, Horus, Set, and so on. The priests were in the best strategic position to acquire great economic and political power for themselves quite naturally. They were the first men of learning – scribes, historians, scientists, architects, physicians, artists, mathematicians, astrologers, and chemists. The temples were places through which flowed much of the national revenue, which explains how and why priest became so politically powerful in Egyptian life that even a great king like Akhenaten could not overcome their opposition. During the Old Kingdom (2686–2181 BCE) artists learned to express their culture's worldview by creating, for the first time, images and forms that endured for generations. Architects and masons mastered the techniques necessary to build monumental structures in stone. Sculptors created the earliest portraits of individuals and the first life-size statues in stone. They perfected the art of carving intricate relief decoration and produced detailed images of animals, plants, and landscapes, recording the essential elements of their world for eternity in scenes painted and carved on walls of temples and tombs. They produced elegant jewelry, finely carved and inlaid furniture, and cosmetic vessels and implements made from a wide range of materials.

Goddesses had been important during the Paleolithic (the period extending from the earliest known use of stone tools, probably by Homo habilis 2.1 to 1.5 million years ago), one of the earliest members of the genus Homo and early Neolithic Era (15,200 to c.3,100), were demoted in the world of gods. Deities represented natural forces and phenomena, and the Egyptians supported and appeased them through offerings and rituals so that these forces would continue to function according to Ma'at, or divine order. Ma'at refers to both the ancient Egyptian concepts of truth, balance, order, harmony, law, morality, and justice, and the personification of these concepts as a goddess regulating the stars, seasons, and the actions of both mortals and the deities who set the order of the universe from chaos at the moment of creation. The opposite of Ma'at is Isfet (evil, troublesome, and disharmonious) and it was believed that the physical representation of Isfet was through the god Seth. Early surviving records indicate that Ma'at is the norm for nature and society, in this world and the next. The traditions of the Egyptian pantheon, goddesses were paired with their masculine counterpart. For example, Thoth was paired with Seshat, goddess of writing and measure. Ma'at represents the ethical and moral principle that every Egyptian citizen was expected to follow throughout their daily lives. They were expected to act with honor and truth in matters that involved family, community, nation, environment, and gods. The development of such rules sought to avert chaos and it became the basis of Egyptian law.

There is little literature that describes the practice of Ancient Egyptian law, but Ma'at was the spirit in which justice was applied. From the Fifth Dynasty (c.2510–2370 BCE) onwards, the Vizier (responsible for justice) was called the

Priest of Ma'at and in later periods, judges wore images of Ma'at. Egyptian laws preserved the rights of women who were allowed to act independently of men and own substantial personal property. Gods rose to the top of this world and goddesses fell. Medusa, in Greek mythology, had been a goddess of fertility and fell to be a monster who could turn men to stone. Pandora, another fertility goddess, became a demon with a box of all the evils in existence. Some goddesses remained powerful but showed attributes of men, almost worshipping their male counterparts, while other goddesses fell to roles as guileful evildoers. In different eras, various gods were said to hold the highest position in divine society, including Ra, Amun, and Isis. The highest deity was usually credited with the creation of the world and often connected with the life-giving power of the sun. The eight gods of the Ogdoad, who represent the chaos that preceded creation, gave birth to the sun god, who established order in the newly formed world. Ptah, who embodied thought and creativity, gave form to all things by envisioning and naming them. Pharaohs are said to be divine and each pharaoh and his predecessors were considered the successors of the gods who had ruled Egypt in mythic prehistory. The pharaoh's divine status was the rational for his role as Egypt's representative to the gods as he formed a link between the divine and human realms. The role of the pharaoh was the protector of Ma'at and the maintenance of the Temple Cult, to prevent Isfet from spreading, by ensuring the cults were performed at defined intervals, which were necessary in preserving the balance of Ma'at against the threatening forces of Isfet.

In Egypt, all the objects of worship are Nubian. Diodorus of Sicily reports that each year, the statute of Amon, King of Thebes, was transported in the direction of Nubia for several days and then brought back, as if to indicate that the god was returning from Nubia. In addition, quoting Egyptian priests, Herodotus stated that of the three hundred Egyptian pharaohs from Menes (c. 3100 BCE) to the Seventeenth Dynasty (1550 BCE), eighteen were of Sudanese origin. Egyptians themselves recognize, without ambiguity, that their ancestors came from Nubia, the land of the Aman (man is equal to ancestor in Wolof). The whole territory of Kush, south of Egypt, was called land of gods by the Egyptians. In reality, it is in Nubia that we find pyramids (similar to those in Egypt), underground temples, and Meroitic writing, which is alphabetical. The city of a hundred gates, Thebes, was the most important single city in the entire history of black people. The history of black Africa might well begin at Thebes, for this was truly the "Eternal City of the blacks," that presented the most compelling evidence that they were the builders of the earliest civilization in Kem, later called Egypt, as well as the civilization in the south. The foundation of Thebes goes so far back in prehistory that not even a general Stone Age period can be suggested. The blacks were also called the Theobald after its greatest city, Thebes, and its people. Thebes also referred to the intellectual center of black Africa – the chief seat of learning science, religion, engineering, and the arts. The war god of Thebes as it was the source of power of the mightiest armies, the proudest and most fearless warriors. From this center of empire alone 20,000 war chariots could be put into the field. Egyptian dynasties were African-founded on African traditional lineage system, matrilineal in character, except when it was made patrilineal after Asian conquests, or the great Egyptian transformation.

Circumcision is of Egyptian and Ethiopian origin and they were none other than Negroes inhabiting different regions of Africa. In Egypt, Abraham had married a black woman, Hagar, mother of Ishmael, the Biblical ancestor of the second Semitic branch, the Arabs. Ishmael was said to be the historical ancestor of Mohammed. Moses, too, wed a Madianite and it was in connection with his marriage that the Eternal asked him to be circumcised. Hence, the idea here is that circumcision was introduced among the Semites only as a result of contact with the black world, which confirms to the testimony of Herodotus. It is said that the Egyptians are especially careful in raising all their children and circumcise the boys and even girls. Both circumcision and excision remove something female from the male and something male from the female. Thus, such an operation is intended to fortify the dominant character of a single sex in a given human being. The matriarchal system is the base of the social organization in Egypt and throughout black Africa. In contrast, there has never been any proof of the existence of a Paleo-Mediterranean matriarchy, supposedly exclusively white. In fact, if the matriarchal system, inherited from some white Paleo-Mediterranean, were anything but a mental fantasy, it would have lasted throughout the Persian, Greek, Roman, and Christian periods, just as it has continued until today in black Africa. But this is obviously not the case. In both Greece and Rome, succession was simply patrilineal although, in reality, there never was a monarchical tradition in Greece, except for the ephemeral reign of Alexander, as the country was never unified. The kings of the heroic epoch of whom Homer speaks were only rulers of cities and village chiefs, such as Ulysses. There is no recorded history of queens during Persian, Greek, or Roman reigns.

In contrast, during those remote epochs, queens were frequent in black Africa. Queen Sobekneferu (d.1802 BCE), her name meaning "the beauty of Sobek," was associated with the Nile crocodile. She was the last ruler of the Twelfth Dynasty and governed Egypt for almost four years from 1806 to 1802 BCE. Queen Hatshepsut (1508–1458 BCE), the second historically confirmed female pharaoh, was the fifth pharaoh of the Eighteenth Dynasty of Egypt and came to the throne in 1478 BCE. Hatshepsut was the chief wife of Thutmose II and ruled jointly with the two-year-old Thutmose III. According to the American Egyptologist James Henry Breasted (1865–1935), Hatshepsut is the first great woman in history of whom we are informed. Queen Tiye (1398–1338 BCE) became the Great Royal Wife of Pharaoh Amenhotep III (1425–1353 BCE), mother of Akhenaten (1427–

1336 BCE), and grandmother of Tutankhamun (1341–1323). Queen Twosret (r.1191–1190 BCE) was the last pharaoh of the Nineteenth Dynasty. Her royal name was Sitre Meryamun (Daughter of Re, beloved of Amun). She is recorded in Manetho's Epitome as a certain Thuoris, who, in Homer, is called Polybus, husband of Alcandra, and in whose time Troy was taken. Queen Candace was a formidable black queen, world famous military tactician, field commander, and Empress of Ethiopia in 332 BCE. When Alexander reached her border, he refused to engage her in battle as he was afraid of being defeated by a woman. Four African queens were known to the Greco-Roman world as the "Candace": Shankdakhete (177–155 BCE), Amanirenas (40–10 BCE), Amanishakheto (10 BCE–1 CE), and Amanitore (1–20 CE).

Champollion the Younger reported the existence in Egypt of a caste of priests call Sen. Nobility and clergy had the same rank. Several pharaohs of the earliest dynasties were Serer, judging from their names: Pharaoh Sar and Pharaoh Sar-Teta (both of the Third Dynasty), Pharaoh Perib-Sen (fifth pharaoh of the First Dynasty), and Osorta-Sen (of the Sixteenth Dynasty). The Serer people are a West African ethnoreligious group. The Serer people believe in a universal Supreme Deity called Roog. Serer religious beliefs encompass ancient chants and poems, veneration and offerings to their gods and goddess, the pangool (ancestral spirits and saints), astronomy, medicine, cosmology, and the history of the Serer people. At the time of those early dynasties, excluding Osorta-Sen, the Negro Egyptian race was still practically free of any racial admixture, as proved by the monuments from those periods which depict a distinctly black type. Yet, all the civilizing elements were already present, including writing and science. Much later, the Scythian, Persian, Greek, Roman, Arab, and Turkish invaders altered the Egyptian type, but it never ceased to retain its basic Negro features (Diop, 1974:199). The political unification of the Nile Valley was affected, for the first time, from the south, from the kingdom of Nekhen in Upper Egypt. Nekhen, or Hierakonpolis, was the religious and political capital of Upper Egypt at the end of prehistoric Egypt and also during the Early Dynastic Period. The capital of the United Kingdom of Egypt was transferred to Thinis near Abydos. This was the period of the first two Thinite dynasties (c.3000–2778 BCE). Nekhen was the center of the cult of a hawk deity, Horus of Nekhen, which raised one of the most ancient Egyptian temples in this city. The first settlement at Nekhen dates from between the late Badri culture (c.5000 BCE) and the Amratian culture (c.4400 BCE). The oldest tomb with painted decoration on its plaster wall was discovered at Nekhen and thought to date between 3500 and 3200 BCE.

By the Third Dynasty (2778–2723 BCE), centralization of the monarchy was complete. For the first time in Egypt, Pharaoh Zoser (Djoser, who is also known as Tosorthros and Sesorthos) introduced architecture in hewn stone. His strong Negro face with characteristic features dominated that period, who had their origin in Sudanese Nubia. The painted statue of Pharaoh Zoser, now in the Egyptian Museum in Cairo, is the oldest known life-sized Egyptian statue, excavated in 1924–5. Zoser's wife was Queen Hetephernebtic and among her titles were "one who sees Horus," "great of scepter," and "King's Daughter," which suggests that she was a sister or half-sister of her husband. Zoser dispatched several military expeditions to the Sinai Peninsula during which the local inhabitants were subdued. Zoser's most famous monument was the "Step Pyramid," which entailed the construction of several "mastaba" (eternal house), one over another. He also reformed the writing system (Diop, 1974:204). With administrative centralization in the Third Dynasty (2686–2613 BCE), there was no longer any noble or privileged class. But the clergy, guardian of the faith that established the king's authority, was a corps apart, well-organized, and relatively independent. Until then, it had exercised its spiritual guardianship at the coronation of the king in the temple at Heliopolis. Heliopolis was one of the oldest cities of ancient Egypt, the capital of the Thirteenth Nome (Province or District). The name Heliopolis is of ancient Greek, meaning city of the sun, as it was the principal seat of the sun god Ra, who was closely related to Atum. Originally, this ancient city was known by the Egyptians as Iunu which means Place of Pillars.

Atum, the self-begotten deity, spat or, according to others, masturbated, producing Shu (who represented the air) and Tefnut (moisture). In turn, Shu and Tefnut mated and brought forth Geb (Earth) and Nut (night sky). The children of Geb and Nut were sons, Osiris and Set, and daughter, Isis and Nephthys, who in turn became couples. The Greek Ennead, denoting nine, was coined by Greek exploring Egypt, its culture and religion, especially after the invasion of Alexander the Great. Hence, Greek terms were used by both Greek and Roman authors to describe Egyptian phenomena. Heliopolis, Egyptian Iunu, was dedicated to the worship of the god Atum and thrived from the time of the Old Kingdom until its decline under the Ptolemaic rulers. Heliopolis was the capital of the Province of Goshen, one of three main store-city locations that grain was kept in during the winter months and the Seven Year Famine discussed in the Joseph narrative in the *Book of Genesis*. The Hebrew name, Beth-Shemesh (where Beth means "house" and Shemesh), means "sun" and was also used to describe Heliopolis by Jeremiah. With the advent of the Fourth Dynasty (2613–2494 BCE), the monarchy had reached its zenith and thereafter, evolved toward feudalism. The feudal system that triumphed with the Fifth Dynasty (2494–2345 BCE) reached its peak with the Sixth Dynasty, which along with dynasties Third, Fourth, and Fifth, constitute the Old Kingdom of Dynastic Egypt (2686–2134 BCE). The Sixth Dynasty was to end with the first popular uprising in Egyptian history, plunging the country into a period of anarchy. Insecurity reigned, especially in the Delta with raids by "Asiatic" (Diop, 1974:205).

The second cycle of Egyptian history covers the period from the Sixth (2181 BCE) to Twentieth Dynasty (1077 BCE). In the course of the Sixth Dynasty, Memphis, the capital in Middle Egypt, temporarily played the role of capital during the Ninth (2160–2130 BCE) and Tenth (2130–2040 BCE) Dynasties. In Upper Egypt, the city of Thebes never failed to act as the guardian of tradition and legitimacy. The Eleventh Dynasty revived the administrative centralization of the Third Dynasty, with all its corollary effects. The Eleventh Dynasty spanned both the early (2134–2061 BCE) and late (2061–1991 BCE) dynasties. The Twelfth Dynasty (1991–1803 BCE) fully established the triumph of administrative centralization. During the reign of the Hyksos ruler, Apophis, hostilities erupted between the "Semitic-Aryan" invaders and the black dynasty of Upper Egypt, which represented the Egyptian people's determination to liberate the nation. The Thirteenth Dynasty of Egypt (c. 1803–1649 BCE) is notable for the accession of the first formally recognized Semitic-speaking king, Khendjer (Boar). The Hyksos, a people that constituted the Fifteenth Dynasty of Egypt, are described by most archaeologists as a mixed West Asian people. The name Hyksos was used by the Egyptian historian Manetho around 300 BCE, who, according to the Jewish historian Flavius Josephus, translated the word as "shepherds kings" or "captive shepherds." However, the word Hyksos probably originated as an Egyptian term meaning "rulers of foreign lands" and it almost certainly designated the foreign dynasts rather than a whole nation. The Fifteenth Dynasty (c. 1650–1550 BCE) was the first Hyksos dynasty, ruled from Avaris, without control of the entire land. The Turin King list indicates that there were six Hyksos kings, ruling some 108 years. The Hyksos were expelled in 1580 BCE and Egypt was reunified for the third time with the founding of the glorious Eighteenth Dynasty (1549–1292 BCE) under Queen Hatshepsut.

The first documented instance of the name Israel in contemporary archaeological record, and the only known mention in ancient Egypt, is an inscription by the ancient Egyptian king Merneptah (r.1213–1203 BCE), discovered by Flinders Petrie in 1896 at Thebes. It is also one of four known contemporary inscriptions containing the name Israel. One of the others, being the Mesha Stele (also known as the Moabite Stone), is an inscription stone of around 840 BCE, set up by King Mesha of Moab. The Books of Samuel record that Moab was conquered by David and retained in the territories of his son, Solomon (d.931 BCE). The stele records Mesha's liberation of Moab from under the suzerainty of Israel in 850 BCE. There is also the Kurkh Monoliths, which are two Assyrian stelae that contain a description of the reigns of Ashurnasirpal II and his son, Shalmaneser III. The Monoliths were discovered in 1861 by John George Taylor, who was stationed in Ottoman Eyalet of Kurdistan, in a town called Kurkh. The Shalmaneser III Monolith contains a description of the Battle of Qarqar and a reference to Ahab, King of Israel. The Dan Stele is a broken inscribed stone which was discovered in 1993–4, during excavations at Tel Dan in Northern Israel, which has generated considerable debates about its age, authorship, and authenticity. On the death of Queen Hatshepsut, the great reign of the Eighteenth Dynasty began under Thutmose III (1481–1425 BCE), whose mother was a Sudanese Nubian. Like the Third Dynasty, the Eighteenth promoted administrative centralization. Thutmose III (meaning "Thoth is born") was the sixth pharaoh of the Eighteenth Dynasty. During the first 22 years of his reign, he was co-regent with his stepmother and aunt. Thoth or Djehuti was one of the deities of the Egyptian pantheon. In art, he was often depicted as a man with the head of an ibis or a baboon, animals sacred to him. His female counterpart was Seshat (goddess of wisdom, knowledge and writing), and his wife was Ma'at (she was truth, order, balance and justice personified).

Thoth's chief temple was located in the city of Khmun, later called Hermopolis magna during the Greco-Roman era, same as the Greek god Hermes. Thoth became heavily associated with the arbitration of godly disputes, the arts of magic, the system of writing, the development of science, and the judgment of the dead. One of Thoth's five titles was the "Thrice Great," translated to the Greek as Trismegistos, or Hermes Trismegistus. But the majority of Greeks, and later Romans, did not accept Hermes Trismegistus in place of Hermes. According to Martin Bernal (1987), Greeks like Aeschylus (525–456 BCE) and Plato (427–347 BCE) appear to have been offended by the legend of colonization because they put Hellenic culture in an inferior position to that of the Egyptians and Phoenicians. The Egyptians and Phoenicians were despised and feared but at the same time, deeply respected for their antiquity and well-preserved ancient religion and philosophy. Starting in the fifth century BCE, at the least, Egyptian deities began to be worshipped under Egyptian names – and following Egyptian ritual – throughout Greece, the East Mediterranean and later, the whole of the Roman world. It was only after the collapse of Egyptian religion, in the second century CE, that other oriental cults (notably Christianity) began to replace it. After the crushing of Neo-Platonism, the Hellenic, pagan descendant of Egyptian religion, and Gnosticism (its Judeo-Christian counterpart), Christian thinkers tamed Egyptian religion by turning it into a philosophy. The process was identified with the figure of Hermes Trismegistos, a euhemerized or rationalized version of Thoth (the Egyptian god of wisdom) written in the last centuries of the Egyptian religion, were attributed to him.

At the beginning of Western civilization, the Frankish kings gradually acquired the habit of arranging their succession in advance, excluding any notion of matriarchy. Thus, in the West, political rights are transmitted by the father. On the other hand, Negro matriarchy is as alive today as it was during Antiquity. In regions where the matriarchal system has not been altered by external influences, such as Islam, it is the woman who transmits political rights. This derives from the general idea that heredity is effective only through matrilineal. Another typical aspect of African matriarchy is the dowry paid by the man a custom reversed in European countries. In Africa, since women hold a privileged position, it is she who receives a guarantee in the form of a dowry in the alliance called marriage. Many temples to the major Egyptian gods and deified pharaohs were built in Nubia. Greek and Roman rulers introduced their own deities to Egypt. The cults of several Egyptian deities – particularly Isis, Osiris, Anubis, the form of Horus named Carpocrates, and the fused Greco-Roman god Serapis – were adopted into Roman religion and spread across the Roman Empire. Thoth was transmuted into the legendary esoteric teacher Hermes Trismegistus, and Isis, who was venerated from Britain to Mesopotamia, became the focus of a Greek mystery cult. In the fourth century CE, Christians suppressed the veneration of Egyptian deities. But many of the practices involved in their worship – processions and oracles – were adapted to fit Christian ideology and persisted as part of the Coptic Church. Many festivals and other traditions of modern Egyptians, both Christian and Muslim, resemble the worship of their ancestors' gods.

According to Diop (1974), Egypt, unlike Greco-Roman and feudal societies, had no servile labor force. In Greco-Latin Antiquity, capitalist production depended on a slave market, ninety-nine percent of which consisted exclusively of white slaves from the north and northwest of Europe. The Egyptian State was responsible for organizing production and achieving the optimum yield from the soil, so the division of labor on the administrative level was extremely sophisticated. It was as a prisoner of war, transformed into a slave, chained, and branded, that the white man first entered Egyptian civilization. Though the white slaves were rather numerous, the Egyptian population could easily absorb them. The 30,000 slaves acquired during the Asian expedition of Usimare Ramses III (1217–1155 BCE) represented a small minority when we consider the density of the indigenous national population was able to remain ethnically black throughout Antiquity, despite a white influx. Ramses III was the second pharaoh of the Twelfth Dynasty and is considered to be the last New Kingdom King to wield any substantial authority over Egypt. His long reign (r.1186–1155 BCE) saw the decline of Egyptian political and economic power, linked to a series of invasions by the so-called Sea People and the Libyans, and internal economic problems. For the third time, Egypt sank into feudalistic anarchy that lasted some three centuries (1090–720 BCE). It ended when a Sudanese Nubian intervened and ignited a rebirth of national consciousness.

Nubians established the Twenty-Fifth Dynasty, which ruled between 760 and 656 BCE, when Pharaoh Bakare Tantamani (d.653 BCE) lost control of Upper Egypt. Psamtik I (r.664–610 BCE) extended his authority into Thebes between 664 to 653 BCE. After having Shabataka (d.690 BCE) assassinated, Taharga (d.664 BCE) ascended the throne in 689 BCE, proclaimed himself the son of Mout

(Queen of Sudan), and erected a temple in her honor. Taharqa was the son of Piye (d.721 BCE), the Nubian King of Napata, who had first conquered Egypt. Napata was a city-state of ancient Nubia on the west bank of the Nile River, at the site of modern Karima, Northern Sudan. Napata was founded by Thutmose III in the fifteenth century BCE, after his conquest of Nubia. Although Taharqa reign was filled with conflict with the Assyrians, it was also a prosperous period in Egypt and Kush. The two snakes in the crown of Pharaoh Taharqa show that he was the King of both the lands of Egypt and Nubia. Taharqa was described by the Ancient Greek historian Strabo as having "Advanced as far as Europe" (Spain). In Biblical descriptions, he is the savior of the Hebrew people (Isaiah 37: 8–9 and 2 Kings 19: 8–9). Taharqa intervened in Asia, in an effort to regain Egypt's international prestige. In 661 BCE Ashurbanipal (685–627 BCE) attacked Egypt and pillaged the city of Thebes. Tanutamon (d.653 BCE), the son of Shabataka, escaped to Napata. The fall of the most venerable city of all Antiquity aroused deep emotion and marked the end of the Nubian Sudanese, or the Twenty-Fifth Dynasty, which also marked the decline of black political supremacy in Antiquity. Egypt gradually fell under foreign domination, without ever having known a republican form of government, or secular philosophy, throughout its three millennia of cyclical evolution.

The Persians, under Darius the Great (c.550–486 BCE), ruled the Persian Achaemenid Empire at its peak. It included much of West Asia, the Caucasus, most of the Black Sea coastal regions, Central Asia, Northeast Africa, and Coastal Sudan, spanning some 5.5 million square kilometers. The Persian Empire was founded by Cyrus the Great in 550 BCE and lasted until 330 BCE. The Persian Empire domination of Egypt lasted from 525 BCE to 404 BCE, with the assistance of Greek mercenaries. The Greeks were to eventually establish their rule over Egypt in 332 BCE, when Alexander invaded Egypt. The Ptolemaic period (332–30 BCE) had been largely one of confusion, the division of power among Greeks, Macedonians, and Egyptians. Towards the end of Greek domination of Egypt, the expansion of the Roman Empire had transferred the real center of power to Rome. Assyria, Persia, Greece, and Rome witnessed the continuing process of transforming an African civilization into a near European civilization long before the Christian era. Psammetichus, who ruled Lower Egypt between 664 and 610 BCE, inaugurated the Twenty-Sixth Dynasty (663–525 BCE). But its most characteristic reign was perhaps that of Amasis (568–526 BCE), under whom Egypt lost its independence with the Persian conquest of 525 BCE. Amasis' popular origins probably explain his secular and democratic conception of government. But, the head of the Persian army, King Cambyses (r.529–522 BCE), son of Cyrus, conquered Egypt and put Amasis to death. It is worth noting that Egypt did not practice feudal or capitalist system of production. In politics, Egypt remained a monarchy and "habeas corpus" was fully recognized. There was no national slavery, as an Egyptian could not be enslaved, as all Egyptians were citizens. There was no solid support for republican ideas and like the rest of Africa, Egypt was unaware of such ideas.

It is impossible to stress all that the world, particularly the Hellenistic world, owed to the Egyptians. The Greeks merely continued and developed, sometimes partially, what the Egyptians had invented. But, by virtue of their materialistic tendencies, the Greeks stripped those inventions of their religious and idealistic shell in which Egyptians had enveloped them. On numerous occasions, reference has been made to the fact that the Greeks borrowed their gods from Egypt. When we say that the ancestors of Black Africans were the first to invent mathematics, astronomy, the calendar, sciences in general, arts, religion, agriculture, social organization, medicine, writing, architecture; that they were the first to erect buildings out of six million tons of stone (the Great Pyramid) as architects and engineers, that they built the immense temple of Karnak, that forest of columns with its framed hypostyle hall, large enough to hold Notre-Dame and its towers; that they sculpted the first colossal statutes, when we say all that; we are merely expressing the plain unvarnished truth that no one today can refute. The color of the Egyptians has become lighter down through the years, like that of west Indian Negroes, but the Egyptian civilization is directly linked to the cultural forms of Black Africa, a specialist would have great difficulties in demonstrating any cultural identity of Egypt with Europe or with Semitic or Chinese Asia. In Egypt, the periods of decay are obvious in two prehistoric ages, in the Seventh to Eleventh Dynasties (2134 BCE), in the Thirteenth (1803 BCE) to Seventeenth Dynasties (1580 BCE), and the Roman age (c.100 BCE–400 CE); in all these we see great decadence, and in all these historic ages there is the absence of public monuments and the shortness of reigns, proving the disturbance, poverty, and trouble.

The account by Hatshepsut states that she had restored that which was in ruin, and completed that which was unfinished, since the stay of the Asiatic who were in the lands of the north and they made a king for themselves in ignorance of Ra, and he did not act according to the orders of the god until the coming of my Majesty. This raises the question as to whether Egyptians placed contemporary dynasties in succession in a continuous list. The evidence that overlapping was avoided by Manetho is seen in the Eleventh Dynasty, which lasted for over a century, but which has only forty-three years, because the Tenth Dynasty was legitimate over the earlier part of the Eleventh Dynasty. Again, Taharqa, who really reigned thirty-four years, is only allowed 18 years by Manetho, because from that point the legitimate line was in Stefinates, great-grandfather of Psamthek I, and the Fifteenth Dynasty (1650–1550 BCE) could not be allowed to overlap the Sixteenth Dynasty. The Turin Papyrus is obviously in accord with Manetho, and they must therefore be taken as supplementing each other. In Manetho the Thirteenth dynasty is of sixty kings, and in the Turin Papyrus after sixty years there is a break, beginning again with the formula "there reigned." Next, the Fourteenth Dynasty (c.1725–1650 BCE) is of seventy-six kings, and the Turin Papyrus after seventy-three, there begins the change to Semitic names, which correspond to the Fifteenth Dynasty of Hyksos in Manetho.

Egyptian Influence

According to Charles Freeman (1996) the rulers of the Middle Kingdom of Egypt (c.1985–1795 BCE) evolved an ideology which underpinned their rule. It centered on the concept of Ma'at, harmony achieved through justice and right living. Hieroglyphs were a formal script used mainly for carving sacred texts on stone, pictures of what the scribe wanted to express – a figure of a man for a man, a bird for a bird. They also carried the sound of the object that they represented. The problem the Egyptians had was that they had no vowels in their script. Pictograms could also represent abstract concept. A papyrus roll stood for writing. Texts from the Middle Kingdom suggest a love of learning for its own sake. Thoth, the god of wisdom, is shown with an Ibis head and a scribe's tools in his hand. At the level of popular religious belief, the Middle Kingdom (2050–1800 BCE) is the period of Osiris – death, suffering, and rebirth as a savior who welcomes those who have lived by his rules to another world. The god native to Thebes was Amun – an unseen god of the air (the word Amun means "the hidden one"). In the Middle Kingdom, Amun became syncretized with the traditional sun-god Ra to form a composite god Amun-Ra. The ram was the sacred animal of Amun. It was Amenhotep's successor, Amenhotep IV, better known as Akhenaten, "Pious Servant of Aten" (1352–1336 BCE), who was to attempt a religious and social revolution, installing Aten as a single god in place of the traditional gods of Egypt. The first temple to Aten was built at Thebes, by Akhenaten. The new religion did not catch on, but Akhenaten's reign was interesting. He was represented with his wife Nefertiti and his family in much more informal and realistic poses than was conventional.

Akhenaten was succeeded by Tutankhaten, who changed his name to Tutankhamun, who by the age of nineteen years old was dead. The last nine kings of the Twentieth Dynasty (1186–1069 BCE) all took the name Ramses, as if they hoped it would prove a lucky token against further decay, but they could do little to stop the decline. After the death of Ramses XI (c.1069 BCE), Egypt underwent a period of increasing fragmentation as provincial families, and above all, the priests of Thebes strengthened their local bases against the power of the central ruler. By the eighth century BCE, Southern Egypt was controlled by a dynasty from Nubia. This Nubian dynasty, the Kushites, originated far in the south. In 727 BCE, their most ambitious King, Piankhi (d.721 BCE), marched against the rulers of the north, claiming that he was leading a campaign on behalf of Amun against rebels to the sun god Ra. He was acclaimed ruler of all Egypt and founded the

Twenty-fifth Dynasty. He built a pyramid tomb for himself and his family at Napata. In the early seventh century, the Assyrian King, Esarhaddon (r.681–669 BCE), was able to invade Egypt across the Sinai desert. Memphis was sacked in 671 BCE, and the Egyptian ruler, Tahargo (747–656 BCE), was forced to retreat south. Between 664 and 663 BCE, the Assyrian's attacked again, this time reaching as far as Thebes, and sacked the religious capital of Egypt. This was a humiliating blow to the Kushite and they withdrew south, where they maintained a kingdom around the city of Meroe for several centuries. The Assyrians ruled Egypt through Greek collaborations.

Through a mixture of diplomacy and force, the Greek Psamtek eventually established his rule over the whole of Egypt, founded the Twenty-sixth Dynasty and was to rule for fifty years. About 620 BCE, Greek traders were allowed by Psamtek I to set up a trading center at Naucratis on a branch of the river Nile near Sais. Greek mercenaries soon formed part of the Egyptian army, together with Phoenicians, Syrians, and Jews, many of whom were refugees from the Assyrian conquests. Greeks began visiting Egypt as tourists and were so overawed by what they saw that some came to believe that their own civilization was descended from Egypt's. In the mid-sixth century, an empire finally arose which managed to conquer and consolidate its hold over the entire Ancient world, including Egypt and North Africa. The Persian Empire was founded by Cyrus II (ruled 560–530 BCE), commonly known as Cyrus the Great. Cyrus II attacked the Babylonians in 539 BCE and found himself master of a vast empire. Among his new subjects were Phoenicians, whose sailors were to provide the manpower for an imperial navy. The Jews rejoiced at their liberation from the Babylonian control and Isaiah proclaimed Cyrus as their deliverer, the anointed one of Yahweh. On Cyrus death, his successor, his son Cambyses, was successful in extending the empire further through the conquest of Egypt and Cyprus. The Persian armies invaded Egypt in 525 BCE, defeating King Psamtek III and besieging his capital at Memphis. The city fell and a new phase in Egyptian history begun, one in which foreign rulers, Persians, Greeks and Romans, would exploit the centuries-old traditions of loyalty to a central ruler to serve their own ends. By 525 BCE, the Persian Empire extended over the whole of western Asia. But, Cambyses faced considerable internal unrest and shortly before his death in 522 BCE there was a coup by one of his generals, Darius. Darius legitimized his rule through the one god, Ahura-Mazda, who was prepared to preside benignly over the lesser gods of the peoples Darius controlled.

Ahura, meaning mighty or lord, and Mazda, meaning wisdom, is the Avestan name for the creator and sole God of Zoroastrianism, the Old Iranian religion which spread across Asia. In 499 BCE, the western part of the empire was shaken by a major revolt by the Greek cities of the Ionian coast. The Greek settled on the coast of North Africa about 630 BCE, in Libya, Herodotus mentions that the women of Cyrene, Libya, followed the Egyptian practice of not eating cow's meat. In the seventh century BCE, Greeks were visiting Egypt not only as merchants, but also as awe-inspiring tourists. Egypt was seen as the font of traditional wisdom and some Greeks believed it to have been the origin of their own culture. The inspiration of the Greeks to be more creative and ambitious with their building material came from Egypt. The opening of Egypt, by King Psamtek 1, encouraged the first major incursion of Greeks, both traders and visitors, into his country. The pyramids of Giza, for instance, were only 120km from the Greek trading post at Naucratis, and visitors would also have had the opportunity to see Psamtek's own massive building program in action. It is also interesting to note that the majority of Greeks who settled at Naucratis were Ionians and a taste for monumental art seems to be found largely in Ionian cities. The temple of Artemis at Ephesus with its double row of columns may be an echo of the columned halls of Egypt, while the famous row of marble icons at Delos seems an almost direct copy of the traditional sacred processional routes of the Egyptian temples.

The Ionians may not have been the only Greeks who borrowed from the Egyptians. A comparison can be made between the columns of the shine of Anubis at the temple of Hatshepsut (1508–1458 BCE), at Deir el-Bagri and the temples to Hera at Olympia (590 BCE) and to Apollo at Corinth (540 BCE). Another Egyptian influence may be seen in sculpture of the seventh century BCE, of small terracotta and bronze statutes, with wigged hair, a triangular face, and a flat skull, which became common in Greece. They face forward in a rigid pose with both feet together. The style is called Daedalic, after a legendary Greek sculptor, Daedalus, although it originated from the east. It can be assumed that the Greeks learnt how to fashion marble after seeing Egyptians working on their native hard stones, granite, and diorite. It would seem plausible to suppose that Egyptian religion collapsed with that of the pharaonic state and Egyptian nationality. However, Egypt had been ruled by foreigners for most of the time since seventh century BCE, like the Ethiopians and the Ptolemaic Greeks, had ruled their whole empire from Egypt, but the Persians were like the Romans in considering Egypt as a – rather special – province. Most rulers considered good relations with Egyptian religion essential to their control of the country. Egyptian religion flourished and expanded throughout this period, reaching a peak in the first half of the second century CE. After four hundred years of Greek rule, the Roman rulers, the Macedonian and Egyptian upper classes – including the priesthood – had fused in a common Hellenic civilization with Egyptian religion. However, after the second century CE, despite the fact that Christianity came from Palestine and was consciously international, it came to represent the poor and middle-class Egyptians against the cosmopolitan Hellenized upper classes with their Egyptian pagan religion.

There is little doubt that social and national factors played a major part in the destruction of organized Egyptian religion; the general belief that the "Old" world was coming to an end and that a new age was about to begin. By the end of the fourth century CE, Gnosticism had been largely extirpated by the Orthodox Church. Pagan Neo-Platonism survived rather longer, but it too had disappeared before the Moslem conquest of Egypt in the 630s. The figure of Hermes Trismegistos as the epitome of knowledge survived in both Christianity and Islam. As with all the descendants of Canaanite monotheism, the Christian Church used euhemerism to diminish and tame the pagan gods at the same time as it allowed them to survive under the new religion. Euhemerus was not the first to attempt to rationalize mythology in historical terms, as euhemeristic views are found in earlier writings, including those of Xenophanes, Herodotus, Hecataeus of Abdera, and Ephorus. Euhemerism holds that many mythological tales can be attributed to historical persons and events, the accounts of which have become altered and exaggerated over time. But the enduring influence of Euhemerus on later thinkers identified him as the traditional founder of this school of thought. Neit/Athena was incorporated as Saint Catherine, Horus/Perseus as Saint George, and Anubis/Hermes as Saint Christopher. However, Thoth-Anubis/Hermes remained outside the Church, as the sage and epitome of Egyptian and Oriental wisdom Hermes Trismegistos. In Islam, Hermes Trismegistos was euhemerized and identified with Idris, a sincere prophet who appears in the Qur'an and was viewed as the "father of philosophers" and "the one who is thrice endowed with wisdom." Indeed, throughout the Middle Ages, Hermes Trismegistos was seen as the founder of non-biblical or "Gentile" philosophy and culture.

The revival of Greek studies in the fifteenth century created a love of Greek literature and language and an identification with the Greeks, but no one questioned the fact that the Greeks had been the pupils of the Egyptians, in whom there was an equal, if not more passionate, interest. Although Copernicus' mathematics was derived from Islamic science, his heliocentricity seems to have come with the revival of the Egyptian notion of a divine sun in the new intellectual environment of Hermeticism in which he was formed. His champion, Giordano Bruno (1548–1600), at the end of the sixteenth century, was more explicit on this and went beyond the respectable Christian Neo-Platonic Hermeticism of Ficino. Appalled by the Wars of religion and Christian intolerance, Bruno advocated a return to the original religion, that of Egypt, for which he was burnt at the stake by the Inquisition in 1600 CE. In Egypt, the stars were used both to align buildings and to calculate time. The "Dog Star," Sirius remains below the horizon in Egypt for some seventy days, reappearing around July 19, which coincided with the beginning of the Nile floods and so for Egyptians, marked the beginning of a new year. The calendar they developed, for administrative purposes, had 365 days, twelve months of thirty days and six hours, which is the correct solar year. Hence, every four years this civil calendar fell one day behind the rising of Sirius and continued to do so until two coincided again, 1460 years later.

Stars are often associated with great and messianic leaders, from Cyprus, who founded the Persian Empire in the sixth century BCE, to the Chinese leader of the eighth century CE, An Lushan (703–757 CE). It is striking to note how often stars appear in association with major leaders during the period of crisis from 50 to 150 CE; from the comet seen as representing the spirit of Julius Caesar to the star of Bethlehem and that associated with Hadrian's new god, the so-called Greek youth Antinous, who was born in Bithynia, Turkey, in 111 CE and died, Mallawi, Egypt, in 130 CE, Hadrian's lover, who was deified after his death. The last messianic leader of Jewish resistance, who led a revolt against the Roman Empire in 132 CE, was known – at least by his enemies – as Simon bar Kokhba, "son of a star." From Plutarch's *On Isis and Osiris*, we know the extreme importance attached to astronomical movements as signs of the ideal world of the stars and geometry and the integral relation seen, at least in late Egyptian religion, between the stars and the gods. Mathematical skills were developed to cope with more complex administrative tasks such as dealing with rations between people of different status. The Egyptians knew that triangles in the ratio of 3:4:5 had a right-angle opposite the hypotenuse and in the measurement of circles calculated pi to 3.16, very close to the actual figure of 3.1416. They could also work out the angles of pyramids and, in general, Egyptian mathematics centered on solutions specific to administration and architectural problems. In agriculture, the mainstay of the economy was conservatism. The system of exchange for surplus goods was based on a unit of weight, the "deben" of about ninety grams. But the Egyptians never developed any exchange system involving coins.

Homer (c.850 BCE) wrote in the Odyssey that medicine in Egypt was more developed than anywhere in the world, and Herodotus (c. 484–425 BCE), a contemporary of Socrates (c.469–399), writing some three centuries later, agreed with him. The family was the living unit of Egyptian society and there was an ideal of care of young for old. "Repay your mother for all her care to you," writes one scribe. "Give her as much bread as she needs and carry her as she has carried you." But infidelity and jealousy were common in ancient Egypt as elsewhere. Marriage took place for women at the onset of puberty, between 12 and 14, while men seem to have been older, perhaps 20. Both families had to provide goods before a marriage contract could be made and within the royal family it was possible for brother to marry sister (the legend of Isis and Osiris legitimized the practice). For commoners, brother-sister marriages were almost unheard of, although marriages between cousins, uncles, and nieces were quite common. Men were specifically warned to leave the running of the home to their wives and women had a right to own and manage property. A woman who was divorced by her husband became entitled to his continued support. In wall paintings, women are usually portrayed much lighter-skinned than their husbands, as a sign that a woman did not have to work in the sun and suggested high status. Children mortality rate was high, especially at the time of weaning, about three years old. When boys reached the age of 14 years old they passed into adult life after a religious ceremony which included circumcision, which was an important *rite de passage* recognized by the whole community.

In Ancient Egypt, the deceased hoped that he would be accepted by Osiris as worthy of life in the fields of Reeds, a lush fertile land somewhere beyond the western horizon, where he would live a more carefree version of what he had already endured. High standards were expected and covered every area of moral behavior. He had to prove he had not killed or stolen, committed adultery, or had sex with a boy. There was no after life without a preserved body. Soon after death the brain and internal organs of the body were removed, although the heart, as the core of the body, was left in place. The whole process, from death to burial, was prescribed to take place within seventy days. Egyptian influences can be found among those that enriched the Hebrew Scriptures, in Book of Proverbs for instance, while Greeks were inspired in their stone working. In the Hellenistic period, Egypt's religious heritage was to become part of the rich spiritual tradition of the Mediterranean world. Isis and Serapis (a composite of Osiris and the bull-god Apis) became popular Greco-Roman cults and it has been argued that the concept of the Christian Trinity is rooted in the syncretism of Amun-Ra. When Rome took over Egypt there was a craze for all things Egyptian. Augustus used a sphinx on his seal and many obelisks, the tall needle-shaped stones which fronted temples, were taken to Rome so that there are now more standing there than are left upright in the whole of Egypt.

The movement among Greeks and other Mediterranean peoples to worship the gods under their Egyptian names began well before Alexander's conquests and the syncretism of Hellenistic times. Early in the fifth century BCE the poet Pindar wrote a *Hymn to Ammon*, which opened "Ammon King of Olympos." This cult of the Libyan variant of the Egyptian Amon was attached to Pindar's (522–443 BCE) native town of Thebes. However, it was also strong in Sparta, and Pausanias (c.110–c.180 CE) wrote about the sanctuary of Ammon in Aphytis in Sparta. Alexander the Great clearly considered himself to be a son of Ammon. After his conquest of Egypt, he set out into the desert to consult the god's great oracle at the Libyan oasis of Siwa. The oracle told Alexander that he was the god's son, which explains why from then on Alexander's coins portrayed him as a horned Ammon. Ptolemy and his successors, right up to the Cleopatra of Caesar and Antony, made great use of Egyptian religion both to gain the respect and affection of their Egyptian subjects and to give them cultural power when dealing with the other states that rose from the fragments of Alexander's empire. The Egyptian mother goddess Isis had been worshipped in Athens since the fifth century BCE by native

Athenians. By the second century BCE, there was a temple of Isis near the Acropolis and Athens was officially encouraging its dependencies to take up Egyptian cults. Indeed, by the second century BCE, Pausanias (c.110–c.180 CE), who made no mention of other Oriental cults, reported Egyptian temples or shrines in Athens, Corinth, Thebes, and many places in the Argolid, Messenia, Achaia, and Phocis. Plutarch (46–120 CE) spelled out in detail the general image of Egyptian religion since the fourth century BCE, which appears to have been common among cultivated Greeks.

In *On Isis and Osiris*, Egypt's religious philosophy was principally concerned not with the ephemeral, material world of "becoming" with its growth and decay, but with the immortal realm of "being" which was especially manifested in numbers, geometry and astronomy. "The Ethiopians, who are illuminated by the first rays of the sun-god as he is born every day, together with the Africans and Egyptians, who excel through having the original doctrine, honor me with my distinctive rites and give me my true name of Queen Isis." As the Neo-Platonist philosopher, Iamblichus Chalcidensis (245–325 CE), a Syrian Neoplatonist philosopher, wrote at the end of the pagan period in the fourth century CE. "Rather think that as the Egyptians were the first of men to be allotted the participation of the gods, the gods when invoked rejoice in Egyptian rites" (Bernal, 1987:120). Thus, the Ancient Greeks, though proud of themselves and their recent accomplishments, did not see their political institutions, science, philosophy, or religion as original. Instead, they derived them – through the early colonization and later study by Greeks abroad – from the east in general and Egypt in particular. In 390 CE, the temple of Serapis and the adjacent great library of Alexandria were destroyed by a Christian mob; twenty-five years later, the brilliant and beautiful philosopher and mathematician, Hypatia (350–415 CE), a Greek mathematician, astronomer, and philosopher in Egypt, was gruesomely murdered in the same city by gang of monks instigated by Saint Cyril (376–444 CE), Patriarch of Alexandria from 412–444 CE. These two acts of violence marked a continuing trend against Egypto-Paganism and the continuing rise of the Christian Dark Ages.

The Ancient Egyptians had developed a complex religious system called the Mysteries, which was also the first system of salvation. As such, it regarded the human body as a prison house of the soul, which could be liberated from its bodily impediments, through the disciplines of arts and sciences, and advanced from the level of a mortal to that of a God. This was the notion of the *summum bonum* or greatest good, to which all men must aspire and it also became the basis of all ethical concepts. The Egyptian Mystery System was also a *Secret Order*, and membership was gained by initiation and a pledge of secrecy. The teaching was graded and delivered orally to the Neophyte and they were forbidden to write down what they had learnt. After nearly five thousand years of prohibition against the Greeks, they were permitted to enter Egypt for the purpose of their education.

There was no doubt that up to the eighteenth century, Egypt was seen as the font of all "Gentile" philosophy and learning, including that of the Greeks, and that the Greeks had managed to preserve only some part of these. The sense of loss that this created, and the quest to recover the lost wisdom, were major motives in the development of science in the seventeenth century. But at the beginning of the eighteenth century the threat of Egyptian philosophy to Christianity became acute. The Freemasons, who made much use of the image of Egyptian wisdom, were at the center of the Enlightenment in its attack on Christian order. It was in opposition to this eighteenth century notion of "reason" on the part of the Egyptophiles that the Greek ideal of sentiment and artistic perfection was developed. Additionally, the development of Eurocentrism and racism, with the colonial expansion over the same period, led to the fallacy that only people who lived in temperate climates – that is, Europeans – could really think.

By the eighteenth century, the Greeks were not only considered to have been more sensitive and artistic than the Egyptians but they were now seen as the better philosophers, and indeed as the founder of philosophy. The Greek War of Independence united all European against the traditional Islamic enemies from Asia and Africa. The Ancient Greeks were now seen as perfect and as having transcended the laws of history and language. Moreover, with the rise of a passionate and systematic racism in the early nineteenth century, the ancient notion that Greece was a mixed culture that had been civilized by Africans and Semites became not only abominable but unscientific. Paradoxically, the more the nineteenth century admired the Greeks, the less it respected their writing of their own history. According to Martin Bernal (1987), the Rose and Cross (secret society – freemasonry), which sprang up in Germany, France and England in the seventeenth century seemed to have been promoting a "true" religion for the elite, in order to avoid the bloody hostility between Catholics and Protestants, that erupted so horribly in the Thirty Years War that ravaged Germany from 1618 to 1648. Like the sixteenth century Hermeticists, the Rosicrucian advocated an elite of enlightened men in possession of true, magical, and scientific knowledge to direct society. In doing this they were following the now familiar succession from the Egyptian priesthoods to the Pythagorean brotherhood to the Platonic Academy.

For Isaac Newton, "The Egyptians were the earliest observers of the heavens and from them, probably, this philosophy was spread abroad. For from them, it was, and from the nations about them, that the Greeks, a people more addicted to the study of philology [*a branch of knowledge that deals with the structure, historical development, and relationships of a language or languages*] than of philosophy; and in the vestal ceremonies we can recognize the spirit of the Egyptians, who concealed mysteries that were above the capacity of the common herd under the veil of religious rites and hieroglyphic symbols." The Freemasons were originally secret societies of masons working on cathedrals and other major buildings in medieval Europe. In most parts of the continent they died out after the Reformation and wars of Religion; they survived in Britain but took on a very different character, with the entry of gentlemen members and the beginning of what was called "speculative masonry," but with a special attachment to Egypt. Egyptians in the Bible were at the core of Masonic mythology. Hiram Abiff, the craftsman of Solomon's temple, was probably part of Masonic legend by the sixteenth century CE. For the Masons, the name of the Hidden God was too sacred or magically powerful to be revealed even to the lower grades of the craft. This name was Jabulon and it is a triple name – its first two syllables being Ja for Yahweh, the God of Israel, and Bul for the Canaanite Ba'al. The last name is On, the Hebrew name of the Egyptian city "Iwnw," known in Greek as Heliopolis and now a suburb of Cairo.

Significantly, the city was a major center of the sun-cult and was associated particularly with Ra, who became associated with Osiris by the Eighteenth Dynasty. In the city of the Sun, Moses, Christ, Mahomet, and other great teachers were revered as magi, but the city was ruled by Hermes Trismegistos as sun priest, philosopher King and lawgiver. In this case the Masonic claim of drawing their traditions from Ancient Egypt has a basis in fact. Hence, one can trace a line from the final syllable of the name of their ineffable God to "Iwnw," the cult center of Ra in Lower Egypt. The ascending mystery of Jabulon from Judeo-Christian to Canaanite-Phoenician, to Egyptian and Osirian rituals for the upper grades – does not mean that the centrality of Egypt to the Freemasons was hidden. Masonic temples have frequently been built in an Egyptian style showing that the "Lodges" are to be seen as Egyptian temples. Their symbols are the eighteenth century conception of purely logical hieroglyphs. Some, like the pyramid and eye still to be seen on the Great Seal of the United States and the dollar bill, were taken direct from Egypt. The concept of "progress" had existed in Europe since the sixteenth century, when people began to realize that they now possessed products and inventions that the Ancients had lacked – sugar, paper, printing, windmills, the compass, gunpowder, etc., all of them introductions from Asia. The century from 1670 to 1770 was one of great economic expansion, scientific and technical development, and increased concentration of political power. Jews like Josephus and Church Fathers like Clement of Alexandria and Tatian, scored points against the Greeks by pointing out the lateness and shallowness of Greek civilization in comparison with those of the Egyptians, Phoenicians, Chaldeans, and Persians. They also stressed Greece's heavy cultural borrowings from the more ancient peoples.

Pantheism could be traced back to Baruch Spinoza (1632–1677) to Bruno and beyond, to the Neo-Platonists and Egypt itself. By the middle of the eighteenth century, a number of Christian apologists were using the emerging paradigm of "progress," with its presupposition that "later is better," to promote the Greeks at the expense of the Egyptians. These strands of thought soon merged with two others that were becoming dominant at the same time: racism and Romanticism. This racism pervaded the thought of Locke, Hume, and other English thinkers. Their influence – and that of the new European explorers of other continents – was important at the University of Gottingen, founded in 1734 by George II, Elector of Hanover and King of England and forming a cultural bridge between Britain and Germany. It was therefore not surprising that the first "academic" work on human racial classification, placed "Caucasians" at the head of the hierarchy, written in the 1770s, by Johann Friedrich Blumenbach, a professor at Gottingen. In the 1770s, other professors at Gottingen also began to publish histories not of individuals, but of peoples, races, and their institutions. These "modern" projects can usefully be seen as an academic aspect of the new Romantic concern with ethnicity, current in German and British society at the time. Eighteenth century Romanticism was not merely a faith in the primacy of emotion and belief in the inadequacy of reason. Clustered around these were feelings for landscapes – especially wild, remote, and cold ones – and admiration for the vigorous, virtuous, and primitive folk who were somehow molded by them. These sentiments were combined with the belief that the landscape and climate of Europe were better than those of other continents. These beliefs were championed by Montesquieu (1689–1755) and Jean-Jacques Rousseau (1712–1778) but took firmest roots in Britain and Germany.

By the end of the eighteenth century, "progress" had become a dominant paradigm and the world began to be viewed through time rather than across space. Although space remained important for the Romantics, because of their concern for the local formation of peoples or "races." They believed that race passed through different ages, but always retained an immutable individual essence. Real communication was no longer perceived as taking place through reason, which could reach any rational person. It was now seen as flowing through feeling, which could touch only those tied to each other by kinship or "blood" and sharing a common "heritage." Although many Ancient Greeks shared a feeling like what would now be called nationalism, it was a feeling qualified by the very real respect many Greek writers had for foreign cultures, particularly those of Egypt, Phoenicia, and Mesopotamia. Ancient Greek "nationalism" was negligible compared to the tidal wave of ethnicity and racialism, linked to cults of Christian Europe with the Romantic Movement at the end of the eighteenth century. The paradigm of "races" that were intrinsically unequal in physical and mental endowment was applied to all human studies, but especially to history. It was now considered undesirable, if not disastrous, for races to mix. To be creative, a civilization needed to be "racially pure." Thus, it became increasingly intolerable that Greece could be the result of the mixture of native Europeans and colonizing Africans and Semites.

In the late eighteenth century and early nineteenth century, Romantic scholars saw the Egyptians as essentially morbid and lifeless. At the end of the nineteenth century, a new contrary but equally disparaging image began to emerge. The Egyptians were now seen to conform to the contemporary European vision of Africans: gay, pleasure-loving, childishly boastful, and essentially materialistic. Another way of looking at these changes is to assume that after the rise of black slavery and racism, European thinkers were concerned to keep Africans as far as possible from European civilization. Where people of the Middle Ages and the Renaissance were uncertain about the color of the Egyptians, the Egyptophile Masons tended to see them as white. Yet despite the triumph of Hellenism and dismissal of Egypt in academic circles, the concept of Egypt as "the cradle of civilization" never completely died. In the eighteenth century and early nineteenth century, Christians were alarmed at the threat of the significance of Egyptian religion. These Christians challenged Greek statements about the importance of Egypt and boosted the independent creativity of Greece in order to diminish that of Egypt. In the 1820s, the Prussian born, Gottingen professor Karl Otfried Muller (1797–1840), who introduced the modern study of Greek mythology, discredited all the ancient references to the Egyptian colonization of Greece by the Egyptians and Phoenicians and attacked reports of Greeks having studied in Egypt. He was greatly influenced by Philipp August Bockh (1785–1867). For these scholars, it was self-evident that the greatest "race" in world history was the European or Aryan one, as it alone had, and always would have, the capacity to conquer all other peoples and to create advanced, dynamic civilizations – as opposed to the static societies ruled by Asians or Africans. These paradigms of "race" and "progress," their corollaries of "racial purity," and the notion that the only beneficial conquests were those of "master races" over subject ones, could not tolerate the Ancient Model. Thus, Muller's refutations of the legends of Egyptian colonization in Greece were quickly accepted.

The Ionians were one of the two great tribes of Greece, the other being the Dorians. In Classical times, the Ionians lived in a band across the central Aegean from Attica to "Ionia" on the Anatolian shore. The Ionians of Attica and Ionia on the Anatolian coast placed great stress on their ancient native origins. All authorities assume the name Ionia to be Greek, despite the fact that it lacks an Indo-European etymology. Herodotus wrote his great *Histories* c. 450 BCE, which explores the relationship between Europe (Greece), Asia, and Africa. He saw this relationship as one of similarities and differences, contacts and conflicts. He asked many questions on these topics during his wide travels in the Persian Empire from Babylonia to Egypt, and on his northern and western fringes from Epirus and Greece to the Black Sea. The Masons, who included almost every significant figure in the Enlightenment, saw their religion as Egyptian, their signs as hieroglyphs, their lodges as Egyptian temples, and themselves as an Egyptian priesthood. Masons have maintained the cult until today, as an anomaly in a world where "true" history is seen to have begun with the Greeks.

Greek Philosophers

There is no one reason why Greek philosophy should have begun in the Ionian world. The cities of the Asian coast were the most prosperous of the sixth century BCE, Greek world. One of the fractions in the civil war, following the overthrow of Miletus, a powerful port, was known as "The Perpetual Sailors." This underlines the fact that many Milesians must have traveled abroad in search of trade, to Egypt for instance, and equally to some of the opulent and sophisticated civilizations of the east. There was a view that material objects could be divided into tiny particles which were themselves indivisible, the Greek used the word *atomos* for such a particle, hence "atom." The concept originated in the mid-fifth century, with Leucippus, a native of Abdera, a small town in the Northern Aegean founded by settlers from Ionia. Leucippus and his younger contemporary, Democritus (460–370 BCE), also of Abdera, went on to argue that the physical world was made up of atoms which were of the same substance but differed in shape and size. However, a brief notice in Diogenes Laertius' life of Epicurus says that on the testimony of Epicurus, Leucippus never existed. But nothing is definitively known about the life of Laertius, who is a principal source for the history of Greek philosophy. Where the Atomists differed from earlier cosmologists was in their belief that the formation of the world was random. The only things that exist are atoms and the empty spaces between them. This was the first developed statement of materialism, the theory that nothing which can be directly grasped by the senses exists beyond the material world. It made the Atomists Marx's favorite Greek philosophers.

A very different approach was provided by Pythagoras (d.495 BCE), another Ionian in origin and a native of the island of Samos. But, it has proved virtually impossible to distinguish between what Pythagoras himself taught and what was added later by Pythagoreans. Pythagoras' theorem of the right-angled triangle, for instance, seems to have had no direct connection with him, and was probably known in essence to Babylonians many centuries earlier. The one teaching which is most likely to have been Pythagoras' own is that of the transmigration of the soul. Pythagoras appears to have believed that the soul exists as an immortal entity separately from the body. The body is simply its temporary home, and on the death of one's body it moves on to another. He believed that the soul is not only immortal, it is rational and responsible for its own actions. It must never let itself be conquered by the desires of the body. The Pythagoreans were therefore ascetics, but unlike many with his leaning, they never cut themselves off from the world. In fact, many Pythagoreans became deeply involved in politics, though the austerity of their beliefs often aroused opposition. Although direct proof of any association of Pythagoras with mathematics is lacking, he is often linked with the theory that the structure of things rests on numbers. It is possible to argue from this that mathematical forms exist unseen behind all physical structures. The possibility that they do and can be grasped by a reasoning soul was to be taken up by Plato. The study of mathematics was to be the core of the education given to his aspiring philosophers. In the sixth century, another Ionian, Xenophanes (c.570–c.480 BCE), suggests that "truth," if the concept could be said to exist at all, was something relative, dependent on the inadequate senses of individual observers or the ways in which they constructed their reasoned arguments. In a famous statement about gods, he wrote:

> Immortal men imagine that gods are begotten and that they have human dress and speech and shape… If oxen or horses or lions had hands to draw with and to make works of art as men do, the horses would draw the forms of gods like horses, oxen like oxen, and they would make their gods' bodies similar to the bodily shape they themselves each had (Freeman, 1996:145).

The fundamental question is then raised to whether there could ever be any agreement over what the gods, or justice or goodness, might be. This was to be the central issue tackled by Socrates and Plato in the late fifth and early fourth centuries. The achievements of these early philosophers need to be placed in context. They had not invented rational thought, which is an intrinsic element of human society, found in every culture. As Freeman stated, quoting the African philosopher, K. Wiredu, "No society would survive for any length of time without basing a large part of its daily activities on beliefs derived from evidence" (Freeman, 1996: 145)). He went on, "You cannot farm without some rationally based knowledge of soils, seeds and climate; and no society can achieve any reasonable degree of harmony in human relation without the basic ability to assess claims and allegations by the method of objective investigation. The truth then is that rational knowledge is not the preserve of the modern 'West' nor is superstition a peculiarity of the African." The Egyptians and Babylonians had evolved a number of mathematical procedures to deal with the practical problems of building, calculating rations, and so on. What was missing was any ability to use numbers in an abstract way. Although a systematic outline of mathematical knowledge was not produced until Euclid's in about 300 BCE, it is clear that some Greeks (mainly Ionians) were thinking about axioms, definitions, proofs, and theorem. In this way, general principles could be formulated which could then be used to explore a wider range of other issues. It was this ability to think abstractly that inspired intellectual progress, not just in mathematics but in science, metaphysics, ethics, and even politics. The argument suggests that once evidence had been written down and a variety of different accounts of an event or a belief could be compared, then rational thinking developed as a way of dealing with these inconsistencies.

According to George Granville Monah James (1954), history is silent on the learning of Thales (620–546 BCE), a native of Miletus, who is credited by Aristotle with teaching that water is the source of all living things and all things are full of God. Anaximander (c.611–546 BCE) is credited with the teaching that the origin of all things is "infinite." Anaximenes (c.585–c.528 BCE) is credited with teaching that all things originated from air. Pythagoras of Samos, moved to Croton, in Magna Graecia, about 530 BCE, established some kind of school or guild, and returned to Samos in 520 BCE. However, most of the information about Pythagoras was written down centuries after his death, so very little reliable information is known about him. Pythagoras has been accredited with the doctrines of Transmigration, the immortality of the soul and salvation. The doctrines of Opposites, the Summum Bonum and the process of purification. The Cosmological doctrine that all things are numbers. The "Eleatic" philosophers such as Xenophanes, who holds that there is an infinite number of worlds, not overlapping in time. He wrote about two extremes predominating world: wet and dry (water and earth), in contrast to Anaximenes' air theory. Parmenides is said to have been born at Elea (c.540 BCE) and to have composed a poem concerning nature which contains his doctrines of the knowledge of truth and the knowledge of the opinion of men. The Physical Doctrine – right (logos) holds that Being is one and immutable. The Doctrine of Truth consists of the knowledge that Being is, and that not Being is not. Hence, "Being" is unproduced and unchangeable. Zeno (c.490–c.430 BCE), was born at Elea and a pupil of Parmenides, little is known for sure about Zeno's life, but is best known for his paradoxes, which were intended to be a contradiction of motion, plurality, and space.

Melissus, whose birth and lifespan is unknown, is credited with introducing the notions of Being and Becoming. The term Eleatic is derived from Elea, a city in Southern Italy, where these men are said to have visited. Xenophanes, born at Colophon, in Asia Minor (Turkey) is accredited with the doctrines of the unity of God and Temperance – plain living. Anaxagoras (c.510–c.428 BCE), a native of Clazomenae, in Ionian, like all the other philosophers, nothing is known about his early life and education. He was the first to bring philosophy to Athens, where he met and befriended Pericles (495–429 BCE), and where, in later life, he was charged with impiety. He escaped from prison and fled into exile in Lampsacus. He described the world as a mixture of primary imperishable ingredients, where material variation was never caused by an absolute presence of a particular ingredient, but rather by its relative preponderance over the other ingredients. He introduced the concept of Nous (Mind) as an ordering force, which moved and separated out the original mixture. Democritus (c.460–c.370 BCE), a native of

Abdera, Thrace, is remembered for his formulation of an atomic theory of the universe, although none of his writings have survived. Like all the other so-called Greek philosophers, nothing seems to be known about his early life and training. His doctrine is associated with the nature of the atoms, creation, life and death, and sensation and knowledge.

The creation story, found in the *Book of Genesis*, speaks of the elements of water, air, and earth as the cosmic ingredients of the chaos out of which creation gradually developed. The date of the Pentateuch, the first five books of the Hebrew Bible: *Genesis, Exodus, Leviticus, Numbers*, and *Deuteronomy*, traditionally ascribed to Moses, are now held by scholars to be a compilation from texts of the ninth to fifth centuries BCE. These so-called Mosaic books take us back into antiquity, and many centuries before the time of these Ionian philosophers. Moses was an initiate of the Egyptian Mysteries and became a Hierogrammat (a writer of hierograms); learnt in all the wisdom of the Egyptian people. The Egyptian name of Moses was given to all candidates at their baptism, and meant "save by water." The Exodus of the Israelites appears to have occurred in the Twenty-fourth Dynasty (732–720 BCE), in the reign of Bocchoris (725–720 BCE), under the leadership of Moses, whose creation story of Genesis is clearly of Egyptian origin. It is therefore clear that the early Ionic philosophers drew their teachings from Egyptian sources. The doctrine of opposites owes its origin to the Egyptian Mysteries, which takes us back to 4,000 BCE, by the pairs of gods in the Mystery System, representing male and female, positive and negative principles of nature. It is clear that the Eleatic philosophers drew their teachings from Egyptian sources. The later Ionic philosophers have been given credit for the doctrines of transmutation from fire, the Nous or Mind and Atoms. These doctrines were by no means produced by the late Ionic philosophers but could be shown to have originated from the Egyptian Mystery System. The Egyptian were fire worshippers, because they believe that fire was the creator of the universe and built their great pyramids (pyr means fire) in order to worship the God of Fire, and the pyramid age goes back to around 3,300 BCE, several thousands of years before Greeks were said to have come into the Mediterranean area.

It was common occurrences for the Athenian government to indict and persecute Greek philosophers for introducing strange divinities. Aristophanes (c.446–c.386 BCE) accused Socrates (d.399 BCE) for being an evildoer, who busied himself with investigating things beneath the earth and in the sky, made the worse appear the better reason, and taught others the same things. It is clear that Socrates was accused of the study of astronomy and probably geology and the other philosophers were persecuted for the same reason. The study of science, however, was a required condition to membership in the Egyptian Mystery System, so if the Greek philosophers studied the sciences, then they were fulfilling a required condition to membership in the Egyptian Mystery System; either through direct contact with Egypt, or its schools or lodges outside of Egypt. In Egyptian Mysteries, the neophyte was required to manifest control of thought and action, the combination of which Plato (427–347 BCE) called Justice, i.e., the unswerving righteousness of thought and action. Steadfastness of purpose, which was equivalent to Fortitude. Identity with spiritual life or the higher ideals, which was equivalent to temperance, an attitude attained when an individual had gained conquest over his passion or nature. Evidence of having a mission in life and of a call to spiritual Order or the Priesthood in the Mysteries, which was equivalent to Prudence or a deep insight and graveness that benefit the faculty of Seership. Freedom from resentment, when under the experience of persecution and wrong, was known as courage. Confidence in the power of the master (as teacher), and confidence in one's own ability to learn; both attributes being known as fidelity, readiness, or preparedness for initiation.

It is now quite clear that Plato drew the four cardinal virtues from the Egyptian ten; also, that Greek philosophy is the offspring of the Egyptian Mystery System. There was a Grand Lodge in Egypt which had associated schools and lodges in the ancient world. Such schools have frequently been referred to as private or philosophic mysteries, and their founders were initiates of the Egyptian Mysteries, the Ionian temple at Didyma, with the schools of Plato and Aristotle (384–322 BCE). It is therefore reasonable to argue that the so-called Greek philosophers formulated no new doctrine of their own; for their philosophy had been handed down by the great Egyptian Hierophants through the Mysteries. We are informed that aspirants for the mystical wisdom visited Egypt for initiation and were told by the priests of Sais that you Greeks are but children in the Secret Doctrine but were admitted to information that would promote their spiritual advancement. We are also informed that various schools or lodges of instructions in different lands visited, greeted, and assisted each other in the secret science, the more advanced being obliged to afford assistance and instruction to their brethren in the lesser Order. It is evident that modern Masonic lodges are copies of the Egyptian temple. The Temple of Luxor stands on a raised platform of brickworks, covering more than 2,000 feet in length and 1,000 feet in width. This rectangular shape became the pattern for all lodges and churches in the ancient world. The temple of Delphi was burnt down in 548 BCE and was rebuilt by King Amasis II of Egypt (r.570–526 BCE), of the 26 Dynasty, the last great ruler of Egypt before the Persian conquest, by donating three times as much as was needed, in the sum of 1,000 talents and 50,000 pounds of alum. It is worth noting that the Greeks regarded the Temple of Delphi as a foreign institution. Hence, they were unsympathetic towards it and, for the same reason, destroyed it by fire. The universal conviction among the ancients was that Egypt was the Holiest of lands or countries and that the gods dwelt there. The Nile became a center for pilgrimages in the ancient world and returned home with the conviction that the Nile was the home of the most profound religious knowledge.

According to GGM James (1954) Pythagoras, whose date of birth is unknown, a native of Samos, traveled frequently to Egypt for the purpose of his education. King Amasis of Egypt secured for Pythagoras an introduction to the Priests of Heliopolis, Memphis, and Thebes, to each of whom Pythagoras gave a silver goblet. According to Herodotus (484–425 BCE), Jablousk and Pliny (23–79 CE), after Pythagoras endured severe trials, including circumcision by the Egyptians, he was initiated into all their secrets. In addition, Plutarch (46–120 CE), Demetrius (337–283 BCE), and Antisthenes (c.445–c.365 BCE) state that Pythagoras founded the science of Mathematics among the Greeks, and that he sacrificed to the Muses, when the Priests explained to him the properties of the right-angled triangle. Pythagoras was also trained in music by the Egyptian priests. According to Hermodorus, Plato at the age of 28 visited Euclid (c.435–c.365 BCE) at Megara in company with other pupils of Socrates; and that for the next ten years he visited Cyrene (present day Libya), Italy, and finally Egypt; where he received instruction from the Egyptian Priests. With regards to Socrates, Aristotle, and the majority of pre-Socratic philosophers, history is silent about their travel to Egypt. The Greeks were civilized by, first, Egyptian, then Phoenicians and Thracians. Phoroneus and Cecrops were Egyptians, Cadmus a Phoenician, and Orpheus a Thracian. Each brought into Greece the religion and philosophical tenets of his respective country. The practice of teaching the doctrines of religion to people under the guise of myths, originated from the Egyptians and was adopted by the Phoenicians and Thracians, and subsequently introduced to the Greeks.

The thunder bolt, the aegis, the trident, the spear, torches, and snakes were the instruments used by the founders of States to terrify the ignorant and vulgar into subjection. The study of the Mysteries of Isis and Osiris proves that it was a pure Fire Philosophy. Zoroaster carried those mysteries into Greece, while Orpheus carried them into Thrace. In each of these places, these Egyptian Mysteries assumed the names of different gods, in order to adapt to local conditions. Hence in Asia, they took the form of Mithra: in Samothrace, the form of the Mother of the Gods: in Boeotia, the form of Bacchus; in Crete, the form of Jupiter; in Athens, the form of Ceres and Proserpine. The most noted of these Egyptian initiations were the Orphic, Bacchic, Eleusinian, Samothracian, and Mithraic. All of these fire worshippers believed that the universe originated from fire, and they lived at a time which antedated the time of the late Ionic philosophers by thousands of years. What is obvious is that the Greek philosophers practiced plagiarism and did not teach anything new. The source of Greek philosophers' teachings was the Egyptian Mystery System. In the history and compilation of Greek philosophy by Aristotle, there is only one other name that is associated with the authorship of an extraordinary number of scientific books, besides Aristotle, and the name is that of Democritus. However, circumstantial evidence points to the fact that the books of Democritus were not written either by him, nor did they contain his teachings. Apart from what was written on the Atom, the name of Democritus is associated with a large list of books, dealing with over sixty different subjects, and covering all the branches of science known to the ancient world. The list also contains books on Military Science, Law, and Magic. The accumulation of such a vast range of knowledge, by a single person, written in a single lifetime is physically and mentally impossible, especially as the method among the ancients of passing on knowledge was by gradual stages, followed by evidence of proficiency, which in turn was followed by initiations, which marked every step in the progress of the Neophyte.

In the history of Greek philosophy, Greek philosophers had direct or indirect association with Alexander the Great, who succeeded his father Philip II to the throne of Macedonia in 336 BCE, possessed a large collection of scientific books. Aristotle tutored Alexander the Great, beginning in 343 BCE, and Anaxarchus (380–320 BCE) accompanied Alexander the Great on his military campaign into Asia in 326 BCE. The history of the ancient theory of "The Four Qualities and Four Elements" provides the world with the evidence of the Egyptian origin of the doctrines of Opposites, change and the life and function of the universe is due to either of four elements: fire, or water, or earth, or air. Socrates was born in Athens, but very little is known about his early life and up to the age of 40, his life appears to be a complete blank. The first mention of him as an adult is when he served as an ordinary soldier in the sieges of Potidaea and Delium between 432 and 429 BCE. He was condemned to death in 399 BCE. The purpose of philosophy is the salvation of the Soul, whereby it feeds upon the truth congenial to its divine nature, escapes from the wheel of re-birth, and finally attains the consummation of unity with God. The Egyptians believed that self-knowledge was the basis of true knowledge, so they wrote on their temples: "Man, know thyself" (James 1954:91). Miletus, who Plato claimed was the chief accuser of Socrates, accused Socrates of committing the crime of not believing in the gods of the city, and by introducing new divinities and the crime of corrupting the youth. Socrates' life of poverty coincided with the requirements of the Mystery System of Egypt and her secret schools, which exacted the vows of secrecy and poverty from all Neophytes and initiates.

All aspirants of the Mysteries had to receive secret training and preparation, and Socrates was no exception. He alone of the three Athenian philosophers deserves the appellation of a true Master Mason. Plato was a great coward and Aristotle was greater still. At the execution of Socrates, in 399 BCE, Plato fled to Megara to the lodge of Euclid, and Aristotle, when indicted, fled into exile to Calchis, a region on the coast of the Black Sea, in present-day western Georgia. It is evident that Socrates' doctrines are eclectic, containing elements from

Anaxagoras, Democritus, Heraclitus, Parmenides, and Pythagoras have been traced to the teachings of the Egyptian Mystery System. Heraclitus (c.535–c.475 BCE), was a native of the city of Ephesus, then part of the Persian Empire, present-day Efes, in Turkey. Little is known about his early life and education. Heraclitus was known for his insistence on ever-present change as being the fundamental essence of the universe. He is accredited with saying, "No man ever steps in the same river twice." He was also committed to the unity of opposites in the world, stating that "the paths up and down are one and the same" (James 1954:96).

Plato is said to have been born at Athens in 427 BCE, but little is known about his early life and training. He is said to have studied the doctrines of Heraclitus, and to have been a pupil of Socrates for eight years, and together with other pupils of Socrates, he fled from Athens to Euclid at Megara for safety, when Socrates was executed in 399 BCE. Plato returned to Athens some 12 years after the death of Socrates in 387 BCE and opened an Academy in a gymnasium on the western suburb of Athens, over which he presided for 20 years. He is said to have taught Political Science, Statesmanship, Mathematics, and Dialectics. However, Plato's writings are disputed by some scholars. Diogenes Laertius, Aristoxenus (c.375–335 BCE), and Favorinus (c.80–160 CE) declared that the subject matter of the Republic was found in the controversies written by Protagoras (490–420 BCE), at the time of whose death Plato was but a boy. The authorship of Plato rests only upon the opinions of Aristotle and Theophrastus (c.371–c.287 BCE), both of whose aims were the compilation of a Greek philosophy with Egyptian material. With regards to the allegory of the "Charioteer and the winged steeds," this is a description of the quality and destiny of the soul as it appears at the bar of justice, in the Judgment Drama of *The Egyptian Book of the Dead*. In this Drama, the Great Chief Justice and president of the Unseen World, Osiris, is seated on a throne, and is attended by the Goddesses Isis and Nephthys, while forty-two assistant judges are seated around.

The doctrines attributed to Plato are scattered over a wide area of literature; being found in piecemeal throughout what are called dialogues, especially in connection with the theory of ideas and its application to natural phenomena which includes the doctrines of the real and unreal, the Nous and Creation. The ethical doctrines concerning the highest good, the definition of virtue and the cardinal virtues. The doctrine of the Ideal State, whose attributes are compared with the attributes of the soul and justice. According to Plato's ethical doctrines, the purpose of man's life is freedom from the fetters of the body, in which the soul is confined and the practice of virtue and wisdom makes him like a God, even while on earth. All virtues may be reduced to the four cardinal virtues: wisdom, fortitude, temperance, and justice. The Ideal State is modeled upon the individual soul and just as the soul has three parts, so also should the state: the rulers, the warriors, and the workers. Just as the harmony of the soul depends upon the proper subordination of its parts, in order to enjoy peace. It is the proper subordination of the different classes, which makes it an Ideal State. The doctrine of Plato is eclectic and point to Egyptian origin – the doctrine of opposites. The main purpose of the Egyptian Mysteries was the salvation of the human soul. The Egyptian believed the human body to be a prison house, where the soul is chained by ten fetters. This condition kept man separated from God and subject him to the wheel of re-birth or re-incarnation.

According to James (1954), in order to escape from the effects of his condition, two requirements had to be fulfilled by the Neophyte. Firstly, he must keep the Ten Commandants taught by the Mysteries, for by such discipline he would gain conquest over the fetters of the soul and liberate it, so as to make its development possible. Secondly, he must undergo a series of initiations, in order to develop his soul from the human stage to that of a God. Such a transformation was known as salvation. According to the theory of salvation, man is expected to work out his own salvation, without a mediator between himself and his God. The doctrines of the Ten Virtues and the Ten Fetters are as old as the Egyptian history itself. Each commandant represented a principle of virtue, and the function of each virtue was to remove a fetter. Plato is credited with having reduced all virtues to four cardinal virtues and assigning the highest place among them to wisdom. Socrates, the alleged teacher of Plato, taught that wisdom was the equivalent of all virtue. The ten principles of virtue are: (i) the control of one's thoughts, (ii) the control of one's action, (iii) one must have devotion of purpose, (iv) one must have faith in the ability of one's master to teach the truth, (v) one must have faith in one's self to assimilate the truth, (vi) one must have faith in one's self to employ the truth, (vii) one must be free from resentment under the experience of persecution, (viii) one must be free from resentment under experience of wrong, (ix) one must cultivate the ability to distinguish between right and wrong, and (x) to cultivate the ability to distinguish between the real and the unreal – a sense of value. When the order in which the cardinal virtues are said to be arranged, the first place which wisdom occupies among the virtues was given to it by the Egyptian Mysteries and not Plato.

From the control thoughts and actions, we derive the virtue of wisdom. From (vii and viii) we derive the virtue of fortitude and from (ix and x) we derive the virtues of justice and temperance. From the doctrine of the Ideal State, it is questionable whether Plato was the author of the republic along with the allegory of the charioteer and winged steeds, as they derived from *The Egyptian Book of the Dead*, in the Judgment Drama. The motion of the scale in the Judgment Drama corresponds with the up and down motion of the winged steeds of the allegory. The opposite qualities weighed on the scale correspond with the opposite qualities possessed by the noble and ignoble steeds of the allegory. The idea of justice symbolized by the scale of Judgment Drama, corresponds with the idea of justice expressed in the allegory. The winged steeds correspond with the monsters of the Judgment Drama. The important question is: from what source did Protagoras drew the ideas of the Republic which were circulated in the controversies? Textbooks on Greek philosophy informed that Protagoras was a pupil of Democritus, in whose writings there is no connection between them and the educational system and the paternal government which are advocated in the Republic. It would therefore be reasonable to conclude that the subject matter of Plato's Republic was neither produced by him nor any Greek philosopher.

According to Diogenes Laertius' Book VIII, pp.399–401, when Plato visited Dionysius at Sicily, he paid Philolaus (c.470–c.385 BCE), a Greek Pythagorean and pre-Socratic philosopher, 40 Alexandrian Mina of silver, for a book from which he copied the whole contents of the Timaeus (c.360 BCE). It could be further concluded that Plato wrote neither the Republic nor the Timaeus, whose subject matter identifies them with the purpose of the Mysteries of Egypt. Greek culture and tradition did not furnish Plato with the idea of the Chariot and winged steeds, for nowhere in their brief military history, up to the time of Plato, do we find the use of such a war machine by the Greeks. The only nearby nation who specialized in the manufacture of chariots and the breeding of horses was the Egyptians. In the time of Joseph, Governor in Egypt (Genesis 41:37–56), the horse and war chariot were in use; and when the Israelites fled from the country, Pharaoh pursued them to the Red Sea in chariots. Both Homer (751–651 BCE), author of the *Iliad* and the *Odyssey*, two epic poems which are the central works of Greek literature, and Diodorus Siculus (90–30BCE), who is known for writing the monumental universal history Bibliotheca historica, between 60 and 30 BCE, visited Egypt. They both testified that they saw great multitude of war chariots and numerous stables along the banks of the Nile, from Memphis to Thebes. A sketch of Greek military history shows that the chariot was not used by them.

The Ionian revolt against Persian rule (499–494 BCE) climaxed in a naval engagement at Lade, where the Ionian fleet was defeated. At the battle of Marathon (490 BCE) the Greeks met the Persians at the bay of Marathon, and after a brief fight with bows and arrows, both belligerents withdrew to prepare for more decisive engagements. At the battle of Thermopylae (480 BCE) the Persians Empire of Xerxes I (518–465 BCE) and the Greeks, led by King Leonidas of Sparta (540–480 BCE), met again to settle their grievances. The Persians had anchored in the Gulf of Pagasae, while the Greeks anchored off Cape Artimesium. A battle followed and Thermopylae was captured by the Persians. Both Persians and Greeks met again at Salamis in 479 BCE and a naval engagement followed, with considerable loss of ships on both sides. Both belligerents withdrew without any decision. The confederacy of Delos and their wars with the Persians (478–448 BCE), was a defensive pack against Persian aggression. They were involved in two naval battles, one at the river Eurymedon in 476 BCE, when the Greeks gained a minor victory, and the other at Cyprus in 449 BCE, when the island was captured by the Persians. No chariots were used in any of these engagements. During a number of internal conflicts, no chariots were used including the Peloponnesian wars, 460–445 BCE, and 431–421 BCE, respectively. These wars were fought between the different Greek states and their major engagements were maritime.

Aristotle was born in 384 BCE at Stagira, a town in Thrace. His father, Neomachus was a physician to Amyntas (r.392–370 BCE), King of Macedonia. There is no record of Aristotle's early education, but we are told that he became an orphan and at the age of 19 years old and went to Athens, where he spent 20 years as a pupil of Plato. Following the death of Plato, Aristotle left for Mysia, where he met and married the niece of Hermeias. Likewise, after the death of Amyntas of Macedon, his son Philip having become King, appointed Aristotle as tutor of his son Alexander, a boy of 13 years, later to be called the Great in consequence of his conquest of Egypt. Following the assassination of Philip in 336 BCE, Alexander became King and immediately started an Asiatic campaign that included Egypt. During this period, Aristotle returned to Athens and founded a school in a gymnasium called the Lyceum. Alexander the Great advanced Aristotle the funds to purchase a large number of books and his pupils were called Peripatetic. Aristotle fled Athens to Chalcis in Euboea, owing to an indictment charge for impiety, brought against him by a priest name Eurymedon. Aristotle died in exile in Chalcis in 322 BCE. Aristotle defines Metaphysics as the science of Being as Being. He names the Attributes of Being as (a) actually (perfection) and (b) potentiality (the capacity for perfection). He states that all created beings are composed of actuality and potentiality. There are four principles of being in the physical realm which are called causes – Matter, Form/Essence, Nature, and Purpose. The world is eternal, because matter, motion, and time are eternal. Nature is everything which has the principle of motion and rest. Nature does nothing in vain, but according to definite law.

The striving of nature is through the less perfect to the more perfect. The soul transcends all material conditions. The soul is the power which a living body possesses, and it is the end for which the body exists. The teleological concept of God (based on perceived evidence of deliberate design in the natural or physical world) has been embraced by Socrates, Plato, Aristotle, and by the peoples of the remotest antiquity. Aristotle introduced the concept of the "Unmoved Mover" in order to prove the existence of God. But the "Unmoved Mover" is none other than the Atum of the Memphite Theology of the Egyptians, the Demiurge (a Being responsible for the creation of the universe), through whose command (logos) four pairs of gods were created out of different parts of his body and who accordingly moved out of him. This act of creation took place while Atum remained unmoved; has he embraced Ptah (he is considered to have existed before all other things). Thus, the family of Nine Gods was created, and has been named the Ennead.

Hence, the concept of the "Unmoved Mover" is derived from the Egyptian Mystery System and not from Aristotle.

The evidence, therefore, would indicate that Greek philosophers were not the authors of Greek philosophy, rather the Egyptian Priests and Hierophants (interpreters of sacred mysteries and arcane principles). Aristotle died in 322 BCE, after he had secured the largest quantity of scientific books from the Royal Libraries and Temples of Egypt. The death of Aristotle marked the death of philosophy among the Greeks; consequently, they were forced to make a study of Ethics, which they also borrowed from the Egyptian "Summum Bonum" or greatest good. Socrates became famous in history as a philosopher and great thinker, but the truth is, he copied his ideas from the Egyptian Temples, and was not the author of *Know thyself*. Plato was also a Greek philosopher who copied his "Four Cardinal Virtues" from the Egyptian Mystery System, which contained ten virtues – Plato's four cardinal virtues are justice, wisdom, temperance, and courage. Most of Greek's philosophies used the teaching of Pythagoras as their model; and consequently, they have introduced nothing new in the field of philosophy.

The Egyptians Mystery System was the first Secret Order in history and the publication of its teachings was strictly prohibited. After receiving his training in Egypt, Pythagoras returned to his native island of Samos, where he established his order for a short time, before migrating to Croton (c.525 BCE) in Southern Italy, until his expulsion. Thales had received his education in Egypt, along with his associates, Anaximander and Anaximenes, both natives of Ionia in Asia Minor, a stronghold of the Egyptian Mystery schools. Similarly, Xenophanes, Parmenides, Zeno and Melissus of Samos (birth and death unknown), were also natives of Ionia, and all migrated to Elea in Italy and established themselves and spread the teachings of the Egyptian Mysteries. In like manner, Heraclitus (c.535–c.475 BCE), was a native of the city of Ephesus, then part of the Persian Empire. It is said that little is known about his early life and education. He was famous for his insistence on ever-present change as being the fundamental essence of the universe. This position was complemented by his stark commitment to a unity of opposites in the world, he is accredited with saying that the paths up and down are one and the same.

Empedocles (c.490–c.430 BCE), was a citizen of Acragas, a Greek city in Sicily. He was a vegetarian and supported the doctrine of reincarnation. His notable ideas were that all matter is made up of four elements: water, earth, air and fire, and the cosmic principles of love and repulsion. Anaxagoras was born in Clazomenae in Asia Minor and was the first to bring philosophy to Athens. He claimed that he did not feel the heat of the sun for it was too far away, for which he was charged with impiety and went into exile in Lampsacus. Democritus was born in Abdera, Thrace, an Ionian colony of Teos. His contribution to philosophy is difficult to distinguish from that of his mentor Leucippus, as they are often mentioned together in texts. None of his writings have survived; only fragments are known from his alleged vast body of work. It is said that Democritus traveled to distant countries, including India and Ethiopia, to satisfy his thirst for knowledge. On his return to his native land, he traveled throughout Greece to acquire a better knowledge of its cultures. Democritus' theory held that everything is composed of "atoms." Consequently, it is clear that Egypt's neighbors had all become familiar with the teachings of Egyptian Mysteries many centuries before the Athenians, who in 399 BCE sentenced Socrates to death, which prompted Plato and Aristotle to flee for their lives from Athens, as philosophy was viewed as foreign to Athenians.

It would seem that both the Ionians and the Italians had a prior claim to philosophy than the Athenians, since it made contact with them long before it did with Athens. It is however interesting to note that neither the Ionians nor the Italians claimed the authorship of philosophy, as they were well aware of its true authors, the Egyptians. It is ironic that philosophy has been accredited to the Greeks, when they were its greatest enemies and persecutors and had persistently treated it as a foreign innovation. Further, from Thales to Aristotle (624–322 BCE), the Ionians were not Greek citizens, but were at first Egyptian subjects and later Persian subjects. Asia Minor or Ionia was the ancient land of the Hittites, who were not known by any other name in ancient days. From Thales to Aristotle, no writer or historian professes to know anything about their early education. It is said that Thales was from Miletus in Asia Minor and one of the Seven Sages of Greece. But it is also said that Thales was a Phoenician, who received instruction from an Egyptian priest, but no writing attributed to him has survived. It is said that Thales used geometry to calculate the heights of pyramids and the distance of ship from shore.

As early as the third century (274–194 BCE) Eratosthenes (d.194 BCE), a Stoic, drew up a chronology of Greek philosophers and in the second century (140 BCE) Appollodorus (c.180–120 BCE) also drew up another. In the first century, 60–70 BCE Andronicus of Rhodes, the eleventh head of the peripatetic school, also drew up another. Apart from the three Athenian philosophers, Socrates, Plato, and Aristotle, we are confronted with confusion. Thales' birth has been recorded as 640, 624 and 600 BCE. For the birth of Anaximenes 588, 560, and 546 BCE. Parmenides is credited as been born in 500 BCE, Xenophanes at 576 and 570 BCE and Zeno at 490 BCE. Heraclitus' birth is placed at 536, 535, or 530 BCE. With regards to Empedocles, his birth is placed at 484 and 490 BCE, while Anaxagoras birth is placed at 500 and 450 BCE. Socrates (469–399 BCE), Plato (427–347 BCE), and Aristotle (384–322 BCE) are the only three philosophers that there seems to be some certainty about their dates of births and deaths. According to Martin Bernal (1987) Thucydides' (460–395 BCE) history, built up to the unprecedented might of his two protagonists, Athens and Sparta, in which he described, "The greatest disturbance in the history of the Hellenes, affecting also a large part of the non-Hellenic world." His whole work was a paean to the uniqueness of Greek achievements, even the destructive ones. Thus, the idea that the Egyptians, whom Athenians could now conquer, or Phoenicians, who formed the most terrible arm of Persian military power – its fleet – should have played a central role in the formation of Greek culture was clearly disturbing to Thucydides' (460–395 BCE) contemporaries. This kind of "nationalism" would seem to be typical in the aftermath of the Persian Wars of the early fifth century BCE and subsequent expansion of Greek power, and from this time onward there is varying degrees of hatred and contempt for "barbarians" among most Greeks.

In such an atmosphere, one would expect Greek writers to play down the legend of cultural indebtedness to Egypt. Further, in the fourth century BCE, the outstanding spokesman for Pan-Hellenism and Greek cultural pride was the Athenian orator Isocrates (436–338 BCE). At the Olympian festival of 380 BCE he called on Spartans and Athenians to drop their differences and join in a Pan-Hellenic union against Persia and the barbarians. He proclaimed: "And so far has our city [Athens] distanced the rest of mankind in thought and in speech that her pupils have become the teachers of the rest of the world. She has brought it about that the name 'Hellenes' suggests no longer a race but an intelligence, and that the title 'Hellenes' is applied rather to those who share our culture than to those who share a common blood" (Bernal, 1987:103). None the less, many cultured Greeks, including Eudoxus (c. 395/390–342/337 BCE), the great mathematician and astronomer of the fourth century BCE, still felt obliged to study in Egypt. Isocrates insisted that *philosophia* (philosophy) was, and could only have been, a product of Egypt and that the Spartans had failed to apply the Egyptian principle of the division of labor and that their constitution fell short of the perfection of the Egyptian model, about which he wrote: "philosophers who undertake to discuss such topics and have won the greater reputation prefer above all others the Egyptian form of government" (Bernal, 1987:105).

In *Phaedrus*, Plato and Socrates declare that "it was He [Theuth-Thoth the Egyptian god of wisdom] who invented numbers and arithmetic and geometry...and most important of all letters." In *Philebos* and *Epinomis* Plato went into detail on Thoth as the creator of writing, even of language and all sciences. Elsewhere Plato praised Egyptian art and music and argued for their adoption in Greece. Plato's republic was based on Egypt, as many of his contemporaries mocked him, saying that he was not the inventor of his republic, but that he had copied Egyptian institutions. *The deeper they [Greeks] went towards the true Hellenic roots of Greece, the closer they came to Egypt.* Despite their ambivalence, if not hostility to the ideas, the two leading intellectual figures of the early fourth century BCE were forced to admit the critical importance of foreign colonization, and massive later cultural borrowing from Egypt and the Levant, and in the formation of the Hellenic civilization they both loved so much. Aristotle, a pupil of Plato, also studied at the Academy under Eudoxus of Cnidus, who is reported to have spent 16 months in Egypt shaving his head in order to study with priests there. Aristotle argued that the Egyptians had created the caste system [division of labor] and hence "Egypt was the cradle of mathematics because the caste of priests was given great leisure, *schole*." According to Aristotle, the priests had invented the *mathe matikai technai* (mathematical arts), which included geometry, arithmetic and astronomy, which Greeks were beginning to process. Aristotle maintained that the Egyptians had developed geometry, the key science, for practical reasons – to measure land after landmarks had been washed away by the Nile Flood.

Among many other things, Aristotle was, of course, the tutor of Alexander the Great. It was immediately after the conquest of the Persian Empire in the 330s BCE that the Egyptian priest Manetho wrote a history of Egypt in Greek, in which he set out the scheme of 33 dynasties, which remains the basis of the historiography of Ancient Egypt. It was also about this time that Hecataeus of Abdera set out his view that the traditions of the Egyptian expulsion of the Hyksos, the *Israelite Exodus* and that of Danaos' landing in Argos were three parallel versions of the same story: "The natives of the land surmised that unless they removed the foreigners their troubles would never be resolved. At once, therefore, the aliens were driven from the country and the most outstanding and active among them banded together and, as some say, were cast ashore in Greece and certain other regions; their teachers were notable men, among them being Danaos and Kadmos. But the greater number were driven into what is now called Judaea, which is not far from Egypt and at that time was utterly uninhabited. The colony was headed by a man called Moses" (Bernal, 1987:109). The early Greeks and Romans copied both religious ideas and architectural designs and during periods of decline or conquests, Asians and Europeans seized and transported from Africa as much of the artifacts of its civilization as they could. For example, Cambyses I, a Persian King of the Achaemenid dynasty, who ruled (c.600–559 BCE), hauled away an estimated one billion dollars of precious historical material from Thebes alone.

Cambyses was only one of countless thousands who invaded the repositories of black history during each of the many periods of foreign invasions and foreign rule. According to G. G. M. James (1954) in the drama of Greek philosophy there are three actors, who have played distinct parts, firstly, Alexander the Great, who by an act of aggression invaded Egypt in 333 BCE and ransacked and looted the Royal Library at Alexandria and together with his companions carried off a booty of scientific, philosophic and religious books. Aristotle made a library of his own with plundered books. Egypt was then stolen and annexed as a portion of

Alexander's empire, which prepared the way and made it possible for the capture of the culture of the African continent. In this way, the Greeks stole the Legacy of the African continent and called it their own. The second actor was the School of Aristotle, whose students moved from Athens to Egypt and converted the royal library, first into a research center and, secondly, into a university and, thirdly, compiled that vast body of scientific knowledge, which they had gained from research, together with oral instructions, which Greek students had received from Egyptian priests, into what they have called the history of Greek Philosophy. When we call the theorem of the Square on the Hypotenuse, the Pythagorean Theorem, it has concealed the truth for centuries from the world, who ought to know that the Egyptians taught Pythagoras and the Greeks, what mathematics they knew.

The third actor, is Ancient Rome, who through the edicts of her Emperors Theodosius (347–395 CE, r.379–395 CE), born at Coca, Segovia, Spain and Justinian (482–565 CE, Byzantine emperor r.527–565 CE), born at Taurisium, Skopje in the Republic of Macedonia, who abolished the Mysteries of the African continent; i.e., the ancient culture system of the world. This lofty culture system of black people filled Rome with envy, and consequently, she legalized Christianity which she had persecuted for five centuries and set it up as a state religion and as a rival of the Ancient Mystery System, its own mother. In keeping with the plan of emperors Theodosius and Justinian to exterminate and forever suppress the culture system of the African continent, the Christian church established its missionary enterprise to fight against what it has called paganism, a euphemism for black. This is why the Mysteries have been despised, because they are all offspring of the African Mysteries, which have never been clearly understood by Europeans, and consequently have provoked their prejudice and condemnation. It is therefore reasonable to argue that pre-Socratic philosophers were unknown because they were foreigners to the Athenian government, or that they never existed. As late as the fourth century BCE, Socrates, Plato, and Aristotle were persecuted by the Athenian government for introducing foreign doctrines into Athens. Hence, any claim by Greeks to the ownership or authorship of the doctrines which they had rejected must be regarded as theft. The so-called Greek philosophy was alien to the Greeks and their conditions of life, from the time of Thales (620 BCE) to the time of Aristotle (384 BCE), the Greeks were victims of internal and external wars and lived in constant fear of invasion from Persians, who were enemy of the city-states. Africa has laid the cultural foundations of modern progress and therefore she and her people deserve the honor and praise which for centuries have been falsely given to the Greeks.

The Romans

According to Charles Freeman (1996), the hills of Rome had been settled for at least 700 years before the city expanded from a relatively small territory on the plain of Latium and achieved the domination of the Italian peninsula in the fourth and third centuries BCE. The achievement, when it eventually came, was, however, a remarkable one. The most formidable obstacle to successful domination has been a mountain range, the Apennines. The Apennines stretch down the peninsula for a 1,000km rising to nearly 3,000 meters in places and are often between 50 and 100km wide. There are pockets of fertile land high in the Apennines so a reasonably sized population could be supported. As a result, Italy has always been a country of unexpected diversity, strong regional loyalties, and well-established local languages. Around the Apennines lie the coastal plains, the richest of which is the Po Valley, which makes up ten percent of the lowland of Italy. Further north, the Alps appear to close the peninsula off from Europe. The most fertile land along the Apennines is that along the west coast, where the soil is volcanic and rainfall good. Between the rivers Tiber and Arno, are to be found some of the richest mineral deposits in the central Mediterranean. The early history of Rome has proved very difficult to reconstruct, and later Roman historians drew on a variety of legends from both Greek and Roman sources to create their own version of the city's foundation.

Rome grew up on the banks of the Tiber at a site where an island divided the river into two narrower channels. In the eighth century BCE, the period in which the legends place the foundation of the city, there is evidence for the arrival of Greek traders. From the eight century through to the end of the sixth century BCE, Rome was ruled by "kings." Almost nothing is known of the early monarchs, but it seems that each new King was acclaimed by the people of Rome, meeting of an assembly of 30 groups of clans. After auspices had first been taken to ensure the King had divine support. He would then have *imperium*, divine authority through which he could exercise his power in practical, military, and religious affairs. The symbol of *imperium* was the *fasces*, a bundle of rods bound round an axe, which was carried in front of the King. King Tarquin I (c.616–579 BCE) is recorded as having migrated to Rome from Etruria and engineered his acclamation as King. Tarquin I was murdered in 579 BCE and his successor, Servius Tullius (575–535 BCE), seized power by force and there is evidence that he expanded the citizen body by enfranchising the local rural population. He also created a citizen army of all those able to afford arms. This was the first legion, with a reported strength of 4,000 men and 600 cavalries. These men were grouped into centuries. The *comitia centuriata*, as this assembly was called later, became the most powerful of the Roman popular assemblies with the formal duty of declaring war or peace and making alliance.

In republican times, it formed the electoral body for the consuls and praetors. This expansion of the citizen body was crucial to Rome's later success. To the astonishment of the Greeks even the descendants of freed slaves would become citizens as a matter of course. Servius' successor, Tarquin the Proud (c.534–509

BCE) was thrown out by the outraged aristocracy in 509. The aristocracy proclaimed themselves the protectors of Rome against tyranny in general and this became central to the ideology through which they justified their political supremacy. In the fifth century, the patrician families consolidated their grip on government. Patricians took ninety percent of the consulships between 485 and 445 BCE. But their growing power was soon challenged by the Plebs, the mass of citizens who by law of custom had become excluded from the magistracies and the senate. The battle between Plebeians and Patricians was marked by a steady retreat by the Patricians, a retreat hastened by a decline in the number of Patrician families as male line failed. Under the kings, Rome had been a successful military state and in 509 controlled about 800 square kilometers, a third of Latium, with an estimated population of between 20,000 and 30,000, larger than any other Latin community, and comparable to the larger Greek cities of Southern Italy. However, the city was challenged by the surrounding Latin tribes, following the fall of their monarchy.

Rome defeated them at the battle of Lake Regillus in 499 BCE, but the victory was Aequi and the Volsci, who successfully disrupted the plain's economy. In 493 Rome agreed with the Latin communities to face the intruders together, but it took until the end of the century to restore order. With order restored, Rome now moved against an old rival, the once wealthy Etruscan city of Veii, which was only 15 kilometers to the north. After an epic year siege, the city fell in 396 BCE. Over 500 square kilometers of land confiscated from Veii had to be integrated into the *ager Romanus* (Roman territory). A new period of warfare began in 343 BCE with a short war against the Samnite, the most formidable and best organized of the inland mountain peoples, after appeals for help by the cities of Campania. The Samnite were quickly defeated but to the fury of the Campanian Rome made peace with them. It was at this time that the Latin states were becoming resentful of the arrogance of Roman rule. Rome suddenly found herself facing a coalition of enemies, Latins, Campanian and, once again, the Volsci. Rome's reputation as a military force was confirmed when she defeated them. It was the settlement of 338 BCE, after this war, which showed Rome's political shrewdness. Her enemies were not destroyed but instead re-organized into what has been described as a "commonwealth" of states which stretched across the coastal plains from the Tiber to the bay of Naples. Everyone accepted the dominance of Rome and agreed to provide armed support when called upon.

Members of these communities became full Roman citizens and could vote in the Roman assemblies. In addition, Rome began to establish colonies (the word derives from the Latin verb *colere*, to cultivate) and by 250 BCE Rome had made alliances with over 150 Italian communities who had either been defeated or forced through fear into surrender. The essence of the settlement of 338 BCE was its flexibility. Rome could draw on a large reserve of manpower at almost no cost to herself while the defeated communities retained enough independence to dampen any desire for revolt. Rome had evolved a system of government and control which was to prove astonishingly resilient in the years to come. With Rome domination in central Italy and the Celts hemmed in through a network of Roman alliances with the cities of Etruria, Roman attention turned south. The Greek cities were now in decline and in the 280s BCE, several of them began to call for help from Rome against the attacks of native populations. As Rome responded, the most prosperous Greek city of the south grew alarmed at this intrusion, and when a Roman war fleet ventured into Tarentum's waters in 282 BCE it was attacked. When Rome counter-attacked, Tarentum was close to being taken, the city appealed to Pyrrhus, the King of Epirus. Pyrrhus arrived with a large and well-equipped army of some 20,000 men. This was the first Hellenistic army the Romans had ever seen, and they proved vulnerable to its power and experience. At two battles, Heraclea (280 BCE) and Ausculum (279 BCE), the Romans were defeated but in each case, Pyrrhus lost thousands of his own precious troops (hence the term Pyrrhic victory). After another battle at Beneventum in 275 BCE, Pyrrhus withdrew and Tarentum fell to Rome in 272 BCE and Roman domination of the south of the peninsula was complete.

By 264 BCE some twenty percent of the land surface of Italy had been made part of the *ager Romanus*, the directly controlled territory of Rome. In much of this land the local population had been enslaved or killed and it was now open to Roman settlement. Between 20,000 and 30,000 adult males may have been given plots of land to farm, with another 70,000 men and their families may have been involved in settling the 19 new colonies recorded between 334 and 263 BCE. However, these colonies and settlements lay in between cities and cultures which still retained their own languages and customs. It was to be another 200 years before Latin became the dominant language of the peninsula. No pre-industrial society has ever mobilized such a high percentage of its male population in war over such a long period of time as Rome. It is estimated that between nine and sixteen percent of male citizens in normal times and twenty-five percent at times of crisis could be supported in their armies. Wars were assumed to be just and the temples built during the Samnite wars were based on Hellenistic victory cults. There were dedications to Victoria, Jupiter, Victor, Bellona (an early Roman goddess), Victrix, and Hercules Invictus (the unconquered Hercules). The religion of Rome was integrated into its political life. The priesthoods were monopolized by leading families and rituals marked the beginning and end of the war-making season. Plunder was used to dedicate and furnish new temples. A victorious general, who had slain at least 5,000 enemies, could claim the right from the senate to extend his *imperium* across the *pomerium* so that he could bring his troops in procession into the city and sacrifice at the great temple of Jupiter on the Capitoline Hill.

In 265 BCE Rome's power extended only as far as Northern Italy where the Celts provided a major barrier to further expansion. But there was no city or people able to challenge the combined strength of her own manpower and that of her allies. Rome had nonetheless already made treaties with Carthage, the major sea power of the western Mediterranean, in which Rome accepted Carthaginian supremacy at sea. Yet in the next 120 years, Rome was to transform herself into a major Mediterranean power with interests as far west as Spain and east as far as Asia and the Aegean. The incident which set Rome on the path to becoming a Mediterranean power was a relatively insignificant one. A group of Italian mercenaries had seized the city of Messene (modern day Messina), which overlooked the straits between Sicily and Italy. In 265 BCE, the ruler of Syracuse, Hiero (c.308–215 BCE), had tried to dislodge them. While some looked to Carthage for help, others appealed to Rome. The senate was reluctant to intervene, as it had already condemned one group of Roman citizens who seized a Greek city. However, it was clear that a Carthaginian takeover in Messina would threaten Roman control of the straits. In the face of Roman response, the Carthaginians withdrew their garrison from Messene and Rome occupied the city. Although Carthage and Syracuse were long-standing enemies, Rome's occupation of Messene was sufficiently provocative to force them into an alliance. The outcome of the siege of Messene was the first Punic War (264–241 BCE) (Punicus is the Latin for Carthaginian and refers to the mixed culture of the Phoenicians and local Africans at Carthage).

Rome's chances of subduing the coastal cities were limited, so long as Carthage was in control of the sea, and it was immediately after the capture of Acragas that Rome decided to build a fleet. A grounded Carthaginian ship had to be used as a model with crews being trained on land as the first 100 quinqueremes were being built. The war could now be fought by Rome at sea and possibly even taken into the heart of the Carthaginian Empire. The first encounter of the two fleet at Mylae off the coast of Sicily in 260 BCE was a Roman victory. It was followed by an even more crushing victory off Cape Ecnomus (on the southern coast of Sicily) in 256 BCE, when 80 Carthaginian ships were sunk or captured. The way was now open for an invasion of Africa, and in 256 BCE troops were landed there. But the invaders were crushed in 255 BCE. Further disasters followed and the war now became one of attrition, symbolized by a nine-year siege by the Romans of the Carthaginian fortress of Lilybaeum on the west coast of Sicily. In 241 BCE, at a battle off the Aegates Islands, the last Carthaginian forces was sunk or captured by the Roman. Carthage could no longer protect Sicily and in the peace that followed, Carthage ceded Sicily to Rome. Syracuse survived as an independent ally of Rome. Within three years Rome had taken advantage of a mutiny among Carthaginian mercenaries to seize Sardinia and Corsica from the Carthaginians.

In 225 BCE, central Italy was faced with a Celtic invasion. The Romans crushed it at the battle of Telamon and exploited their advantage by conquering the Po valley and establishing Roman colonies at Cremona and Placentia. When the Carthaginians, under Hannibal, who had succeeded his father Hamilcar, besieged and took the city of Massilia in 219 BCE, Rome quickly protested. But neither side appeared to have had any inhibitions about going to war again, but the Second Punic War (218–202) was the result. Hannibal crossed the Alps, but perhaps a third of his army was lost on the way, with some 25,000 men finally descending on the Po plain, where the Celts rallied to Hannibal as their liberator. In the first major encounter with the Romans at Trebbia (218 BCE), west of the new Roman colony at Placentia, over half the Roman army was lost and with it the north of Italy. In 217, Hannibal, now in central Italy, lured a large Roman army into the narrow plain between Lake Trasimene and the mountains and slaughtered it. According to one source, the senate raised eight legions each of 5,000 men and together with 80,000 allied men marched south to Apulia where Hannibal was ravaging the land. Hannibal drew the Roman armies on to an open plain at Cannae where he knew he could use his cavalry effectively. The Romans hoped that the sheer weight of their numbers would be enough to overwhelm the Celts and Spaniards who were holding Hannibal's center. However, the Romans found themselves enveloped by African infantry stationed on the two wings and the Carthaginian cavalry who had routed their Roman counterparts. In a devastating defeat, all but 14,500 of the Roman army was wiped out. Hannibal's greatest prize was Capua, the second city of Italy, and a number of other cities of Campania either came over to him or were captured in the aftermath of the battle. Hannibal was now in a position to march on Rome, but he never made the move. This was to be Hannibal's greatest military error, as this was the last time he would be in a position to capture Rome and possible Italy.

In 172 BCE, the Romans shipped over an army and forced the Macedonian King Perseus (212–166 BCE) into a war he had never desired. Although he held out successfully for some time, in 168 BCE Perseus' army was destroyed at the battle of Pydna on the Macedonian coast. It was in the settlement after Pydna that Roman power was first imposed effectively in Greece, and in that sense 168 BCE marked a turning point. Macedonia was split up into four republics, each ruling itself through elected representatives and allowed only limited contact with the others. The Molossians of Epirus who had aided Perseus found their cities plundered and, 150,000 of their inhabitants sold into slavery. The Seleucid King Antiochus IV (215–164 BCE), who had invaded Egypt in 168 BCE without Roman approval, suddenly found himself confronted on the spot by a Roman envoy, Gaius Popillius Laenas, who drew a circle around the astonished King and forbade him to leave it until he had agreed to make peace and withdrew. Other kings were exposed to greater humiliation, including Prusias II of Bithynia (182–

149 BCE) and Eumenes, King of Pergamum (d.160 BCE). Julius Caesar (100–44 BCE), his name transmitted into later European history as Kaiser and Tsar and incorporated into the western calendar (July), with his assignation remaining one of the most vivid folk memories of European culture. By 59 BCE, Caesar had marked himself out as a remarkable man. Caesar introduced a number of land laws, which allowed for the settlement of Pompey's veterans and distributed public land in Campania to some 20,000 citizens, mostly veterans and poor.

In 58 BCE, Caesar left Rome to take up his command, with immense potential for glory, had there had been continuing unrest among the Celtic tribes in Gaul. It was to be another nine years before he returned to Rome. By 57 BCE, Caesar brought virtually the whole of Gaul under Roman control. However, the Battle of Carrhae, in 53 BCE, between the Roman Republic, under the command of Marcus Licinius Crassus and the Parthian Empire, was one of the most humiliating of all Roman defeats and news of the disaster filtered back to Rome at a time of essential disorder. On January 10, 49 BCE, Caesar crossed a small river, the Rubicon, which marked the boundary of Cisalpine Gaul within which he could exercise *imperium* and the rest of Italy where he could not. He had, in effect, declared war on the Republic. Once Caesar had taken the initiative there was no reason to delay. The summer of 49 BCE was spent by Caesar eliminating Pompey's armies in Spain and this important success was followed by the submission of Sicily and Sardinia. However, there was a major setback in Africa. Caesar found himself facing not only the local Pompeian commander but King Juba of Numidia (d.46 BCE). Africa for the first time was lost to Caesar. It took all of Caesar's formidable power and leadership to regroup his forces and finally bring Pompey at Pharsalus in Northern Greece in August to heel. Although he was outnumbered by 47,000 to 24,000, Caesar inflicted a crushing defeat on Pompey, killing 15,000 of his men and capturing another 24,000. Pompey fled, first to Lesbos and then to Egypt, where on stepping ashore he was killed, on the orders of the Egyptian authorities. When Caesar arrived a short time afterwards in Egypt he was presented with Pompey's embalmed head.

Egypt was still an independent kingdom ruled, in theory, jointly by a 21-year-old Queen, Cleopatra, and her brother, the 15-year-old Ptolemy XII, but the two had fallen out. In 47 BCE, Caesar returned to Italy from Egypt, via Asia Minor and Greece. Caesar paused in Rome and then set out in late 47 for Africa, where resolute supporters of Pompey still held out. Caesar faced immense logistical problems in landing a force large enough to take on the 14 legions awaiting him, but he rounded on his enemies and the final battle at Thapsus in April 46 BCE was a massacre. The Republican forces of the Optimates, led by Quintus Caecillius Metellus Scipio, were decisively defeated by the veteran forces loyal to Julius Caesar. Shortly after the defeat, Scipio and his ally, Cato the Younger, committed suicides. In March 45 BCE, Caesar arrived in Spain, where after a short but savage campaign, which ended in the battle of Munda, a hard-won victory was achieved. The old order was dead. On March 15, 44 BCE, three days before Caesar was due to leave on campaign, he was murdered by senators. Caesar fell bleeding to death at the foot of a statute of Pompey. The conspirators claimed that they had killed Caesar in the cause of republican liberty.

It was Mark Antony, with the support of Lepidus, Caesar's master of the Horse, who now held the initiative. In the early 30s BCE, both Antony and Octavian were preoccupied with the consolidation of their rule. By fostering traditional Roman values Octavian was implicitly condemning the influence over Rome of the east. When Antony had assumed command in the east, he had worked hard to restore order among the client states of the empire. One of these was Egypt, and so Cleopatra was summoned to Antony in 41 BCE. Antony spent the winter of 41–40 with Cleopatra in Alexandria, and she bore him twins. The couple spent four years apart, between 40 and 36 BCE, a period when Antony was married to Octavian's sister, Octavia. In 39 BCE Parthian forces invaded Syria and even entered Jerusalem. Antony launched a major invasion of Parthia in 36 BCE which ended in disaster and Antony was forced to withdraw his forces with the loss of 22,000 legionaries, a third of his men. The final act between Octavian and Antony came at Actium, a cape on the western coast of Northern Greece. Octavian's forces managed to cut Antony off from the Peloponnese and Antony was reduced to trying to break out with his fleet. When the breakout failed, he and Cleopatra abandoned their forces and fled to Egypt. A year later Octavian arrived in Egypt and seized Alexandria and the treasures of the Ptolemies. Mark Antony stabbed himself, while Cleopatra had herself bitten by a poisonous snake. Caesarian was later murdered. Egypt, the last of the great Hellenistic kingdom, was now in the hands of Rome. At last, wrote the poet Quintus Horatius Flaccus (65 BCE–8 CE) in one of his odes, the time for drinking and dancing had come. Octavian was granted a new name, Augustus, the name by which he became known through history. Augustus was given numerous titles, but one which he valued was the title *Pater Patriae*, "Father of the Fatherland," in 2 BCE.

Although senators continued to fill almost all the senior posts in the empire, including the governorships of the provinces and the commands of the legions, an exception was Egypt. Egypt was treated as the personal conquest of Augustus, the source in fact of much of his wealth, and it was governed on his behalf by an equestrian (Freeman, 1996:385). Augustus built many new towns, among them Aosta, Turin, and Verona, to consolidate Roman control over the rich plain of the Po. Stability also allowed the continued spread of Latin, which acted as a lingua franca among the many local languages of the peninsula and gradually displaced many of them. Beyond Rome and Italy stretched the empire. To the east and beyond direct Roman control, was Parthia, the only state which could meet Rome as an equal. It was one of Augustus' major achievements that he came to terms with Parthia, in 20 BCE. In the west, Roman control was still limited. In Spain, some areas were still unpacified, even though the Romans had nominally controlled the peninsula for 200 years. Others such as Gaul still had not been consolidated for tax purposes. All this was put in hand. Spain was pacified with great brutality. The southern borders of the province of Africa were also stabilized, an important achievement in an area which, along with Italy, Sicily, and Egypt, supplied most of the grain of Rome. In the north, the borders of the empire, from the Balkans to Germany, had never been properly defined. It was here the empire was most vulnerable. These tribes, Celtic, German, and Sarmatians who were Asiatic in origin, were fiercely independent and able to offer determined resistance to the Romans.

With the exceptions of the conquest of Britain (from 43 CE) and Dacia (present day Romania, in 105–6 CE), and the absorption of clients' states, no further permanent additions were made to the empire. In 43 CE, 40,000 troops were ferried over the Channel and the conquest of Southern Britain was effectively done and soon the southern part of the country was under Roman control. Claudius' son, born in 41 CE, was renamed Britannicus in the exultation of a victory which was proclaimed on coins throughout the empire. Claudius allowed a temple in his honor to be built at Colchester, to provide a focus for the emotions and loyalties of a people shattered by their defeat. Claudius was in power for 13 years, and in addition to Britain two more provinces in Mauretania (North Africa), as well as Thrace (comprises Southern Bulgaria, Northeastern Greece and part of Turkey) and Lycia (present day Antalya and Mugla on the southern coast of Turkey), were added to the empire in his reign. In October 54 CE, Claudius died, the victim, it was said, of a dish of poisonous mushrooms fed to him by his wife Agrippina. Nero, still aged only 16, was proclaimed emperor. Britannicus, four months under age, could not succeed with him, but the day before he reached the required age of 14 he died at a banquet. Nero passed off the cause of Britannicus' death as an epileptic fit.

In 59 CE, egged on by his mistress, Poppaea, Nero decided to murder his mother. But after the first attempt to drown her in a collapsible boat ended in a farce, she was beaten to death. Soon, a reign of terror began. When a fire destroyed much of Rome in 64 CE, it was rumored that Nero had started it. Nero did not start the fire but he used it to scapegoat the small Greek-speaking Christian community of the city and persecuted them so brutally that he simply did his own image further damage. His response to the devastated center of Rome was the building of a vast imperial palace, the Domus Aurea, the "Golden House." In 68 CE, a revolt broke out in Gaul, which was led by Gaius Julius Vindex, a Romanized Celtic aristocrat who had established links with the governor of one of the Spanish provinces, the 71-year-old Servius Sulpicius Galba. The senate and the Praetorian Guard rallied to Galba and proclaimed him the new emperor. Nero, waiting in a suburban villa for a boat to take him from Italy, killed himself. Nero had no obvious successor within the family and the imperial throne was there to be fought over. By early 69 CE the legion along the Rhine had revolted and declared their own candidate for the throne, the governor of the province of Lower Germany, Aulus Vitellius. One of Galba's leading supporters, Marcus Salvius Otho, was so frustrated by events that he won over the Praetorian Guard, who proclaimed him emperor, and then used them to assassinate Galba in the Forum. What was most remarkable about the political struggles of 69 CE, was how little they shook the institution of the empire. There were three Flavian emperors, Vespasian (r.69–79 CE) and his sons, Titus (r.79–81) and Domitian (r.81–96). They personified a new phase in the development of the empire, power could be achieved through merit.

Emperor Hadrian (ruled 117–138 CE) succeeded his cousin emperor Trajan (53–117 CE). But while he was still in the east, four senators appeared to challenge his succession in Rome and they were executed. Hadrian toured Gaul, the German border, Britain, Spain, Mauretania and Greece, the emperor's favorite part of the empire. He returned to Italy in 126 CE, but between 128 and 134 CE, he was away again. This time his travels included Greece, Egypt, and Palestine, where he rebuilt Jerusalem, a deserted site since 70 CE, as a Roman colony. Hadrian is supposed to have forbidden the castration of slaves and the practice of shackling agricultural slaves in prisons. Capital punishment was used not only to eliminate undesirables but to act as an example to others. Crucifixions provided a slow public death. Like most societies of the ancient world, Rome was very brutal. When a slave murdered his master, it was the custom to execute all the other slaves in the household. In 61 CE, the wealthy City Prefect, Lucius Pedanius Secundus was murdered by one of his slaves, and 400 of his slaves, including women and children, were put to death. Romanization spread throughout the empire via the army, law, citizenship and the growth of a uniform urban culture, although it was a slow and uneven process, partly because the Romans tolerated local culture. The Greek world was particularly resistant to Roman ways. Even after the experience of the Jewish revolts, the Jews were still allowed their own laws and to practice their religion. Egypt was another area which remained distinct from the rest of the empire. It had a civilization of far greater antiquity than any other, which had survived under the rule of the Ptolemies. It was of special interest to Rome, along with the rest of Africa, because of the supply of corn on which Rome depended.

Much of Egyptian culture remained intact under Roman rule. Egyptian temples continued to be built and hieroglyphic texts written. At the same time an overlay of Greek culture remained. Alexandria, Naucratis, and Ptolemais were Greek cities. There was only one new city founded by the Romans, Antinopolis, in Egypt, created by Hadrian in memory of his beloved Antinous who had drowned in the Nile. However, the lack of new cities may have been the result of a determination not to disturb the agricultural economy. The bulk of the tax fell on the poorest population, with Roman citizens and citizens of the three Greek cities exempt. The Egyptian ruling elites were allowed to exploit the poor. In times of peace the empire could survive without problems, but when it came under threat there was always the risk that the poor would revolt, which, arguably, is what happened in later centuries. The most urbanized part of the empire was North Africa (now Northern Tunisia), with some 200 towns at an average distance from each other of only ten kilometers.

Traditional Roman religion remained highly ritualistic with the emphasis on the propitiation of the gods through ceremonies which had to be carried out with absolute precision. This approach was reinforced through the rise of the imperial cult, which took different forms in different reigns. In Africa, dedications to emperors were inscribed on temples alongside those to Jupiter, Juno, and Minerva. A mass of temples, oracles, centers of healing and remote shrines also survived alongside the official religion of the state. In Egypt animal worship persisted. At Didyma on the coast of Asia, a great temple to Apollo remained crowded with worshippers seeking the advice of the oracle there. Oracles sustained the belief that the will of a god could be known and that there were gifted individuals who might be able to proclaim it, an approach which was to have its own influence on Christians. In Syria people honored a Holy and Just Divinity, who was portrayed with attendant angels. In the Celtic world, water and river gods remained popular. Roman cults either co-existed with or were superimposed on these beliefs. The Romans were prepared to identify foreign gods with their own, for instance, in the east, Jupiter with Zeus, Venus with Aphrodite. In the west, Celtic gods were also incorporated within the Roman pantheon. The major Celtic deity Lug became associated with Mercury and in the city of Aquae Sulis (Bath in England) the local water goddess Sulis was identified with Minerva. Individuals could participate in a variety of different cults without any sense of impropriety. There were also the mystery cults, which appealed to those who sought a more personal salvation. These cults shared common features which may be traced back to the Greek world, for instance, to the ceremonies involved in the worship of Demeter at Eleusis.

The gods and goddess who were worshipped in these mystery cults tended to come from outside the Greek world. The cult of Isis spread from Egypt and vied with long-established cult of Cybele (whose origins were in Anatolia) for those who wanted the protection of a mother goddess. Isis tells Apuleius, "I am nature, the universal mother, mistress of all the elements, sovereign of all things spiritual, queen of the dead, queen also of the immortals, the single manifestation of all gods and goddess that are" (Freeman, 1996: 490). By the second century CE, this elevation of one god or goddess above all others was a common feature of religious belief. Humans had been conceived by gods in both the Egyptian and Greek world. Stories of miraculous healings, shared meals of believers, and even resurrections and the promise of an afterlife for the initiated would have been commonplace to anyone who had contact with mystery religions. But, while belief in one mystery religion did not preclude involvement in another, Christianity did require rejection of other gods and an exclusive relationship with Christ and his God. The Romans were traditionally suspicious of religious activities which took place in private. Christians made no such compromises and their worship of a man who had claimed to be a King aroused instant distrust.

Threats to Rome

Between 138 to 313 CE, threats to the Roman Empire came from two sources. First, there were the tribes of Northern Europe. The Romans gave the name German to the wide variety of peoples who occupied the area from the Rhine and Danube valleys to the North Sea and the Baltic and as far-east as the river Vistula. The Romans had long accepted that the Germans could not be incorporated into the empire. According to Freeman (1996), instead a variety of relationships had been built up. Trading and diplomatic relationships were underwritten with Roman subsidies. During the second and third centuries CE, however, there were important changes taking place in the societies of Northern and Eastern Europe, although these are still impossible to define clearly. In the Black Sea area, the Goths appeared in the early third century CE. Research suggests that they were an amalgam of various migratory peoples, Eastern German tribes and the original settlers of the Black Sea region. In Southeastern Europe, they came into conflict with the Sarmatians, nomadic peoples on the Hungarian plain. The Sarmatians in their turn were pushed towards the Roman frontier. This period also sees the emergence of new Germanic cultures further north. One of them, the so-called Przeworsk culture which appeared in the late second century CE, between the Vistula and Oder rivers, standout because of its rich warrior burials. Another is the so-called Oksywie culture on the lower Vistula. Archaeological evidence suggests that a new tribe, the Burgundians, emerged on the Elbe to the west of the Vistula about the same time, as the home of the Oksywie culture became deserted.

Similarly, another German tribe, the Vandals, may have been the successors of the people of the Przeworsk culture. The emergence and expansion of these peoples put the German tribes along the Roman frontier under increasing pressure. One result was to force the smaller scattered peoples into larger tribal units. The central German tribes were drawn together as a confederation known as the Alamanni (all men), first attested in 213 CE. The franks emerged slightly later along the lower Rhine while the Saxons appeared along the coast of the North Sea. For the first time, the Germans could face the Romans with some confidence, and as pressure built up on them from the north, the riches and lands of the empire became more alluring. By the middle of the third century, the Romans were vulnerable along the whole northern border from Saxons, Franks, Alamanni, Sarmatians, Goths, and other smaller tribes. The border was so extended it could not be effectively guarded along its whole length. The Romans were forced to try a variety of policies from straightforward military confrontation to making treaties with individual tribes or buying them off with payments of cash. Garrisons were sometimes stationed over the border in German territory, so that trouble could be snuffed out before it reached the empire, while on other occasions invaders were allowed to settle within the empire, in the hope that they would defend their land against any future incomers. But none of these policies provided a permanent solution.

The Roman Empire also faced a fresh threat from the east. Campaigns by the Romans against the Parthians in the 160s and 190s CE were relatively successful but this was partly because the Parthian empire was in decay. It was under threat from the Kushan empire (encompassed much of Afghanistan and part of Northern India) in the east and it also faced internal disintegration because of its policy of relying on independent local leaders who were allowed their own armies and control of their own finances. In the early third century, the last of the Parthian kings, Artabanus V, was overthrown by one Ardashir (180–242 CE), King of a tiny state in the southern province of Persis. Ardashir was succeeded by Shapur I (CE 239–270), a forceful ruler who extended the state into Armenia and Georgia. Until the middle of the third century, the empire managed to defend itself with some success.

When Antoninus Pius (b.86 CE and r.138–161 CE) became emperor, the succession was smooth. Marcus Aurelius (121–180 CE) had been groomed for the role, but while he had learned the conventions of court life, he had never been given any military command and, at first, he relied heavily on his adoptive brother Lucius Verus (130–169 CE), who seemed to have the dash needed for military action. But Aurelius' confidence was misplaced. When the Parthians invaded in 161 CE, Verus was dispatched east to deal with them, but he only managed to beat them off with difficulty. Verus died in 169 CE, and despite his inexperience, Marcus Aurelius took on the challenge of defending the empire, and for most of his reign, he was campaigning along the Danube borders. When he died in 180 CE, the borders were intact and there were Roman forces stationed in the territory of two of the major tribes, the Marcomanni and the Quadi. Marcus Aurelius had made his son, Lucius Aurelius Commodus (161–192 CE) co-emperor three years before he died. Commodus was, according to the historian Dio Cassius (155–235 CE), "a greater curse to the Romans than any pestilence or crime." Commodus attempted to create an image of himself as a divine emperor. It aroused little support and without allies in the army, the senate or even within his family, he was vulnerable (Freeman, 1996:468). In 192, Commodus was assassinated in Rome and was followed by a provincial *coup d'état.* The Praetorian Guard sold off Commodus' property, including his concubines and youths he kept for his sexual pleasures.

Publius Helvius Pertinax Augustus (August 126 – March 193 CE), Roman Emperor for the first three months of 193 CE, following the assassination of Commodus, was the first to serve as emperor during the tumultuous "Year of the Five Emperors." Born the son of a freed slave, Pertinax originally worked as a teacher before becoming an officer in the army. He was murdered by the Praetorian Guard, who auctioned off the imperial title, which was won by the wealthy senator Didius Julianus (137–193 CE), whose Latin name was Marcus Didius Sevrus Iulianus Augustus and reigned for sixty-six days. Julianus was ousted and sentenced to death by his successor, Septimius Severus Augustus (April 145 – February 211 CE), who was born in Leptis Magna, in Libya. As a young man, Septimius advanced through the *cursus honorum* – the customary succession of officers – under the reigns of Marcus Aurelius and Commodus. After deposing and killing the incumbent emperor Iulianus, Septimius fought his rival claimants, the generals Pescenius Niger (140–194 CE) and Clodius Albinus (150–197 CE). Niger was defeated in 194, at the battle of Issus in Cilicia. Three years later, Albinus was defeated at the battle of Lugdunum in Gaul. Severus waged a brief war in the east against the Parthian Empire, sacking their capital in 197 CE, and expanding the eastern frontier to the Tigris. In 202 CE, he campaigned in Africa and Mauretania against the Garamantes, capturing their capital Garama and expanding the *Limes Tripolitanus* along the southern frontier of the empire. Late in his reign, he traveled to Britain, strengthening Hadrian's Wall and re-occupying the Antonine Wall. In 208 CE, he invaded Caledonia (Scotland). He fell ill in 210 CE, and died early in 211, at Eboracum (York) and was succeeded by his sons Caracalla and Geta.

The Severan dynasty lasted 193–235 CE, which ended with the assassination of Marcus Aurelius Severus Alexander Augustus in March 235 CE. Following the death of Alexander Augustus, there were at least 18 emperors, between 235 and 84, who could lay some claim to legitimacy. Their average reign was only two-and-half-years. The crisis of the third century was as much an internal as external one. As many resources were used fighting rivals as in confronting invading enemies. The effects of this continuous unrest are difficult to quantify, but one response to the increasing costs of war had been the debasement of coinage. By the reign of Gallienus (218–268 CE), a typical "silver" coin only contained two percent silver. This led to the hoarding of old coins and the rejection of the new, which caused soaring inflation. Gallienus was killed by his officers in 268 CE. His successor, a cavalry general, Claudius II (r.268–70 CE), won a major victory over the Goths but died in the following year at his Balkan headquarters, Sirmium, of the plague. After his death, a series of emperors continued the struggle to resume control of the empire. The first of the new victorious emperors to gain control was Aurelian (214–275 CE), who defeated an invasion by the Alamanni and finally brought to an end the two independent parts of the empire, the Gallic empire and

Palmyra. Once the empire was restored, Aurelian brought back riches plundered from Palmyra to display in a great triumph in Rome with Zenobia and the last of the Gallic emperors, Tetricus (r271–274 CE), among the prisoners. A successor of Aurelian, Probus (r.276–82 CE), achieved further success against the Germans through a mixture of victories and concessions and the inclusion of Germans in his armies. But, both Aurelian and Probus were killed by their own soldiers and Probus successor, Carus (r.282–3 CE), who had continued the fight back by launching a successful invasion of Persia, died on campaign. Carus was the first emperor not to seek formal recognition by the senate, and his successor followed suit.

The elder, Carinus, was given charge of Italy and the western provinces. The younger Numerian accompanied his father on campaign against the Sarmatians and then on the invasion of Persia. When his father died, he was declared emperor, but while the army was returning home, he was found dead in his litter, having reigned as emperor between 283 and 284 CE. The chief suspect was the Praetorian Prefect Lucius Aper, who was challenged by the commander of the household cavalry, one Diocles. Aper was summoned before the assembled armies at Nicomendia in November 284 CE, and Diocles, after obtaining the support of the troops, stabbed Aper to death himself. Acclaimed as Augustus, Diocles defeated Carinus, eldest son of Carinus, six months later and found himself sole emperor. He took the name Diocletian. He had the good fortune to stay in power for 20 years and he was to establish the empire in a form which was to survive in the west for almost 200 years and in the east for very much longer. A fellow Balkan commander, Maximian, was appointed as a joint, but clearly junior, Augustus in 286 CE. Seven years later, two more younger commanders, Constantius and Galerius, were added as Caesars and designated as successors to the Augusti. This Tetrarchy, or rule of four, was consolidated through marriage alliances between the four families. Although the empire remained a single political entity each was given a sphere of operation. Diocletian took the east; Maximian, Italy and Africa; and the two Caesars, Galerius and Constantius, the Danubian provinces, Britain, and Gaul respectively. Four new imperial capitals appeared, Trier near the Rhine, Milan in Northern Italy, Sirmium on the Danube border, and Nicomedia in Asia Minor. Rome was now a backwater so far as the political needs of the empire were concerned. In the 290s CE, the Tetrarchs achieved between them a succession of victories which quelled the Germans, and ended in 297 CE, with a massive defeat of the Persians by Galerius, which brought peace on the eastern frontier for decades to come.

In 305 CE, Diocletian abdicated, persuading a reluctant Maximian (250–310 CE) to do likewise. He retired to a palace at Split, parts of which still stand. When Diocletian and Maximian abdicated, Diocletian's carefully structured system of succession was put into operation with Constantius and Galerius being appointed

Augusti and they in their turn naming two new Caesars. But when Constantius died in 306 CE, instead of one of the Caesars succeeding him the troops of Britain and Gaul acclaimed his son, Constantine (272–337 CE), as Augustus. Meanwhile in Rome the son of Maximian, Maxentius, also had himself proclaimed emperor. By 308 CE, there were no less than seven rival emperors contending for power. The winner was to be Constantine, an intensely ambitious and determined man with little time for power sharing. By 312 CE, he was in Italy and after crushing Maxentius at the Milvian Bridge, the senators voted him a triumphal arch which still stands near the Colosseum. The arch marks the appearance in art of the new imperial ethos, the emperor as semi-god, removed from his people. The inscription on Constantine's arch attributes his victory to "inspiration of the divinity and the nobility of his own mind." On the arch Constantine is shown making a sacrifice to the goddess Diana, but there is also a representation of the sun god. Constantine was to issue coins with *Sol Invictus*, the unconquered sun, portrayed on them, as late as 321 CE. In the third century, the imagery of the sun god had also been used by Christians. Constantine convened the Council of Nicea, in 325 CE, which affirmed the doctrine that Jesus, the Son, was equal to God the Father. The details of the period 354 to 378 CE are well known thanks to the Roman historian Ammianus Marcellinus (330–395), who was Greek by birth, and a native of Antioch. Having served with the Roman army he spent the last years of his life in Rome and wrote in Latin. Ammianus' history began in 96 CE, the date at which Tacitus' history had ended. The humiliating Roman defeat at Adrianople, in August 378 CE, is often seen as a turning point in the story of the Roman Empire, the moment when the Romans finally lost the initiative against the invaders.

The Fall of the Roman Empire (Western Half)

Emperor Theodosius (347–395 CE) was the last emperor to rule over both the eastern and the western halves of the Roman Empire in 395 CE. On his death in 395 CE, his two sons were declared joint emperors and the empire was split into two administrative areas. Arcadius (c.378–408 CE), the eldest son became eastern emperor from 395 to 408 CE. In the north, the division was made along the boundary of Illyricum, roughly were Greek replaced Latin as the predominant administrative language. The two halves of the empire were never to be reunited. The western empire was ruled by Honorius (384–423 CE), which was to "fall" in 476 CE, when it lost control of virtually all its territories outside Italy and relied on German soldiers to lead their own depleted troops. Romulus Augustulus, a boy emperor, who ruled the western empire from October 31, 475 to September 4, 476, was deposed by a Germanic soldier, Flavius Odoacer (435–493 CE). One explanation for the "fall" of the Western Empire suggests that continuous pressures along its extended borders on the Rhine and Danube, which by 395 CE had lasted over 200 years, since the war against the Marcomanni in 160s CE.

Reoccupation with the Goths had left the western government paralyzed while far more serious incursions were taking place to the north.

The collapse of the Roman defenses was said to have been viewed with dismay in Britain, which was itself suffering raids from Saxons and others. By 430 CE, urban life in Britain was in decay and rival invaders, Scots, Saxon, and Angles Jutes took over the country and no central rule was to be re-imposed for centuries. Germans had served as mercenaries for centuries, making their fortunes in Roman service and then returning to their homes. More recently prisoners of war, Sueves, Sarmatians, and Burgundians among them, had been settled and bound to military service but now there were also whole contingents of Franks and Goths serving under their own officers. Up to the fifth century the bishops of Rome, though maintaining some authority in the church as a whole as the proclaimed successors of Peter, had played little part in formulating Christian doctrine. The Christian world was predominantly Greek, the great councils of the church at which doctrine had been decided took place either at Constantinople or even further east, Nicaea (325 CE), Ephesus (431 CE) and Chalcedon (451 CE). The dominant figures in these councils had been the emperors, not individual bishops.

It was not until the Council of Chalcedon in 451 CE, when the so-called *tome* (letter) of Leo was read, that for the first time Rome took a determining role in the definition of Christian dogma. But the council held in Constantinople under Justinian's auspices in 553 CE, conducted its business totally independently of Rome. When in 590 CE, a new bishop of Rome, Gregory (540–604 CE), was consecrated, it seemed that the supremacy of the Greek east in defining Christianity would continue. Gregory was a Roman aristocrat and his affection and concern for the city remained strong. Despite his stay in Constantinople, he was not learned in Greek and represented the new clerical culture of the west, in which learning in the Latin classics was combined with a devout and somewhat austere Christianity, but remained always subservient to it. The bishop of Rome was to be the presiding force in Christian Europe with his fellow but subordinate bishops strengthened as leaders of the Christian communities. The foundations had been laid for the medieval papacy. They were reinforced by the widening doctrinal split with the east. Later, in the seventh century CE, Rome's position was further strengthened by the eclipse of two traditional rivals, the bishoprics of Alexandria and Antioch, by the Arab invasions. Yet in the late sixth century, few could have predicted the later supremacy over Europe of these popes.

The Lombard had overrun many of the larger Italian cities and Gregory had only the most fragile of contacts with the rest of Europe. The mission he sent to England which successfully converted the Anglo-Saxons was in the circumstances a magnificent achievement. Freeman (1996) argues that there is no doubt that Gregory's reign marks a turning point in the history of Christianity, not least of his achievements and that of his fellow bishops, who ensured the survival of classical

Latin as the language of church law and administration in the Middle Ages and beyond. In 813 CE, a council of bishops at Tours ruled that sermons had to be in *rustica Romana lingua*, colloquial Latin, while the rest of the service continued in classical Latin. It was from the local dialects of Latin that the Romance languages appear to have emerged in those areas where the Roman population was a majority, the Iberian Peninsula, Italy, France, and Romania. A barrier between these areas and that further north where German became the majority language has lasted from the sixth century to the present day, which is a reminder that despite the collapse of the empire its legacy in Europe persisted.

Eastern Half

The half of the empire which was placed under the rule of the younger brother, Emperor Honorius, in 395 CE, was one of the geographical and cultural complexity. It encompassed the Danube provinces, Illyricum, the Balkans, Greece, Asia Minor, Syria, Palestine, and Egypt. Latin remained as a language of the army and law, but the main spoken language of administration was Greek, which had spread widely in the east after Alexander's conquests. Antioch, the second city of the empire, and Alexandria were both Greek-speaking and prided themselves on a Greek heritage which was much older and richer than that of Constantinople. Christianity was a religion where the written text was important and local languages developed their own Christian literature. Syriac was used for a wide variety of Christian writings, including the lives of the saints, sermons, and church histories. Greek texts were translated in Syriac and vice versa while Syriac texts were in their turn translated into Armenian, Georgian and later into Arabic. In Palestine, the Jewish teachers understood Greek but debated in Hebrew and conversed in Aramaic. In Egypt Coptic, which is essentially Egyptian, written in a Greek script, had appeared in the late third century as the medium used by the Christian church to communicate with Egyptian-speaking masses. Many Egyptians were bilingual in Greek and Coptic became more widespread until the Arabic invasions of the seventh century. Yet, despite the cultural complexity, the eastern part of the empire saw itself as the proud heir of Rome. Its inhabitants called themselves *Romaioi* or Romans, right up to the fall of Constantinople to the Turks in 1453 CE. A scholarly elite survived in Constantinople for centuries and it is through their careful copying of Greek texts that so much of the works of Plato, Euclid, Sophocles (496–406 BCE) and Thucydides (460–395 BCE) has been saved. In the fourth century, a model of Christian kingship was adopted by Constantine's successors. The emperor was God's representative on Earth. God regulates the cosmic order, the emperor regulates the social order, bringing his subjects together in a harmony which mirrors that which God has designed for all creation. Leo I (r.457–74 CE) was the first of the emperors to be crowned by the

Patriarch of Constantinople, a ceremony which took place before "the people" in the Hippodrome.

The heaviest financial burden on the state was that of defense, as the empire remained under continuous military threats. The Danube provinces to the west were ravaged by a succession of Goths, Huns and later Bulgars, Avars, and slaves. Theodosius I had launched a determined attack on paganism but many areas of the eastern empire still remained pagan and only gradually succumbed to Christianity. In the fifth century Athens, it was still possible for a Platonist such as Proclus (412–485 CE) to have his own school and conduct his own pagan rituals, including prayers to Asclepius, the Greek god of medicine. The Athenian school of philosophy survived into the sixth century when it was finally closed down by Justinian. By the late fourth century, the gymnasia of the Greek world had disappeared while the church's influence over education steadily increased. Local temples continued to be closed down by determined bishops or sacked by vigilante groups made up of monks. The centuries old culture of Egypt was also finally stifled. The temple of Isis at Philae was closed in 536 CE and at Karnak, wall paintings and relics were covered with rough plaster and the temple buildings adopted to the use of convents and monasteries. The spread of Christianity introduced many important social changes. In cities, the bishops assumed responsibilities of the old classical elites. As in the West, bishops tended to come from the traditional ruling classes, for whom personal relationships were an art form in themselves. The demise of the old city government also left bishops responsible for the maintenance of order.

The Jews were one target. The empress Eudocia was met in Jerusalem by an enormous anti-Jewish demonstration led by Barsauma (d.491 CE), a Syrian monk. A glimpse of the relationship between church and state can be seen in surviving records from Southern Egypt. When raids into the empire from Nubia caused a mass of refugees to flee northwards up the Nile, the well-known abbot Shenoute took responsibility for feeding them for three months from the bakehouses of his monastery. Another instance was when bishop Apion of Syene is found petitioning the emperor for more troops with which to protect his churches and people. The petition went all the way to Theodosius II and was endorsed by him and then sent to the military commander of Southern Egypt for action. In both cases church initiatives received state responses. The emperor's role was to maintain the religious unity of his people and it was now accepted that this could best be done through a council of bishops whose decision would then be enforced as orthodox. A council held in Ephesus, where Mary had spent her later life, in 431 CE, accepted the concept of Mary as *Theotokos* (derived from the Greek terms: *Theos* "God" and *tiktein* "to give birth"). Usually the term is translated into English as "Mother of God." However, Greek-speaking Christians also used the equivalent Meter Theou. The title, Mother of God, was first used by Christians in Egypt.

Nonetheless, this title was also used for the goddess Isis, mother of Horus, before it was sanctioned by the Ecumenical Council of Ephesus of 431 CE, where the Church declared that both divine and human natures were united in the person of Jesus, the son of Mary. Hence, Mary called Theotokos. A second council of Ephesus, held in 449 CE, took the Monophysite position, the concept that Christ, while appearing in human form, was predominantly divine. But this position was then condemned by the bishop of Rome, Leo I, as "a robber council."

Two years later yet another council was held, this time at Chalcedon (a city in Bithynia, on the Asian side of the Bosporus, in Turkey). Here the pendulum swung back and Christ was proclaimed to have two natures, human and divine, within the same undivided person and Mary's title as mother of God was confirmed. By taking a compromise position, the Council of Chalcedon (451 CE) had isolated extremists on both sides. One group continued to emphasize the distinct human nature of Christ, eventually formed the separate "Church of the East," most of whose adherents were in Persia, survived for many centuries and sent missionaries to as far as China in the thirteenth century. Meanwhile, the Monophysite, those who emphasized the divinity of Christ, claimed the adherence of many in Syria and Egypt, and separate churches, the Coptic, and Syrian Orthodox churches, eventually emerged. The Council of Chalcedon had therefore succeeded in creating a religious division which made a mockery of the emperor as ruler of a people united in a single church. The whole debate had been marked by high levels of violence and intimidation and any further compromise was to prove impossible. The Monophysites, in particular, were intransigent and any move to accommodate them within the church now risked offending the church in the west, which remained (and still remains to this day) resolutely Chalcedonian.

The first "great" achievement of Justinian (482–565 CE), a Byzantine emperor from 527 to 565 CE, was his codification of Roman law. For Justinian, a unified system of law, based on Roman tradition, was essential to the security of the state, and in 528 CE he set codification in hand. The code brought together all imperial decrees in a single volume. Henceforth only those cited in the code could be used in the courts. The digest is a compilation and rationalization of the opinions of jurists. Three million words of opinion were reduced and consolidated into a million. In order that there should be no further confusion, Justinian forbade any further commentaries on these opinions, although they could be translated into Greek. In order that lawyers would be able to use the *Code* and *Digest* a separate volume, the *Institutes* were drawn up to serve as textbook for students. The *Digest* and *Institutes* were promulgated in 533 CE. It was this codification, together with a fourth volume of the laws which Justinian enacted after 534 CE, which was to pass through the medieval Italian schools of law and became part of the legal tradition of many European countries. More importantly it was a symbol of Justinian's determination to bring an administrative unity to his empire based on

Roman, not Greek, principles. The main barrier to unity within the empire was Monophysitism, still strong in the eastern provinces of the empire. As early as the 550s CE, Justinian had been trying to find a way of bringing back the moderate Monophysites into the Orthodox Church. His best hope seemed to be to launch a new condemnation of "Nestorianism," of the variety preached by the Church of the East, behind which he could rally the Monophysites.

Nestorianism is a Christological doctrine that emphasizes the disunion between the human and divine natures of Jesus. It was advanced by Nestorius, Patriarch of Constantinople from 428–431 CE. Justinian target was the so-called Three Chapters, texts written by three fifth-century bishops in which sympathy for Nestorianism might be detected. Although these three bishops were cleared of any heresy at the Council of Chalcedon, Justinian called a new council to meet in Constantinople in 553 CE, to revive the issue. The emperor browbeat the attending bishops into accepting his interpretations of these texts. This caused a split between the western (Catholic) and eastern (Orthodox) churches, while only confirmed in the eleventh and twelfth centuries, it was one step nearer. The late sixth century can be seen to mark the transition from the classical to the Byzantine world, one in which a predominantly Christian, Greek culture was precariously maintained by autocratic state beset by enemies. The word Byzantine derives from Byzantium, the name of the Greek city on which Constantinople was built. Classical culture was by now largely dead and a more intensely Christian atmosphere pervaded the empire. In the cities, resources now seemed to be targeted almost exclusively at Christian buildings. Christian liturgies and the music that accompanied them became an important part of general culture and it was clear that they were used by whole congregations, not just an educated elite. The icon, a picture of Christ and the Virgin Mary normally painted on wood, became increasingly popular at all levels of society. When Constantinople was besieged in 626 CE, the city's icons were paraded before the enemy and portraits of the Virgin Mary were carried around the walls. The city survived.

After Justinian's death, Latin gradually became forgotten and court titles became Greek. When the defenders of Constantinople had finally triumphed in 626 CE, they sang the great Greek hymn *Akathisto*, which still survived to be used in services in Lent. This was a time of increasing isolation and attacks were unrelenting. The early seventh century saw the crumbling of the Danube borders and the most successful Persian attack ever on the empire, with both Jerusalem and Alexandria lost. Asia Minor was ravaged and even Constantinople was nearly captured. Under the emperor Heraclius (610–41 CE), a miraculous recovery took place which brought the Sasanian empire close to collapse. Hardly had Heraclius' success been celebrated than an onslaught of a totally unexpected nature came from the south. Islam had been born in the deserts of Arabia and after the death of its founder, Muhammad, exploded northwards. The Byzantine rulers had had no time to successfully restore order to their southern provinces after the Persian invasions and their largely Monophysite population remained resentful over the imposition of religious orthodoxy.

The Jews, increasingly persecuted by the Christian state, had no reason for loyalty and even may have welcomed the invaders. Under the double edict, issued by Constantine II, in concert with his brothers, Jews were limited in owning slaves. They could not marry Christian women and were prohibited from converting Christian women. Defeat of the Byzantine army at the Yarmouk River in 636 CE left Syria and Palestine open to Islamic conquest. The Sasanians Empire (ruled by and named after the Sasanian dynasty from 224 to 651 CE) were crushed shortly afterwards. In 642 CE, Alexandria capitulated to Islam and over the next century the Arabs spread inexorably along the coast of North Africa, eliminating Byzantine rule in its wake and then across the Straits of Gibraltar. Only the victory of Charles Martel at Poitiers in 733 CE, finally halted an advance which also destroyed Visigothic Spain. At first the Arabs ruled as an elite for whom conversion was not an immediate priority. They used Greek administrators and Greek inscriptions sometimes alongside texts in Arabic, which survived longer than the conquest. Culturally, a New World was in the making and it is one which still survives today. Islamic culture remains predominant in North Africa and the east. Orthodox Church still exists in the east and the split from Christian churches of the west. However, Christianity remains the single most influential and current legacy of the ancient Mediterranean world.

Jews in the Ancient World

The origin of the Israelites is obscure and outside of their own writings there is virtually no mention of them as a people before the ninth century BCE (there is a single reference to them from Egypt about 1200 BCE). According to the Bible, the Jews settled in the land of Goshen and became shepherds of the Pharaohs' flocks, after being chased from Palestine by famine and attracted to the Nile Valley. Many of the events recorded as history in the Hebrew Scriptures have no archaeological or documentary evidence to confirm them. According to their own sources, they appeared first in Egypt, divided into 12 tribes. They were led out of Egypt by Moses across the Sinai desert and then wandered for forty years before finding a home in the land of Canaan. Among their early enemies in Canaan were the Philistines, Sea Peoples, who had come to settle along the southwestern coast of Canaan. After the death of Joseph and the Pharaoh "Protector" and facing the proliferation of the Jews, the Egyptians grew hostile. Israelite, in the broadest sense, is a Jew, or descendant of the Jewish patriarch Jacob, whose name was changed to Israel (Genesis 32: 28). Once in Canaan the 12 tribes gave allegiance to a simple King, first Saul, then David, and much later Solomon. Little mention of David has been found in any document or inscription of the period, outside the

Hebrew scripture. But there is some evidence to support the reputation given to Solomon, in the Book of Kings, as a builder.

After Solomon's death, his kingdom was split into two. In the north, ten tribes preserved the name *Israel*. In the south, the kingdom of Judah emerged, with Jerusalem a short distance within its territory. The citizens of Judah were known in Hebrew as *Yehudi*, and from this, by way of the Greek *ioudaios* and the Latin *Judaeus*, come the English "Jew." The two kingdoms co-existed for two centuries, although they were often at war with each other. After 930 BCE and the establishment of two independent Jewish kingdoms in Palestine, the ten northern tribes constituting the Kingdom of Israel, to distinguish them from Jews in the Southern Kingdom of Judah. The Northern Kingdom was conquered by the Assyrians in 721 BCE, and its population was eventually absorbed by other peoples. Thereafter, the name Israelite referred to those who were still distinctively Jewish, namely, descendants of the Kingdom of Judah. In 722 BCE, the Assyrians annexed the Northern Kingdom and extinguished its national identity. Judah survived, but as a subject kingdom of the Assyrian empire. The Israelites' creation story, narrated in the *Book of Genesis*, has parallels with a similar account in the Babylonian epic *Enuma Elish*. In both myths, God (Yahweh) fashions the world from a primordial abyss and his work of creation lasts six days, after which he rests on the seventh. Genesis 1:1–3, describes the state of chaos immediately before God's act of creation, which is closely related to the Enuma Elish, which also left traces on Genesis 2, as both begin with a series of statements of what did not exist, at the moment when creation began.

Genesis 2 has close parallels with a second Mesopotamian myth, the Atra-Hasis epic, parallels that extend throughout Genesis 2–11, from the Creation to the Flood and its aftermath. The two share numerous plot details – the divine garden and the role of the first man in it, the creation of the man from a mixture of earth and divine substance, the chance of immortality – and have a similar overall theme: the gradual clarification of man's relationship with God(s) and animals. The Atrahasis can be dated to between 1646 and 1626 BCE. Further, the narrative in Genesis 1 and 2 were not the only creation myths in ancient Israel. The biblical evidence suggests two contrasting models. The first is the "logos" ("speech") model, where a supreme God "speak" dormant matter into existence. The second is the "agon" ("combat") model, in which it is God's victory in battle over monsters of the sea that mark his sovereignty and might. Genesis 1 is an example of creation by speech, while Psalm 74 and Isaiah 51:9–10 are examples of the combat mythology, recalling a Canaanite myth in which God creates the world by vanquishing the water deities. However, the idea that God created the world out of nothing is central today to Judaism, Christianity, and Islam. Yet, it is not found directly in neither Genesis, nor in the entire Hebrew Bible.

The range of the scriptures is wide, from prehistorical accounts of the formation of Israel and Judah to the gentle eroticism of the Song of Solomon, from the intensity of the *Book of Job* to the exultations and thanksgivings of many of the Psalms. As a varied collection of texts, they evolved over a period of some six to eight-hundred years and were eventually brought together as a single body of writings, the Hebrew Old Testament, about the second century BCE. The most outstanding feature of these writings and what gives them a coherent theme is that they focus on one god, Yahweh becomes associated with the people of *Israel*. Gradually Yahweh becomes associated with the national identity of the Israelites, and other gods are seen as those of Israel's enemies, to be despised as such. Central to the worship of Yahweh was the concept of covenant, an agreement which bound two people together. In this concept, it was an agreement made between Yahweh and his people, Israel. The books of the prophets, Isaiah and Jeremiah are dominated by warnings of the catastrophe about to fall on Israel because of its wrongdoings. The Assyrian empire fell, at the hands of the Babylonian King, Nebuchadnezzar II, who ruled from 604–562 BCE, and was responsible for the final defeat of the Assyrians at Carchemish. Among Nebuchadnezzar's conquests was Judah, in 597 and 587 BCE, and according to the *Book of Kings*, ten thousand inhabitants were carried off to Babylon, which undermined the new image of Yahweh as one who could abandon his people to their suffering.

The first dispersion of the Jews was to establish an experience of exile which was to recur throughout their history. Under the Persians the Jews had been tolerated and references in the Bible to the Persians are favorable. But, for the first one-hundred-and-twenty years after Alexander's death, Palestine was under Ptolemaic rule and was subject to the same intrusive bureaucracy suffered by the Egyptians. One result was a new diaspora of Jews throughout the Mediterranean world. The descendants of Zadok, founder of the Jewish priesthood of Jerusalem, when the First Temple was built by Solomon (tenth century BCE), are hereditary priests. Zadok is related to Aaron, the first Jewish priest, who was appointed to that office by his younger brother Moses. According to Diop (1974), the Bible states that they were employed on construction work, serving as laborers in building the city of Ramses. The Egyptians took steps to limit the number of births and eliminated male babies. Henceforth, the Jewish minority withdrew within itself and became Messianic by suffering and humiliation. According to Diop, this race of shepherds, without industry or social organization, armed with nothing but sticks could envisage no positive reaction to the technical superiority of the Egyptian people. It was to meet this crisis that Moses appeared, the first of the Jewish prophets, who, after working out the history of the Jewish people from its origins, presented it in retrospect from a religious perspective. Thus, he caused Abraham to say many things that he could not have possibly have foreseen. For example, the four-hundred years in Egypt.

Moses lived at the time of Tell el Amarna, a city built 190 miles above Cairo in 1396 BCE, as the new capital of Akhnaton's empire, when Amenophis IV (Akhnaton) was trying to revive the early monotheism which had been discredited by sacerdotal ostentation and the corruptness of the priests. Sacerdotalism is the belief that propitiatory sacrifices for sin require the intervention of a priest, a segregated order of men, called the Levitical Priesthood, who are the only ones who can commune directly with God or the gods. Moses was probably influenced by this reform and from that time on, he championed monotheism among the Jews. The Jews had created the world's first sustained monotheistic religion, as the Egyptian King Akhenaten's dominant sun god had died with him. It was, however, a concept which left many unsolved philosophical problems about the nature of the one God. For some, he was the source of both good and evil, "I make good fortune and create calamity," writes Isaiah. The lesson of the Babylonian exile was that only through the admission of guilt and the acceptance of just punishment could the relationship be restored in a new covenant. In the prophecies of both Isaiah and Jeremiah, a messiah is talked of, one who will bring everlasting justice and peace.

If, argues Diop, the Egyptians persecuted the Jews as the Bible says, and if the Egyptians were black sons of Ham, it is not difficult to see the historical causes of the curse upon Ham. The curse entered Jewish literature considerably later than the period of persecution. It is not by chance that this curse on the father of Mesraim, Phut, Kush, and Canaan, fell only on Canaan, who dwelt in a land that the Jews have coveted throughout their history. Where would Moses have found the name Ham (Cham) or (Kam)? It was in Egypt where Moses was born, grew up, and lived until the Exodus. It is a fact that the Egyptians called their country Kemet, which means "black" in their language. Mizraim is the Hebrew and Aramaic name for the land of Egypt. But, in the Amarna tablets, it is called Misri and Assyrian records called Egypt Mu-sur, while the Arabic word for Egypt is Misr. According to Genesis 10, Mizraim was the younger brother of Cush and elder brother of Phut and Canaan. Hence, it is easy to find Kam in Hebrew, meaning heat, black, burned. The inhabitants of Egypt, symbolized by their black color, Kemet or Ham of the Bible, would be accursed in the literature of the people they had oppressed. What is interesting is, according to the need of the cause, Ham is cursed and blackened, but he is whitened whenever one seeks the origin of civilization. The Jewish people, that is, the first branch called Semitic, descendants of Isaac, seem to have been the product of crossbreeding. The largest Jewish community outside Palestine was in Alexandra, but there were communities in Asia and as far north as the Black Sea. Inevitably the scattering led to the losing of roots with traditional Judaism and many Jews became Hellenized and even forgot Hebrew.

The Torah and the Hebrew Bible were translated into Greek. This was the world where 200 years later Paul, a Hellenized Jew and a Roman citizen, was to be born, in Tarsus in Cilicia. In Judaea, itself the Ptolemies were replaced by the Seleucids in 200 BCE, who were to set about imposing Greek culture. King Antiochus IV (215, r.175–163 BCE), who was humiliated by the Romans in 168 BCE, when he tried to invade Egypt, was desperate to rebuild his dwindling kingdom around a unified Greek heritage, went too far, when he tried to ban Jewish observances and dedicate the temple at Jerusalem to Zeus in 167 BCE. Guerrilla warfare broke out under the leadership of Judas Maccabaeus (d.160 BCE). Giordano Bruno (1548–1600), was an Italian Dominican friar, philosopher, mathematician, poet and astrologer, and a supporter of Egypto-Paganism: "Do not suppose that the sufficiency of the Chaldaic magic derived from the Kabbalah of the Jews; for the Jews are without doubt the excrement of Egypt, and no one could ever pretend with any degree of probability that the Egyptians borrowed any principle, good or bad, from the Hebrews" (M. Bernal, 1987: 159). The collapse of Egypto-Pagan religion happened with remarkable speed between 130 BCE and 230 CE. By the middle of the first century CE, Jews formed between five and ten percent of the population of the Roman Empire. However, in 116 to 117 CE, there was a huge revolt in the Jewish Diaspora, far greater than the better-known ones of the Zealots and Bar Kokhba in Judaea of 66 to 77 CE and 132–5 CE. The revolt of 116–7 CE was followed by repression in Cyprus, Cyrene, and above all, Alexandria which completely destroyed the brilliant culture of Hellenized Jewry.

The Egyptian Jews were middlemen, between the ruling Greeks and the Egyptian people. Jews did not begin to count in history until David and Solomon, or the beginning of the first millennium BCE, the epoch of Queen Makeda of Sheba. Egyptian civilization was already several millennia old. Solomon was but a minor king, ruling a small strip of land; he never governed the world as the legends claim. He had joined with the merchants of Tyre in building a merchant marine to exploit overseas markets, during which Palestine prospered under his reign. That was the only important reign in Jewish history down to the present. Later, the country was conquered by Nebuchadnezzar, who transferred the Jewish population to Babylon; this was the period known as the Captivity. The Jewish state went rapidly into eclipse and did not reappear until modern Zionism under Ben-Gurion.

The Moors

The Sahara, far bigger than the United States of America, was once a land of lakes, rivers, forests, green fields, farms, villages, towns, and cities. It was a great land, yet only a part of an even greater African world. Geologists, archaeologists and other specialists have all advanced various theories to explain the great mystery of the transforming Sahara. But every explanation seems to project still another puzzling question. That is, just how did the Albion Sea disappear in the Sahara? The great story of the Sahara is yet to be told, as archaeologists have hardly scratched the surface beneath which a lost civilization lies buried under several thousand feet of sand and rocks. What is known is that the migrations from the Sahara, while heavily concentrated in Upper Egypt and the Eastern Sudan, also spread out over Africa in and through the Western Sudan. African migrations were not always all black, as some were Afro-Asians, some had few white Asians and other groups were entirely Afro-Berber or Afro-Arab. There were also some Berber groups and, later, Arabs who migrated from the Sahara to favorable locations in the African interior. There was a general mixing of peoples from the earliest times, and the progenies of Africans and white Berbers and Arabs became known as Moors, Tuaregs, and Fulani.

The original Moors, like the original Egyptians were Black Africans, but as amalgamation became more and more widespread, only the Berbers, Arabs, and Afro-Berbers and Afro-Arabs were called Moors, while the darkest and black-skinned Africans were called "Black-a-Moors." Eventually, "Black" was dropped from "Blackamoor." In North Africa, all Muslim Arabs, mixed Afro-Arabs, and Afro-Berbers are regarded as Moors. Medieval and early modern Europeans variously applied the name to Arabs, North African Berber, and European Muslims. During the colonial era, the Portuguese introduced the names "Ceylon Moors" and "Indian Moors" in Sri Lanka, and the Bengali Muslims were also called Moors. The Tuareg people inhabit the Sahara Desert, in an area stretching from southwestern Libya to Southern Algeria, Niger, Mali, and Burkina Faso. Small groups of Tuareg are to be found in Northern Nigeria. The Tuareg adopted Islam in the seventh century CE, after its arrival with the Umayyad Caliphate, and belong to the Sunni Islamic sect. They also helped to spread Islam into Western Sudan.

The Fula or Fulani people are one of the largest and widely dispersed Muslim ethnic groups in Sahel (the eco-climatic and biographic zone of transition in Africa between the Sahara to the north and the Sudanese Savanna to the south) and West Africa. They are the largest ethnic group in Guinea, Senegal, Mali, Burkina Faso, and Niger and are present as a significant ethnic group in Mauritania, Ghana, Cameroon, Ivory Coast, Chad, Central African Republic, Liberia, Togo, Sierra Leone, South Sudan, and Egypt. The Fula people reflect a genetic intermix of people with West African, North African and Arabian origins and have been a part of many ruling dynasties, particularly in the Sahel and West Africa. During the ensuing migrations, Africans, instead of moving *en masse* to the seacoasts and maintaining the dominant position there, they moved en masse toward the interior, first to the remaining oases in the desert and later into Northern and Southern Ethiopia (Egypt and Sudan), and to the south, central, and western regions. The Berbers, Arabs and their Afro-Asian progenies, now firmly held the entire northern, western, and eastern seaboard of Africa. Social and economic mobility came from the circumstances that Africans made up the strongest contingent of the Berber and Arab armies. Most males were castrated or removed from possible contact with all females. The African labor force relieved the Asians from all labor.

During the Persian, Greek and Roman invasions large numbers of Egyptians fled to the desert, the mountain regions, Arabia and Asia Minor, where they lived, and secretly developed the teachings which belonged to their mystery system. In the eighth century CE, the Moors invaded Spain and took with them the Egyptian culture which they had preserved. During the classical period, the Romans interacted with, and later conquered, parts of Mauretania, a state that covered modern Northern Morocco, Western Algeria, and the Spanish cities of Ceuta and Melilla. The Berber tribes of the region were noted in Classical literature as Mauri, which was subsequently rendered as "Moors" in English and in related variations in other European languages. The name acquired more general meaning during the medieval period, associated with "Muslim," similar to association with "Saracens." During the context of the Crusades and the *Reconquista*, the term Moors included the derogatory suggestion of "infidels." In 711 CE, troops mostly formed by Moors from North Africa led the Umayyad conquest of Hispania. The Iberian Peninsula then came to be known in classical Arabic as Al-Andalus, which at its peak included most of modern-day Spain, Portugal, and Septimania. The fall of Granada in 1492 marked the end of Muslim rule in Iberia, although a Muslim minority persisted until their expulsion in 1609.

During the Moors' occupation of Spain, they established schools and libraries which became famous throughout the medieval world. The schools of Cordova, Toledo, Seville, and Saragossa attracted students from all parts of the western world. The Moors were the recognized custodians of African culture, to whom the world looked for enlightenment. Consequently, through the medium of the ancient Arabic language, philosophy and various branches of science were disseminated. In addition, the Moors kept up constant contact with Egypt, by establishing a Caliphates at Cairo in Egypt, as well as at Baghdad and Cordova. It should be noted that European scientists like Roger Bacon, Johann Kepler, Copernicus, and others obtained their science through Arab Berber sources and European knowledge of medicine came from these same sources. However, in 1567 King Philip II of Spain directed Moriscos (Muslims who converted to Christianity) to give up their Arabic names and traditional dress and prohibited the use of Arabic. Apart from these historic associations and context, Moor and Moorish designate a specific ethnic group speaking Hassaniya Arabic. They inhabit Mauritania and parts of Algeria, Western Sahara, Tunisia, Morocco, Niger, and Mali.

Early Christians

According to Charles Freeman (1996), Christianity was born in the Roman Empire and its authority was based on a tradition that St. Peter, Christ's chosen successor, had been martyred in Rome. By the time of the Edit of Milan (313 CE), Christianity had survived in an empire which had been at best indifferent to it and at worst actively hostile for nearly three-hundred years. Its origins, like so many of the religious beliefs that spread into the Greco-Roman empire after the first century, lay in the east. It was inspired by Jesus, a Jew who lived and preached in Galilee, part of Roman Palestine, before being crucified in Jerusalem in the reign of Tiberius Claudius Nero (42 BCE–37 CE) Roman Emperor from 14 to 37 CE. Jesus was his given name – Christ, from the Greek *Christos*, the messiah or anointed one, was used by his followers only after his death. The sources for Jesus' life are, like those for most aspects of the ancient world, inadequate. References to Christianity in contemporary non-Christian sources are very few, just enough to give confirmation that Jesus existed. Of the 20 "gospels" believed to have been written (the word derives in English from the Anglo-Saxon "godspell," the Greek original means "good news"), only four, those of Matthew, Mark, Luke and John, have survived since antiquity while another, later, collection of sayings of Jesus (the so-called "gnostic" gospel of Thomas) was rediscovered only in 1945, among the documents of the Nag Hammadi library, so called from the Egyptian town near where they were found (most of these other gospels were composed in the second century CE and were rejected as the "Canon" of accepted New Testament writings was consolidated in later centuries).

As a historical source the gospels have serious drawbacks. They were written down two generations after Jesus' death (most scholars date the gospels to between 65 and 100 CE, with John's account traditionally placed much later than the other three), and for local Christian communities distant from Jerusalem and Galilee where the events they describe took place. (Tradition relates that Mark's gospel was written in Rome and Matthew's in Antioch). They appear to be based on collections of sayings, some of them in the form of parables. With the exception of a few surviving phrases in Aramaic, the language Jesus spoke, they are written in Greek. Inevitably much of the original meaning of what Jesus said and the context in which he said it must have been lost in the transfer from one culture and language to another. There was an emphasis on distinguishing Jesus from other holy men and cults which were pervading the ancient world. This was done through highlighting stories of a virgin birth, of a "transfiguration" (the moment when God himself appears to have recognized Jesus' status), and of his powers as a miracle worker. Jesus' death and his resurrection are also given special prominence, with a focus on his mission as an innocent man, put to death but come to life again to proclaim God's message of salvation. There was also a concern with establishing Jesus as the longed-for messiah. The degree to which such needs and pressures shaped the "facts" presented in the gospels is the subject of immense scholarly dispute. At one extreme there are those who claim that the gospels are historically reliable, even when they describe events as distant and seemingly irrecoverable to the gospel writers as Jesus' conception and birth. At the other, radical theologians such as Rudolf Bultmann (1884–1976) have seen the events of the gospels as largely the creation of the gospel writers.

Jesus was brought up in Galilee, a northern region of Palestine, which was governed by a series of client kings, first, at the time of Jesus' birth around 5 CE, Herod the Great (d.4 BCE), and then his son Herod Antipas (20 BCE–39 CE), who is best known for his role in events that led to the executions of John the Baptist and Jesus. Caravan routes to the east ran through the region and there was some contact with the wealthy trading cities of the coast. The Galileans had the reputation of being a tough and rather unsophisticated people, looked down upon by the more highly educated Jews of Jerusalem to the south. Jesus had little in common with the devout Jewish sectarians such as the Pharisees who laid immense emphasis on rigid adherence to Jewish law, the Torah. He was more in the tradition of the *Hasid*, the holy man, an individual who has the power to cure illnesses, exorcise devils, and heal the sins which Jewish teaching believed was their root cause. He moved freely among the local outcasts. The news of Jesus' healing powers and his message spread quickly and crowds gathered to listen to him. The world in which Jesus moved was a tense one. Judaea to the south had now become part of the Roman Empire, with a Roman governor, Pontius Pilate, the fifth perfect of the Roman province of Judaea from 26–36 CE. The Jewish people were divided in their response to Roman rule. At one extreme the Sadducees, a wealthy and aristocratic group with conservative religious and social ideas, were prepared to tolerate Roman rule as offering the best chance of their survival as an elite. They dominated the councils of Jerusalem. The Sadducees are often compared to other contemporaneous sects, such as the Pharisees and Essenes. At the other extreme the Zealots were actually prepared to countenance armed rebellion against the Romans. In between these two extremes, other sects such as the Pharisees concentrated on maintaining their religious principles intact without offering any open opposition to Roman rule.

When Jesus moved his ministry out of Galilee to Jerusalem, the center of conservative Jewry and during festivals of the Roman administration, in about 30 CE, the risks were high. Neither Sadducees nor Romans could afford to allow a popular leader to upset the delicate political situation. The resulting crucifixion, the punishment meted out to thousands of rebels before Jesus, was probably a collaboration between the authorities to keep the peace after Jesus' dramatic entry into the temple. Jesus, with no institutional power base in the Jewish world, was an easy victim. When given the choice, the crowd at Jerusalem roared for the freeing of the local Barabbas, instead of Jesus, the Galilean whom they did not know. Three gospels state that there was a custom at Passover during which the Roman governor would release a prisoner of the crowd's choice; Matthew 27:15, Mark 15:6 and John 18:39, but this is not recorded in any historical document other than the gospels. Barabbas' name appears as *bar-Abbas* in the Greek texts of the gospels, which is derived ultimately from the Aramaic "son of the father." Some ancient manuscripts of Matthew 27:16–17 have the full name of Barabbas as "Jesus Barabbas." However, the story of Barabbas is problematic, because it has been used to lay blame on Jews for the crucifixion of Jesus. Jesus' followers were shattered by his death, in particular by its humiliating form. Early stories circulated that, though taken down dead from his cross and buried, he had come to life again and had been seen by a favored few before ascending into heaven. The belief in this "resurrection" persisted to become a central doctrine of Christian belief. Meanwhile Jesus' closest disciples remained in Jerusalem and struggled to keep their community intact.

One early leader was the former fisherman Peter, who, according to Matthew's account, had been picked out by Jesus as the first leader of the movement. By 40 CE the dominant figure in the community appears to have been Jesus' brother, James, who died in martyrdom in 62 or 69 CE. The earliest traditions, the Gospel of Mark and the Acts of the Apostles record Jesus as having brothers and sisters, but these traditions were later obscured by the belief that his mother, Mary, remained perpetually virgin in her marriage. Another role for Jesus emerged in these early years, that of messiah. The coming of a messiah who would deliver the Jews from bondage, had long been part of Jewish belief, but the Jewish messiah had always been seen as a powerful King coming in triumph. Jesus' life and death could hardly give him this status but he could be seen in a different sense, a messiah who redeemed through his own suffering. Several of the Psalms of David provide precedents for a suffering messiah. In this sense, Christians now talk of a "New" covenant between God and his people to replace the traditional one of the Hebrew Scriptures. These different conceptions of the messiah were to be one of the issues which helped maintain a division between Christians and Jews. The early Christian community of Jerusalem was viewed with suspicion by many traditional Jews, especially when Christians such as Stephen argued that the new covenant brought by Christ was needed because Jews had failed to adhere to the old one. Its converts were mainly among Greek-speaking Jews, and soon small congregations appeared outside Jerusalem, in Jewish communities of large cities such as Damascus and Antioch, the capital of Syria and the third city of the empire.

The term Christian appears to have been first used in Antioch. The synagogues in these large cities traditionally attracted gentiles (non-Jews) to their services and it may have been in this way that the story of Jesus reached the gentile world. The Jerusalem leaders, Peter and James insisted that Jesus was only for those who were circumcised and who obeyed Jewish dietary laws. It took Paul, a Greek-speaking

Jew from Tarsus in Cilicia and a citizen of the empire, to break this taboo. Paul was a Pharisee who had come to Jerusalem to train as a rabbi. At first, he had shared the Pharisees' distrust of Jesus and joined in persecution of Christians but then, on the road north from Jerusalem to Damascus, he had a vision of Jesus and became a believer. Paul was born about 10 CE, but never known Jesus. In his letters to the early Christian communities, he makes almost no reference to Jesus as a historical person. But, Paul had few doubts as to who Jesus was and what his message meant. For Paul, Christ had come to redeem those, Jews and Greek, slave and free, male and female alike, who showed faith in him. Those who put their trust in Jesus would be saved. Paul's emphasis is thus on faith rather than rigid adherence to Jewish law. Paul insisted that uncircumcised gentiles could become Christians. He got his way when he agreed that his gentile churches would collect money for the church in Jerusalem. But, the relationship between the two missions was a tense one, as Paul later told the Galatian Christians of a public row he had had with Peter in Antioch.

Luke, an educated Greek, attempts to place the Christians' story within the context of world history and more than any other gospel writers, he showed a detailed knowledge of the Roman world. His account of Paul's shipwreck on the way to Rome is a valuable piece of historical evidence in its own right. Paul, however, is the central character in Acts and his energy and beliefs transformed the early Christian communities. He moved on his missionary journeys through Galatia, Asia, Macedonia, Greece, and even as far west as Rome, inspiring the first Christians. He was so successful that the Jerusalem Christian community was soon eclipsed. It had no real future within the Jewish world and in the revolt against Rome in 66 CE, it was accused by traditional Jews of being unpatriotic. The break between church and synagogue was complete by about 85 CE, although scattered and isolated communities of Christian Jews continued to exist in Syria and elsewhere for some time. By the second century, the gentile communities represented mainstream Christianity. Christians believed, like Jews, that there was only one god, who deserved exclusive worship, and that those who believed were a people set apart. Christians retained the Hebrew Scriptures, valuing them for what were seen as references – in Isaiah, for instance – to the coming of Jesus. The Old Testament remained an integral part of the body of Christian scripture, even if the god of the Old Testament sits ill at ease with the gentler and approachable god preached by Jesus.

Women seem to have made up a large part of the membership of early Christian communities, as they probably did in the mystery religions. An ascetic streak in early Christianity appears to have attracted virgins and widows in particular. It was precisely women of this status who were most marginal in traditional Greco-Roman society, with its focus on marriage and childbearing, and so the church offered them a home denied elsewhere. The poor were also welcomed. In Rome, some 1,500 poor were being fed by the church in the middle of the third century and some fifty years later, the community at Antioch was providing food for 3,000 destitute people. The first Christian communities were spread mainly over the eastern part of the Roman Empire, though there was a Greek-speaking Christian church in Rome by the middle of the first century CE. These communities were exclusively urban (among the meaning of the word "pagan," eventually used in a derogatory sense by Christians and non-Christians, as country dweller, though the word also means civilians as against a soldier) and most kept a low profile so as not to invite persecution. An opponent of Christianity, Celsus, writing about 180 CE, recorded wool-workers, cobblers and laundry workers among the congregation. He argued that Christianity was only suitable for the most ignorant, slaves, women, and little children. It has been suggested that, perhaps two percent of the empire were Christians by 250 CE, though there are some estimates as high as ten percent, with virtually no Christian presence in the west of the empire or along its northern frontiers.

In the decorated baptistery, the earliest known representation of Christ survives, and he is portrayed as a breadless young man extending his hand over the man "sick of the palsy." Christians took care over their burials, favoring the Jewish custom of preserving the body rather than burning it. One early Christian burial site by the Appian Way bore the name "by the hallow" and the Greek for this gives the word "catacomb." The word was used to describe the hundreds of galleries constructed around Rome as the Christian community in the city grew in the second and third centuries. Christians inherited from Judaism the concept of elders, known as presbyters, from the Greek *presbuteros,* "old man." This confirmed the early church as male-dominated (there is little evidence to suggest that women played any officiating role in the early church). The role of the presbyter was to look after the affairs of the community, overseeing baptisms, managing the offerings, and corresponding with churches. This was the origin of the bishop and by the middle of the second century, it was accepted that there should be a single bishop at the head of each community. There was no supreme bishop, although those of the larger cities, Jerusalem (in the early days), Antioch, Ephesus, and Alexandria, claimed some form of pre-eminence in their region. In the late second century, these cities were affronted when Victor, bishop of Rome (d.199 CE), a Berber born in the Roman Province of Africa, tried unsuccessfully to impose the date of Easter adopted in Rome on the rest of the Church. By the mid-third century CE, the bishop of Rome further justified their primacy over the rest of the Christian world by arguing that Christ had proclaimed Peter as his successor and Peter had gone on to found the Church of Rome.

There is no direct evidence that Peter ever visited Rome. In the Acts of the Apostles, Peter is mentioned as having been imprisoned in Jerusalem, but miraculously released. Then after one reported speech he disappears from the text.

In the 90s CE, there are two sources: one, the letter of Clement written in Rome, the other, John's Gospel (Chapter 21), which make clear that he was martyred, but no clear indication is given as to where. Although Luke describes Paul's journey to Rome in meticulous detail, he made no mention of Peter's journey, which if it did happen, would have been about the same time, 60 CE. The strongest, and perhaps most persuasive supporting evidence for Peter's martyrdom in Rome is that no other place has claimed the honor and that other Christian cities were prepared to accept the tradition. By the second century, Christians had had to defend themselves against Gnosticism, a movement which reached its height in the second century. Gnostics taught that souls of human beings were imprisoned in their earthly bodies, but could be liberated through the acquisition of "knowledge" (gnosis). Christ, whom the Gnostics believed had had no earthly existence, was one of the mediators between man and the divine. The first century had seen a revival of Platonism (first to third century Platonism is normally known as Middle Platonism to distinguish it from the later Neoplatonism of Plotinus 205–70 CE). Plato's "the good" was for these later followers a supreme reality, whose existence transcended human thought. Middle Platonism gave the name *theos* to "the good" and this can be translated as "God." In this sense, Platonism was echoing the elevation of deities seen in the mystery religions. From now on "the Good" will be given a capital, to suggest its elevation to a supreme spiritual force. Middle Platonism began to permeate the writings of Christians.

Clement of Alexandria, who was influenced by Hellenistic philosophy and writing around 190 to 200 CE, argued that it was possible to grasp the nature of God through the reading of the Hebrew Scriptures, and had shown that his existence could be defended through the use of reason. Platonists did not mention Christ, as the idea that "the Good/God" could influence human history through the activity of a human being was alien to Platonism. Christians had therefore to find their own method of integrating Christ into the Platonist principles they had absorbed. One view, first articulated in John's gospel and later taken up by the church in Alexandria, was that Jesus represented the *logos. Logos* was a concept developed by Greek philosophers (Stoics as well as Platonists) to describe the force of reason which, they argued, had come into being as part of creation. It is often translated as "the word." *Logos* existed in human beings as the intellectual power with which they were able to understand the divine world. In this sense, Logos overlapped both the physical world and the divine Christ created by God in human form and sent by him into the world to act as an intermediary between god and man. However, this still left aspects of Christ's relationship with God unclear, as to whether Christ was an indivisible part of God, or a separate entity. These speculations may have helped gain Christianity intellectual credibility but did little to help the security of individual Christian communities at a time of tension. As early as 64 CE Christians were used as scapegoats by Emperor Nero, when seeking to allocate blame for the fire at Rome. The real problem with Christians was their refusal to honor traditional gods. Christians were therefore viewed as a threat to the state, by refusing to worship the emperor.

In North Africa, in particular, there are signs of a collective willingness among Christian communities to face death for their beliefs, with others attracted to Christianity as a result of the example of martyrdom of Vibia Perpetua and Felicity, a slave imprisoned with her and pregnant at the time, in the arena of Carthage in 203 CE. The significance of Perpetua's and Felicity's martyrdom is that they defer their roles as mothers to remain loyal to Christ. The persecution of Christians reached its fullest extent in the third and fourth-centuries. It was inevitable that those who refused to sacrifice to the gods would be confronted, when continuing defeats of the empire suggested that those gods were deserting Rome. The refusal of converted soldiers to honor the cult of the emperor was particularly intolerable. There was a major persecution under Emperor Decius in 250–1, with bishops as the prime targets, and another under Diocletian and his successor Galerius between 303 and 312. Christians were often thrown to the lions in front of howling crowds. Persecution can also be seen as a response to the success of Christianity in infiltrating official institutions such as the civil service and the army. Bishops were becoming well-known local figures, running large and well-organized communities and distributing alms among their members. Christian communities may also have been filling gaps left by the decay of traditional institutions. There was general agreement by 200 CE on a basic creed affirming by all seeking baptism which included acceptance of God as the father, Jesus Christ as the son, the Holy Spirit, and the resurrection. The Holy Spirit refers to the activity of God shown in the world, typically as the power of healing, casting out devils, or prophesying through the medium of ordinary human beings, but also as the instrument through which Mary conceived Jesus.

Gradually the sacred writings of the church were gathered into a Bible of selected books of the Old and New Testament. The Greek word *biblia* means "the book," although the disputes over which early Christian writing should or should not be included took some time to resolve. Those not accepted were gradually discarded or in some cases declared heretical. Most have now disappeared. Although the bishops of Rome, Antioch, and Alexandria had gained some prominence in their local areas, with the right to consecrate the bishops of similar cities, there was still no supreme human leader of the church. For Cypian, bishop of Carthage, who argued in his treaties on the unity of the Catholic church (251 CE), that the church was the only body capable of authoritative Christian teaching and no true Christian could exist outside of it. "He no longer has God for his father, who does not have the church for his mother." This claiming of exclusive authority over all Christians was to have immense implications for the future. Ever since the fall of the Severan dynasty, which was founded by the Roman general Septimius

Severus, in 193 CE, who rose to power as the victor of the civil war of 193–7 CE, rivals for the imperial throne had bid for support by either favoring or persecuting Christians. For example, Emperor Diocletian (244–312 CE), by proposal of Emperor Galerius (260–311 CE), issued a persecutory edict in 303, which prescribed the destruction of churches and the burning of Holy Scriptures, among other things, the confiscation of church property. However, before Emperor Galerius died in 311 CE, he issued the Edict of Toleration. Further, when in February 313 CE, Emperors Constantine I (272–337 CE), and Licinius (263–325 CE) met in Milan, among other things, they agreed to change policies towards Christians, in line with the Edict of Toleration.

Hence, when Constantine and Licinius offered toleration for all sects, including Christianity in 313 CE, the church, even though it still had only a minority of the population, was in a strong position to exploit it. With the support of Constantine, Christianity came into its own and enjoyed a political and social status it had previously lacked. It is most likely that without imperial support Christianity would most likely be a religion of a minority. Constantine I was not a Christian emperor and was not baptized until shortly before he died and the vast majority of his subjects were not Christians and most of them had still probably never heard of Christ. But, over the next century, it was to become the only officially tolerated religion of the empire. After Constantine's victory at the Milvian Bridge, he was prepared to recognize Licinius as Augustus in the east. The two Augusti met at Milan, and in the tradition of marriage alliances established by the Tetrarchy, Licinius married Constantine's sister. But, in 324 CE, Constantine moved east to defeat Licinius and became sole emperor. Although Constantinople was founded to commemorate Constantine's victory, the centuries-old Greek town of Byzantium was an ideal base from which the defense of the empire in the east could be directed. There were excellent road links both to the east and west and the city could also be supplied by sea. Constantine spent most of his remaining life in Byzantium until his death in 337 CE.

Constantine relieved Christians of any obligation to serve on city councils and taxation. There was also financial help for the building of churches and bishops were able to receive bequests, some congregations became extremely wealthy. It was the emperor himself and his family who funded the first great Christian buildings. Constantine donated land from the old imperial palace of the Lateran, while the mother of the emperor, Helena, visited Palestine in 326 CE and set in hand the building of appropriate memorials to the life of Jesus at Bethlehem and on the Mount of Olives. Constantine himself was responsible for the great Church of the Holy Sepulcher at Jerusalem, over the supposed burial place of Jesus. As early as 333 CE pilgrims were visiting these sacred sites. The martyrs of the great persecutions had not been forgotten. The Vatican Hill, the traditional burial place of Peter, saw a great church rising from a site which had to be levelled for the purpose. Saint Peter's was another of Constantine's foundations, and one source suggests that a mosaic with the emperor presenting the church to Christ adorned the central triumphal arch. These churches borrowed the traditional Roman hall, the basilica, as a model. Rome still has two fine fifth century examples of basilicas, those of Santa Maria Maggiore and Santa Sabina.

Round about 313 CE, Constantine was approached by a group of Christians from North Africa, known as the Donatists. They questioned the right of a man who had surrendered the scriptures to the authorities during a time of persecuting to be appointed as a bishop. One such had been appointed in Carthage and the Donatists refused to accept him and appointed their own bishop, creating in effect, a schism. Constantine consulted bishops on the matter and eventually ruled against the Donatists. The Donatists ignored the emperor's ruling and continued in schism into the next century. But, the precedent had been created that the emperor was prepared to intervene in matters concerning the Christian churches. A doctrinal dispute arose in the 320s, concerning the relationship of Christ to God the Father. The question hinged on whether Christ has been part of God from the beginning of time or whether he had been created by him at a later date and with a distinct substance. One view was that Christ occupied an indeterminate position somewhere between the creator and what had been created, neither fully god nor fully man. Another view was that the son had existed eternally and that there was no separate act of creation. The church provided no satisfactory way of resolving it. Constantine heard of the debate and volunteered to convene a council of bishops in order to reconcile the opposing fractions. They eventually met at Nicaea, near to Constantine's eastern base at Nicomedia, as Constantinople was still under construction, so that the emperor could attend in person.

The Council of Nicaea (325 CE), was the first great ecumenical council of the church with 220 bishops in attendance, most of them from the east where the dispute was most intense. The bishop of Rome, still on the margins of the largely Greek-speaking Christian world, did not attend. While details of the council are obscure, it seems that it was Constantine himself who urged the declaration that Christ was "consubstantial (Latin: consubstantialis), of one substance, with the father," in effect a refutation of the view that Christ had been created by him at a later date and with a distinct substance. Two bishops opposed the resolution, but Constantine used his imperial powers to exile them, thereby establishing imperial responsibility for upholding Christian doctrine. It was emperor Theodosius who used the Council of Constantinople of 381 to declare opposition to Constantine's ruling of 325 CE a heresy. When Constantine died in 337 CE, he left three sons to succeed him and all three were Christians. Constantine II took the west of the empire, Constantius the east, and the central provinces of Africa, Illyricum and Italy went to the youngest Constans. They eliminated many of their close relatives, in order to secure their position. In 340 CE, Constantine invaded Italy, in the hope of adding it to his share, but he was killed. Constans died in turn in 350 when fighting a usurper, Magnentius. The following year Constantius and Magnentius met in the great battle of Mursa where Magnentius was defeated but both armies suffered enormous losses. Constantius ruled as sole emperor until his death in 361 CE. For much of his reign he was preoccupied in the east where the Sasanian King Shapur II (309–379 CE) was energetically raiding into Mesopotamia. This meant that the northern borders of the empire were neglected and Gaul was frequently ravaged.

In 356, Constantius nominated his cousin Julian as Caesar and given charge of Gaul. Both the Franks and the Alamanni suffered major defeats at Julian's hands and by 360 order had been restored to the borders. Constantius, still hard pressed in the east, now tried to remove some of Julian's troops. They revolted and declared Julian an Augustus in 361. When Constantius died in 361, Julian found himself sole emperor by default. Although Julian had been brought up as a Christian, he had reverted to paganism and had attempted to re-establish the traditional cults of the empire. But, he was only to last 18 months before dying at the hands of an unknown assailant in 363 CE, while on campaign against the Sasanians. Julian was the last emperor of the pagan empire. It was in Theodosius' reign that the emperor was confirmed as the upholder of Christianity, not only against the "pagan" but also against variants of Christian belief declared heretical. The Greek word *hairesis* originally meant simply "choice." It now developed the meaning of "unacceptable choice." Constantine's sons, though Christian, had continued to tolerate paganism. It was only in the 350s that Constantius launched a determined attack on paganism, in particular the practice of divination. When the "pagan" emperor Julian came to power, he banned Christians from teaching rhetoric and grammar and abolished the exemption of clergy from taxation. Revenues were restored to the temples and Julian set about the revival of animal sacrifice with some enthusiasm. But in his short reign he never developed the rapport with the pagan elites which would have ensured the restoration of the traditional cults to a central place in state ceremony. With Jovian, his successor, came a restoration of Christianity and there were to be no more pagan emperors.

In the reign of Theodosius I (b.347, r.379–395 CE), who was the last emperor to rule over both the eastern and the western halves of the Roman Empire, a wide variety of heresies were first defined and a vigorous onslaught launched against pagan cults. In Egypt, bands of fanatical monks wrecked the ancient temples. The serapeion (Latin: serapeum), near Alexandria, one of the great temple complexes of the ancient world dedicated to the syncretic Greco-Egyptian deity Serapis, who combined aspects of Osiris and Apis, in a humanized form that was accepted by the Ptolemaic Greeks of Alexandria, was dismantled in 392 CE. In North Africa, Christian vigilantes raided pagan centers and ridiculed traditional beliefs. There was also growing Christian intolerance to Jews and by the beginning of the fifth century, Jews were banned from the civil service. The political power of the emperor had become intertwined with the spiritual power of the church. Some of the manifestations of pagan culture in the fourth century are explained in the early chapters of Saint Augustine's *Confessions*. Saint Augustine was attracted to the cult of Manicheism, which was founded by the Persian religious leader Mani in the third century. The Manicheans believed that the world was divided between good and evil, light and dark. "Good" had been shattered by the forces of evil, which also had their physical forms. Augustine was appointed professor of rhetoric in Milan in 385 CE and it was there that he became drawn to Neoplatonism.

Plotinus (205–70 CE) early studies took place in Alexandria, Egypt, but his later years were spent in Rome, where he attracted a circle of devoted admirers. For Plotinus "the Good" was an entity which had existed since before the creation of the physical world. Within "the Good" was the power of love, which reached out to those who searched for it. Once the mind of human believer met with "the Good" a transformation, a profound mystical experience, could take place. As Plotinus put it, "when in this state the soul would exchange its present state for nothing in the world, though it was offered the kingdom of all the heavens: for this is 'the Good' and there is nothing better." It was clear that orthodox Christianity shared a vast territory with their pagan counter-part. There is no evidence that Christian marriage customs were any different from pagan ones, though Christian influence seemed to have impelled emperors to tighten the divorce laws. Christians continued to own slaves and as late as 580 CE the emperor Tiberius, launching a persecution of pagans, using the traditional Roman punishment of crucifixion. Until the Edict of Theodosius (Latin Flavius Theodosius Augustus 347–395 CE), also known as *Cunctos populos*, was issued on February 27, 380 CE, which ordered all subjects of the Roman Empire to profess the faith of the bishops of Rome and of Alexandria, making Nicene Christianity the state religion of the Roman Empire. The Emperor Constantine 1 converted to Christianity in 312 CE, and together with his eastern counterpart Gaius Valerius Licinianus Licinius Augustus (c.263–325), issued the Edict of Milan, which granted religious toleration and freedom for persecuted Christians.

By 325 CE Arianism – the concept that asserts that Jesus Christ is the Son of God, who was created by God the Father at a point in time, is distinct from the Father and is therefore subordinated to the Father. Arian teachings were first attributed to Arius (250–336 CE) a Christian presbyter in Alexandria. The teachings of Arius were contradictory to the prevailing theological views held by proto-orthodox Christians, regarding the nature of the Trinity and the nature of Christ. The Nicene Creed is the official doctrine of most Christian churches, including the Roman Catholic, Eastern Orthodox, Oriental Orthodox, Church of the East and Anglican Communion, as well as Lutheran, Reformed, Evangelical and most mainline Protestants, with regards to the ontological status of the three persons or hypostases of the Trinity: Father, Son and Holy Spirit. In Europe, Egyptian divinities were corrupted with Greek and Asiatic names and mythologies and reduced to vague pantheistic personalities, so that Isis and Osiris had retained very little of their Egyptian origin. Consequently, as they failed to advance Egyptian Philosophy, so they also failed to advance Egyptian religion. At the end of the fourth century CE, Theodosius ordered the closure of Egyptian temples, and Christianity began to spread more rapidly and both the religion of Egypt and that of Greece began to decline. But, on the island of Philae the Egyptian religion was being practiced by its inhabitants, the Blemmyans and Nobadians, who refused to accept Christianity and the Roman government paid tribute to them. But, during the sixth century CE, Justinian (L. Flavius Petrus Sabbatius Iustinianus Augustus (c.482–565 CE), who wanted to revive the empire's greatness, issued a second Edict which suppressed this remnant of Egyptian worship and propagated Christianity among the Nubians. With the death of the last priest, who could read and interpret the writings of the words of the gods (hieroglyphics) the Egyptian faith sank into oblivion.

The Edicts of Theodosius in the fourth century and that of Justinian in the sixth century, abolished both the Mystery System of Egypt and its philosophical schools, located in Greece and elsewhere, outside of Egypt. The abolition of the Egyptian Mysteries was to create an opportunity for the adoption of Christianity. For GM James (1954), the abolition of both the Egyptian Mysteries and the schools of Greek philosophy, shows that the nature of the Egyptian Mysteries and Greek philosophy was identical and that Greek philosophy grew out of the Egyptian Mysteries. Hence, the western world, copied and relabeled African culture, and claimed it as their own. According to Bernal (1987), the belief in Egypt as a powerful, if not the most powerful, center of magic survived the conversion of Western Europe to Christianity. Both scarabs and a barbaric head of a bull with a solar disc on his forehead, which has been identified with Apis, were found in the pagan tomb of Childeric I (440–481 CE), the father of Clovis I (466–511 CE), the first Christian King of France, who united the Franks and founded the Merovingian dynasty. About three-hundred years later, the great seal of Charlemagne (742–814 CE), represented the head of the late Egyptian Jupiter Serapis. West Europeans, from the fifteenth century to the seventeenth century CE, were far more concerned with travels in Egypt than they were with those in Greece. In some circles, having traveled to the sources of knowledge in Egypt provided a legitimacy for attacks on conventional wisdom.

Christian Africa

Africans' conception of God was on a scale too grand to be acceptable to western minds. So, they had to reduce it by using a term that is equated with paganism, "primitive," backwardness and barbarism. The word is "animism," but, in documenting animism as the chief characteristic of the religion of Africans, from the remotest times they are also documenting the fact that Africans' belief in the existence as well as the nature of one Universal God. Animism, as applied to Africans, is the belief that the spirit of the Creator or the Universal God permeates all of His creations, living and dead. Hence, any object, animate or inanimate, may be sacred. Indeed, precisely the same African religious belief becomes the doctrine of "Immanence" in Christian Civilization. The Bakuba (people of Kuba) believed that two contending spirits affected man: the spirit of good and the spirit of evil. Religion was involved in the practice of medicine, as in every other aspect of African life. Disease was believed to be the result of some misdeed on the part of the individual himself or the working of an evil spirit. If widespread, the community as a whole may have sinned. Songs, dances and sacrifices were communal activities designed to re-establish the proper relationship between the people and the unseen power. "Magic" was another form of prayer, song, or dance in the appeals to supernatural powers for help. However, Africa was among the first areas to which Christianity spread. It was next door to Palestine, and from earliest times, there had been the closest relations between the Jews and Africans, both friendly and hostile.

The pre-Christian religious concepts took place easily and, due to the residence of so many ancient Jewish leaders in Ethiopia, almost naturally Abraham, Joseph and brothers, Mary and Jesus, and the Lawgiver Moses, who was not only born in Africa but married the daughter of an African priest. The religious belief in sacrifice for the remission of sins was an African belief and practice at least 2,000 years before Abraham. Practically all of the Ten Commandments were embedded in the African constitution (Ancient African Mysteries) ages before Moses went up to Mount Sinai in Africa in 1491 BCE. From the early African perspective, there was nothing earth shaking or extraordinary about the establishment of still another cult – the cult of Christians. The only unusual thing about the new cult of Christians was that while they disclaimed being of the Jewish faith, they worshipped the Jewish tribal god – the God of Israel. The Christians seemed to be expanding the role of a god that had been concerned only with the Jews as his "Chosen People" to a God of the Universe and thus competing with the African God of the Universe – The Sun God. The Christians were not really different even in the central religious beliefs of the African and Jews of the period in sacrificing sheep, goats, bulls, and sometimes humans, for the remission of sins. For while the Christians had given up the slaughtering of animals for offerings, the very cornerstone of their faith was that Jesus Christ, the Son of God, was sacrificed for the sins of man and that his blood was shed for this purpose alone.

Drinking of the blood (now wine) and eating of the body (now bread) are all fundamental aspects of man's most ancient religion. The spread of Christianity in the land below the First Cataract gained momentum after the destruction of

Ethiopia as an empire in the fourth century BCE. In 332 BCE, Alexander the Great arrived in Egypt and, having broken the imperial power of Persia elsewhere, had no trouble taking over Egypt. A Greek was crowned Pharaoh in 334 BCE, as Ptolemy I. The Greek ruled for almost 300 years before the expansion of the Roman Empire into Egypt ended their dominion in 30 BCE. Africans were prevented from accessing theological schools and educational opportunities. In religion, as in every other fields, the system deliberately prevented Africans from achieving qualifications in order to exclude them from certain position in the Christian Church. European administration and control of African Christianity was assured by establishing the head of the Church in Lower Egypt (the Patriarch of Alexandria) with power to appoint all bishops in Africa. The bishops' appointees were always European or Mixed-European, until token appointments of Africans to lesser posts, such as deacons. This was the last phase of the processes of Europeanisation in Egypt that was so thorough going that both the Africans and their history were erased from memory by foreign rulers, including the Asians; Hyksos; Assyrians; Persians; Greeks; Romans; Arabs and others. The Romans ruled for seven-hundred years, with the Arabs ruling over one thousand-three-hundred years exemplifies the long struggle to take from Africans whatever they had of human worth; their land and all the wealth therein; their bodies and minds – a process of steady dehumanization.

When Cyriacus was "King of Kings" in 745 CE, Omar, the governor of Egypt, stepped up the persecution of Christians in Egypt, in what amounted to be a Muslim Holy War, destroying churches or converting them into mosques and putting the Patriarch in prison. When the African King headed an army of 100,000 men and marched on the Arab center of power in Lower Egypt, the governor of Egypt quickly freed the Patriarch and promised to leave the Christians and their churches alone. It is worth noting that thousands of Africans remained in both Lower and Upper Egypt, who accepted a slave or inferior status in the society as their lot. It was these Africans that Aristotle had in mind when he referred to men who were born to be slaves; on the other hand, those Africans who migrated or fought to the death rather than accept slavery were those who were born to be free! Yet, Greece and Rome, having made the exclusion of the Africans from Egypt permanent, appeared to have no conquest ambitions in the African country of the south. It would seem that whoever held the seacoasts; whether Asian, European or Egyptian, controlled world trade and put Ethiopia in a state of economic dependence, no matter how vast the flow of goods was from the south. However, a storm was threatening farther south as the Roman Legions withdrew from Egypt. Now, for some centuries Arabs and Jews (the latter called "Solomonids" by most historians) had been swarming into the southeastern region, pushing through the middle in such a way that even in Abyssinia Africans were pressed southward. The Asians and Afro-Asians held Northern Abyssinia, with the center of power in the strategic kingdom of Axum, from where the Arabs prepared their forces for the destruction of a now – weakening Ethiopian empire. In 350 CE, the Arabs, with their Jewish allies, destroyed Meroe, and an epoch in history ended.

Christianity and Sex

The first public Christian art shows Christian themes mingled with pagan symbolism and motifs. Images of the Virgin and Child appear to be derived from those of the Egyptian goddess Isis and her son Horus. While many Christians enjoyed being in and of the world, exercising their power as bishops or advisers to the emperor, a minority saw the world as a haven of wickedness. Their response was to leave it. The Egyptian Antony, so-called "father of the monk," lived 70 of his purported 105 years in the desert, remote from any human contact. In Syria, some holy men climbed pillars and lived on top of them for years with hundreds of curious or devout visitors coming to stare. But, not all could bear the lack of immediate human contact. In Egypt, the withdrawal from the world took place in communities. Hundreds of ordinary men crowded into settlements where they lived according to a routine of prayer and manual labor. These were the first monasteries. However successful an individual might be in escaping from other human beings he or she still had a physical body to contend with. Some Greek philosophers long asserted that the desires of the flesh hampered them in their search for the spiritual world. By the fourth century, the preoccupation had become an obsession and it seems that celibacy was practiced by some Jewish communities, such as that at Qumran.

The act of sex in itself was now viewed by many with intense distaste. The church viewed sex between married couples as acceptable, but only as a means of creating children. But the fulfilment of sexual desire as an end in itself was morally wrong. This left women in an ambiguous position. On the one hand, they could be cast, in the tradition of Eve, as temptresses to be avoided. On the other hand, those who make a commitment to virginity could achieve a certain status denied to their more carnal sisters. In these same years, the cult of Jesus' mother Mary as perpetually virgin appeared, even though Jesus had brothers and a sister. In the late fourth and early fifth century, a number of converts to Christianity deployed their classical learning in the service of the church. Of these Augustine of Hippo (354–430 CE), who converted to Christianity in 386 CE. He helped to formulate the doctrine of "original sin" and "just war." He detailed his spiritual experiences in Milan and his eventual conversion to Christianity, in the *Confessions*, written in the late 390s CE, after he had returned to his native Africa. Augustine presents himself as a deeply unworthy man, tormented by his sexuality and harried by the looming power of God. Augustine argued that as a result of Adam and Eve's transgressions in the Garden of Eden, God had burdened all human beings with an "original sin," which was passed on from generation to generation. Although the concept of original sin had never been mentioned by Jesus, Augustine relied on one verse from Saint Paul (Roman 5: 12) for support.

Human beings, according to Augustine, were tied by original sin to the earthly pleasures of the world and only the grace of God could liberate them from the burden of these pleasures. This grace could be passed on through the sacraments especially those of baptism and the Eucharist, which was a gift from God, not the right of any individual, however good his or her life. This view of God was very selective and only a few would be saved. What would happen to those who did not get this grace of God remains problematic. Although there were many flaws in Augustine's argument, he managed to get his view accepted as the official doctrine of the western church, after the emperor Honorius (384–423 CE) insisted the Italian bishops adopt it. The concept of original sin received no support in the east and was never adopted by any other monotheistic religion. The logic of Augustine's views suggested that membership of the church did not guarantee salvation and that those who did not join the church were not necessarily deprived of God's grace. In 394 CE, the emperor Theodosius had been challenged by a usurper in Gaul, Flavius Eugenius, who although was a Christian, supported Roman polytheism. Theodosius met the forces of Eugenius at the River Frigidus in the Alps and crushed them. The battle was seen by contemporary Christians as the confirmation of the triumph of their faith.

This was to signal a New World order of spiritual authority and a growing preoccupation with the elimination of paganism and heresy, resulting in stifling of the rich diversity of Greco-Roman spiritual experiences and Jews were increasingly isolated. The state and church authorities initiated measures to segregate the Jews from mainstream Christian society with consequences that were, in the long term, profound. The Greek and Roman world had seen a variety of gods whose relationships and conflicts had often diverted them from human affairs. The single Christian god was portrayed as if he had few other concerns than the behavior and attitudes of individual human beings. Their sexual behavior in particular seemed of particular concern to him. It was perhaps at this moment that intense guilt replaced public shame as a conditioner of moral behavior. Ever more lurid descriptions of the horrors of Hell accompanied the shift. Soon consuming fires and devils with red-hot instruments of torture entered European mythology. There was tension over the way Christian society used its resources, whether for the relief of the poor, as the gospels would seem to suggest, or the glorification of God in gold and mosaic. These shifts in beliefs helped determine a framework of social, economic, spiritual, and cultural life which has persisted even into the present day.

Islamic Invasion of Africa

Muhammad (c. 570–632 CE) was orphaned at an early age; he was raised under the care of his paternal uncle, Abu Talib. At age 40, he reported being visited by Gabriel in a cave, where he stated that he received his first revelation from God. Three years later, Muhammad started preaching these revelations publicly, proclaiming that "God is One," that complete "surrender" (Islam) to him is the only way acceptable to God, and that he was a prophet and messenger of God, similar to the other prophets in Islam

The six articles of the Islamic faith mentioned in the Qur'an are:

1. Belief in Allah (One God)
2. Belief in the Angels
3. Belief in Divine Books
4. Belief in the Prophets
5. Belief in the Day of Judgment
6. Belief in Allah's predestination

The first five are mentioned together in the Qur'an and by Muhammad, in the following manner in the Hadith of Gabriel:

> Iman is that you believe in God and His Angels and His Books and His Messengers and the Hereafter and the good and evil fate ordained by your God.

In a Hadith, Muhammad defined Iman as "knowledge in the heart, a voicing with the tongue, and an activity with the limbs." Faith is confidence in a truth which is real. When people have confidence, they submit themselves to that truth. In the Qur'an, Iman is one of the ten qualities which cause one to be the recipient of God's mercy and reward. The Qur'an states that no one can be a true believer unless he loves the prophet more than his children, parents, and relatives. A person who only professes faith through words is not regarded as a true believer (mu'min), and so it is essential that a person's deeds also testify to his faith. Muslims believe that the first prophet was Adam (Adem). Many of the revelations delivered by the 48 prophets in Judaism and many prophets of Christianity are mentioned in altered form and with different names. Elisha is called Alyas, Job is Ayyub, Jesus is Isa, Moses is called Musa, and David is called Dawood. None of the seven Jewish prophetesses are mentioned in the Qur'an as prophets. For Muslims, every prophet in Islam preaches the same main Islamic beliefs, the Oneness of God, worshipping of that one God, avoidance of idolatry and sin, and belief in the Islamic Day of Resurrection and life after death. The beliefs of charity, prayer, pilgrimage, worship of God, and fasting are believed to have been taught by every prophet who has ever lived. Sunni scholars agree that prophets were all males.

The Islamic Isa (Jesus) did not die on the cross like the Christian Jesus but deceived his enemies and ascended to heaven. Muslims believe that the *Tawrat* (Torah) was revealed to Moses and *Zabur*, (Psalms) the Holy Scripture, was revealed to David. *The Book of Enlightenment*, The Books of Divine Wisdom, *Injil (Gospel)* was the holy book revealed to Isa. Scrolls of Abraham are believed to have been one of the earliest bodies of scripture and used by Ishmael and Isaac. The Scrolls of Moses, containing the revelations of Moses, now lost. To escape persecution, Muhammad sent some followers to Abyssinia before he and his followers migrated from Mecca to Medina [known as Yathrib] in the year 662 CE. This event, the Hegira, marks the beginning of the Islamic calendar, also known as the Hijri calendar. The migration to Abyssinia, also known as the First Hegira, was where Muhammad's first followers (the Sahabah) fled from the persecution of the ruling Quraysh tribe of Mecca. They sought refuge in the Christian Kingdom of Aksum, present-day Ethiopia and Eritrea (formerly referred to as Abyssinia, a name derived from the Arabic Al-Habash). The Aksumite Monarch who received them is known in Islamic sources as the Negus (a royal title king).

The Arab General Amr ibn-al-As, in 639 CE, marched into Egypt, facing off with the Byzantines in the Battle of Heliopolis, that ended with the defeat of the Byzantines and opened the door for the Muslim conquest of the Byzantine Exarchate of Africa. The Muslim conquest of Egypt was to change the character of Egyptian civilization radically and was to have a disastrous impact on the dignity and destiny of Africans, as a people. Colonization and Islamization progressed and as Egypt became the main center of Arab power, which found concrete expression in Arab-Islamic expansion over North Africa, into Spain, and southward into what remained as "The Land of the Blacks." Ethiopia now began at the First Cataract in the north and extended south into present-day Ethiopia. It was bound by Upper Egypt, the Red Sea, and the Libyan Desert. The geography of Nubia, between the First and Sixth Cataracts, is much like that of present-day Sudan and beyond. The land of the south of Egypt had developed a strong economy, enriched by a thriving export trade in paper, ivory, gold, ebony, emerald, copper, incense, ostrich feathers, and decorated earthenware. All the Arabs that swarmed into Africa across the Red Sea and Indian Ocean were refugees – fleeing for their lives. In 831 CE, King Zakariya, alarmed at great incursions of Arabs into Nubia, sent a delegation headed by his nephew and heir to the throne to the Caliph at Baghdad, asking that the Treaty of 652 CE be respected and Arab migrations halted. The highest ranking of the 13 kings under the "King of Kings" was the Eparch of Faris, Lord of the Mountain, whose special mission was to bar Arab migration and settlement in the land of Makuri (Nubia). However, by the ninth century CE, the Arabs had been passing the Lord of the Mountain and his garrisons for many decades, that by then Arabic was being generally spoken below the First Cataract.

Once settled, the Arabs formed an ever-increasing population base for the Muslim leaders whose aim was to establish Islamic rule over the whole of Africa. They were to follow the Christian strategy of concentrating on the conversion of African kings and other leaders, in the belief that as the king goes, so goes the nation. Black kings were already dropping their African names for "Christian" names – the first step towards self-effacement. Northern Ethiopia (Nubia) was now split into three major states: Nobatia bordering Egypt at the First Cataract, with its capital at Pachoras, was initially the most exposed to the influence of Arabization and Islamization and over time, the people gradually converted and married into Arab clans. But, by the eighth century CE, Nobatia was under the control of its neighboring kingdom – Makuri. Makuri covered the area along the Nile River from the Third Cataract to somewhere between the Fifth and Sixth Cataracts. It had control over the trade routes, mines, and oases to the east and west. Its capital was Dongola, the name by which the kingdom is sometimes known. Unlike Nobatia, by the end of the sixth century CE, it had converted to Christianity, but by the seventh century, Egypt was conquered by the Islamic armies, and Nubia was cut off from the rest of Christendom.

In 642 CE, an Arab army invaded Mukuri, but it was repulsed. They again invaded in 652 CE, Makurians inflicted another defeat on the Arab army. Eventually a treaty, known as the baqt, was signed, creating relative peace between the two sides. These battles were two of the most decisive battles of history but they are not mentioned in any history book. These two defeats on the hitherto undefeated Arab forces was so disastrous for the Arabs that they sought peace in a treaty, which lasted until the thirteenth century CE. The Makurian king agreed to give Arab traders more privileges of trade in addition to a share in their slave trading, while the Arabs were to send manufactured goods south. Between seven hundred CE and twelve-hundred CE, Makuri was more empire than kingdom, as it was organized into 13 major states, with a sub-king over each and the "King of Kings" over all. But, increased aggression from Egypt, and internal discord led to the collapse of the kingdom in the fourteenth century. The third kingdom, Alodia, also referred to as Alwa or Aloa, with its capital at Soba, was located near the confluence of the Blue and White Nile. These southern kingdoms continued the expansion of caravan routes for external trade across the Sahara to Western Africa, to offset the Egyptian seacoast monopoly, replacement of vast temple building programs with equally vast church building programs and continued development of iron industries and better-equipped armies.

African Retreat

Initially, the Africans who had fled below the First Cataract, to escape the various conquests, never seemed to accept those conquests as final, and attempted to retake Egypt from time to time. But, having reconquered the Asian dominated Lower Egypt, African Pharaohs sought integration with the Asians, instead of driving them out of the country. The second threat was economic, as Egypt's flourishing export trade, both by sea and caravans, depended heavily on her imports from the south. To cut these off would mean economic panic in an otherwise prosperous land. Hence, the Afro-Asian (Egyptian) conquest of Nubia might remove the military and economic threats, but, insofar as the Nile was concerned, it would settle nothing. Like Upper Egypt, Nubia was a land of cities and towns, of temples and pyramids. The Old Kingdom's raiders could not destroy all of the temples and other monuments and any outstanding African creations that could not be converted and claimed as the work of Egyptians were destroyed, for now "Egyptian" meant "Asian or European." The Arabs were to carry out the work of eradication in a far more thoroughgoing manner at a later time.

Napata was a beautiful city, located below the Fourth Cataract. The city itself was regarded as the "Holy of Holies," the capital of what the Egyptians called "The Land of the Gods." It was to this area that African leaders, including priests of various cults, retreated when things got too difficult in Egypt. Here also certain African kings preferred to stay even when their position and power in Egypt were unchallenged. Most of the royal burials in pyramids were at Kurru. The largest pyramid in Ethiopia is that of King Taharqa (d.664 BCE) at Nuri. After the Assyrian-Greek invasion in 590 BCE, the city was almost completely destroyed again. The capital now moved on the other side of the river, to the other historic industrial center at Meroe. Even after the onslaught by the Assyrian and their allies, the Africans were to rebuild, from the new capital city of Meroe, a civilization greater than the one just destroyed. One African state defied the slow onslaughts of the Sahara, for over 2,000 years, hanging on to its fringes far into historic times. Geographers were among the first foreigners to arrive in the region in the tenth century CE. The Arab and European practice of naming countries and peoples often displayed both arrogance and ignorance. So, they called this country "Ghana" – which means "warrior" the name given to their ruler. Ghana's actual history goes far back beyond its known record. Ghana, properly known as Awkar, was located in what is now Southern Mauritania and Western Mali. According to Williams (1974), that record listed 44 kings before the Christian era and this alone would extend Ghana's known history beyond the Twenty-Fifth Dynasty, when the last Black Pharaohs ruled Egypt, in the seventh century BCE. It surpassed many others in social organization, military power, and economic wealth.

The introduction of the camel to Western Sahara in the third century CE, gave way to great changes in the area that became the Ghana Empire. By the time of the

Muslim conquest of North Africa in the seventh century CE, the camel had changed ancient and irregular trade routes into a trade network running from Morocco to the Niger River. Control of caravan trade routes to the north, east, Ethiopia and Egypt were probably the most important factor in the ever-growing wealth of the empire. There were import and export taxes, a system of weights and measures, and control of the flow of gold. This African empire had expanded territorially by both conquests and peaceful alliances with neighboring countries, including dependencies such as Tekur and desert tribes of Berber were made tributaries. Kumbi Saleh, the capital, was a city of stone mansions, temples, mosques, and schools, along with the thatched roof huts of the masses. It was a mixed economy of agriculture: wheat, millet, cotton, corn, yams, and cattle raising. There were numerous crafts: blacksmiths, goldsmiths, coppersmiths, stonemasons, brick masons, carpenters, weavers and sandal-makers, dyers, furniture makers, and potters. Imports were salt, textiles, cowrie shells, brass, dates, figs, pearls, fruit, sugar, dried raisins, and honey. The chief exports were gold, ivory, rubber, and slaves. Under the Emperor Tenkamenin (1037–75 CE), who is considered to have been the most powerful Ghanaian Emperor, came to the throne in 1062 CE, and had an imperial army of some 200,000, of which half were mounted cavalry and 40,000 were expertly trained archers.

The Cordoban scholar, Abu Ubaid al-Bakri, gave a detailed description of the Ghanaian Empire in the eleventh century CE. The world-renowned University of Sankore was at Timbuktu. The destruction of the capital by Muslim in 1076 CE and the great migration from the country are part of the story; but only a part, because the Muslims did not stay in force.

Another part that affected the stability and growth of the country was the continuous raids by Semitic nomads of the desert, mostly Berbers and Arabs. As the empire declined, it was finally made a vassal to the rising Mali Empire at some point in the thirteenth century. Mali was the second of the "Great Three" West African empires that became well known in the medieval world. Although its history has been traced back to Paleolithic times through rock paintings, carvings and other archaeological finds, such as the "Asselar Man" skeleton, discovered by Theodore Monod and Wladimir Besnard in 1927, which has been dated to c.6,400 BP, making it no older than Holocene (c.11,700 BP). The Mali Empire rose in the thirteenth century CE, with the decline of the Ghanaian Empire. Among the contestants for succession to the disintegrating empire of Ghana were two of its rebelling provinces, Kaniaga – the kingdom of the Mandinka – and Diara. The Kingdom of Tegrur, under the leadership of Sumanguru, who captured the capital of Ghana, Kumbi Saleh, in 1203 CE. Sumanguru was defeated by the Mandinka King, Sundiata, at the historic Battle of Kirina in 1240 CE, which was to mark the beginning of the Malian Empire.

The Egyptians were convinced of having the same ancestor as the Blacks, who then inhabited the land of Punt. Until the close of the Egyptian Empire, the kings of Nubia (Sudan) were to bear the same title as the Egyptian Pharaoh, that of the Hawk of Nubia. Amon and Osiris were represented as coal-black; Isis was a black goddess. The god Kush had altars in Memphis, Thebes, and Meroe under the name of Khons, god of the sky to the Ethiopians, and Hercules to the Egyptians. In Wolof, Khon means "rainbow," it means "to die" in Serer, in modern-day Senegal. There is also a land named Khons on the Upper Nile. Accordingly, Nubia appears to be closely akin to Egypt and the rest of Black Africa. So, we find many civilizing features common to Nubia, whose kingdom lasted until the British occupation. Right after the end of Egypto-Nubian Antiquity, the Empire of Ghana soared like a meteor from the mouth of the Niger to the Senegal River, about the third century CE. Viewed from this perspective, African history proceeded without interruption. Nubia remained the sole source of culture and civilization until about the sixth century CE, and then Ghana seized the torch from the sixth century until 1240 CE, when its capital was destroyed by Sundiata Keita. This heralded the launching of the Mandingo Empire (capital Mali) of which Maurice Delafosse (1922) would write "this little village of the Upper Niger was for several years the principal capital of the largest empire ever known in Black Africa, and one of the most important ever to exist in the universe" (Diop, 1974:147).

Under the Emperors Sundiata Keita (1217–1255 CE) and Mansa Uli (r.1255–1270 CE). Mansa is a Mandinka word meaning "Sultan" (King) or "emperor." Under these two emperors there was systematic reorganization, consolidation, and expansion of the Mali Empire, so that when Mansa Musa came to the throne in 1312 CE, he had a solid foundation upon which to build what was to become one of the greatest empires of the time. It must be noted that both Ghana and Mali empires included strong Arab-Berber tribal states under their rule. These states occupied the surrounding strategic points of power and were able to harass and raid the great caravans conducting the vast import and export trade across the Sahara. One solution of this problem, it was believed, was for African kings to become Muslims, as the

Muslims controlled the all-important caravan trails and all African ports of trade with the world. The fact that many of these desert tribes were nominally a part of the empire, or tributaries to it, made matters worse. Pretending to be loyal to the emperor when this served their purpose, they could play it both ways. As Muslim "brothers," they secured important posts in government. Here, as elsewhere, "brotherhood" and "integration" were most beneficial. Another important fact to be noted is that the Arab-Berber position near and within the empire was the base from which the fanatical Almoravids spread the Islamic religion in West Africa, with an uncompromising aggressiveness unmatched in the history of religion.

Their proselytizing brotherhoods were camps of military missionaries. They were hostile to the black masses because they actively resisted conversion to Islam. The Almoravids established an empire in Morocco, Algeria, and Andalusia (Spain) in the eleventh century and were in turn driven out by Almohads in the twelfth century. Baranmindanah was the first Mansa (king) of Mali to embrace Islam in 1050 CE. He urged that all succeeding mansas do the same. The mansas who came after Baeanmindanah did indeed become Muslims, mainly for trade and security. Many became as fanatical as any of the semi-barbarous Almoravids of the deserts, such as the great Mari Jalak, known as Mansa Musa. Between 1307 and 1322 CE, Mali evolved from an expanding kingdom to an expanding empire. It extended north over the all-important salt mines of Taghaza, eastward to the Hausa States of Nigeria, and westward to cover the strong Tegrur and the countries of the Fulani and Tucolor peoples. The expansion of Mali meant the expansion of Islam in the Western Sudan, and in countries outside of the empire. The spread of Islam replaced African traditional laws and the Qur'an was now the new constitution. But, after 1550 CE, Mali, as an empire, was little more than an inspiring memory, and just as Mali had spread over the former Ghanaian empire, Songhay was to spread over Mali.

Next came the Empire of Gao, which preceded that of the Songhay Empire, in the Middle Niger. In the ninth century CE, it was considered to be the most powerful West African kingdom. Towards the end of the thirteenth century CE, Gao lost its independence and became part of the expanding Mali Empire. In the fourteenth century CE, Ali Kulun, the first ruler of the Sunni dynasty, rebelled against Mali hegemony, and was defeated. In the first half of the fifteenth century CE, Sunni Sulayman Dama threw off Mali rule. His successor, Sunni Ali Ber (1464–1492) greatly expanded the territory under Songhay control and established the Songhay Empire. The story of Songhay is like retelling the stories of Ghana and Mali. Their small state, with its capital at Kukya, was east of the Niger River bend, between Gao and Agadis, can be traced back to the seventh century CE. The sixteenth ruler, Dia Kossoi, was crowned at Gao early in the eleventh century CE and the capital moved there. The capture of that city-state from the Sorko people in the seventh century CE was the early beginning of Songhay expansion. Gao was the important caravan center for international trade, and it dominated the commerce of the central regions of the Western Sudan, controlling the flow of gold and ivory from the southern forests and the precious salt trade from the Taghaza mines in the northern desert.

In 1325 CE, Mansa Musa (1280–1337 CE) used military force to bring Gao and other Songhay territories within the Mali Empire. The defeated Songhay pretended loyalty to the Mali Empire while busily rebuilding and reorganizing their armies and political structures. In 1335 CE, they started a new leadership with the kingly title of Sunni. The second Sunni, Suleiman-Mar, was able to break away from Mali and declare Gao's independence in 1375. When Sunni Ali came to the throne in 1464 CE, he became a nominal Muslim for the same economic reasons that influenced other African kings, especially as the Muslims controlled trade with Asia and Europe. The wealth of the nation depended very largely on cooperation with them. The challenge faced by all African kings was how to be a Muslim without alienating the people. It was clear to the Arabs and Berbers that Sunni Ali's real loyalty was to the traditional religion of the Africans. At the close of his reign in 1492 CE, the Songhay Empire rivalled that of Mali in wealth and territorial expansion.

Sunni Ali was succeeded by Sunni Bari in 1492, who refused to compromise with Islam and defended the African religion. He was deposed after a year, paving the way for Sunni Ali's chief minister, general and most ardent and sincere African Muslim, Muhammad Ture (1443–1538 CE), who became emperor in 1493 CE. He extended the empire eastward over the Hausa States across Northern Nigeria, northward over the Sahara beyond the Taghaza salt mines and westward to the Atlantic Ocean. After a thirty-five-year reign, at age 80, he was deposed by his eldest son in 1528 CE, and died ten years later. His successors were generally weak and had short reigns, which resulted in internal conflicts, social, political, and economic disorganization. In 1582 CE, the Hausa States regained independence and within a few years, the Mossi States renewed their attacks. The Sultan of Morocco, Mulay Ahmad, now saw an opportunity to capture the salt mines of Taghaza and the gold of Songhay. Armed with guns and cannons – then not available to African armies – the Moroccans met the army of Songhay, under Askia Issihak, at Tondiki, in 1594 CE. Spears and arrows had to give way to gunfire, and the Songhay of glorious memory was no more, as Islam continued their triumphant in Africa, destroying its basic institutions whenever it was possible to do so.

The two principal seats of learning, Timbuktu and Jenne, had been included in Songhay's northward and westward sweep. It was at Timbuktu that two of the great African writers of the period wrote their famous histories in Arabic. Tarikh al Fattash, by Mahmud Kati, and Tarikh Al Sudan, by Rahman as Sadi. Songhay's greatness was the grand scale on which the revival of learning spread among the people of West Africa – over a territory larger than the continent of Europe. Three of the principal centers of learning were at Jenne, Gao and Timbuktu, where the world-famous University of Sankore was located. It is worth noting that the renaissance in Africa occurred at the same time it developed in Europe – between the fifteenth and sixteenth centuries CE – and that both in Europe and Africa Islamic sources were the catalysts. For the Arabs, like the early Greeks, had advanced their civilization by systematically drawing heavily on pre-existing cultures and civilizations with which they came in contact with, as they spread out from the deserts of Arabia to distant lands. In Africa, as elsewhere, whenever

Asian and European influence prevailed, the destruction of African Civilization was real. But, in this widespread destruction, something was generally missed – enough to give posterity a clear idea of the state of things which were. During the period of destruction, three great African writers escaped the "Blackout" – Mahmud Kati, Rahman as Sadi and Ahmad Babo – the last President of the University of Sankore. In the Muslim destruction of the Songhay Empire, the main centers of learning with all their precious libraries and original manuscripts were destroyed. They seized all men of learning and skilled craftsmen for enslavement and service to the conquerors. Foremost among those captured and carried off to the Maghreb, was Ahmad Baba al-Massufi al-Timbukti (1556–1627 CE), where he was treated as an honored guest and instructed to use his great learning in the service of his conquerors, the Moors.

The Mossi States was made up of five "core" kingdoms – Wagadugu, Yatenga, Fada-Gurma, Mamprussi, and Dagomba, with each becoming a kingdom independently of the others. The union of these kingdoms was inspired by the bonds of kinship – a common Mossi origin. Although the Mossi was almost surrounded by the expanding empires of Mali and Songhay, neither was able to subdue and bring the Mossi within their respective empire. But, as Arabs overran Eastern Sudan, a period of crisis began, between the twelfth and seventeenth centuries. This was a long period during which migrating Africans undertook to form new and stronger states all over the continent, and some succeeded while others struggled to survive. By the 1500 CE, the Mossi became a dominant power and one of the most industrious nations of the period. Africa-wide concept of the basis for legitimate rule was held as a means of social control and national unification, as well as the basis for all authority. It all traced back to the founders of the nation, in this case Ouedraogo and Oubri. They had the Nam – the God given power to lead men, therefore, inherit the right to rule. Since the nabas of the five core states claimed equality and were all fiercely independent in both spirit and action, the early contests were over what state should become the leader (primus inter pares) of them all and provide the Mogho Naba (King of Kings).

The Mogho Naba was God's son and therefore scared and all must prostrate themselves before him. He became, therefore, the Mogho Naba of the united Mossi Kingdoms, each of which was virtually autonomous. The Ouidi Naba (Prime Minister) was next in authority under the Mogho Naba. In relation to Muslim, all their trading activities were restricted, no foreigners could settle in Mossi territory and the religion of Islam was rejected, its teachings or conversations to it forbidden. The Mossi saw Islam and Christianity as the white man's vehicles of conquest. It was the only African empire to see the threat of these religions. The Mossi held steadfastly to their own African religion and institutions and survived for over 500 years into the twentieth century, until it was finally overrun by France. The Mossi recognized the principle that no matter how powerful the conquerors of a territory might be, the land belonged to the people whose homeland it was. The Mossi's political system was unsurpassed by any state anywhere in the world and was developed by Africans. The family was the smallest socio-economic and political unit and the extended family council settled all cases involving offences by members which affected only the family, as unacceptable behavior by one member was a reflection on the rest of the family. The village was the next political unit, with an elected headman and a Council of Elders, who were the representatives of the various family sections or wards that made up the village. The districts were the next and larger divisions, varying in size, and having many villages and towns. Any number of districts made up the provinces and kingdoms which formed the nation. The great Nanamse (plural of Naba) headed provinces and kingdoms. All, from the village chief to the King of Kings, were elected by their respective councils and subject to their will.

Through all these millenniums of ups and downs, of trials and errors, of great victories and defeats, through it all, the central drive of this once all-African land was in the direction of consolidation and progress. Africans battled the invading Asians decade after decade and century after century until their resistance to conquest and enslavement extended over four thousand years. A distinguished line of African leaders followed Tanutamun to the throne in 653 BCE, including Atlanersa (r.653–640 BCE), to Karkaman (r.503–488 BCE). Two of the greatest temples were built by King Aspalta (r.573–553 BCE) at Meroe: The Sun Temple and the Temple of Amon. The royal tombs, as in Egypt, were the repositories of the nation's history. These monuments were of the highest importance and were elaborately decorated outside with both the first form of writing, hieroglyphics, and the more advanced inscriptions in their own invented writing. There were twenty-three characters or letters in the African alphabet – four vowel signs, seventeen consonants, and two signs of the syllable. There was also a developed system of numerical symbols for mathematics. However, conquest and domination brought with it the imposition of the conquerors' speech and writing – the first step in the process of conquering both the conquered minds and bodies.

This was made easy because "key people" among Africans eagerly grasped Arabic, Portuguese, Spanish, English, French, or German as the best route to status in a new civilization. For Williams (1974), Africans made the first step in their own self-destruction, in 1272 CE, when Shakandu, the King's nephew, secured an alliance with the Sultan of Egypt to invade his country. Sultan Baibars (1223–1277 CE), the fourth in the Mamluk Bahri dynasty, and one of the commanders of the Egyptian forces that inflicted a defeat on the Seventh Crusade (1248–1254 CE) of King Louis IX of France, did not hesitate to organize a strong invading expedition, with Shakandu at its head, and entered Makuri. The Sultan's strategy was to make it appear as a civil war between African rivals. Shakandu succeeded to the crown, but the kingdom was divided into two parts, the Sultan taking the northern region as his personal fief. Muslim rule now extended over Egypt and into Nubia. There were those among the Makurian who were quite willing and ready to surrender their people to Arab invaders, in exchange for "high office" and limited consideration.

In 1304 CE, a self-serving African leader journeyed to Lower Egypt (Cairo) to have himself crowned as the servant king of the Makurians by the Mamluk Sultan an-Nasir Muhammad (1285–1341 CE) and was crowned King Amai of Dongola. The days of African immortals seemed to have passed forever. Mental pygmies again occupied the African throne, once held by Menes, Piankhi, Shabaka, and Kalydosos and Queen Candace. In order to put an end to the endless coups and countercoups among Makurians, the decision was made to overwhelm the south with united armies from both Lower and Upper Egypt and set up the Islamization of Africans. In 1316 CE, when Dongola was again razed to the ground for the fifth time and Kerembes, the last Nubian Christian King, was replaced by an African Muslim, Abdullah, who was made temporary king, while awaiting the pleasure of the powerful Chief Kanz ad-Dawlah. His pleasure was to put the African Muslim King to death and assumed the kingship himself. Africans were no longer masters of their own fates. The Mamelukes were a class of warrior-slaves, mostly of Turkic or Caucasians origin, who served between the ninth and nineteenth centuries, in the Islamic world. The term Mamluk, means "slave" in Arabic, and comes from the root malaka, meaning "to possess." Slave-warrior armies were raised in barracks, away from their homes and separated from their ethnic groups. But, the intense loyalty within the Mamluk regiments sometimes allowed them to band together and bring down the rulers themselves.

In 1249, the French King Louis IX launched a Crusade against the Muslim world, but was wiped out by Mamluks shortly after the Battle of Fariskur in April 1250 CE. Fariskur resulted in the complete defeat of the crusader army and the capture of Louis IX, who was later ransomed. On September 1260, the Mamluks triumphed over the Mongols of the Ilkhanate at the Battle of Ayn Jalut and marked the southwestern border of the Mongols' conquests. The Ilkhanates later converted to Islam. The Funj state arose with a suddenness and proceeded with policies and programs, so daring that it shocked both the Arabs and the now encroaching Ottoman Turks. The latter, after overthrowing Mameluke rule, took over Egypt. The state of Funj annexed and brought the Arab tribal states in Lower Gezira region and the areas around present-day Khartoum under their control. In the interest of trade and foreign commerce, Funj kings began to accept Islam and take the Arabic title of Sultans. Thereafter, the kingdom was called the "Funj Sultanate." Funj traders roamed far and wide in the great game of buying and selling. Having become Muslim, if only in name, the Funj merchants were readily received everywhere in the increasingly Islamized world in Africa and Asia. Unlike Makuria and Alwa, the Funj Sultanate did not resist Islamization but welcomed it. Yet, its African nationalism transcended Islam, as a significant number of sultans and notables, rejected Arabic names. But, as Arabization spread among the Africans so did slavery and slave trading.

The flight of Africans from the Sudan increased as the Arab hordes continued to sweep in during the thirteenth century and Islamization was more aggressively pushed. This led to an increased number of African leaders – kings and nobles – divested themselves of a tradition of civilization that went back beyond history into Paleolithic times and, for expediency or self-interest, were humbly grasping at the robes of the Arabs, their language and their religion. The Arabs not only tolerated these Africans Muslim rulers, Sultans and emirs, but found it expedient to use them as fronts in controlling the remaining African population. The real rulers were the various Arab tribes that were now scattered all over the Sudan. The Funj is just another example of the role played by Africans that not only guaranteed their own domination, but also made their re-unification for nationhood, or anything else a most difficult undertaking. The Funj kingdom, because of its Muslim shield and "war-making machine" survived as an African state between 1504 and 1761 CE. The centuries were characterized by all the ups and downs, internal power struggles, coups, and countercoups that beset other states. Sometimes an Arab dynasty ruled, sometimes it was an Afro-Arab line, and other times, most often it was an African dynasty, or what the Arabs called the Homaji (uncivilized/barbaric).

The end of Funj came at the hands of the Ottoman Turks, in their reign of terror in the Sudan and the seizure of Sennar, a town on the Blue Nile, by Muhammed Ali, who was one of the first mass murderers of Africans on the African continent. His massacre of men, women, and children was on such scale that even the Caucasian world protested. The focus here is on the decline of the African civilization, before the final collapse of the Ethiopian empire in the fourth century BCE, and before the three "infant" states that were born as their imperial mother deceased. The main characteristics of the history of Africans are reflected in those states: building of an advanced system of life, then having it destroyed, building again, destruction again, migrating and building somewhere else, only to be sought out and destroyed again; moving, moving always moving, rebuilding and moving again, and again; countless thousands giving up the struggle as utterly hopeless. Internal strife increased as external pressures and threats to existence increased, with an every-man-for-himself philosophy replacing that of eternal brotherhood in some societies. But, the Africans were still rebuilding their own civilization when that of Asia and Europe was being imposed on them.

The record of over four hundred years in Kuba showed that in each and every case where the rule of exclusion was relaxed and Asians or Europeans were admitted under whatever pretext, the ultimate fate of Black Africans was sealed. First a lone Portuguese came, "seeking trade." The exploring expeditions up and down the rivers did not cause alarm. Instead of invading the country, the Europeans, ringed the country with trading posts along the country's borders. To these outposts, missionaries assembled to form missions (for God and the empire) and were later followed by armed detachments to protect the trading routes and new markets from imaginary raiders. With regards to Kuba, the Portuguese offer to buy all of the captured rebels and other troublemakers and the replenishing of a drained treasury by the sale of these war prisoners. The first would tend to end civil strife and restore domestic peace, and the second was a new source of great wealth. For such reasons the unforgivable sale of Africans into slavery by Africans began. The fact that African kings and chiefs had quite different conceptions of slavery than that of Caucasians does not excuse them; as in time they had to know that Caucasians treated slaves differently.

In Africa, persons who were captured and enslaved, were integrated into families, became members of any of the crafts, had rights to farm land, hold offices and, in fact, had all the rights and privileges enjoyed by their original captors. Hence, African slave sellers may not have known the fate to which they were consigning their brothers, but in time they did learn, yet they continued to sell their brothers. For this reason, these Africans stand condemned forever before the bar of history. Kuba revealed an African imperialism in Africa and without outside influence. There existed a microcosm of all the conquests of Africans by Africans, the oppression and enslavement of Africans by Africans – all of which left us the heritage of suspicion, distrust, and hatred that accounts for "tribalism," disunity, fear, and unrest today. The history of Africans in Egypt and elsewhere was being repeated in Kuba – and exactly the same way Africans had learned nothing from their previous experiences with Caucasians and were therefore doomed to repeat the same big mistakes over and over. As the last days of the kingdom show, separatist chiefdoms, struggling for power, actually sought alliances with Caucasians to overcome other African fractions. They did this in Egypt and lost!

Before the sixteenth century, most Africans on the continent of Africa had never seen a real white face, especially as in many societies all devils and other evil spirits were white. Over a thousand years had passed since Assyrians, Persians, Greeks, Romans, Arabs, and Turks had taken over Egypt, and Arabs now also ruled the Eastern Sudan. Arab-Hebrew rule was steadfast in isolated Abyssinia, while the Arabs along the East Coast, operating from their Zanzibar stronghold, had not themselves ventured far into the interior. Their Afro-Arab agents generally spearheaded slave-hunting operations. Ghana and Mali had disappeared, and now Songhay was making its last stand against Arab, Afro-Arab, and Berber armies from across the desert. Even where African armies clashed with invading white armies, the masses never saw white people. The Portuguese were the first European people to arrive in West and Central Africa. They were not long in adopting the Arab strategy in dividing Africans against themselves – a strategy since adopted by all Europeans. The Portuguese arrived at the mouth of the great Congo River in West Africa in 1488. Africa had been secure from invasions from this quarter during all the centuries the western world believed that the earth was flat. But, in 1434, Gil Eanes (b.1395) sailed around Cape Bojador, a headland on the northern coast of Western Sahara. The Portuguese were surprised to find highly advanced states in West Africa, such as the Kingdom of Kongo, which was prosperous, carrying on external trade by both land and rivers, with states farther north, east, and west. The states to the south, later to become Angola, were in an uneasy commotion, due to the increasing presence of foreigners on the coast, on nearby islands, and now sailing up the rivers toward the interior.

The Portuguese painted their monarch as the greatest King in a world that had advanced to a pinnacle of civilization under the guidance of a universal religion that was headed by a Supreme Pontiff who was appointed by the Son of God himself. They also argued that the Head of the Church would welcome the King of Kongo and his people into the great Christian fold and send missionaries and teachers to help make his kingdom the greatest in Africa. But, nothing could have been farther from Portugal's real objective than bringing Christianity and a higher civilization to Africa. Portugal's presence in West and Central Africa aimed at nothing less than building an empire across Africa from west to east – from the Atlantic Ocean to the Indian Ocean – a vast swathe across the continent that would also serve directly as the imperial highway connecting with the projected Indian Empire. The African-Indian Empire was Portugal's grand design. The major and immediate Portuguese aim in Africa was the destruction of Arab power in Africa and the Islamic control of almost all of the overland trade routes to the east. The Portuguese sought to use religion as the usual spearhead and unite the Christian forces of Europe with those of Africa in an all-out war against the Arabs. Such as the kingdom of Axum, which expanded to become the Empire of Abyssinia that was ruled alternatively by Christian Arabs and Afro-Hebrews. It must be noted that not all Arabs were Muslims, or all Hebrews Jews in religion. African Hebrew and Christian Arab communities were in Southern Arabia and Yemen. However, the Portuguese did not reach the African Christian kingdom, so they began to create an African Christian kingdom in their own image in Kongo.

By 1512, the Portuguese King, Manuel, made his plan clear in a document: *The regimento*, a detailed blue print for the conquest of Africa and Africans. Manuel moved to make certain that his *Code de Kongo* was carried out and sent his ambassador, Simao de Silva, in effect, his viceroy of Kongo. Simao de Silva real functions were covered over by the usual title of courtesy: Advisor to the King or the King's Counsellor. In this capacity, he was the supreme judge and had control over the army and finance. He was to have a comprehensive geographical survey of the country to determine the extent of its natural wealth for direct exploitation. But, the Portuguese settler population desired the quicker riches that would flow from the increasing demands for African slaves. The settlers pursued a more aggressive course of action. Up to the sixteenth century, the people here referred as slaves were laborers who were either captured as prisoners of war or persons imprisoned for various offences. During this initial stage of the slave trade, many African chiefs and kings actually thought they were supplying workers needed abroad and at a great profit to themselves. Although they had no experience with Europeans' slave system or its equation with race, as the decades passed many Africans became enmeshed in the horrors of the trade and in the pursuit of guns and became as brutal as the Europeans in dealing with their fellow country men, women and children. Africans were insistent in their demands for guns as articles of trade, but there was a silent embargo on arms to Africans – a sort of white "gentlemen's agreement." The demand for guns by kings and chiefs was pitted against the demand for slaves by Europeans and Arabs. Some traders were willing to arm certain strategically located kingdoms and chiefdoms, in the interest of wealth.

The Kongo interlude was merely a needed stepping stone and base of operations. The first task of the Portuguese was to convert Africans into Christians, which changed them into westerners and the European image, the outcome of which caused the Africans to reject and become ashamed of both their culture and themselves – the only people on earth to do so. The process of westernization began with missionaries converting kings and nobles, in the case of the Kongolese, who were so anxious for the new education and its vehicle, Christianity, that the priests found their tasks easy. To become a Christian, one had to be baptized and given a "Christian" name, which were western names, and they all took the form used in the conquering country. The first Kongolese King to become a Christian was Nzinga Kuwu (r.1470–1509 CE) in 1491, taking the Portuguese name of Joao I (John I). Other notable Kongolese kings who became "Black Portuguese" were Afonso, Pedro (Peter), and Diogo. Born Mvemba a Nzinga (c.1456–1542 or 1543) known as King Afonso I (r.1509–1542 or 1543), who succeeded his father, Nzinga Kuwu. Although Afonso I was initially opposed to slavery, he eventually relented in order to sustain the economy of the Kongo. At first, Afonso sent war captives and criminals to be sold as slaves to the Portuguese, but the increased demand from the Portuguese exceeded the country's supply, prompting raids on neighboring regions for captives. Apart from his involvement in the slave trade, Afonso is known for his vigorous attempt to convert Kongo to a Catholic country, by establishing the Roman Catholic Church in Kongo, and providing for its financing from tax revenues, and creating schools.

Significantly, religious brotherhoods (organizations) were founded in imitation of Portuguese practice. By 1516 there were over a thousand students in the royal school, and other schools were located in the provinces, which were restricted to the children of the elites. Afonso's efforts to introduce Portuguese culture to the Kongo (Congo) was reflected in the Portuguese names adopted by Kongolese aristocracy, titles, coats of arms, and styles of dress. Youths from elite families were sent to Europe for their education. Toward the end of his life, Afonso's children and grandchildren began to maneuver for the succession. He died toward the end of 1542 or the very beginning of 1543, leaving his son Dom Pedro to succeed him, but Pedro was soon overthrown by his grandson Diogo in 1545. The Portuguese Christianization of the Kongo created a revolting mess. To begin with, priests were some of the leading slave traders and slave ship owners who carried their African human cargoes off to distant lands. Priests also had their harems of enslaved African girls – they were called "house servants" by these "holy fathers." The slave situation became increasingly desperate as every white man down to the lowly worker became a trader. Builders sent to erect fortifications and other permanent installations for the Portuguese – stone and brick masons, carpenters, engineers, painters, metal and other craftsmen were all slave traders. Sailors and unskilled Portuguese workers had their own quotas of slaves – especially slave girls.

One of the main attractions of slavery, and the magnet that drew thousands of white men on, was their sexual freedom with all the African women and girls, who were under the total control of their masters. These "wholesale raids" on African womanhood continued to swell the Mulatto population, the majority of whom – as in the case of Egypt and the Sudan – became the faithful servants and loyal representatives of the conquering race to which their fathers belonged. The strategy for destruction seldom varied, the practice of having white groups spread out over the country into the various provinces, heavily laden with gifts of goodwill, and getting themselves attached to the courts of local chiefs as friendly advisors who were going to guarantee the security of the chiefs and their people, and even extend their power over other peoples – all of which would mean great riches for these chiefs. A few old guns replacing spears seemed to be sufficient evidence that these whites were indeed saviors as well as friends. The identical activities that had been carried out in Egypt some three-thousand years before would be repeated all over Africa. The aim was to provoke war between Africans, pitting the gun-armed groups against those who only had shields and spears, and thus increasing the number of captives for slavery from a few thousands to millions. Entire provinces were depopulated and their formerly proud and free citizens marched off in chains, collared and joined together with heavy poles. According to African tradition, leader and people were one and the same, sharing a common lot, but only to the members of one's tribe and not to Africans outside of the tribe – another tragic fact of African history. This is why the chiefs and kings would secure prisoners of war by attacking other states, which fitted well with European plans to keep Africans divided.

The idea of divine kingship was promoted through the anointment and crowning of kings by Portuguese bishops. Kings now ruled as "sons of the Church," chosen by divine decree to serve it. This means serving the Portuguese by meeting their demands. In addition to the widespread use of Portuguese names, important Portuguese titles appeared, such as dukes and infantes (the title and rank given in the Iberian kingdoms to the sons and daughters of kings), hitherto never used in Africa, because the western conception of royalty was absent. As the fifteenth century moved on toward the nineteenth century, the Europeans became less and less "white devils" and more and more "white masters," backed up by awesome firepower. "White" was no longer the face of evil in the African world. It had been transformed and now "Black" was the badge of evil. To make a white man look evil one had to dress him in black; life's final tragedy, death, called for mourning in black; happy events, such as baptism and weddings, required the wearing of white. God himself, being white, had cursed the Blacks and made them the servants of man – man being the white man, for was not he made in the "image of God?" hence, to worship God was to, in effect, worship the white man. These are, according to Williams (1974), examples of little psychological gimmicks that are now so deeply embedded in cultural thought that they are taken as a simple matter of course and require no comment. Yet, they have been more devastating in conquering Africans and reducing them to an inferior status than arms might have done.

Blacks now throughout the world join whites in glorifying all things white and condemning all things black, including themselves. Hence, in attempts to replace his own values with those of the white man's, the black man lost his own personality and his manhood. The Kongolese opposing their kings were fighting both slavery and the Christian Church that promoted it. Even the broader education they all so passionately desired turned out to be a farce, as the "schools" rigidly restricted in number and attendance, were nothing more than Catholic historical classes, under semi-literate priests who were themselves slave traders. All of King Afonso's efforts to get at least one good school established in the Kongo were blocked. In 1556, war broke out between the major conflicting groups. Royal Portuguese forces allied with those of Kongo against Portuguese trader forces allied with Ndongo – Portuguese against Portuguese and Africans against Africans. So it appears, but the simple truth is that it was a war of Africans against Africans, with the Portuguese forces safely in the rear. According to royal order from Lisbon, black troops were to be used in all dangerous situations and white lives safeguarded wherever possible.

The Kongolese were defeated and Ndongo and the slave traders now controlled the whole trade. The defeat of Kongo was the defeat of Kongo, not Portugal. In 1575, Angola became a colony of Portugal by a royal decree and mother Kongo could only weep at the permanent loss of her greatest progeny. The disintegration of the Kongolese state seemed to be complete, but it was not. For although the conquest of Angola was ordered by Lisbon in 1571 and began in 1575, the Portuguese had to fight their longest and bloodiest war before Angola was finally taken, nearly fifty years later. They had not counted on the new Queen of Ndongo, Anna Nzinga. After 1608, the commander-in-chief, the Portuguese Bento Cardoso, planned to depopulate Angola by a massive onslaught for slaves through a closely coordinated system in which every chief in the land would be "owned" by a Portuguese and directly responsible to him for a stated quota of slaves. This would bypass the Angolan King (of Ndongo) to whom the provincial chiefs paid their taxes in slaves. This would also mean increased warfare between the chiefdoms, in order to meet the increased quotas demanded by raiding each other's territories. Chiefs failing to secure the required number of slaves were themselves enslaved. Over a hundred chiefs and other notables were sold into slavery in a single year and another hundred murdered by the Portuguese. The Angolan King, who had been cooperating with the slave traders, now saw himself losing his people and his profits, began to resist the Portuguese. Both the Portuguese and their Jaga allies were checked and the war dragged on year after year.

In 1619, a new Portuguese commander murdered over a hundred chiefs. At this point, even Pope Paul V (b.1550, Pope 17/09/1550–1621 CE), the pope who persecuted Galileo Galilei (1564–1642 CE), intervened, insisting that the wholesale slaughter be ended and peace pursued, not, it will be noted, the slave trade. In 1622, a new governor (Joao Correia de Sousa) was sent from Lisbon to make peace. The conference was held at Luanda with the Angolan delegation, headed by Anna Nzinga, sister of the King. Even before the conference the Portuguese governor had decided on a studied insult, by providing only chairs in the conference room for himself and his councilors, with the idea of forcing Princess Nzinga to stand before his noble presence. As if they had expected this, her entourage quickly rolled a beautifully designed royal carpet they had brought before Nzinga, after which one of them went down on hands and knees and expertly formed himself into a "royal throne," upon which she sat. She spoke as a ruler of the land and did not recognize the existence of a Portuguese "colony of Angola." The Ndongo's terms for peace were presented as uncompromising demands. Before any kind of treaty was signed, Portugal had to agree to evacuate Kabasa, the capital, and all nearby fortifications. Portuguese were to wage war against the Jaga, their former allies in trying to crush Ndongo, and all chiefs who had become vassals of the Portuguese King were to be freed and enabled to return to former tributary status at home and, finally, the important concession Nzinga made was to return the Portuguese prisoners of war she held. The treaty of 1622 was supposed to end all fighting in the whole of West Central region. But the governor marched off to invade Kongo again almost immediately. Nzinga's brother died the following year and she became Queen of Ndongo, in 1623, and went into action at once.

The Dutch were themselves heavily involved in the slave trade and their main aim was to break the Portuguese monopoly and secure their share of the slave trade and the mineral wealth of West and Central Africa. The Dutch formed an alliance with Pedro II (r.1622–1631 CE) of the Kongo, in his war against the Portuguese, which gave Queen Nzinga time to prepare for war. In 1624, she declared all territory in Angola over which she had control Free Country, all slaves reaching it from whatever quarter were forever free. She infiltrated the Portuguese African armies, causing whole companies to rebel and desert to the Queen, taking with them much needed guns and ammunition. The Queen's armies were further strengthened by the runaway slaves who entered her land. However, in July 1626, Queen Nzinga's forces were defeated and she fled the country. Aidi Kiluanji was crowned King Philip I of Ndongo, after the Portuguese had ousted Queen Nzinga. The Portuguese offered a big reward for the capture, dead or alive, of Queen Nzinga and their slave troops were given the special inducements of land and freedom for her capture. Realizing the consequences of her capture, Queen Nzinga instructed her lieutenants to spread the word everywhere that she fled the country, mistakenly entered the territory of an enemy, and had been killed. The masses and the Portuguese believed the story to be true. A special mass, in celebration of this news was called by the Bishop, and the colony of Angola could at last be organized after some fifty years of obstruction. But, in 1629, Queen Nzinga burst upon the Portuguese from the grave, sweeping all opposition before her. The Portuguese were completely defeated and Queen Nzinga retook her country.

She had, meanwhile, become Queen of Matamba, having replaced their Queen Mwongo; she was now an empress of two countries. She now redoubled her campaign against slavery and the slave trade by making both Ndongo and Matamba havens for all who could escape from their captors. The Portuguese, fearful of losing every foothold in the area, declared that their wars against the Queen had been unjust and in 1639, sent a high-level delegation to the Queen. She received them, listened to their protestations of eternal friendship, but was not fooled. It is, however, unfortunate that Queen Nzinga's anti-slavery crusade did not extend to herself, as she owned captives in bondage, including Portuguese and African chiefs, who were allies of the Portuguese. She did not hesitate to sell such chiefs and their followers into slavery. But, she continued her campaign against the Portuguese and, aided by the Dutch, captured the Portuguese stronghold of Masangano in 1648. Finally, in 1656, Queen Nzinga signed a treaty with the Portuguese, which was acceptable to her. In 1663, Queen Nzinga died and over three hundred years later, the Angolans were still fighting the Portuguese. Queen Nzinga was the first African to see that the Portuguese conquests, the slave trade, and the Catholic Church were all inseparably one and the same. According to

Joseph C. Miller (1975), Nzinga of Matamba faced hostility from her Mbundu people and the opposition of neighboring tribal rulers. Her gender disqualified her from many Mbundu political offices, reserved for males, and her lineage. But she overcame these disadvantages by skillfully manipulating the threats of alien forces on the Mbundu borders – Imbangala warrior bands, the Portuguese, and Dutch – while dominating Mbundu politics and diplomacy until her death in 1663. She officially ruled Ndongo 1624–1626 and 1657–1663.

The Kingdom of Mutapa

The Kingdom of Mutapa was a Shona Kingdom (1430–1760 CE), which stretched from the Zambezi through the Limpopo rivers to the Indian Ocean in Southern Africa, in what are the modern states of Zimbabwe, South Africa, Lesotho, Swaziland, Mozambique, and parts of Namibia and Botswana; stretching into modern Zambia. The empire had reached its full extent by the year 1480 CE, and the Emperor Mutope had left a well-organized religion with a powerful priesthood, which revolved around ritual consultation of spirits and royal of ancestors. The Portuguese dominated much of Southeast Africa's coast by 1515 CE, and their main goal was to dominate the trade with India. The Portuguese entered into direct relations with the Mwenemutapa in 1569 and by 1561, a Portuguese Jesuit missionary managed to make his way into the Mwenemutapa's court and convert him to Christianity. This did not go well with the Muslim merchants in the capital, and they persuaded the King to kill the Jesuit a few days after the Mwenemutapa's baptism. This was all the excuse the Portuguese needed to penetrate the interior and take control of the gold mines and ivory routes. The Portuguese, after a lengthy preparation, launched an expedition of a thousand men, under Francisco Barreto, in 1568. They got as far as the Upper Zambezi, but the expedition was decimated by disease and forced to retreat.

In 1572 CE, the Portuguese attacked Swahili traders and massacred them and replaced them with Portuguese and their Afro-Portuguese progenies. In 1629 CE, the Mwenemutapa attempted to throw out the Portuguese, but failed and were overthrown, leading to the Portuguese installing Mavura Mhande Felipe (r.1629–1652 CE). He ceded gold mines to the Portuguese, and remained nominally independent, though practically a client state of Portugal. The belief that the mines of King Solomon were inside the Mwenemutapa Kingdom in Southern Africa was one of the factors that led to the Portuguese exploration of the hinterland of Sofala in the sixteenth century, and contributed to early Portuguese control of Mozambique, as the legend was used to recruit colonists back in Portugal. Sofala, presently known as Nova Sofala, is located on the Sofala Bank, in Sofala Province of Mozambique, which was founded by African and Indian Ocean traders, including Swahili and Somali merchants and seafarers. Sofala was founded about 700 CE and was part of a long line of trading centers, stretching from Kismayu, incorporating Mombasa, Malindi, and Zanzibar. The Buzi River connected Sofala to the internal market town of Manica, and from there to the gold fields of Great Zimbabwe. In the 1180s, Sultan Suleiman Hassan of Kilwa (in Tanzania) seized control of Sofala and brought it into the Kilwa Sultanate and the Swahili cultural sphere. The Swahili used their dhows to ply the Buzi and Savi rivers to ferry the gold extracted in the hinterlands to the coast. A Portuguese spy, Pero da Covilha, was the first known European to have visited Sofala in 1489. He sent a secret report to Lisbon, identifying Sofala's role as a gold emporium. In 1502, Pedro Afonso de Aguiar led the first Portuguese ships into Sofala's harbor.

When in 1663 CE, the Emperor Domingos tried to resist the Portuguese; he was murdered. The highly organized African religion under a priesthood that had been so powerful that it had blocked the spread of Islam for over two hundred years was now swept aside by the aggressively pushed Christian missions in almost every village. In the same year, the Portuguese were attacked by Chanagamires, who reconquered most of Monomotapa and a vigorous anti-Portuguese policy was adopted. However, the Monomotapa kingdom came under new threats from the British and Dutch, who had moved inland from the Cape, and from the rapid rise and expansion of the Zulu Empire, under Shaka. The great Zulu Emperor was ruthless in his fights to unify the African people, in an empire that would be greater and stronger than the failing Monomotapa empire, that would not only serve as one vast and impregnable fortress against Europeans, but a fortress from which they could attack kings and chiefs who could not see the need to unite, under Zulu imperial rule. However, the overall scene was one of British-Dutch pressures on the African empire in South Africa. The Portuguese still held on to their strongly fortified posts, especially along the Zambezi, and were able to reach a partition agreement with the British in 1890, by which the Portuguese gained Mozambique. By 1902, British power was firmly established and the last African empire had become European controlled, with Rhodesia (now Zimbabwe) and its southernmost territory was now under the iron rule of the Dutch invaders of South Africa.

Slavery

Slavery was an integral part of the ancient world, especially of the Greco-Roman world. Slaves had been accumulated as the plunder of wars and in the early days of Rome, slaves were defeated enemies, whom the victor had the right to kill, but chose to preserve, under a suspended death sentence. In Roman ideology, the defeated were seen as object in themselves. One estimate is that there were between two and three million slaves in Italy in the first century BCE, as much as forty percent of the population. They came from far afield as Arabia, Ethiopia and India. Many of these slaves were eventually freed and became absorbed within the Italian population. There are relatively few references to slaves in Britain and in

Gaul slaves are to be found only in cities. There is virtually no evidence of any challenge to the institution of slavery in the Greek or Roman world during the first century, although some Stoics did advocate that the slave be recognized as a human being. There was little economic rationale for slavery, where the mass of the society was poor. Rome was not a slave society in the sense that slaves made a unique economic contribution to society. The mines in Spain may have been worked largely by slaves, but those in Gaul were probably not. Attitudes to slaves may have been conditioned by their large numbers and memories of the great slave revolts of the Republic, those in Sicily in the 130s BCE and the uprising of Spartacus in 73 BCE, both of which attracted more than 70,000 slaves.

Slaves were treated as if they were naturally deceitful and needed constant supervision. In the domestic setting, the position of individual slaves was more complex. Many of these jobs in the home offered the opportunity of direct human contact on a one-to-one basis with the master or mistress and slaves may have taken pride in belonging to one of the grander families of Rome. While slaves could not be legally married, liaisons, with children born to them, were common, and many owners condoned these "family" arrangements, preferring slaves who had been born into slavery to those brought in from the outside world. The children of slaves could be sold separately from their parents and the plucky slave-girl, Fotis, who initiates and enjoys sex with the "hero" Lucius in Apuleius' *The Golden Ass*, cannot be assumed to be typical. Trimalchio boasts that his freedom was granted after he had satisfied the desires of both his master and mistress. Where Rome differed from Greece was that slaves could be freed and their descendants become full citizens. Manumission was an ancient concept found as far back as the fifth century BCE. An owner could set a slave free by means of a declaration in front of the magistrate or through the terms of his will. Alternatively, by offering the owner compensation from whatever he might have saved. The number of slaves an owner could free through a will was limited, by a law of Augustus. An owner with between 30 and 100 slaves could free no more than a quarter, and one with over 100 slaves could only free a fifth. Manumission brought freedom for only a minority of slaves and inevitably those who were freed during an owner's lifetime tended to be those who had earned his respect. Marriages between freedmen and freedwomen were common and their children enjoyed the full rights of any citizen. The army was one avenue through which a man might reach some of the highest posts in the empire and in troubled times even become emperor. The emperor Diocletian was said to have either been born a slave or was the son of one, and yet managed to use the army as a stepping stone to supreme power, such as in the case of Publius Helvius Pertinax Augustus (August 126–March 193 CE), Roman Emperor for the first three months of 193 CE, following the assassination of Commodus, was the first to serve as emperor during the tumultuous "Year of the Five Emperors." Born the son of a freed slave, Pertinax originally worked as a teacher before becoming an officer in the army.

Christianity made little difference, other than to transfer the institution of slavery into a new context. "Slaves, be obedient to the men who are called your masters in this world, with deep respect and sincere loyalty, as you are obedient to Christ, not only when you are under their eye, as if you only had to please men, but because you are slaves of Christ and wholeheartedly do the will of God." From the following scriptures, it would seem that Christianity is pro-slavery. "And if a man sells his daughter to be a maidservant, she shall not go out as the menservants do. If she please not her master, who hath betrothed her to himself, then shall he let her be redeemed: to sell her unto a strange nation he shall have no power, seeing he hath dealt deceitfully with her" (Exodus 21:7–8). Further: "And if a man smites his servant, or his maid, with a rod, and he die under his hand; he shall be surely punished. Notwithstanding, if he continues a day or two, he shall not be punished: for he is his money" (ibi. 20–21). "Both thy bondmen, and thy bondmaids, which thou shalt have, shall be of the heathen that are round about you; of them shall ye buy bondmen and bondmaids. Moreover, of the children of the strangers that do sojourn among you, of them shall ye buy, and of their families that are with you, which they begat in your land: and they shall be your possession. And ye shall take them as an inheritance for your children after you, to inherit them for a possession; they shall be your bondmen forever: but your brethren the children of Israel, ye shall not rule one over another with rigor" (Leviticus 25: 44–46).

Further, "When thou goest forth to war against thine enemies, and the Lord thy God hath delivered them into thine hands, and thou hast taken them captive, And seest among the captives a beautiful woman, and hast a desire unto her, that thou wouldest have her to thy wife; Then thou shalt bring her home to thine house; and she shall shave her head, and pare her nails; and she shall put the raiment of her captivity from off her, and shall remain in thine house, and bewail her father and her mother a full month: and after that thou shalt go in unto her, and be her husband, and she shall be thy wife. And it shall be, if thou have no delight in her, then thou shalt let her go whither she will; but thou shalt not make merchandise of her, because thou hast humbled her" (Deuteronomy 21: 10–14). "Let as many servants as are under the yoke count their own masters worthy of all honor, that the name of God and his doctrine be not blasphemed" (1 Timothy 6: 1). "Exhort servants to be obedient unto their own masters, and to please them well in all things; not answering again" (Titus 2: 9). "Servants, be subject to your masters with all fear; not only to the good and gentle, but also to the forward" (1 Peter 2: 18). Freedom comes for the Christian in the next world, not this one.

The Arabs' insatiable and perpetual demands for slaves had long since changed slavery from an institution that signaled a military victory by the number of captured prisoners to an institution that provoked warfare expressly for the enslavement of men, women and children for sale and re-sale. Human beings had now openly become very profitable articles of trade and the slave dealers had found shorter routes to quicker riches. The Funj, like many other African states then and since, found added wealth in the slave trade, and a new reason for waging war on its neighbors for "prisoners of war" to further the trade. Islamic Sharia law allows slavery, but prohibited slavery involving other pre-existing Muslim; as a result, the main target for slavery were people living in the frontier areas of Islam in Africa. The conquest of the Arab armies and the expansion of the Islamic state that followed have always resulted in the capture of war prisoners, who were subsequently set free or turned into slaves and servants, rather than taken as prisoners, as was the Islamic tradition in wars. According to Islamic law, slaves were allowed to earn their living if they opted to do so, otherwise it is the owner's duty to provide for his slave. They could not be forced to earn money for their owners, unless with an agreement between slave and his owner (mukharajah). In 641 CE, there was a treaty between the Christian state of Makuria and the Muslim rulers of Egypt. Makuria was a kingdom located in what is today Northern Sudan and Southern Egypt. By the end of the sixth century, Makuria had converted to Christianity, but in the seventh century Egypt was conquered by the Islamic armies, and Nubia was cut off from the rest of Christendom. The period from about 750 to 1150 CE saw the kingdom stable and prosperous, but internal discord led to the collapse of the state in the fourteenth century. Makuria had to provide 360 slaves per year to Egypt, to be of the highest quality with no old ones or children, a mixture of male and female.

The Umayyad, Muslim dynasty that ruled the Islamic world from 660 to 750 CE and Moorish Spain from 756 to 1031 CE, claimed descent from Umayya, a distant relative of Muhammad and Abbasid, the third of the Islamic caliphates to succeed the Islamic prophet Muhammad, caliphs recruited many Zanj slaves as soldiers, and as early as 696 CE. Zanj slaves reached as far as China, from the Hindu kingdom of Srivijaya in Indonesia (Srivijaya was a dominant thalassocratic city-state on the island of Sumatra, which influenced much of Southeast Asia). Srivijaya was an important center for the expansion of Buddhism from the eighth to the twelfth century CE. In Sanskrit, *Sri* means "fortunate," "prosperous," or "happy," and *vijaya* means "victorious" or "excellence." It has been suggested that between the eighth and nineteenth century, ten to 18 million people were brought by Arab slave traders and taken from Africa across the Red Sea, Indian Ocean, and the Sahara Desert. The Arab slave trade occurred mainly in Western Asia, North Africa, Southeast Africa, the Horn of Africa, and certain parts of Europe (Iberia and Sicily), beginning in the era of the Roman Empire and continuing until the early 1960s. The trade was conducted through slave markets in the Middle East, North Africa and the Horn of Africa, with slaves captured mostly from Africa's interior.

The slave trade across the Sahara and the Indian Ocean has a long history, beginning with the control of sea routes by Arab and Swahili traders on the Swahili Coast, during the ninth century CE. These traders captured Bantu peoples (Zanj) from the interior in present-day Kenya, Mozambique and Tanzania and brought to the littoral. These enslaved Africans were sold throughout the Middle East (Egypt, Arabia, the Persian Gulf), India, European colonies in the Far East, the Indian Ocean islands, Ethiopia and Somalia. The Zanj were for centuries shipped as slaves, by Arab traders, to all the countries boarding the Indian Ocean. Bantu adult and children slaves (jareers) were purchased in slave markets exclusively to do undesirable work on plantations, harvesting lucrative cash crops such as grain and cotton. In Ethiopia, during the second half of the early nineteenth century and early twentieth century, slaves shipped from there had a high demand in the markets of the Arabian Peninsula and elsewhere in the Middle East. They were mostly domestic servants, but some of these slaves worked as officials or bodyguards of the emirs, or business managers for rich merchants. Beside Javanese and Chinese girls, Ethiopian young females were among the most valued concubines. A small number of eunuchs were also acquired by the slave traders in the southern parts of Ethiopia and commanded the highest prices in the Islamic global markets. They served in harems or holy sites.

By the fourteenth century, an overwhelming number of slaves came from sub-Saharan Africa, leading to prejudice against black people, in the works of several Arabic historians and geographers. For example, the Egyptian historian Al-Abshibi (1388–1446 CE) wrote that it is said that when the black slave is sated, he fornicates, when he is hungry, he steels. Ibn Battuta, who visited the ancient kingdom of Mali in the mid-fourteenth century, recounts that the local inhabitants vie with each other in the number of slaves and servants they have. But others have challenged this racist view of Arabs, including Abdel Majid Hannoum, who argues that such attitudes were not prevalent until the eighteenth century. In the Central African Republic, during the sixteenth and seventeenth centuries Muslim slave traders began to raid Southern Ethiopia, as part of the expansion of the Saharan and Nile River slave routes. Their captives were shipped to the Mediterranean coast, Europe, Arabia, the Western Hemisphere, or to the slave ports and factories along the west, north, and south of Africa, the Ubanqui, and Congo rivers. Hence, the Arab slave trade in Africa, the Indian Ocean, the Red Sea, and the Mediterranean Sea, long predated the arrival of any significant number of Europeans on the African continent.

From Arab literature, manifestations of racism and racist discrimination subsequently followed within the Arab world. Ethnic prejudices developed among Arabs because of their extensive conquests and slave trade. The influence of Aristotle's idea of final causes, which argues that slaves are slaves by nature. A refinement of Aristotle's view was put forward by Muslim philosophers such as

Al-Farabi (c.872–950 CE) and Avicenna (c.980–1037 CE), particularly in regard to Turkic and black peoples, and the influence of ideas from the early Medieval Geonic academies regarding divisions among mankind between the sons of Noah. The Geonic academies were two great Babylonian Talmudic Academies of Sura and Pumbedita, in the Abbasid Caliphate. Ethnic prejudice among elite Arabs was not limited to dark-skinned people, it was also directed towards fairer-skinned "muddy people," including Persians, Turks, and Europeans. Whilst the Arabs referred to themselves as "swarthy people," the concept of an Arab identity did not exist until modern times. Until 1884, the Sultans of Zanzibar controlled a substantial portion of the Swahili Coast, known as Zanj, and trading routes extending further into the continent, as far as Kindu on the Congo River. That year the Society for German Colonization forced local chiefs on the mainland to agree to German protection, following on from the Berlin Conference and the *Scramble* for Africa.

In 1886, the British and Germans secretly met and discussed their aims of expansion in the African Great Lakes, with spheres of influence already agreed upon the year before, with the British to take what would become the East Africa Protectorate (modern day Kenya), and the Germans to take present-day Tanzania. By 1888, the Imperial British East Africa Company took over the administration of Mombasa. In the same year, the German East Africa Company acquired formal direct rule over the coastal area previously submitted to German protection. This resulted in a native uprising, the Abushiri Revolt, which was crushed by a joint Anglo-German naval operation, which heralded the end of Zanzibar's influence on the mainland. Arab slave traders traded between one and one-and-a-quarter million enslaved Europeans, between sixteenth and nineteenth century, captured by Barbary corsairs, who were vassals of the Ottoman Empire. Periodic Arab raiding expeditions were sent from Islamic Iberia to ravage the Christian Iberian kingdoms, bringing back booty and slaves. In a raid against Lisbon in 1189, the Almohad caliph, Abu Yusuf Yaqub al-Mansur, took 3,000 female and child captives, while his governor of Cordoba, in a subsequent attack upon Silves (Portugal) in 1191, took 3,000 Christian slaves. Under Islamic law, if a non-Muslim population refuses to pay jizya, a per capita yearly tax, levied by Islamic states on certain non-Muslim subjects, that population is considered to be at war with the Muslim Ummah (nation), and it becomes legal to take slaves from that non-Muslim population.

The Ottoman wars in Europe and Tatar raids brought large numbers of European Christian slaves into the Muslim world. In 1769, a last major Tatar raid saw the capture of 20,000 Russian and Polish slaves. Domestic slavery was not as common as military slavery. Rural slavery was largely a phenomenon endemic to the Caucasus region, which was carried to Anatolia and Rumelia after the Circassian migration in 1864. Many Circassians were exiled by Russia to lands of the Ottoman Empire, where the majority of them live today. The majority of Circassians are predominantly Sunni Muslim but the Circassians refer to themselves as Adyghe. The Crimean Khanate maintained a massive slave trade with the Ottoman Empire and the Middle East until the early eighteenth century. In a process called "harvesting of the steppe," Crimean Tatars enslaved Slavic peasants. The Polish-Lithuanian Commonwealth and Russia suffered a series of Tatar invasion, the aim of which was to loot, pillage, and capture people to enslave. It is estimated that up to seventy-five percent of the population of Crimea consisted of slaves or freed slaves.

Slavery had been abandoned in Northern Europe by the twelfth century but it was still common around the Mediterranean and English and Irish traveling there were often enslaved by Muslims. Although Islamic law forbade the forcible enslavement of fellow Muslims, non-Muslims were fair game. Slavery had always been about "inferior" peoples – for the Greeks, it was the "Barbarians," for Jews, the "Gentiles" – but Muslims believed that they had identified the most inferior of all; "Africans!" The Arabs were the first to develop a specialized long-distance slave trade from sub-Saharan Africa. In almost all cultures, color of skin was seen as an indicator of status, the darker one's skin the more likely one was to be a lowly field worker, with lighter skin associated with skilled indoor work, or not to work at all. Increasingly dark-skinned African slaves were given the most degrading form of labor by their Muslim masters. According to Aristotle, some peoples were "natural slaves" – like tame animals, unable to look after themselves, they needed masters. The characteristic of these "natural slaves," as suggested by Aristotle – excitability, emotional immaturity, lack of reason, sometimes sullen stupidity – were being applied to Africans. From the early thirteenth to the mid-fifteenth century, Italian merchants transported tens of thousands of Slavic people to the Mediterranean region, a good proportion of them were used for the production of sugar. But the capture of Constantinople in 1453 stopped this flow.

Almost from their first voyage of discovery, Portuguese mariners had been bringing enslaved Africans back to Lagos to be sold as slaves. In 1444 CE, 253 enslaved Africans were landed in the Algarve, with 46 – the "royal fifth" – being given to Prince Henry the Navigator (1394–1460 CE), who rejoiced at the prospect of their conversion to Christianity, as well as the income he got from selling them on. A great number ended up in Lisbon and by the sixteenth century, slaves numbered 10,000 a tenth of the population and marriages between these enslaved Africans and Portuguese was not forbidden. But a large number ended up working in the sugar cane fields. Sugar has a long association with slavery. The cane carried by the Muslim expansion into the Mediterranean was largely slave-grown and slave-processed. When wages skyrocketed after the "Plague" in the mid-fourteenth century, the labor-intensive industry relied even more on coerced workers. When the Portuguese and Spanish started growing sugar on the Atlantic islands, enslaved African labor became the norm for the crop. The institution of slavery requires the suppression of spirit, intelligence, and initiative on the part of the victims. The mind-numbing, repetitive, and physically exhausting tasks demanded exactly the same thing. Hence, sugar and slavery were found to be the perfect fit.

Apart from slaves, Cape Verde traded in goods between Africa, Europe, and America. The important trading islands were Santiago, Fogo, and Maio. Cape Verde had one home-produced product and that was cotton, which was grown by slaves who then wove it into cloth of the finest quality. The cloth from Cape Verde was marketed along the West African Coast and Brazil and it became the chief currency for trading in Africa. This gave Cape Verde a continuing hold on the slave trade, with English and French ships forced to stop at the archipelago to obtain cloth for barter on the African mainland. The right to extract slaves from the African coast was awarded by the Portuguese Crown as a single, monopolistic contract which lasted for six years. Contractors paid a lump sum and agreed to supply a few incidentals to the Crown, including slaves for the King and some money donated to the Church. The Portuguese Crown received customs duties when contractors deposited slaves at Cape Verde and also export duties from those who brought them (Irwin and Campbell, 2003: 13). Over the following centuries, tens of thousands were put to work growing food and cotton. By 1582, there were 13,700 slaves on the islands of Santiago and Fogo, under a regime of 100 European. Increasingly, in the latter part of the sixteenth century, the Portuguese who stopped there were on their way to open up the treasure of Brazil. The Spaniards were ferrying goods and people to and from the vast new empire they were creating in South America. This arrangement was to last until 1721, when the rules on trade were relaxed so that people could trade with whom they wished.

After Columbus reached the "New World" in 1492, Portugal and Spain agreed the Treaty of Tordesillas (1494 CE) to avoid conflict over new maritime discoveries. This divided the world along a line drawn 2,000 kilometer west of Cape Verde Islands, with the Spanish keeping west of the line and Portugal to the east. The Treaty allowed Portugal to claim Brazil after its discovery in 1500 (Haywood, 2008:160). The Atlantic slave trade accounted for the largest forced migration in history, with an estimated 14 million enslaved Africans transported by Europeans to work on plantations in the Americas and the West Indies, between the sixteenth and nineteenth centuries. When slavery was justified by the Catholic Church, most infamously in the Papal Bull of 1454, the issue of slave conversion was hugely important, as the Christian scheme of enlarging the flock cannot be carried out without it. In the same way, in defense of slavery, it was argued that the slaves' condition was bettered by being removed from Africa to the West Indies and was also underwritten by the idea that the slaves would be Christianized. In 1511, the Spanish Crown licensed the dispatch of fifty enslaved

Africans to the island of Hispaniola for work in the mines, but larger consignments followed, for sugar production and for gold mining on the island of Puerto Rico. From the 1520s onward, sugar was produced on Hispaniola as an export commodity, with between eighty and a hundred enslaved Africans, who were employed at each *ingenio* or mill. In 1500, Portuguese ships reached Brazil and it was claimed for the Portuguese Crown. The solution to the labor problem in Brazil was inevitably found in the resort to enslaved Africans, the first of which were imported in the 1530s, and whose numbers would rapidly increase with the expansion of the sugar industry in the 1570s.

Portugal was engaged in the slave trade longer than any other European state and had control over Angola, a major source for enslaved Africans and colonial control over Brazil, the largest market for them. In the sixteenth century, while the leading Lisbon merchants were preoccupied with trading for gold in Africa and spices in Asia, the less glamorous business of buying, transporting, and selling enslaved Africans was left to others, among them Portuguese "New Christians" – Jews who had been forcibly converted in 1497. As with the persecuted Protestants in France, their own experience as victims failed to deter some of them from profitable engagement in the slave trade. Even the development of slave-based sugar production in Brazil was financed by the Dutch, partly through the commercial enterprise of Jewish families with members in both the Netherlands and Brazil. Lisbon trading houses increasingly became agents of British suppliers to the Brazilian market. The Atlantic slave trade began in the 1460s, when Portuguese began transporting enslaved West Africans to work on sugar plantations on Cape Verde Islands. But, the first enslaved Africans were transported across the Atlantic by the Spanish in 1517, to work on sugar plantations in the West Indies and Mexico. The Spanish had initially enslaved native Indians but found them unsuitable because of their vulnerability to European diseases. In 1534, the Portuguese started to transport enslaved Africans to Brazil to work on sugar plantations and later coffee plantations. Brazil became by far the biggest importer of enslaved Africans: over 3.6 million. In the seventeenth century, other Europeans, including England, France, the Netherlands, and Demark, began shipping enslaved Africans to their West Indian and North American colonies.

In 1500, a Portuguese ship was blown off its course and carried to the east coast of South America, on landing they planted their flag and named the place *Brazil*, because of the red wood that they found. Both France and Spain demonstrated a lack of respect for Portugal's claim to sovereignty over Brazil. In 1521, the Portuguese established a garrison at Pernambuco and in 1530 dispatched five ships to explore the 3,000 miles' eastern coast. By 1549, Brazil had sixty sugar mills and a population of between 17,000 and 25,000 Portuguese, 18,000 Indians, and 14,000 enslaved Africans. In 1630, the Dutch seized Pernambuco and rapidly extend their control northward. Technologically, the most advanced people of the time, they introduced new ways of growing and processing sugar and imported substantial number of enslaved Africans to provide the labor. In 1640, a Papal Bull against any traffic in Indians slaves was issued, which resulted in riots in Rio de Janeiro, Sao Paulo, and Santos, but there were never enough Indians to enslave for the plantations and mines. In the sixteenth century, only 50,000 enslaved African had been imported, but in the succeeding centuries, Brazil imported over three and a half million enslaved Africans. It is estimated that about thirty-eight percent of all enslaved African transported to the hemisphere were landed in Brazil (Segal, 1995:72). Labor was not the only use to which enslaved Africans were put. They were sexually used on such a scale that Brazilians proclaim miscegenation as having been a major factor in the making of their national identity. Portuguese emigration to the territory during the sixteenth and seventeenth centuries consisted almost entirely of men, who took first Indian and then increasingly enslaved African women as concubines and wives, with the blessing of the authority. However, it was the whites who made the rules, and the rules, written or not, reflected a presumption of black inferiority. Phrases in common usage revealed the contemptuous equation. A "person of infected blood" (*pessoa de sangue infecta*) or someone possessing a "defect of blood" (*defeito de sangue)* was accordingly a "person of the lowest social standing" (*pessoa de infima condicao).* It is ironic that those persons of infected blood were in reality those Europeans, whose blood carried diseases, who were to result in the deaths of millions of indigenous people of the Americas.

Both slavery and sugar pre-date the colonization of the Caribbean and both were exported to the New World from Europe. The origins of slavery are to be found in Ancient Egypt, Greece, and Rome, where legal doctrines authorized the enslavement of conquered peoples or those barbarians whom Aristotle defined as "natural slaves." The early Christian Church endorsed the institution of slavery, which survived in parts of Europe alongside other forms of coercive labor such as feudalism and serfdom into the fifteenth century. Before slavery was adopted as the preferred solution to the Caribbean's labor shortage, strenuous attempts were made to ensure a steady supply of European workers. From the 1620s onwards, the system of indenture labor was widespread in English and French islands. According to Williams, quoting Merivale, slavery has been too narrowly identified with the Negro, with a racial twist given to what is basically an economic phenomenon. Slavery was not born of racism; rather, racism was the consequence of slavery. He argues that "unfree" labor in the New World consisted of white, black, brown, and yellow, Catholic, Protestant, and Pagan. The first instance of slave trading and slave labor in the New World involved Indians. However, they rapidly succumbed to the excessive labor demanded of them, along with insufficient diet, the white man's diseases and their inability to adjust themselves to the new way of life (Williams, 1943: 7). Both England and France, in their colonies, followed the Spanish practice of enslavement of the Indians. There was one conspicuous difference – attempts of the Spanish Crown, however ineffective, to restrict Indian slavery to those who refused to accept Christianity and to the warlike Caribs on the specious plea that they were cannibals. But Indian slavery was never extensive in the British dominions.

The Spanish discovered that one enslaved African was worth four Indians, as a prominent official in Hispaniola insisted in 1518 that permission be given to bring Negroes, a race robust for labor, instead of natives, so weak that they can only be employed in tasks requiring little endurance, such as taking care of maize fields or farms. The future staples of the New World, sugar and cotton, required strength which the Indian lacked. Africans, therefore, were stolen from Africa to work the lands stolen from the Indians in the Americas. The immediate successor of the Indian, however, was not enslaved Africans, but poor whites. The white servants, so-called because before departure from England, they had to sign a contract, indentured by law, binding them to service for a stipulated time in return for their passage. Others known as "redemptioners" arranged with captains of ships to pay for their passages on arrival or within a specified time thereafter. However, if they did not, they were sold by these ships' captains to the highest bidder. Others were convicts, sent out by the deliberate policy of the British government, to serve for a specified period. This emigration was in tune with mercantilist theories, which strongly advocated putting the poor to industries and useful labor and favored emigration, as more profitable occupations abroad for idlers and vagrants at home and would also relieve the poor rates. In a State Paper delivered to James 1, in 1606, Francis Bacon emphasized that by emigration England would gain "a double commodity, in the avoidance of people here, and in making use of them there" (Williams, 1943: 10). Many of these servants were manorial tenants, and Germans running away from the Thirty Years' War. A regular traffic developed in these indentured servants.

Between 1654 and 1685, ten thousand sailed from Bristol alone, chiefly for the West Indies and Virginia. In 1683, white servants represented one-sixth of Virginia's population and two-thirds of the immigrants to Pennsylvania during the eighteenth century were white servants. It has been estimated that more than a quarter of a million persons were of this class during the colonial period, and probably constituted one-half of all English immigrants. As commercial speculation entered the picture, abuses crept in: kidnaping became a regular business in such towns as London and Bristol. Convicts provided another steady source of white labor, especially as feudal laws in England recognized three hundred capital crimes, including picking a pocket for more than a shilling; shoplifting to the value of five shillings; stealing a horse or a sheep; poaching rabbits on a gentleman's estate. It is difficult to resist the conclusion that there was some connection between the laws of England and the need for labor in the colonies. Settlers in the West Indies were prepared to accept all and sundry, even the spawn of Newgate and Bridewell. The political and civil disturbances in England between 1640 and 1740 augmented the supply of white servants. Political and religious nonconformists paid for their beliefs by transportation, mostly to sugar islands in the West Indies. This was also the fate of many of Cromwell's Irish prisoners and the vanquished in his Scottish campaigns. Religious intolerance sent more workers to the plantations. In 1661, Quakers refusing to take the oath for the third time were to be transported, or a fine of one hundred pounds was decreed and in 1664, for the third offence for persons over sixteen assembling in groups of five or more under pretense of religion.

Many of Monmouth's adherents were sent to Barbados, with orders to be detained as servants for ten years. A similar policy was resorted to after the Jacobite rising of the eighteenth century. These white servants were packed like herrings during transportation. A petition to Parliament in 1659 describes how seventy-two servants had been locked up below deck during the whole voyage of five and a half weeks, amongst horses, that their souls fainted in them. Merchants and justices were in the habit of straining the law to increase the number of felons who could be transported to sugar plantations they owned in the West Indies. They would terrify petty offenders with the prospect of hanging and then induce them to plea for transportation. By the end of the seventeenth century, the mercantilists were arguing that the best way to compete with other countries was to pay low wages, which a large population tended to ensure. The fear of overpopulation at the start of the seventeenth century gave way to a fear of under-population in the middle of the same century. Servitude, originally a free personal relation, based on voluntary contract for a definite period of service in lieu of transportation and maintenance, tended to pass into a property relation which asserted a control of varying extent over the body and liberties of the person during service, as if that person was a thing. Planters agreed to pay the passage of poor agricultural laborers, who were contracted to serve terms of between three or five years in return for subsistence and a small wage and a land grant, averaging four acres. During the term of service, the laborer was the legal property of the planter, forbidden to leave the plantation or to sell his services elsewhere. In England, rural poverty, unemployment, and under-employment and the effect of the enclosures pushed an estimated 110,000 white servants towards the Caribbean colonies between 1610 and 1660. Some white laborers were kidnapped or press-ganged and others were political or religious dissidents who were transported to the Caribbean islands to work on plantations.

The backers of new colonies needed able and willing hands – to clear land, build forts, and plant crops. Under the system of indenture, developed by the Virginia Company in the 1620s, young men and women contracted themselves to work for a master, for a period ranging from three to nine years. In return, they were given passage to the colonies and subsistence during their tenure. Some were paid annual wages, but most were promised a one-off payment – usually around ten pounds – or some land (in Barbados it was ten acres) at the end of their contract. During the reign of Charles 1 (1625–1649), some 30,000 indentured servants went to the Caribbean, with a similar number going to the North American colonies. Although among them there were dissenters and those who were politically disaffected, most were from the rural poor, adversely affected by severe economic and social troubles in England during the 1620s and 1630s, which included depressions and bad harvests. The majority of these servants were from the West Country, East Anglia, or Ireland. There were others who saw emigration as a route to a new freedom, be it religious, political, economic, or social (Parker, 2011: 25). In the 1630s, there were ready supplies of willing immigrants, but the following decade witnessed a declining birth rate in England, death from the Civil War and a rise in wages, meant there was a shortage of indentured laborers. At the same time, the switch to sugar increased the demand for labor. The result was that growing numbers of those arriving in Barbados were now unwilling immigrants (Parker, 2011:47).

On the sugar plantations of Barbados servants spent their time grinding at the mills and attending furnaces, or digging, having nothing to eat but potatoes, nor to drink but contaminated water, being brought and sold from one planter to another, or attached as horses for the debt of their master's pleasure and sleeping on sties worse than hogs in England. The servants were regarded by the planters as "white trash" and were bracketed with enslaved Africans as laborers. The Council of Montserrat in 1680 declared that not one of these colonies ever was or ever can be brought to any considerable improvement without a supply of white servants and Negroes. Daniel Defoe stated that the white servant was a slave. But, the servant's status could not be passed on to his off-springs and at no time did the master have absolute control over the person and liberty of his servant, as he had over his Negro slave, as the white servant had limited rights. The laws in the colonies maintained a rigid distinction between white servants and Negro slaves. At the end of his contracted term, the servant could aspire to a plot of land, or a one-off payment, but there was no end in sight for enslaved Africans. For most black people in the Caribbean, their experience of the British Empire was mediated by their experience of slavery and colonialism. In late seventeenth and eighteenth centuries, Caribbean, about ninety percent of all enslaved Africans, with the exception of children under six, a few aged, and invalids, work on sugar plantations was the norm. Some Caribbean islands were little more than one vast sugar plantation. The major exception was Britain's largest sugar island, Jamaica, which was always diversified and became more so over time.

In the late eighteenth century, the proportion of Jamaica's enslaved Africans on sugar plantations was about sixty percent and declining. The secondary crop was coffee, which employed a sizeable number of enslaved Africans in Jamaica, Dominica, St. Vincent, Grenada, St. Lucia, and Trinidad, that had a less arduous work regime than on sugar plantation. Generally, slave societies in the Caribbean distributed their captives roughly seventy to eighty percent field hands, ten to twenty percent in skilled, semi-skilled, and supervisorial position and about five to ten percent in domestic service, which varied considerably from place to place. Individuals were allocated jobs according to gender, age, color, strength, and birthplace. Men dominated skilled trades, and women generally came to dominate field gangs; age determined when children entered the workforce, progression from one gang to another, when field hands became drivers, and when drivers were pensioned off as watchmen. Those slaves of mixed heritage, or mulatto (white fathers and enslaved African mothers) were often allocated to domestic work or, in the case of men, to skilled trades. Island planters would almost never work mixed heritage slaves in the field. Mixed heritage slaves were the most likely of any slaves to be freed, thereby producing the greatest divide among slaves and the slave system's greatest anomaly, a third party in a structure built for two. Drivers were taller and often stronger than men and women who labored in work gangs. Those slaves in plantation societies who lived in towns and cities ranged from five to ten percent in most Caribbean territories and women usually outnumbered men. In the highly polarized world of a slave society, standardized patterns of interaction and codes of behavior arose quickly to govern relations, both between Caucasians and enslaved Africans, and among enslaved Africans themselves.

The law was one vital means of institutionalizing interactions between the free and the enslaved. The British West Indies territories, with Barbados the prototype, were the first to develop elaborate slave codes. Police regulations lay at the heart of the slave system and some of the common features of the slave codes were the prohibition and suppression of authorized movement of enslaved Africans, large congregation, the possession of guns and other weapons, the playing of horns and drums and the practice of secret rituals. The highly personalized mechanism of coercion; the whip, was the main instrument of brutality and sadism, which was widely spread in the British West Indies where the behavior of the owners of enslaved Africans went unchecked by any external authority. Jamaica, soon to be the prize among England's Caribbean possessions, was seized from the Spanish colonists, in May 1655, when an English fleet bearing 7,000 men sailed into Kingston Harbor and captured Jamaica for Cromwell. Nine years later, systematic English settlement began. From the outset, it was envisioned that sugar was to be the principal crop and a settler with a wife was granted ninety acres, but a capitalist with one hundred enslaved Africans was granted three thousand acres. Sugar production accounted for the vast bulk of the labor used in this slave society. For its first adventure in aggressive, state-sponsored imperialism, England had put together a wretched army of the poorest quality soldiers, which were ill equipped and ill led. One English officer called the men of the army the "very scum of scums, and mere dregs of corruption" (Parker, 2011: 107). Between 1671 and the 1680s, sugar production had increased tenfold in Jamaica. The number of sugar works had jumped from 57 in 1671 to 246 in 1684.

Thirty years after Barbados, the Sugar Revolution had arrived in Jamaica and from the 1680s the profits, political and social power were in the hands of sugar plantation owners, such as Francis Price, Peter Beckford and the Drax family. By the 1680s, a Governor of Jamaica, Sir Hender Molesworth (c.1638–1689) was writing about the regular supply of enslaved Africans, provided by the Royal Company. Many of these enslaved Africans were from the Coromantee people, derived from the name of the Ghanaian coastal town "Koromantse," also called Coromantins, Coromanti, or Koromantine, enslaved and brought from the Gold Coast (modern Ghana). Coromantins were from several Akan ethnic groups – Ashanti, Fanti, Akyem, and others. Coromantin groups or states were not all the same, but they shared a common political language and mythology, such as there being a single, powerful God, Nyame, and Anansi stories. These Anansi stories would be spread to the New World to become, Anansi Drew, or Br'er Rabbit stories in Jamaica. Akans also shared the concept of Day Names. Akan slavery, and Ashanti slavery in particular, was a condition based on circumstance. The enslaved person had rights and could own property and the child of an enslaved person was a free person. Akans tried to ultimately incorporate a slave from another tribe into their own by making the child of a slave a free person. Many were sold as war captives, owing to their militaristic culture and common Akan language. In one year alone, 1686–7, more than 6,000 enslaved Africans were imported by the Royal Company.

Ransoming Christian and Muslim Captives

According to James W. Brodman (1986), the threat of capture, whether by pirates or coastal raiders, or during one of the region's intermittent wars, was consequently not a new but rather a continuing threat to the residents of Catalonia, Languedoc and other coastal provinces of Medieval Christian Europe. Capture could occur at any time or place that marked the convergence of hostile people, which was increasingly between Christian and Muslim peoples. By the twelfth century, a captive was almost axiomatically a slave of his religious enemy – a Christian held by a Muslim or a Muslim by a Christian. Along the shifting frontier that came to delimit the zones of Christian and Islamic power, three occasions are identified that might have given rise to the capture of a Christian or of a Muslim, which were formal battles, raids and piracy. Battles had the potential to produce many captives, especially great battles between Christian and Muslim Spain like those at Zallaca (1086), Valencia (1102), Ucles (1108), Saragossa (1118), and Fraga (1134). Muslim chronicles tell of victorious forces of the Muwahhid Caliph Ya'qub who captured between five and twenty-four thousand Leonese and Castilian soldiers at Alarcos in 1195. Raids and sieges were frequent in occurrence, and chronicles have left accounts of the casualties produced by this type of campaign. For example, the last of the Murabit sultans, Tashufin (1143–45), in a raid against Toledo, attacked the castle of Azeca and in the process of taking it, killed three hundred of its Christian defenders and sent the rest as captives to Cordoba and then to Morocco.

In another series of raids, Ali ibn Yusuf (1106–1143) assaulted the Christian towns of Talavera, Olmos, and Canales, and took many captives and booty. A raid by the Muwahhid fleet against Lisbon in 1181 yielded 20 ships, much booty, and a lot of Christian captives, while Alfonso VIII's forays in Andalusia in 1182 are said to have brought him over 2,000 Muslim captives and 2,775 dinars in ransoms. Ibn Khaldun reports that in 1195, the Muwahhid's army took nearly 5,000 Christians captive near Badajoz. In another raid against Lisbon in 1189, the Muwahhid Caliph Ya'qub al-Mansur is reputed to have left with 3,000 female and child captives, while his governor of Cordoba, in a subsequent attack upon Silves in 1191, won 3,000 prisoners and 15,000 head of cattle. These and the numerous other examples contained in Medieval sources illustrate the pan-Iberian character of the phenomenon; any Christian or Muslim near the frontier zone stood at least some danger of capture. The extension of the wars of re-conquest from interior battlefields to the periphery of Granada and to the high seas marks only a new phase in a continuing Christian-Islamic struggle, because the new seats of Muslim military activity in North Africa had always been associated, politically and culturally, with Hispanic Islam. In the twelfth century, the unity between peninsular and African Islam that had been achieved under the Murabits and Muwahhids can be seen in the free flow of Christian captives from one region to the other.

Christians captured by the Murabit Sultan Tashufin at Azeca, for example, were taken first to Cordoba in Spain and from there to Morocco. Even after the collapse of this trans-Mediterranean Berber empire in the early thirteenth century, the movement of Christian captives from Spain to Africa continued. By all accounts, direct pirate attacks from African ports became relatively more important as Islamic territory in Spain shrank and as Christians re-occupied the coastal regions of Valencia, Murcia, Andalusia, and the Balearics. Christian shipping and populations were the targets of pirates and of more official naval forces of Muslim sultans and emirs. Ibn Khaldun described how groups of North Africans built ships and chose brave leaders, who then led them in attacks upon the coasts of Spain, France, and Italy. They arrived by surprise and took off all they could get their hands on; they also attacked the ships of the infidels

(Christians), very often seizing them and returning with them filled with booty and prisoners. A confirmation of this from the Christian side comes in Pope Clements III's indulgence of April 22, 1188, granting to those of Tarragona who defended the city against the raids made each summer by Muslim pirates. Concern for coastal defense against such incursions also motivated James I to approve in 1257 the appointment of an official by the city of Barcelona to supervise such preparations, which explains the patent issued to one Guillan Grony of Barcelona in 1263 that gave this seaman license to prey upon the lands and ships of Tunis.

Cross-border and coastal raiding, land and sea battles, piracy and the detention of otherwise peaceful merchants all were causes of captivity. Whatever the particular circumstances of a captive's seizure, his ultimate fate was much the same – slavery. The experience of one Esteban de Matrera, a Christian captured in 1285, is perhaps typical. His captor took him to Algeciras, where he was sold to one Bovac the Hunchback for four doblas; his new master then transported Esteban to Tangiers, where he was sold to a resident for eight doblas. A similar fate befell a Muslim of Honein, who was seized in the early 1360s by a galiot captained by Bernat Marti of Donia. The Muslim was taken to Cagliari in Sardinia and, there, was sold to Esteve Sa Basa for 32 livres; the new master then returned to Barcelona with his slave. Slavery was the invariable result of captivity, because those so taken were considered to be spoils of war to be used or sold to the profit of the captor. From medieval sources, we learned that slavery was sometimes viewed, by the captive, as worse than death. In 1327, Catalan captives at Tlemcen wrote to their King, Alfons III, that the physical torments of captivity made death seem preferable to life. Some captives, especially those who found honorable employment with their Muslim lords, were able to maintain their Christianity. Reverter (1090–1142), a Catalan noble taken captive by the Murabits, served the Muslims as commander of all Christian mercenaries and eventually became general in the army of the Sultan, Ali ibn Yusuf (1106–1143). But less fortunate individuals might be tempted to forswear their faith, in order to escape from captivity.

Normally, the captive's ability to convert was limited, as exceptions were made principally for those captives whose freedom would be useful, such as soldiers. Another option for captives was to escape, but few attempted this route, because the price of failure, usually the loss of an eye or nose, was higher than most were willing to risk. The most practical means to gain freedom was redemption – through the payment of a ransom in money or in kind, or through the exchange of a suitable captive held by the other side. Redemption was an ancient practice, for which provision was made in both Roman and Visigothic law. The effort to institutionalized and regularize what had been chiefly a private endeavor was itself a response to the increasingly bitter Muslim-Christian conflict engendered by crusader enthusiasm and Berber revivalism. The natural desire on the part of the captive and his family for liberation combined with the inclination of captors to turn a profit from the now abundant supply of prisoners made redemption a mutually acceptable alternative to the slave market. As early as the Castilian *fuero of Escalona* (1130) and the Aragonese *feuro of Calatayud* (1131), towns tried to guarantee the right of a captive's family to purchase, at a fair price, a locally held Muslim slave who could be exchanged for the Christian.

In addition, laws were designed to help provide a captive with a ransom, and these frontier towns also sought to facilitate the actual negotiation of a redemption. Town councils made use of those Christian and Muslim merchants who maintained the flow of trade across the military frontier. As early as 1104, the count of Barcelona, Ramon Berenguer III (1082–1132), granted a monopoly over ransoming, between his and Islamic lands, to four Jewish merchants. The towns of the Aragonese and Castilian frontiers also relied upon merchants, to whom they gave the title of *exea*, an Arabic word that means guide or companion. In the thirteenth century, the sole remaining Islamic state in the peninsula, Granada, the *exea* and the *alfaqueque* became less municipally licensed merchants and more royal officials, but this in no way changed the redemptionist function of the office. In 1277, two charters of Pere II (1178–1213), the Catalan monarch granted permission to two Muslims to reside permanently in Valencia to arrange for the ransoming of their coreligionists held there and in the second, thanked them for negotiating the redemption of Pere de Moncada, the master of the Knights Templars (known as "The Poor Fellow-Soldiers of Christ and of the Temple of Solomon," Hugues de Payens Godfrey of Bouillon (1070–1136). The first Grandmaster, with Saint Bernard of Clairvaux (1090–1153), drew up the code of the Templars, which was founded in 1119 and ceased operation in 1312). The *Ordenamiento* of Toro of 1369 speaks of the *alfaqueque* mayor of the lands of the Moors. By the fifteenth century, we have examples of such officials and of their delegates, or *alfaqueque menores*, to whose care smaller segments of the frontier were given.

Thus, at least until the end of the Middle Ages, there existed in the *alfaqueque* and *exea* a publicly licensed official who was able to carry out ransoming by virtue of the safe conduct that permitted his secure crossing of the frontier and of his oath to act honestly and justly. With the Christian occupation of much of the northern coast of the western Mediterranean, captivity after the mid-thirteenth century increasingly occurred at sea and at the hands of Muslims from Granada and North Africa. For those unable to afford the cost of redemption, twelfth century society devised a second method, organized by the church, by elevating ransoming from a work of civic importance to an act of religious charity, with a sharp distinction between Christians and infidel Moors. With captives now numbered among the religiously deserving, various efforts to raise alms for captives began to appear along the twelfth century frontier. Christian scripture supported the use of ransoming, as testified by the following scripture: "And after he is sold he may be redeemed again; one of his brethren may redeem him: Either his uncle, or his uncle's son, may redeem him, or any that is nigh of kin unto him of his family may redeem him; or if he be able, he may redeem himself" (Leviticus 25: 48–49).

One of the first efforts to apply the institutions of religious charity to ransoming grew out of the initiative of Alfons I (1073–1134) of Catalonia-Aragon and of Alfonso VIII (1158–1214) of Castile to entrust this work to the military orders of the realms. Alfonso VIII established a number of religious ransoming centers in the Trans-Tagus region of Castile and entrusted these to the knights of Santiago. The first of these so-called Hospitals of Mercy was founded and royally endowed at Toledo in 1180; a second appeared in 1182 at Cuenca, a third at Huete in 1198, a fourth at Alarcon in 1202 and a fifth at Moya in 1215. By 1227 there were seven frontier hospitals being operated by Santiago. The King of Leon, Alfonso IX (1171–1230), himself established two during his drive into *Extremaudura*, one at Castrotoraj and another at Salamanca. The Knights of Calatrava, the first military order founded in Castile and received papal approval in September 1164 by Pope Alexander III, had by 1214 a ransoming hospice at Evora in the Portuguese Alentjo and another at Salvatierra in the Sierra Morenas. Military redemptionism advanced the development of organized ransoming in three main ways. Firstly, it facilitated royal intervention into the work of ransoming, by establishing and endowing such hospitals, the Hispanic monarchs acknowledged the seriousness of captivity and thus society's general responsibility to promote redemption. Secondly, these hospitals of mercy were entrusted to religious orders, helped to establish ransoming as a legitimate and meritorious work of charity that was properly the work of the entire Christian community. Thirdly, military redemptionism, tied closely as it was to individual municipalities, was the charitable complement to the other facilities offered by these same towns to their more affluent captured residents.

The treatment of captives as Christ's poor and the resulting religious and ecclesiastical interest in ransoming appear first and most prominently in Catalonia, where as early as 957 the canons of Vich were admonished to assist captives. Twelfth century wills provide ample testimony that Catalans had come to consider captives, alongside the poor, to be fit objects of their charity and statistical studies of thirteenth century wills confirm what was emerging in the twelfth century. In 1144, Berenguer of Ripoll, among his bequests were a bed to be given to the hospital at Narbonne, belonging to the Order of St. John, a lance, shield, sword, and a small amount of money for the Templars. In the thirteenth century, episcopal redemptionism was replaced, in the main, by the work of the new orders. There arose, alongside the new hospitable orders of St. Anthony, the Holy Spirit, Roncesvalles, Aubrac, and other redemptionist orders of the Holy Trinity and of Santa Eulalia of Barcelona. The order of the Holy Spirit was founded by John de

Matha, at Cerfoid, northeast of Paris and approved by Pope Innocent III in 1198, with its members coming to work in the hospital and people who handled ransoms in thirteenth century France and Spain.

The Middle Ages

The history of the Middle Ages, the period between the fifth century and the fifteenth century, is said to begin with the fall of the Western Roman Empire and merged into the Renaissance and the Age of Discovery. The Middle Ages is the middle period of the three traditional divisions of Western history: classical antiquity, the medieval period, and the modern period. The medieval period is itself subdivided into the Early, High, and Late Middle Ages. The Early Middle Ages witnessed large-scale movements of people, including various Germanic tribes – Teutonic, Suebian, or Gothic – who formed new kingdoms in what remained of the Western Roman Empire. In the seventh century, North Africa – Algeria, Egypt, Libya, Morocco, Sudan, Tunisia, and Western Sahara – and the Middle East – the transcontinental region centered on Western Asia and Egypt, once part of the Byzantine Empire. The term "Middle East" may have originated in the 1850s in the British India Office. During the High Middle Ages, which began after 1000 CE, the population of Europe increased greatly and trade flourished. Manorialism – the organization of peasants into villages that owed rent and labor services to the nobles – and feudalism, the political structure whereby knights and lower-status nobles owed military service to their overlords in return for the right to rent from lands and manors, were two of the ways society was organized in the High Middle Ages. Kings became the heads of centralized nation states, reducing crime and violence, but making the ideal of a unified Christendom more distant. The theology of Thomas Aquinas (c.1225–1274 CE), the paintings of Giotto (c.1266–1337 CE), the poet Dante (c.1265–1321 CE) and Chaucer (c.1343–1400 CE) and travels by Marco Polo (1254–1324 CE) and the Gothic architecture of cathedrals such as Chartes, France, are among the outstanding achievements toward the end of this period.

The Late Middle Ages was marked by difficulties and calamities including famine, plagues, and wars, which significantly diminished the population of Europe, between 1301 and 1500 CE. In the later Middle Ages, the people of England knew that the ideals of the gospel of Love were far removed from prevailing reality. The Holy Roman Empire was falling into the quagmire of political dependence. The world was ruled by brigandage, superstition and the plague. The violent tenor of medieval life lent a tone of excitement and passion to everyday life, which oscillated between despair and distracted joy, between cruelty and pious tenderness, which characterizes the Middle Ages – the lepers with rattles, the beggars in churches, the public executions, the hellfire sermons, the processions, the steeple bells and the street criers, the stench and the perfume.

According to Southgate (1954), life in the Middle Ages was in the main co-operative and communal. The individual was a member of a group, to which he was expected to be faithful and obedient. The Catholic Church was the only accepted religion. With the passing of the Middle Ages, this communal spirit gave way to individualism. Protestantism challenged the authority of the Catholic Church. Individuals learned to think and act for themselves, as commercialism replaced custom and new occupations came into existence. The discontent of the poor was shown in various revolts which occurred in the middle of the Tudor period. The Kett Rebellion (July–August 1549), which occurred during the reign of Edward VI, in the county of Norfolk, was caused by the extension of enclosures and the rise in rents. A third of the agricultural land of the country changed hands in the course of a few years and the economic effects of the dissolution of the monasteries were of great importance. Every aspect of medieval economic life – agrarian, industrial, commercial – was subject to regulation. Towards the close of the Middle Ages the idea of nationality became increasingly more distinct.

The spirit of nationality developed in most parts of Christendom – as separate political, religious, and economic entities – and private interests could not be permitted to take precedence over considerations affecting the well-being of the nation as a whole. The direction of political and economic affairs in the interest of the nation was impossible without an authority sufficiently strong to exercise control. This authority was monarchical in character, which prevailed in most of the countries of Europe, from the sixteenth to the eighteenth century and in some cases to the nineteenth century. The system that was developed in England was later called mercantilism, which involved the control of English activity, political as well as economic, in order that England might be powerful. The full national consciousness which developed in the sixteenth century under the influence of the autocratic rule of Tudors at home and of the opposition to Rome and to Spain aboard found partial expression in the mercantilism which flourished from the sixteenth to the eighteenth century. Mercantilists' aim, the development of national power, called for State action in many directions, especially in the maintenance of a large and healthy population. Hence, the maintenance of the national food supply could not be permitted to be dependent upon the goodwill of other nations. The importance of naval strength was not overlooked by the mercantilists and there was no sharp distinction between fighting ships and trading vessels, as it was common practice for merchant ships to be armed for defense against piratical attack. By a series of Acts of Parliament, the State encouraged the building of merchant vessels, which might be pressed into the King's service when required. Attention was given to the manning of ships and for the purpose of training seamen.

Overseas trade was subject to State control, by entrusting foreign trade to monopolistic chartered companies. Great attention was paid by economists of the

Tudor and Stuart periods to the question of treasure, as it was felt that an adequate supply of gold and silver was essential to the safety of the State. Treasure was needed for the waging of war. Spain possessed it in abundance, through the control of Mexican and Peruvian mines. Every year a Spanish treasure fleet, bearing the year's produce of these mines, sailed for Spain. One of the aims of commercial regulation was to promote trade with the one group and to discourage it with the other. The mercantilists were prepared to distinguish the effects on national well-being of different kinds of trade. The importation of raw materials, which might be worked upon by English artisans and ultimately re-exported with their value enhanced, was to be commended. The export of English raw material was disliked, as it was held that such materials should be worked upon and exported in a manufactured form. Settlement overseas was sanctioned only if it conformed to mercantilists principles. Colonial products that could not be grown in England and were needed in England were to be sent only to England. These actions by the state were to have far-reaching consequences for the later Atlantic slave trade.

In the Middle Ages, the failure of a harvest might result in starvation of the inhabitants of a manor. Such cases of destitution as occurred in the Middle Ages were relieved without recourse to State aid. Guild members who fell into poverty were assisted by the fraternity, or to the widows and orphans of deceased brethren. Monastic Charity was opened to all who needed their help, and many lords and ecclesiastics kept open house to all comers. Hospitals and lazar houses existed for the sick. With the passing of the Middle Ages, the number of destitute persons increased. The increase in pastoral farming in some parts of the country involved the expulsion of many of the villagers from their holdings. Without occupation, they drifted into towns or became vagrants or robbers. During the Hundred Years' War (1337–1453), a series of conflicts between the House of Plantagenet of England and the House of Valois of France, over the succession of the French throne. The Hundred Years' War was one of the most notable conflicts of the Middle Ages, involving five generations of kings from both rival dynasties. Additionally, the Wars of the Roses (1455–1487) were another series of conflicts for control of the throne of England, fought between the royal House of Lancaster and the House of York. The power struggle was, to some extent, caused by the financial problems following the Hundred Years' War, combined with the mental infirmity of Henry VI, which revived interest in Richard, Duke of York's claim to the throne. At the end of these conflicts, Henry Tudor (1457–1509) seized the English crown on August 22, 1485 and became Henry VII, the first monarch of the House of Tudor. Under the firm rule of the Tudors, retinues were dispersed, and the countryside swarmed with able-bodied beggars.

Charities were inadequate to deal with the problem which had arisen, gilds were in decline, and monasteries were soon to disappear. It was assumed that able-bodied beggars were lazy individuals who preferred idleness to work. Henry VIII

(1491–1547) ordered that beggars should be punished for not being in settled employment. The law of 1531 required that every person found begging without license should be whipped twice, after which a license would be issued allowing this person to beg from place to place until he reached his native town or village, where he was expected to settle down to work. Disabled and wounded soldiers who were unable to work were given a license to beg. This brutal law had little effect in reducing the number of beggars. A further law was enacted in 1536, which classified the poor into three categories: the disabled for whom alms were to be collected in each parish, the able-bodied for whom work should be provided, and the lazy who were to be punished. The children of paupers were to be apprenticed. In 1547, in the reign of Edward VI (1537–1553), it was enacted that a person caught wandering without employment should be branded with the letter V (for vagabond) and be compelled to work as a slave for his captor for two years, during which time he was to be fed on bread, water, and broken meats and to be kept at work with stripes. For a further offence, he was to be branded with the letter S (for slave) and was to be enslaved for life.

"The nation-state" and "nationalism" are terms which are frequently applied, or misapplied, to the sixteenth century. But they are more appropriate to the nineteenth century, when they were invented by historians looking for the origins of the nation-states of their own day. They should not, however, be used to convey premature preoccupations with ethnic identity. What they can properly convey is a strong sense of sovereignty which both monarchs and subjects assumed, as the unity of the Middle Ages disintegrated. Their overriding *raison d'état* had economic dimension associated with mercantilism, as well as the purely political one. Mercantilism, or "the mercantile system," is a label that had little currency until popularized in the late eighteenth century. Yet the set of ideas which Adam Smith (1723–1790) was to criticize formed the main stock of economic thought of the early modern period. Mercantilism, in essence, referred to the conviction that in order to prosper, the modern state needed to manipulate every available legal, administrative, military and regulatory device. In this sense, it was the opposite of the *laissez-faire* system, which Smith would later advocate. Mercantilism is also underpinned by the idea that a country's wealth and power depended on amassing gold. In another, it concentrated on improving the balance of trade by assisting exports, penalizing imports, and encouraging home manufactures. In all forms, it was concerned with strengthening the sources of economic power – colonies, manufactures, navies, tariffs – and was expressly directed against a country's commercial rivals. It was argued that the ordinary means to increase England's wealth and treasure is by foreign trade. To sell more to strangers yearly than we consume of theirs in value.

The English Church

The Englishman John Wyclif (1330–84), sometime master of Balliol College, railed against the wealth of the Church, rejected papal supremacy and denied the doctrine of transubstantiation of the Eucharist. He was burned as a heretic, but only posthumously. The "Twelve Conclusions of the Lollards of 1395 contains a direct attack on the medieval English Church's involvement with magic." Wyclif, the Lollards' guru, translated the Bible into English to make it accessible to all. Yet three-hundred years later, in Cromwell's Puritan England, the sales charts were topped by William Lilly's astrological almanac, the "Merlinus Anglicus," and by his collection of "Ancient and Moderne Prophecies." Magic held its own throughout the Reformation era. After Wyclif came Luther's attack on indulgences and Calvin's dismissal of transubstantiation as "conjury." Since Protestant Christianity was supposedly magic-free, Protestantism's enemy, "Popery," was judged equivalent to black magic; the pope was a wizard, and the Catholic Mass was a branch of devil worshipers. But it proved difficult to abandon the sign of the Cross, oaths in court, or the "churching" of women after childbirth. It proved virtually impossible to abandon the consecration of church buildings, of battle standards, of food, of ships and of burial grounds. Protestantism was due to create a new form of Christianity, with emphasis on conscious belief; but magic was never eliminated. According to Davies (1996), witchcraft developed in parallel to Christian mysticism and for some of the same reasons. Witches, black and white, were undoubtedly a hangover from the pagan animism of pre-Christian countryside, as was the firm belief in pixies, elves, sprites, and hobgoblins. By openly entering into combat with witchcraft, the Church inadvertently fostered the climate of hysteria on which the alleged witches and sorcerers thrived.

The crucial Bull, *Summis Desiderantes,* which landed the Church's official counter-offensive, was issued by Innocent VIII in 1484. The standard handbook for witch hunters, the *Malleus Maleficarum,* was published in 1486, by the Dominicans. Thereafter, all Christendom knew that the legions of the Devil were led by evil women, who anointed themselves with grease from the flesh of unbaptized children, who rode stark naked on flying broomsticks or on the backs of rams and goats, and who attended their nocturnal "Sabbaths" to work their spells and copulate with demons. Women were classified as weak, inferior beings, who could not resist temptation. Once the Church gave public credence to such things, the potency of witchcraft was greatly increased. Hence, after that, for three hundred years, witchcraft and witch-hunting were endemic to most parts of Europe. Yet, no medieval institution, suggests Davies (1996), has attracted greater opprobrium from later ages than the "Holy inquisition." The ferocity aroused during the pursuit of heretics, Jews, or witches is often incomprehensible. Yet, a little reflection suggests that the phenomenon is not exclusively medieval. The definition of "normal" and "deviant" is always subjective and people whose unconventional conduct threatens entrenched interests can easily be denounced as "mad" or "dangerous" (Davies, 1996:454).

Il Principe [The Prince], written in 1513, by Niccolo Machiavelli (1469–1527), argues that "The nearer people are to the Church of Rome, the more irreligious they are. War should be the only study of a prince. He should look upon peace only as a breathing space which…gives him the means to execute military plans." The French wars of religion were spectacularly un-Christian. Persecution of the Huguenots had begun with the *Chambre ardente* under Henri II (b.1519). But the King's sudden death in 1559, and that of the Duke of Alencon, provoked prolonged uncertainty about the succession. This in turn enflamed the ambitions of the Catholic fraction led by the Guises, and of the Bourbon-Huguenot fraction led by the King of Navarre. Eight wars in thirty years were peppered with broken truces and foul murders. Given the persistence of religious pluralism in Britain, France, the Netherlands, and Poland-Lithuania, it is erroneous to view Europe in this period in term of a simple division between the "Protestant North" and the "Catholic South." The Irish, the Belgians and the Poles, among others, have every right to insist that the north was not uniformly Protestant. Both Orthodox Christians and Muslims have good reason to object to the south being classified as uniformly Catholic. The Protestant – Catholic divide was an important feature of Central Europe, but it cannot be applied with any precision to the Continent as a whole. Attempts by Marx or Webber to correlate it with later division, based on social or economic criteria, would seem to be German-centric. One thing was clear, senseless bloodletting in the name of religion inevitably sparked off a reaction in the minds of intelligent people. The wars of religion offered fertile soil for the fragile seeds of reason and science. In 1529 King Henry VIII of England initiated the policy which was to separate the English church from Rome. The initial cause lay in Henry's obsessive desire for a male heir and in the Pope's refusal to grant him a divorce.

The Act of Annates (1532) cut financial payments to Rome. The Act of Appeals the following year curtailed Rome's ecclesiastical jurisdiction. The Act of Supremacy (1534) abolished papal authority completely, raising the King to be Supreme Head of the Church of England. Subjects such as Thomas More (1478–1535) or Cardinal John Fisher (1469–1535), who decided to accede, were executed for treason. The Act of Ten Articles (1536) and of Six Articles (1539) asserted the inviolability of the Roman Mass and of traditional doctrine. The direct association of Church and State – later called Erastianism – brought Anglicanism closer to Orthodox than to Catholic practice. Erastianism is the doctrine that the state should have supremacy over the Church in ecclesiastical matters, wrongly attributed to Erastus in the New Testament. Henry VIII died in 1548 and the reign of the boy King Edward VI produced much confusion. The interval of the ultra-Catholic Queen Mary resulted in a crop of Protestant martyrs. Under Elizabeth I, the Church settlement enshrined in the Act of Uniformity (1559) and the Thirty-Nine Articles (1571) reached a judicious synthesis of Erastian, Lutheran, Zwinglian, Calvinist, and traditional catholic influences. From then on, Anglicanism has always provided an umbrella for two competing tendencies – the "High Church" of Anglo-Catholicism and the "Low Church" of Calvinistic evangelicals. Despite merciless persecution under Elizabeth I, both recusant Catholics and non-conformist puritans survived underground. The latter re-emerged in force in the seventeenth century and, under Cromwell's Commonwealth (1650–8), briefly controlled the state. Thanks to the efforts of John Knox (1513–72), Calvinism became the sole established religion in the kingdom of Scotland in 1560, in the form known as Presbyterianism.

The effects of Protestantism can be observed in every sphere of European life. By emphasizing the necessity of Bible reading, it made a major impact on education in Protestant countries and, hence, on popular literacy. In the economic sphere, it made a major contribution to enterprise culture and, hence, on the rise of capitalism. In politics, it proved a major bone of contention both between states and between rival groupings within states. By dividing the Catholic world in two, it spurred the Roman Church into Reform, which it had repeatedly postponed. Above all, it dealt a fatal blow to the ideal of a united Christendom. Until 1530s, Christendom had been split into two halves – Orthodox and Catholic. But, from the 1530s onwards it was split into three: Orthodox, Catholic, and Protestant. The Protestants themselves were split into ever more rival fractions. The Council of Trent, met in three sessions, 1545–7, 1551–2, and 1562–3, which provided the doctrinal definitions and the institutional structures which enabled the Roman Church to revive and to meet the Protestant challenge. It confirmed that the Church alone could interpret the Scriptures and that religious truth derived from Catholic tradition as well as from the Bible. It upheld traditional views of original sin, justification, and merit. It rejected the various Protestant alternatives to transubstantiation during Eucharist.

Critics of the Council of Trent point to its neglect of practical ethics, its failure to give Catholics a moral code to match that of Protestants. By the acts of 1547, 1552, and 1557, attempts were made to organize the collection in church of voluntary alms for the necessitous poor. By a further act of 1563, it was ordered that those who declined to give alms should be compelled to do so. In 1572, a compulsory levy was ordered, bringing the poor rate into existence. This act further ordered that severe measures should be taken against vagrants, who were to be whipped and branded, and, for repeated offences, hanged. An act of 1576 ordered that employment should be given to the workless and houses of correction were to be set up in every county. Vagabonds were to be committed to them and after being whipped, were to be set to work. A further act was passed in 1597. The Society for the Propagation of the Gospel prohibited Christian instruction to enslaved Africans in Barbados. Thomas Sherlock (1678–1761), later Bishop of London, assured the planters that: "Christianity and the embracing of the Gospel does not make the least difference in civil property" (Williams, 1943: 42). The return of the Anglican supremacy put limits on toleration, characterized by the Clarendon Code and Test Acts (England), which proscribed conduct perceived as threatening, harmful, or otherwise endangering to the property, health, safety, and moral welfare of people. In Scotland and Ireland, there was the re-imposition of episcopacy. In foreign policy, there was great dissension over fighting the Dutch on religious and strategic grounds. All these issues came to a head after 1685, when Charles II was succeeded by his brother James II (r.1685–8) (1701) – a militant Catholic and a client of Louis XIV. When the King tried to widen, the toleration acts to include Catholics, the dominant Protestant and Parliamentary party in England – known as "Whigs" – forced a showdown on their royalist opponents – henceforth known as "Tories."

James II mobilized French support and succeeded in fleeing abroad at the second attempt. The Protestant victory was secured by the firm action of the Dutch stadholder, William of Orange (1650–1702), the husband of James' daughter Mary, who was determined to stop England from falling into Louis' net. Landing at Torbay on November 5, 1668, with a powerful mercenary army, he cleared London of English troops without resistance and established a position of unassailable strength. He summoned the Convention Parliament which carried out the "glorious" and "bloodless" revolution which offered him the English throne jointly with his wife. The "Revolution" was confirmed by the Declaration and the Bill of Rights and by another Toleration Act, which admitted Protestant dissenters but not Catholics. For Davies (1996), the religious map of Europe did not change significantly and established churches continued to operate according to rigorous state laws of toleration and non-toleration. Members of the official religion gained preferment, having sworn oaths and passed strict tests of conformity; non-members and non-jurors, when not actively persecuted, lingered in legal limbo. In Catholic countries, Protestants were generally deprived of civil rights. In Protestant countries, Catholics suffered the same fate. In Britain, the Church of England and the Church of Scotland formally barred both Roman Catholics and their respective Protestant dissenters. The horror of the age occurred in 1685, when Louis XIV revoked the Edit of Nantes, and all of France's Huguenots were driven into exile.

In England, the Congregationalists or "Independents" surfaced in 1662, initially on condition that their chapels were located at least five miles from any parish church. Following the remarkable career of George Fox (1624–91), the Society of Friends or "Quakers" suffered numerous martyrdoms until gaining the right to worship, like other dissenters, from the Toleration Act of 1689. The General Body of Dissenters – Independents, Presbyterians, and Baptists – was organized in London in 1727. The Moravian Church re-emerged in Holland, in England, and the experimental community of Herrnhut (1722) in Saxony. In the Anglican world, the Methodism of John Wesley (1703–91) threatened to tear the Church of England apart. Wesley had created a spiritual method for his "Holy Club" of students at Oxford and had visited Herrnhut. His lifetime of evangelism, touring the remotest parts of the British Isles, fired the neglected masses with enthusiasm. The Roman Catholic Church settled into a routine that no longer sought to recover Protestant lands but directed its energies to the Jesuit missions in South America, South India, Japan to 1715, China, and North America. In Europe, the Vatican could not cope with the growing centrifugal tendencies of the Church provinces. Pope Innocent XI (1676–89), was driven in 1688 to excommunicate Louis XIV, in secret for occupying Avignon in the *regalia* dispute. Another, Pope Clement IX (1700–21), was pushed against his better judgment to issue the Bull *Unigenitus Deifilius* (1713) condemning Jansenism. Wesley's rejection of episcopacy caused a schism at the first Methodist Conference assembled in London in 1785. Within the British Isles, Ireland was a country apart. Both Catholics and Protestants had suffered foul persecution during the religious wars. After 1691, the Protestant supremacy was bolstered by draconian penal laws which denied Catholics the right to office, property, education, and intermarriage.

Ireland was excluded from the Union of 1707. It retained its own Parliament but was subject to the ancient "Poynings' law" of 1494, which gave automatic control of legislation to the King's ministers in London. With the sole exception of Protestant Ulster, where Huguenot refugees started the prosperous linen industry, it did not participate directly in Britain's industrial revolution. In Ireland, the "Glorious Revolution," was achieved by bloody conquest and the triumph of "King Billy" and his "Orange men" at the Battle of the Boyne in July 1690, which has become a national holiday in Northern Ireland, held on July 12 each year. The "Glorious Revolution" of 1688–9, was neither glorious nor revolutionary. It set out to save the political and religious Establishment from James' radical proposals; and it was brought to fruition through the only successful invasion of England since 1066. From 1701, Louis XIV formally recognized the claims of James Edward Stuart, the "Old Pretender" or James III (1688–1766), whilst the death of Mary (1694), of William III (1702), and of all 17 children of Queen Anne (1665–1714, r.1702–14) rendered the Protestant Stuarts heirless. William of Orange [1650–1702] became King William III (r. 1689–1702) of England, was born in the middle of a Dutch revolution, eight days after his father had died of smallpox. The Act of Union (1707) between England and Scotland largely came about as a result of common frustration in London and Edinburgh at the welter of dynastic settlements being floated. As the price of its disbandment, the Scottish Parliament was able to secure English acceptance of free trade between the two countries,

English cash for settling Scotland's huge debt, English agreement to the separate existence of Scots law and the Presbyterian Kirk. Henceforth, the United Kingdom of Great Britain was to be ruled by a joint Parliament at Westminster.

The famines of 1726–9 and 1739–41 foreshadowed the disaster of the 1840s. Ireland was forcibly incorporated into the United Kingdom through the second Act of Union in 1801. The Orange Order was founded in Armagh in 1795. Like the earlier "Peep O'Day Boys," it aimed to preserve the Protestant supremacy in Ireland. Its hero was "King Billy" [William III]: its watchword, "No Surrender." For two hundred years, the Orange Order has held its annual parades on the anniversary of the Boyne on July 1, 1690. Marchers in bowler hats and orange sashes tramp defiantly through Catholic quarters to the whistle and beats of fife and drum and the old toast is raised; "To the glorious, pious, and immortal memory of the great and good King William, who saved us from popery, slavery, knavery, brass money, and wooden shoes. And a fig to the Bishop of Cork." Discriminatory laws against Catholics dating from the seventeenth century were removed in most Protestant states, and Protestants gained equivalent rights in most Catholic states. In Great Britain, Roman Catholics were largely emancipated by Act of Parliament in 1829 and the Jews in 1888; though both continued to be excluded from the monarchy.

The general trend towards literacy strengthened religious, as well as secular education; and missionary campaigns were targeted as much on the poor and lapsed souls of the new industrial town as the pagans of distant continents. The revivalist movements such as German Pietism or English Methodism now gripped whole districts. In Ireland, popular piety became associated with national resistance. The Catholic heartlands of Spain, Italy, Austria, Poland, and Southern Germany were less immediately affected by industrialization and modernization. Under Pius IX (b. 1792, r.1846–78) the doctrine of the Immaculate Conception of the Virgin was promulgated in 1854. In 1864, the *Encyclical Quanta Cura* asserted the Church's supremacy over all forms of civil authority. In 1870, by the doctrinal constitution Pastor Aeternus passed by the General Vatican Council, the dogma of papal infallibility was introduced in matters of faith and morals. Under Leo XIII (r.1878–1903) the Church moved closer to modern thinking on political and social issues, including affirming the positive aspects of democracy and freedom of conscience. The Church of England was never dis-established, except in Ireland (1869) and in Wales (1914). With regards to slavery, the Bishop of Exeter retained his 655 enslaved Africans, for whom he received over £12,700 compensation in 1833. In 1756 there were 84 Quakers listed as members of a company trading to Africa, among them the Barclay and Baring families. In 1729, the Attorney General ruled that baptism did not bestow freedom or make any alteration in the temporal condition of the enslaved Africans, in addition the slave did not become free by being brought to England.

The Scientific Revolution

The scientific Revolution, which is generally held to have taken place between the mid-sixteenth century and mid-seventeenth century, has been called "the most important event in European History," since the rise of Christianity (Herbert Butterfield, 1947, in *The Origins of Modern Science, 1300–1800*). It followed a natural progression from Renaissance humanism and was assisted to some extent by Protestant attitudes. Its forte lay in astronomy and in those sciences, such as mathematics, optics, and physics, which were needed to collect and to interpret astronomical data. It began with observations made on the tower of the capitulars Church of Frauenburg in Polish Russia in the second decade of the sixteenth century, and it culminated at a meeting of the Royal Society at Gresham College in London on April 28, 1686. Mikolaj Kopernik (1473–1543) had studied both at Cracow and at Padua, established that the Sun, not the Earth, lay at the center of our universe. His heliocentric ideas coincided with the Common astrological habit of using the sun as the symbol of unity. He proved the hypothesis by detailed experiments (Davies, 1996: 507). Kopernik theory of heliocentrism, first advanced in 1510, was fully supported with statistical data in *Derevolutionibus Orbium Coelestium* (On the Revolution of the Celestial Spheres, 1543). At a stroke, it overturned reigning conceptions of the universe, dashing the Aristotelian ideas about a central, immobile, and unplanet-like Earth. Johann Kepler (1571–1630), established the elliptical shape of planetary orbits and enunciated the laws of motion underlying Copernicus (Kopernik). But it was the Florentine, Galileo Galilei (1564–1642), one of the first to avail himself of the newly invented telescope, who really brought Kopernik to the wider public. "The astronomical language of the Bible," he suggested to the dowager Duchess of Tuscany, was "designed for the comprehension of the ignorant."

In 1616, Galileo was summons to Rome, where he received a papal admonition. But, when Galileo persisted and published his *Dialogo dei due Massimi Sistemi del Mondo* (Dialogue on the two main World System, 1632), which expounded the superiority of Kopernik over Ptolemy, he was formally tried by the Inquisition and forced to recant. His supposed parting comment to the inquisitors was, "*Eppur si muove*" (Yet it does move) in apocryphal. Although practical science remained in its infancy during the era when Copernican theory was in dispute, some important assertions were made. Francis Bacon (1561–1626), sometime Chancellor of England, stated the proposition that knowledge should proceed by orderly and systematic experimentation and by deductions, based on experimental data. In this he boldly opposed the traditional inductive method, where knowledge could only be established by reference to certain accepted axioms sanctioned by the Church. But, he held that scientific research must be complementary to the study of the Bible (Davies, 1996:508). Important advances were also made by philosophers with a mathematical bent, notably by Rene

Descartes (1596–1650) and Blaise Pascal (1623–62) and their successor Benedict Spinoza (1632–77), a Sephardic Jew. Descartes, a soldier-adventurer, lived much of his life in exile in Holland. He is most associated with the rationalist system, named after him (Cartesianism) and elaborated in his *Discours surla methode* (1637). Having rejected every piece of information which came to him through his senses, or on the authority of others, he concluded that he must at least exist if he was capable of thinking: *Cogito, ergo, sum* (I think therefore I am), is the Launchpad of modern epistemology. Descartes emphasized the mechanistic view of the world which even then was taking hold. He viewed both human and animals as complex machines.

Pascal took the mechanical ideal to the point where he was able to produce the first "computer" *"Le Coeur a ses raisons,"* he wrote, *"que la Raison ne connait point"* (The heart has its reasons which Reason cannot know). Amidst growing hints about the conflict between science and religion, he proposed his famous gamble in favor of faith. If the Christian God exists, he argued, believers will inherit everlasting life. If not, they will be no worse off than unbelievers. In which case, Christian belief is worth the risk. Spinoza, a lens grinder by profession, had been expelled from Amsterdam's Jewish community for heresy. He shared Descartes' intensely mathematical and logical view of a universe formed by first principles concept of a social contract. He viewed God and nature as indistinguishable. The highest virtue lay in restraint guided by a full understanding of the world and of self. Evil he believed derived from a lack of understanding. "The Will of God" was the refuge of ignorance. In England, the advocates of "experimental philosophy" began to organize themselves in the 1640s. An inner circle, led by Dr. John Wilkins (1614–1672) and Dr. Robert Boyle (1627–1691), formed an "Invisible College" in Oxford during the Civil War. They joined together in 1660 to found the Royal Society for the Improvement of Natural Knowledge. Their first meeting was addressed by the architect Christopher Wren (1632–1723). Their early membership included Isaac Newton (1642–1727), the magician.

The Enlightenment, according to Immanuel Kant (1724–1804), was the period in the development of European civilization when "Mankind grew out of its self-encumbered minority." But, according to Davies (1996), perhaps the Enlightenment is best understood by reference to the darkness which this "light of reason" was trying to illuminate. The darkness was provided by all the unthinking, irrational, dogmatic attitudes with which European Christianity had become encrusted. These attitudes including bigotry, intolerance, superstition, monkishness, and fanaticism, were summed up in the most pejorative word of the age, "enthusiasm" (Davies, 1996: 596). The key concept – *lumen naturate* or "natural light of reason" – has been traced to one of the works of Melanchthon (1497–1560), *De lege nature* (1559) and via Melanchthon to Cicero and the Stoic philosophers. Together with the fruits of the Scientific Revolution and the rational methods of Descartes, it formed the core of an ideology which held center stage from the 1670s to the 1770s. It led to the conviction that reason could uncover the rules that underlay the apparent chaos of both the human and material world. Hence, the law of natural religion, of natural morality of law. Beauty was order, and order was beautiful, was the true spirit of Classicism, which could be traced back to the Egyptian Ma'at. The philosophy of the Enlightenment was primarily concerned with the theory of knowledge (epistemology) – or how we know what we know. In Britain, the basis for debate was supplied by the Englishman John Locke (1632–1704) and the Scotsman David Hume (1711–76), sometime secretary of the British Embassy in Paris. As empiricists, they all accepted that the scientific method of observation and deduction should be applied to human affairs and hence the precept of their contemporary, Alexander Pope (1688–1744): "Know then thyself, presume not God to scan, the proper study of Mankind is Man" (Davies, 1996: 597).

Religious thought was profoundly influenced by rationalism – especially in the sphere of biblical scholarship. The initial problem was how to distinguish between the rival claims of Catholics and Protestants, both of whom gave scriptural backing to their dogmas. In due course, reasoning about religion gave rise to an intellectual fashion for Deism – the religious belief in a "Supreme Being," in God the Creator, or in Providence. The struggles of *the philosophes* against the authorities of Church and State inevitably created the impression that Catholicism and absolute monarchy were united in their blind opposition to all reason and change. Rational economics stood high on the Enlightenment list of priorities. At the micro-level, gentlemen were absorbed by the rising science of estate management, convinced that their properties could be transformed into thriving businesses. Land reclamation by the Dutch or on the Dutch model changed the face of several low-lying regions, including the Fens of East Anglia. The enclosure movement gained speed, threatening the peasantry, but promising larger agrarian units suitable for commercial cultivation. Systematic stockbreeding, plant selection, soil nutrition, crop rotation, and drainage, as practiced by "Farmer George." At Windsor in the 1770s, or by Thomas William Coke (1754–1842) of Holkham in Norfolk, was rewarded by dramatically improved yields. At the macro-level, mercantilism of the autocratic variety long held sway. But the conviction grew that economic life could not expand beyond a certain point unless shorn of artificial theory was long associated with support for absolute monarchy, which accorded well with the classical spirit of order and harmony. It was seeking for the most efficient means of cutting through the maze of local and feudal privilege. John Locke's two Treatises on Government (1590) proposed that government should be subject to natural law and opposed the hereditary principle. He developed the idea of government through a social contract and hence the principle of consent, the cornerstone of liberalism.

Further, he advocated the separation of powers and the need for checks and balances between the executive and the legislative. Adam Smith (1723–90), together with his friend David Hume (1711–76) were the stars of the Scottish Enlightenment in an era when English academic life slumbered. He entered the realm of economics by asking himself about the implications of human greed and how could self-interest work for the common good. His 900 pages of *The Wealth of Nations* (1776) were essentially an extended essay in pursuit of that quest. It shattered the protectionist philosophy of mercantilism, which had reigned supreme in economic thought for two hundred years. Smith's speculations led him to postulate the existence of "society," in whose mechanisms all people participate and to formulate the laws of "the market." He outlined the workings of production, of competition, of supply and demand and prices. He paid special attention to the organization of labor, as shown in his famous description of a pin factory. Rationalized tasks and specialized skills enabled the workforce to produce 48,000 pins a day, where each of the workers might individually produce only two or three. He also stressed the self-regulating nature of the market, which, if unhindered, would foster social harmony. "The demand for men," he wrote, "necessarily regulates the production of men." The science of economics has been exploring the issues raised by Adam Smith ever since. The trail leads from David Ricardo (1772–1823), Reverent Thomas Malthus (1766–1834), and Karl Marx (1818–1883) via John Atkinson Hobson (1858–1940), Frederic Bastiat (1801–1850), and Alfred Marshall (1842–1924) to Thorstein Veblen (1857–1929), Joseph Schumpter (1883–1950) and John Maynard Keynes (1883–1946), and the list goes on.

Education was the sphere to which the ideas of the enlightenment were most readily applicable. The Church held a virtual monopoly in the curricula of schools and universities. In the Catholic, Jesuit, and Piarist schools for boys and Ursuline schools for girls, were set in their ways. The Enlightenment was pitted almost everywhere against a strongly entrenched religious tradition in education. In the long run, under the influence of the Enlightenment religious teaching was separated from general education, modern subjects were introduced to supplement the classics, and in Jeremy Bentham's (1748–1832) long campaign for the University of London, higher education was divorced from ecclesiastical patronage. By 1778, when both Voltaire (b. 1694) and Jean-Jacques Rousseau (b.1712) died, the Enlightenment was starting to run out of breath. Pure reason was felt to be inadequate to the task of understanding the world and of reading the auguries of upheaval. Romanticism refers to the titanic cultural movement which set in during the last quarter of the eighteenth century, in reaction to the waning Enlightenment. Its prime concerns were often directed to those spiritual and supernatural spheres of human experience which religion also addressed and which the Enlightenment neglected.

The French supremacy in Europe lasted for the greater part of two hundred years. It began with the personal rule of the young Louis XIV in 1661 and lasted until the fall of Napoleonic Wars, France was not definitively replaced as the single most powerful state of Continental Europe until her submission to Bismarck's Germany in 1871. For most of that time, Paris was the unrivalled capital of European politics, culture, and fashion. France's lengthy pre-eminence can be partly explained by its large territory and population and by the systematic nurture of her economic and military resources. It can also be explained in part by the disarray of major rivals: the decay of Spain, the ruin of Germany, by the divisions of Italy, by Austria's pre-occupation with the Ottomans. It was also assisted by the extraordinary longevity of the ruling Bourbon kings – Louis XIV (r.1643–1715), Louis XV (r.1715–74), and Louis XVI (r.1774–92) – who supplied a focus for unity and stability. In the end, it was undermined by the growing tensions within French society and by the appearance of new powers – notably Great Britain, the kingdom of Prussia, and the Russian Empire, none of which had even existed in 1643. In the British Isles, the capital event of the period, the founding of the United Kingdom (1707), occurred as the culmination of complicated religious and dynastic constitutional conflicts. The Restoration of the Stuarts, after the Civil Wars, had ushered in an uneasy stand-off, and the reign of Charles II (d.1685) survived two Dutch wars.

The Formation of Western Europe

After 1248, in Spain, the Moorish armies had retreated to the Sierra Nevada, in whose shadow the emirate of Granada could flourish for another two centuries, which was the only Muslim-ruled state in Iberia. The Kingdom of Portugal, independent since 1179, controlled the Atlantic seaboard, where it conquered the Algarve in 1250. The kingdom of Navarre, which straddled the Basque districts of the Northern Pyrenees, was subject from 1234 to French rulers, who maintained their independence until 1516. In 1340 at Salado, Alfonso XI (1312–50) achieved the first Castilian victory over the Moors for almost a century, and crossed the Straits of Algeciras. Thanks to the sturdy African merino sheep which grazed on the uplands of the Meseta or Plateau, Castile became Europe's principal exporter of wool, which was carried from Bilbao and Santander to Flanders. The kingdom of Aragon, in contrast, turned to the sea. James I, the Conqueror (1213–76) occupied Minorca and Majorca in the Moorish war, where he gave Murcia to Castile. Peter III (1276–85) was given the throne of Sicily in 1282, following the expulsion of the French. Sardinia was taken from the Genoese in 1316. Alfonso V (1416–58) took Southern Italy from the Angeuins in 1442. Aragon's domination of the western Mediterranean created an inimitable maritime community, based on

Barcelona, Palermo and Naples, where Catalan was the lingua franca and where nobles enjoyed a regime of remarkable liberality. Disputes between monarchs and their subjects were referred to the Justiciar of Cortes. In 1287, by the Privilege of Union, the nobles were empowered to take up arms against any King who infringed their rights. In the fifteenth century, Aragon controlled both the largest city in Iberia – Barcelona – and the largest city in Europe – Naples. In the five kingdoms of medieval Spain, three main religions were practiced: Christianity, Islam and Judaism; and six main languages were spoken: Castilian, Gallego, Catalan, Portuguese, Arabic, and Basque. The Christian population, dominated by the ranchers and soldiers of the central Plateau, was generally much rougher than the more urbanized and civilized moors of the fertile south. The Spanish Jews, who had gained a foothold through the tolerance of Muslim rulers, spread throughout the Peninsula and played a prominent part in administration, medicine, learning, trade, and finance. In the fifteenth century, a large caste of *conversos* or New Christians – the Lunas, Guzmans, Mendoza, and Enriquez – filled the highest offices of Church and State.

Granada, two and a half thousand feet above sea level, is six miles to the east of Santa Fe. The city was more like those of Muslim North Africa than Christian Spain. Granada was the capital of an emirate, which had come into being in the thirteenth century, in the shadow of the fall of other Muslim monarchies in Cordoba, Valencia, Jaen, and Seville. Granada paid gold to Castile until 1480, in order to be allowed to continue her separate being. But, under siege in 1491, it was the last stronghold of a Muslim empire which had once stretched to the Pyrenees and beyond and included Galicia and Asturias. After nearly eight hundred years, the Muslim reign in Spain ended with the defeat by the Christian triumph. The Christian victory derived from many things: the Muslims' farming in the Vega had been ruined by repeated Spanish raid, which had destroyed wheat and olives, carried out after 1482 from newly conquered city of Alhama. Castilian pressure had been effective, especially with the capture of the port of Malaga. Pope Sixtus 1V (Niccolo Franco) (1414–1484) had talked in the 1470s of the danger of the survival of a Muslim enclave in Spain, at the same time as he had spoken adversely of the Jews in Castile. The Pope had issued a crusading bull calling for war against Granada in 1479 and repeated it in the *Orthodoxae Fidei*, of 1482. Christianity played a central role in the Castilian army and soldiers were preceded in battle by a silver cross, which had been a present from the late Pope Sixus IV. Priests were always available to sing a *Te Deum*, and archbishops and bishops were present in battles (Thomas, 2003: 10).

When King Juan died in 1454, he was succeeded by Isabel's half-brother, Enrique IV (1425–1474), who was perhaps a homosexual and his first mirage to Blanca of Navarre had been annulled because of impotency (Thomas, 2003: 17). King Enrique accepted Isabel as his heiress, instead of his own daughter Juana, aged five, as there was doubt about Juana's real father. Isabel (1451–1504) decided on Fernando of Aragon (1452–1516) as a husband, which would strengthen Castile rather than would have occurred had Isabel married the King of Portugal, even though she was the cousin of Fernando. Fernando was a second cousin of Isabel, on his paternal side. Isabel and Fernando were married in 1469, which caused King Enrique IV to disinherit Isabel and declared his daughter heir. But, in 1474, both Isabel and Enrique spent Epiphany together in Alcazar of Segovia. In December 1475, King Enrique died suddenly in the small town of Madrid. In a deal signed on December 15, 1475, the Crown of Castile was vested in the Queen, but both Isabel and Fernando could jointly issue decrees and approve coins and stamps. Should Fernando die, Isabel would inherit the Crown of Aragon. But it was understood that, should Isabel die, her eldest son or daughter would succeed, not Fernando (Thomas, 2009: 23). It is hard to distinguish important matters on which Isabel and Fernando differed. Their motto *"Tanto monta, monta tanto, Isabel como Fernando"* (It comes to the same thing, Isabel is the same as Fernando), which indicated their equality: that both monarchs could rule in both realms and also in that of the other (ibid: 30). Internationally, the King of Portugal was restrained after the defeat in the 1470s and no longer constituted a threat to Castile or to Spain's control of the Canary Islands, even if Tenerife and La Palma remained to be conquered. As Thomas (2003) points out, the peace with France and England was tied to Castile by a treaty of mutual protection against France, signed in Medina del Compo in 1489. These successes were partly due to Fernando establishing regular ambassadors in five European capitals. The unification of Castile and Aragon represented a powerful monarchy internationally.

It is difficult to say how many soldiers were assembled at Santa Fe in 1491, for the final battle against Islam in Spain, but there were perhaps between six and ten thousand knights and ten to sixteen thousand infantrymen, in an army possibly some eighty thousand. There were three main military orders, Santiago, Alcantara, and Calatrava, which had played an important part in earlier wars against Granada for the last time. There were an army of servants and slaves who attended Isabel and Fernando. These slaves included Canary Islanders, Muslims captured in earlier wars and Africans. Members of the Spanish court, the nobility and trades people, the clergymen and bakers all usually owned one or two slaves each and in the case of the nobility, man more. The Duke of Medina Sidonia in 1492 had ninety-five slaves, many of them Muslims, and nearly forty Africans. In 1490, there were about one hundred-thousand slaves in Spain, with Seville having the largest number. Some slaves were from Eastern-Europe, who had been sold in Western Europe during the Middle Ages, giving the word *"Slav"* to this status of service, in place of the old Latin *"Servus."* There was a diversity of medieval slaves, including Bosnians, Poles, and Russians. There were slave markets in Barcelona and Valencia in Spain and Genoa and Naples in Italy. Others, principally Berbers, came from Spain's outpost in the Sahara. African slaves were probably brought from merchants in Lisbon, as Portuguese had been trading people whom they acquired on the west coast of Africa, anywhere between Senegal and the Congo, for the last two generations. Many were sold by Florentine and Genoese merchants in Portugal, or by their representatives in Seville. The high number of slaves in Spain had been boosted by the centuries of war in Spain between the Christians and the Muslims, as they both made slaves of their captives. Many slaves were employed as domestic servants, but others worked in the sugar mills on the Atlantic islands – the Azores, Madeira, and the Canary Islands. Some slaves were hired out by their masters for wages. Both Christian and Muslim laws indicated the place a slave should occupy in society. Sometimes slaves held properties or brought their freedom and sometimes they were treated better than servants by their masters. Masters were not allowed to kill or mutilate their slaves. No Jews or Muslim in the Christian kingdoms could have Christians as slaves. It was obligatory to treat slaves humanely (Thomas, 2003: 37).

On November 28, 1491, terms of surrender, the *"Capitulaciones,"* were ratified by both sides and signed by both monarchs and witnessed by Hernando de zafra. The Christian monarchs would accept all those who lived in Granada as their vassals and *"natural subjects."* Boabdil and all his people would live in their own religion and not permit their Mosques to be taken from them. The conquered people would also continue to be judged by their own laws. Those who wanted to go and live in North Africa would be allowed to sell their property and make such profits as they could. Christians would not enter Mosques without permission (Thomas, 2003: 80). Lawsuits between Muslims would be judged by their own law, and any suit between people of the two religions would have both a Christian and a Muslim judge. No Muslim would be forced to be a Christian against his or her will. No one be called to account for anything which happened before the surrender and all prisoners were to be released. Muslims would not be conscripted for military service on behalf of Castile against their will. Christian and Muslim slaughterhouses would remain separate. On January 1, 1492, Gutierre de Cardenas, escorted by Almulih and Ibn Kumasha, rode into the palace of Alhambra, to accept the surrender of the last Muslim city of Western Europe. The fall of Granada was an event which was celebrated throughout Europe and in Rome it seemed almost to make up for the loss of Constantinople in 1480, when 12,000 of the inhabitants were allegedly put to death by Muslims with horrible tortures.

For England, according to Davies (1996), the era of the Hundred Years' War was crucial in the formation of a national community. At the outset, Plantagenet England was a dynastic realm, which in cultural as well as political terms was little more than an outpost of French civilization. By the end, shorn of its continental possessions, Lancastrian England was an island kingdom secure in its separateness and confident in its newfound Englishness. With Geoffrey Chaucer (1340–1400),

English literature began its long career. Under Richard II (1367–c.1399) and the three Lancastrians – Henry IV (1367–1413), Henry V (r.1413–22), and Henry VI (r.1422–61) – the war in France provided a safety valve for energies left over from the violent struggles of monarchy and barons. Richard II was forced to abdicate, and later murdered at Pontefract. Henry IV, the usurper son of John of Gaunt, seized the throne with the aid of a false genealogy. Henry V was cut short in his endeavor to conquer France. Henry VI, another infant King, was eventually deposed. Within England the Island Britain, the Welsh formed the only community which could not be fully assimilated. In 1400–14, at the height of the French wars, they staged a promising rebellion with links to the King's other enemies in Northumbria, Ireland, Scotland and France. Under Owain ap Gruffydd, Lord of Glyndyvrdwy (c.1359–1416), who was known to the English as "Owen Glendower," they revived the vision of a liberated Wales, and briefly reconstituted an independent principality. In 1404–5 a sovereign Welsh parliament was summoned to Machynlleth. But within a decade the enterprise was crumbling. Its fate was sealed by the English victory at Agincourt, after which, the royal castles in Wales were recovered. Hence, although culturally and linguistically impervious, Wales was to form an integral part of the English realm. From 1450 onwards, England was laid low by a fratricidal war. An insane king and a disputed succession set the Lancastrians and Yorkists at each other's throats. The Wars of the Roses did not leave England free to benefit from growing prosperity until the rivalries of the three contenders – Edward IV (1442–1483), Richard III (1452–1485) and Henry VII (1457–1509) – was settled. Much of the fighting took place at St. Michael's Mount in Cornwall, and in Wales – at Denbigh, Harlech, Carreg, Cennen, and Pembroke, the birthplace of Henry Tudor, who eventually triumphed (Davies, 1996:425).

The British Civil War

The British Isles, increasingly dominated by the English, were taken closer to the unification which had beckoned once or twice already. Having lost its foothold on the continent, the Kingdom of England turned its energies into affairs of its immediate neighbors and into overseas ventures. A typical composite polity of the era, consisting of England, Wales, and Ireland, it lacked the national cohesion which Scotland already possessed. But under the Tudors, it manifested great vigor. Henry VIII (1509–48) and his three children – Edward VI (r.1548–53), Mary I (r.1553–8) and Elizabeth I (r.1558–1601) – created the Church of England, the lasting symbiosis of monarchy and Parliament and the Royal Navy. The Stuarts, who had ruled in Scotland since 1371, accepted the Personal Union of Scotland and England (1601), after the Tudors ran out of heirs. Mary's son James I of England and VI of Scotland (r.1586 (1601)–1625), succeeded by general consent to the inheritance that had escaped his mother. His son Charles I (r.1625–49), and his grandson Charles II (r.1649–(60)–85), ruled from Holyrood and from Whitehall in parallel. The integration of the dependent principalities did not proceed smoothly. Wales, which was shirred by Henry VIII, entered the community of English government without demur, as the Anglo-Welsh gentry were reasonably content with their lot. But, Ireland whose parliament had virtually broken free of English control since the Wars of the Roses, was only reined in with difficulty.

In 1534, the same year when both the Church of England and the counties of Wales came into being – Henry VIII declared himself "King of Ireland." The policy of turning Irish chiefs into Earls and Barons was little more than a palliative, especially when Irish customs and language were curtailed. Resentment against the Protestant reformation fueling a series of revolts. The Nine Years' War, 1592–1601, was waged round the Ulster rising of Hugh O'Neill, Earl of Tyrone. It closed amidst the devastating reprisals of Queen Elizabeth's lieutenant, Lord Mountjoy, who abolished Irish law and started a policy of systematic colonization. A prosperous decade of reconciliation in the 1630s, under the Earl of Strafford, was followed by a further insurrectionary decade in the 1640s, when the Irish profited from England's troubles to introduce religious toleration and an independent parliament. However, Ireland was brutally conquered by Cromwell in 1649–51, and effectively annexed. The new colony in Ulster was largely peopled by Scots Presbyterians, seeking the same sort of refuge offered by the English colonies across the Atlantic, in Virginia and New England. The foundation of Maryland (1632) was followed by Jamaica, which was seized from Spain in 1655, the Carolinas (1663), New York, formerly Dutch New Amsterdam (1664), and New Jersey (1665). The Navigation Act of 1651, insisted, among other things, that Dutch ships salute the English flag.

Scotland was the scene of bitter religious and political conflicts which eventually provoked the "British Civil wars" of the mid-seventeenth century. Knox's Presbyterian kirk had been founded on the Genevan model and was designed by its Calvinist founders as a theocracy. But a resentful court part repeatedly trimmed its aspirations. In 1572, the year of Knox's death, a regent forced the Kirk to accept bishops, thereby causing ceaseless strife between Church and state. In 1617, James VI imposed his five Articles, which insisted on a number of practices such as kneeling at communion. In 1637, Charles I, imposed a modified version of the Anglican liturgy and prayer book. When the liturgy was introduced at St. Giles' Cathedral in Edinburgh on July 23, 1637, it caused a riot. In due course, it led to the formation of "the Tables," a revolutionary committee of all estates, and in February 1638 to the signing of "the Covenant." Then recruited an armed league which was sworn to defend its statutes to the death. They sought to protect the Presbyterian kirk from the King and bishops and Scotland from the English. They claimed the allegiance of all true Scotsmen and set up a parliament without royal warrant. In August 1640, the first of several armies of Covenanters crossed the Tweed and invaded England. In this way, Scotland's religious wars became embroiled with the equally long-running constitutional struggle between King and Parliament in England. The winning of political initiative by the House of Commons under James I, put an end to Parliament's subservience and parliamentary control of taxation was to prove decisive. In 1629–40, when Charles I decided to rule without Parliament, no one had the means to oppose him. But, in April 1640, when the cost of the Scottish war forced the King to recall the English Parliament and to beg for money, the storm broke. Court talk about the divine right of kings was opposed by parliamentary lawyers quoting Magna Carta.

Bulked on all sides, Charles I attempted to arrest the contumacious members of the House of Commons but failed: "I see the birds have flown," he stuttered (Davies, 1996: 551). Defied by the parliament which he had not wished to summon, he abandoned the tradition of kings accepting the advice of their councils, and raised his standard at Nottingham, in the summer of 1642. The conflict was to cost him his life. The "English Civil War" is a misnomer which inadequately describes the nature of a very complex conflict. It did not start in England and was not confined to England. It embraced three separate civil wars in Scotland, Ireland, and England, and involved interrelated developments within all parts of the Stuart realm. The militancy of English parliamentarians was heightened by their knowledge of the King's despotic policies in Scotland and Ireland. Catholics and High Church Anglicans felt the greatest loyalty for the King, whose monarchical prerogatives were under attack. English puritans and Calvinist Scots provided the core support of Parliament, which they saw as a bulwark against absolutism. The gentry was split down the middle. There were several key issues on which neither Parliament nor the King was prepared to show any margin of tolerance. The "low-taxation philosophy" of the parliamentarians did not provide the means for the King to govern effectively. Also, the dominant English establishment was only interested in England, and careless of the separate interest of Ireland and Scotland. Above all, in religious matters, both sides were determined to persecute their opponents in the hope of imposing a single religion. The War "was not fought for religious liberty, but between rival groups of persecutors." Nor was the war free of horrors. Well-documented atrocities such as the general massacre at Bolton (June 1644) perpetrated by the troops of prince Rupert of the Rhine, or the fearful sack of Drogheda (1649), where Cromwell slaughtered the entire population of an Irish town, were accompanied by the less-publicized practices of killing prisoners and razing villages.

Four years of fighting saw large number of engagements involving both local and central forces. The royalists, with their Headquarters in Christ Church, Oxford, initially held the upper hand in most of the English counties. But the parliamentary forces, aided by the Scots' League of Covenanters, held an impregnable base in London, and hence the organs of central government. In due course, they were able to raise a professional New Model Army, whose creator, Oliver Cromwell (1599–1658), gradually assumed a commanding role in political, as well as military affairs. Parliament often controlled the towns and the King the countryside. Parliament reaped the benefits of superior organization, an invincible general, and Scots alliance. After initial clash at Edge Hill, on September 24, 1642, north of Oxford, the decisive battles were contested at Marston Moor, in Yorkshire, on July 2, 1644 and at Naseby, June 14, 1645. Once the King had surrendered to the Scots at Newark in 1646, all open resistance from the royalists ceased. As the fighting slowed, the political situation accelerated with revolutionary speed. But, unable to pin the King to a firm agreement, Cromwell decided on his execution, which was carried out in front of Whitehall Palace on January 31, 1649, thereby initiating the Commonwealth. Unable to control the Long Parliament Cromwell purged it. Unable to win over the Irish and Scots by persuasion, he invaded first Ireland then Scotland. His victory over the Scots at Worcester (1657) left him totally triumphant in the field. Yet, he could never engineer a political settlement to match his military triumphs. Unable to carry the Barebones Parliament of picked supporters, he dissolved it. The parliamentary cause was politically bankrupt, Cromwell ruled as Lord Protector through the colonels of eleven military districts. On his death, the royalist cause revived. There was no alternative to a return of the *status quo ante bellum.* Both King and Parliament had to be restored. Charles II returned from exile on July 29, 1660, on the terms of an Act of Indemnity and Oblivion. Both King and Parliament had to relearn the rules of watchful cohabitation. The British Civil Wars were symptomatic of strains which surrounded the growth of a modern state in numerous European countries. But they did not inspire any Continental emulators and must be judged a tragedy of essentially regional significance.

The Anglo-Spanish War

On August 3, 1553, Mary entered London in triumph as Queen of England and soon returned the country to Catholicism. Mary married Philip II of Spain on his father's, Charles V, abdication in 1556 and assumed the title of "Philip and Mary, by the Grace of God, King and Queen of England, Spain, France, Jerusalem, both the Scillies and Ireland, Defenders of the Faith, Archdukes of Austria, Dukes of Burgundy, Milan and Brabant, Counts of Habsburg, Flanders, and Tyrol." Mary also became "Queen of the Spanish East and West Indies and of the Islands and Mainland of the Ocean Sea." In England, Elizabeth Tudor cleared the way to become Queen, by signing the death warrant of her half-sister Mary on February 1, 1557, the daughter of Katherine of Aragon (1485–1536) and Henry VIII (1491–1547). Elizabeth Tudor (1533–1603) was crowned Queen at Westminster Abbey on Sunday, January 15, 1559 – the daughter of King Henry VIII and Anne Boleyn (1501–1536), who was beheaded on Tower Green on Friday, May 19, 1536, on what was widely seen as trump-up charges of treason, adultery, and incest with her brother George Boleyn (c.1503–1536), who was also executed. The Act of Supremacy and the Act of Uniformity made attendance at church compulsory for all and the 1552 Prayer Book in English was the only religious liturgy allowed in England and Wales. In the name of Elizabeth I, more than two hundred Catholics and their priests were executed during her forty-four-year reign – butchered on the scaffold as traitors to her Crown. This created a schism with Rome and aided an expensive nineteen-year war with Spain.

On February 25, 1570, Pope Pius V (1504–1572) signed the papal bull *Regnans in Excelsis,* which excommunicated Elizabeth I – "that servant of all iniquity." Pope Pius had instructed Elizabeth's Catholic subjects that to obey her or her laws would automatically invoke their excommunication – "utter separation from the unity of the body of Christ." Elizabeth I countered with the Second Treasons Act of 1570, which made it a crime to imagine, invent, devise, or intend the death or destruction, or any bodily harm to the queen, or to deprive or dispose her from the style, honor or kingly name of the imperial Crown of this realm.' It was also treasonous to claim that Elizabeth was a "heretic, schismatic, tyrant, infidel, or a usurper of the Crown." It was a criminal act to import papal bull or writings, instruments and other superstitious things from the See of Rome. According to Hutchinson (2013), in the spring of 1582, a plan was considered by Walsingham to transport recusants to a new colony in North America. The plan was seen as the ideal solution to many of Elizabeth's domestic and international problems. A patent under the Great Seal of England to colonize nine million acres (36,000km sq.) in Florida was granted. The fact that Florida was already claimed by Philip and was occupied by Spanish troops was beside the point. In August 1580, Lisbon was captured and Portugal annexed to Spain, which produced an important new maritime base in the Iberian Peninsula's Atlantic Coast and well-equipped fleet to augment existing Spanish sea power. (Hutchinson, 2013: 29). In January of 1586, Santa Cruz was ordered by Philip of Spain to produce estimates of the extent of forces necessary to successfully invade England. On March 12, 1586, Santa Cruz asked for one hundred and fifty-six ships plus 55,000 troops to land in England, supported by four hundred auxiliary vessels.

Santa Cruz estimated that invading England would cost four million ducats (about £3bn at 2013 prices). The Spanish Armada is claimed to have changed the course of European history. The Armada was a mix of religion, economics, and spurned love. Philip II of Spain was rejected by Elizabeth as a prospective husband, and she was viewed as a heretic illegitimate Queen. Hence, the Anglo-Spanish war of the 1580s was also a personal conflict between two monarchs who reviled each other but both were strapped for cash. On the July 29, 1588, the

Spanish Armada was sighted off Cornwall's Lizard Peninsula, and two days later, the first shots were fired, as Howard attacked the Spanish Armada. Much has been written about the Spanish Armada, and I do not intend to explore this period of history in any depth or then to highlight the fact that many enslaved Africans were involved in the Spanish Armada. It is known that Moncada's flagship, the *San Lorenzo,* had some four hundred and fifty enslaved Africans on board, many of whom were oarsmen, about fifty of whom were slain in fighting, near Calais. By August 10, 1588, the Armada's crews began to return to Spain, having suffered a resounding naval defeat. By the end of August 1588, Elizabeth I had ordered the disbandment of her army, and Parma had stood down his invasion fleet. On September 13, 1598, King Philip died near Madrid, aged 71, after reigning as King of Spain for 42 years, 240 days. Elizabeth I died on March 24, 1603, at Richmond Palace, aged 69, after reigning for 45 years, 127 days. On August 28, 1604, James I of England ratified the Treaty of London, ending the 19-year Anglo-Spanish war, which was to signal a new era in European relationships. At the start of the seventeenth century, Spanish control of the Caribbean was still intact, although under regular attack by French and English pirates and privateers.

Columbus' New World

Portugal was the pioneer of European overseas expansion, founding its first colonies in the fifteenth century. Thousands of Portuguese migrated to colonies in Africa, South America, and Asia. Portuguese maritime expansion was initiated by Prince Henry the Navigator (1394–1460) in 1418, in order to find new trade routes, which could end Muslim control of trade with Asia and to strengthen Christendom by converting pagan peoples to Christianity. The first maritime discoveries were Madeira (1419) and the Azores (1427). In 1456, the Cape Verde Islands were discovered and colonized. The Cape Verdes are an arrow-shaped archipelago of ten islands, five islets and various rocks and stacks that poke out of the eastern Atlantic on a band of latitude that runs between Senegal in the east and the Caribbean, 3,600km to the west. They stretch between 14 and 18 degrees north, 22 and 26 degrees west. The Canaries, off Morocco, are over 1,000km away, while the Azores, parallel with Portugal, are about 2,500km away. The islands are widely spaced, with the most easterly 460km from Senegal and the most westerly 830km. the largest island is 990km sq., with the smallest 35km sq. The total land area is 4,033km sq., scattered over 58,000km sq., of ocean. Several famous mariners claimed to have discovered Cape Verde in the 1450s and 1460s, such as the Venetia, Cada Mosto (1432–1488) in 1456, or the Genoese Antonio de Noli (b.1415), who may have stumbled on them in 1455 or 1461. But, whatever the truth, all the islands were discovered between 1455 and 1461 (Irwin and Wilson, 2009:6). The Portuguese begun to colonize the islands in 1462, with Spanish and Genoese settlers on the island of Santiago. The Portuguese gave settlers exclusive trading rights along the creeks and shores of the West African coast between Senegal and Sierra Leone.

Genoese merchants dominated Mediterranean commerce and a number of popes had their origin in Genoa, including Nicholas V (1397–1455), Sixtus IV (1414–1484), and Innocent VIII (1432–1492). Many Genoese merchants traded in African gold, sugar, silk, olive oil and dyes, soap, wheat, and wool. Others sold slaves and founded settlements on Cape Verde Islands. Many Genoese traded slaves in the Crimea, Chios, Tunis, Centa, Malaga, and Granada, men, women and children of all hues and races. Cristoforo Colombo (c.1451–1506), or Cristobal Colon, to use his Spanish name, was a serious Christian sailor, who preferred not to work on Sundays. Although there is uncertainty about his birth, it is widely accepted that he was from Genoa. Columbus, as he is known in the English-speaking world, first maritime exploit was in 1472, when he was 21, he was involved in the capturing of a ship belonging to merchants from Barcelona. Columbus sailed to Chios, in the Aegean, an island port concerned with the sale of Atlantic sugar and slaves. He also sailed to Lisbon in 1476 and to Ireland the following year. In 1478, Columbus was employed selling sugar in Madeira, where there was a sugar mill since 1452, Madeira being the Portuguese for wood and the Azores mean "the hawks." By 1470, the pursuit of African slaves had come to be an important part of these adventures off the west coast of Africa, as well as a way of attacking Islam from its rear. Columbus read, as well as traveled, and certainly examined Polo del Pozzo Toscanelli's (1397–1482) summary of information and his memoir. Polo del Pozzo Toscanelli, a Florentine astronomer, mathematician, and cosmographer, wrote in a letter of 1474, to a Portuguese cannon, Fernao Martius, one of King Alfonso V's chaplains, that a western route to China was possible. Toscanelli added, in another letter, that the Emperor of China thought that this western route from Europe to his country might be about 3,900 nautical miles, but that he himself considered that a sensible figure might be 6,500 miles.

Toscanelli was the decisive influence on Columbus, who mentions him again and again in his letters, although Toscanelli was wrong in his estimate of the distance from the Canary Islands to Japan. In 1484, Columbus put a scheme of sailing west to Cipanyu (Japan) and China to King Joao (1455–1495) of Portugal, who had devoted more attention than any other monarch to the idea of discovery. Indeed, Portuguese explorers had already discovered sophisticated principalities, such as Benin and observed colossal African rivers, such as the Senegal, the Gambia, the Niger, and the Congo. Columbus' scheme was put to a committee in Lisbon (*the Junta dos Matematicos*) who rejected Columbus' scheme, saying that no expedition could be fitted out with food and water to travel across so enormous an expanse of sea. Rebuffed in Portugal, Columbus decided to approach the monarchs in Spain, which he had not previously visited. The Portuguese accepted Castilian control of the Canary Islands by the Treaty of Alcacovas in 1479, as well as the modern territory of Sahara. In return, Castile accepted the Portuguese possession of the Azores and Madeira, and her monopoly of the trade with the rest of West Africa. Those "Canarians" are mysterious, were they Berber, African, or even European in origin? No one can say for sure, or even what they looked like. But, numerous Canary Islanders had been kidnapped since the 1450s and sold as slaves in Andalusia. Columbus arrived in Huelva in the second half of 1485 and made his way to the Franciscan monastery of La Rabida, which was a kind of maritime university. The first discussion between Columbus and the monarch on January 20, 1486, in the Cardinal's palace did not prosper, as Columbus may have under-estimated the royal preoccupations with the war against Granada. The Catholic King's relations with the Republic of Genoa were also at the time poor (Thomas, 2003: 71). The committee of inquiry met during the winter of 1486–7, in Salamanca and its conclusions were negative, as those of the similar body in Lisbon. They thought that Columbus' claim about the distance of China and the ease of travel there could not be true. This bad news was communicated to Columbus in August 1487. The committee concluded that they did not exclude the possibility that one day, when the Crown's war with Granada was won, their judgment might be reconsidered.

Early in 1488, King Joao sent Columbus a safe conduct to Lisbon. But back in Lisbon by October 1488, Columbus was once again thwarted, as King Joao had half-changed his mind about the value of an Atlantic route to China. Failing yet again to find the backing which he needed, Columbus contemplated an approach to the King of France and England. On January 1, 1492, Gutierre de Cardenas, escorted by Almulih and Ibn Kumasha, rode into the palace of Alhambra, to accept the surrender of the last Muslim city of Western Europe. The fall of Granada was an event which was celebrated throughout Europe, and in Rome, it seemed almost to make up for the loss of Constantinople in 1480, when 12,000 of the inhabitants were allegedly put to death by Muslims with horrible tortures. In early April 1492, a court constable was sent to fetch Columbus. In Santa Fe, the monarch, Isabel, received Columbus and instructed Juan de Coloma to draw up warrants by which Columbus was charged to carry out the discoveries which he had always desired. According to Hugh Thomas (2003), the King and Queen of Aragon and Castile founded the Spanish Empire in the Americas when, on April 17, 1492, at Santa Fe, they committed themselves to support the expedition of Columbus. The document had five items, which were, (1) Columbus was named "Admiral of the Ocean Sea" and any islands and mainlands, which he had already discovered; (2) Columbus would be named "Don"; (3) Columbus would have a right to a tenth of everything found in the new territories; (4) On all ships taking part in commerce with those new territories, Columbus would be able to load an eight of all goods; and (5) Columbus would be informed of any lawsuit which might take place as a result of commerce, in or to those territories. The expedition planned by Columbus would not cost much; only two million maravedis in all. But Columbus' two million were raised in a roundabout way (Thomas, 2003: 85). For example, two senior treasurers of Aragon (Santangel) and Castile (Pinelo) respectively, a *converso* and a Genoese, would raise 1.1 million maravedis, from profits from the sale of indulgences in the province of Extremadura.

The port of Palos, on the Rio Tinto, north of Huelva, owed the Crown the service of two ships for a year. It was agreed that Palos should settle this debt, which had been assumed by the Crown of Castile, by providing two ships to serve with Columbus. The rest of the sum required for the journey was raised by Columbus himself. Columbus was given the title of "Admiral, Viceroy, and Governor," in a document of April 30, 1492. The town of Palos provided Columbus with two ships, the Pinta *(painted lady)* and the Nina *(girl)*. They were each about 70ft long by 25ft wide and 11ft in depth and both had three masts. The Pinta belonged to Gomez Racou, a *converso* family and Cristobal Quintero, a seafaring family of Palos. The Nina was owned by Juan Nino, after whom it was named. These two ships would be captained by two brothers. A third ship was hired by Columbus himself, the *Santa Maria*, also known as the *Maria Galante*, which was about 100 tons, with a round hull, built in Galicia and was hired from Juan de la Cosa. Having found his ships, Columbus went ahead to seek crews and was helped by the Pinzons who founded most of the eighty or so men who sailed. The majority of the crews came from Moguer and Huelva, as well as Palos, but there were also a few from Seville. There was a few *converso,* Torre Luis and Juna de Penalosa. But no priest sailed on this voyage. Columbus voyage of discovery started "half an hour before sunrise" on August 3, 1492. Twenty-six men were on the Pinta, twenty-four on the Nina, and forty on the Santa Maria. Experienced crews were paid 1,000 maravedis per month and 600 if they were novices. But, none were to be paid before 1513. There provisions included salted cod, bacon, and biscuits. They also had flour, wine, olive oil, and water enough for a year.

Columbus' journey between August and October 1492 began with a week's sail from the Rio Tinto to the Gran Canary, where he remained with his three ships for almost a month. Columbus and his three ships finally left La Gomera on September 6, 1492, after praying at its large new parish church, San Sebastian. The trade wind *(las brisas)* filled his sails. The Nina was captained by Vicente Yanez, while his brother, Martin Alonso Pinzon, captained the Pinta. On October 10, 1492, Columbus announced that he would give a coat of silk to the man who first saw land. Two hours after midnight, with a full moon, Juan Rodrquez Berinejo, a sailor from Seville, on the Pinta, saw "a white stretch of land" and shouted, "Land! Land!" The next day, October 12, 1492, Columbus made landfall, on what is now known as Watling Island, known to its inhabitants as Guanahani, but in the tradition of all Europeans, going back to the Greeks, Columbus renamed it "San Salvador." He saw inhabitants whom he called "Indians." These inhabitants of the Bahamas were later wiped out by contact with Spaniards. Columbus took possession of San Salvador in the names of the King and Queen of Spain and raised the flag of those monarchs: a green cross with an F and a Y crowned on a white background. Mistaking the Bahamas for Asia, from this moment on, the peoples who inhabited the Caribbean archipelago were to be known generically and erroneously, as "Indians" and the region as the Indies, or more recently, the West Indies. Columbus stopped at several other islands, in what is now the Bahamian archipelago, including Santa Maria de la Concepcion. But these islands all had indigenous names already. Columbus received presents of cotton and in return he gave his usual glass beads and trinkets. On October 24, 1492, Columbus left what he thought would turn out to be Cipangu (Japan) for a larger island that he called Colba (Cuba). When Columbus reached Cuba on October 28, 1492, he decided that it must be part of the Asiatic mainland, and called it Juana, which he thought resembled Sicily. He found dogs, which did not bark and good houses with palm roofs. He also observed silver ornaments hanging from the noses of the indigenous people. On November 12, 1492, Columbus set sail for what turned out to be Inagua Grande, then sailed west before returning to Cuba, where they spent another two weeks, kidnapping a few more natives to take back to Spain.

Columbus left Cuba on December 5, 1492, for an island the indigenous people called "Haiti" and which Columbus called "Little Spain" (*La Espanola*), although he believed Haiti to be Cipangu (Japan). On Christmas Eve 1492, the largest of Columbus' ships, the Santa Maria, was wrecked on a coral reef off the northern shore of Haiti, which left Columbus with only one ship, the Nina, as the captain of the Pinta had sailed off on November 21, 1492, without leave. On the December 26, 1492, the word *Caribe* or *cannibal* first entered Columbus' log (Thomas, 2003: 110). Faced with the impossibility of carrying all his men back to Spain in one small boat, Columbus founded a settlement, which he called "*La Navidad*." Thirty-nine men would remain there collecting gold and await the next expedition from Spain. In early January, 1493, Columbus left his first European settlement in the Americas in the hands of Diego de Arana (1468–1493), along with a doctor. Sailing east along the north coast of Haiti, on the Nina with 15 men, Columbus encountered the errant Alonso Pinzon (c.1441–1493) and the Pinta, just inside what is now the Dominican Republic. On January 13, 1493, when the now reunited expedition of the Pinta and the Nina reached a peninsula off Haiti, they had their first armed clash with indigenous people in the New World. The resistance convinced Columbus that these were those Caribs who eat men. Thus, for the next generation, any indigenous people who resisted the Spaniards would be considered a cannibal, fit to be enslaved. In February 1493, the Nina sailed into the harbor of Santa Maria, in the Azores, but the Pinta, with Pinzon, had once again disappeared. After some difficulties with the Portuguese authority, Columbus left the Azores on February 20 and sailed into Lisbon on March 4, 1493.

On his return to Spain, Columbus sailed first to Palos and then to Seville and then made his way to Barcelona, via Cordoba, Murcia, Valencia and Tarragona. He had seven of his Indians still alive to exhibit in Barcelona. The captain of the Pinta arrived in Spain, at Baiona in Galicia, near Vigo, a few days before Columbus reached Seville. Pinzon disputed Columbus' story and wrote to the monarchs that he had discovered what he knew to be mainland China, as well as islands. But, Pinzon died as soon as he reached Seville (Thomas, 2003: 118). On September 24, 1493, Columbus set sail from Cadiz, with a fleet of two naos (three/four masts, ocean-going ship) and 15 caravels. The naos was the flagship *Marigalante* and *Gallega.* On November 3, 1493, Christopher Columbus landed on a rugged shore on an island that he named Dominica. He also landed at Marie-Galante, which he named Santa Maria la Galante. He sighted and named many islands, including Montserrat, Antigua, Saint Martin, and Santa Cruz. He also sighted and named the Virgin Islands, and present-day Puerto Rico, on November 19, 1493. He returned to Hispaniola, where he found his men at La Navidad had fallen into dispute with natives in the interior and had been killed. He left Hispaniola on April 24, 1494 and arrived at the island of Cuba, which he had discovered and named during his first voyage, which he believed to be a peninsula off China rather than an island. In the spring of 1496, Columbus returned to Spain, principally to refute growing accusations of incompetence and corruption which were being levelled against him by opponents at court. The Spanish monarchs were clearly less than happy about the modest riches which had so far materialized from Columbus' enterprise. But, Ferdinand and Isabella were prepared to entrust a further expedition to Columbus, who continued to insist that in Cuba he had discovered the China of the legendary Great Khan. Finally, on May 30, 1498, Columbus had gathered enough finance to undertake a third voyage. Columbus' third expedition was in part comprised of convicts whose death sentences or imprisonment were commuted and replaced by a one-way passage to the colonies. Some white slaves, particularly women, were also brought to the islands with the intention of providing non-Taino wives for the colonists.

Hence, the first slaves brought to the Caribbean thus arrived from Spain and were Christians, who were mainly enslaved Africans or their descendants who had been captured on the west coast of Africa by Portuguese slave-traders and then brought to Spain. This trade had been in existence since the 1450s, and it has been estimated that a hundred shiploads of slaves arrived each year in the port of Seville. Early colonists sometimes arrived with slaves, used as servants or companions. Half of the fleet of six ships sailed directly to Hispaniola; the other three, under Columbus's command, set sail for the Portuguese-owned Cape Verde Islands and then sailed across to the mainland of South America. He explored the Gulf of Paria, which separates Trinidad from mainland Venezuela, Tobago, and Grenada. During Columbus' term as Viceroy and Governor of the Indies, he had been accused of governing tyrannically and as a result, he was placed in chains and removed from his post on October 1, 1500, along with his two brothers and sent back to Spain. Columbus and his brothers were jailed for six weeks in Spain, before King Ferdinand and Queen Isabella ordered their released. They were pardoned by both the King and Queen, who restored their freedom and wealth and agreed to fund Columbus' fourth voyage. But, he was not reappointed as governor of the Indies and as an added insult, the Portuguese, Vasco da Gama, won the race to the east, when he returned in September 1499 from a trip to India, having sailed east around Africa.

Columbus left Cadiz on May 12, 1502 and arrived at Santo Domingo on June 29, 1502. After a brief stop at Jamaica, he sailed to Central America, arriving at Guanaja, off the coast of Honduras on July 30, 1502. He spent two months exploring the coasts of Honduras, Nicaragua, and Costa Rica, before arriving in Panama on October 6, 1502. Columbus was to visit Jamaica again, in May 1503, on his way back from the American mainland, when it became clear that his two battered, worm-eaten caravels *Capitana* and *Santiago* were in no state for an Atlantic crossing. He tried to sail for Hispaniola but, battered by a storm off the west end of Cuba, ran for Jamaica instead, reaching Discovery Bay on June 23, 1503. Columbus and his crew, including his sons Ferdinand and Bartholomew, and his brother, watched his vessels fill with water and sank in the soft sand of the bay. The Indians proved friendly and gave them fresh supplies of food each day in exchange for cheap ornaments and trade goods. Eventually, two volunteers, Diego Mendez and Bartolome Fieschi, made the hard and dangerous journey to Hispaniola. However, it was over a year before Columbus knew for certain that they had made it. Meanwhile, at St. Ann's Bay, sickness broke out among the ships' company and discontent grew and turned to mutiny. The mutineers were led by the brothers Francisco and Diego Porras, seized ten dugout canoes together with all the provisions on hand, set off eastward along the coast intending to attempt the crossing to Hispaniola. They ran into bad weather soon after they started and decided to lighten their canoes by throwing their Indian paddlers overboard and chopping off their hands when they attempted to cling to the sides of their boats.

Forced back to land the mutineers ran riot through the island. Knowing from a book on astronomy he had with him that there would soon be an eclipse of the moon, Columbus decided to play on the fears of the Indians. Calling them together he told them that the God he served was angry with them for stopping the supply of food and intended to punish them severely, as a proof of which the moon they loved so much would soon be turned to blood. On the night predicted, February 29, 1504, the moon went into eclipse and the Indians were terrified and with loud cries of distress begged Columbus to plead with his God on their behalf. Columbus deceit against the Indians had succeeded and from then on, the food supply never failed. However, the governor of Hispaniola, Don Nicolas de Ovando, hated

Columbus and made no effort to provide Diego Mendez with a rescue ship, but he did send a small caravel to St. Ann's Bay to spy out the position and report back to him. The caravel spent less than a day off the shore of St. Ann's Bay, then sail away, leaving behind a slab of salt pork and a cask of wine, which proved to Columbus that Diego Mendez and Bartolome Fieschi had reached Hispaniola. Columbus and his stranded crew were eventually rescued toward the end of June 1504. Columbus sailed for Spain in September 1504 and was never to see the New World again. He died at Valladolid, Spain on May 20, 1506 and in accordance with his wish his remains were taken from Spain to Hispaniola in 1542 and placed in a vault in the Cathedral of Santo Domingo, which is said to contain Columbus' bones.

The Caribbean

Stretching from the coast of South America up to the tip of Florida, an arc of islands follows its curved course through the Atlantic Ocean, listing and dividing into two off the northwest coast of Haiti, a northerly chain heading off to the Florida Straits. To the north and east the islands look out to the broad expanse of the Atlantic, their coastlines battered and eroded by tireless wind and waves. To the south and west they encircle the more placid Caribbean Sea, bounded by the mainland, which runs down from Mexico to Guyana. This fragmented mix of land and sea makes up what we know as the Caribbean. The Caribbean comprises at least 7,000 islands and Cays (low insular banks or reefs of sand) and a region of extraordinary diversity. There are volcanic islands, which rise steeply out of the sea, their mountainsides covered with dense forest and scarred by fast-running rivers. There are also coral limestone islands, flat, featureless, and dry, where only cactus and scrub resist the heat. Individual islands can contain a surprising range of microclimates. The Caribbean contains high mountains and pine forests, volcanic lakes and salt ponds, marshes and coastal wetlands. It is argued (Ferguson, 1999) that the geological formation of the present-day archipelago began to take place some seventy million years ago, when pressures in the earth's crust forced up vast areas of rock from the seabed. This process created the fertile islands of Hispaniola, Jamaica and Puerto Rico, whose mountains follow in a chain from those of Mexico and Central America to the west.

Southern Cuba also belongs to this geological structure, but its northern part has more in common with Bahamas, an arc of low-lying coral limestone islands. Volcanic activity on the larger islands, known collectively as the Greater Antilles, ceased millions of years ago, but on the islands of the Lesser Antilles, which stretch down from the Virgin Island to Grenada, violent eruptions are not uncommon and this part of the region remains geologically volatile. There are also many natural features throughout the Lesser Antilles, including hot springs, boiling lake and several *Soufriere* or volcanic vents with their distinctive sulfurous odor. The Eastern Caribbean island chain consists of two separate chains, one volcanic and the other limestone. The volcanic chain runs down from Saba to Grenada. To the east, runs a line of flatter islands, encompassing Anguilla, Antigua, Barbuda, and Barbados, while the western half is unmistakably volcanic. The limestone arc can be traced upwards to meet the Bahamas archipelago, made up of some 2,700 islets and cays, which sit in the shallow seas of the Bahamian Platform. Their golden beaches, made of powered coral, are more akin to those celebrated in tourist brochures than the mostly black sand of the volcanic islands. All the Caribbean islands, apart from Trinidad, are defined as oceanic rather than continental, never having been attached to the mainland, which explains the absence of large animal life. Trinidad lying only seven miles off the coast of Venezuela, was until recently joined to the South American continent. When the ice age ended and sea level rose it became separated from the mainland, but its rich animal life is still that of the mainland. Apart from the northern tip of the Bahamas, all the Caribbean islands have a tropical climate and vegetation, with the prevailing trade wind coming from the northeast nearly all year round, with heavier rainfall to the north and east of the mountainous islands and the low-lying receiving less rainfall.

All the islands and their peoples live in fear of the hurricane season, which normally lasts from August until November, with September the most active month. Hurricanes rise in the Atlantic, where the trade winds from both hemispheres meets and gather strength around an updraught of warm air which begins to gather speed as it moves across the ocean. By the time hurricanes reach the Caribbean, they can move at 200km per hour with bursts of almost 300km per hour. The earliest known inhabitants of what is now known as the Caribbean were the Siboneys, who migrated from Florida and spread throughout the Bahamas and the major islands. They were hunters and gatherers, living on fish and other seafood, small rodents, iguanas, snakes and birds. They also gathered roots and wild fruits, but they did not cultivate plants. They worked with primitive tools made out of stone, shell, bone, or wood. The Siboneys were eventually absorbed by the advancing Arawaks from the south. The people known as Arawaks migrated from the Guianas to Trinidad and on through the island arc of Cuba. Their population expanded due to the fertility of the islands, their agricultural skills in cultivating and improving wild plants, the abundance of fruit and seafood, and their boat-building and fishing skills. They were healthy, tall and lived to a ripe old age. Arawak society was essentially communal and organized around families, but each village had a headman, called a *cacique*, whose duty it was to represent the village when dealing with other tribes, to settle family disputes and organize defense. The division of labor was usually based on age and sex. The men would clear and prepare the land for agriculture and be responsible for defense of the village, while women cultivate the crops, make mats, baskets, bowls and fishing nets. Women were in charge of raising the children, especially the girls, while the men taught the boys traditional customs, skills and rites. The inhabitants of the Bahamas were generally referred to as Lucayans and those of the Greater Antilles as Tainos, but there were many sub-groupings. The inhabitants of the Lesser Antilles were referred to as Carib and were described to Columbus as an aggressive tribe, who sacrificed and sometimes ate the prisoners they captured in battle.

Archaeological evidence suggests that the first people to inhabit the region arrived around 500 BCE, reaching the Bahamas and the larger islands of the Greater Antilles, who established small settlements along the shore where they lived from fishing and hunting. Remains of the largest known settlement, numbering about a hundred people, have been discovered in Cuba. Another group of people who traveled up the islands from the mouth of the Orinoco River, stopping first in nearby Trinidad and moving up to Grenada and northwards, about the same time as the Ciboney, were the Tainos (men of the good), who have been called Arawaks by some historians. The Taino-Awarak people can be divided into three main sub-groupings of which two were offshoots from the main basic group: the Tainos themselves, who inhabited Jamaica, Hispaniola, and Cuba; the Lucayans, who settled on the Bahamas; and the Borequinos, who lived in Puerto Rico. The Tainos had formidable canoes, which they made from a single huge tree trunk, measuring as much as 25 meters and capable of carrying fifty people. Using these canoes, they moved in successive waves from the South American mainland up as far as Cuba and the Bahamas. This process took hundreds of years as discovery followed discovery. Eventually, the Tainos came to replace earlier societies such as the Ciboneys. Unlike the Ciboneys, the Tainos were skilled farmers who brought with them certain plants such as guava and animals like the agouti. Their staple food was cassava or manioc, which provided the flour for their baking after the poisonous juice had been extracted. Other basic crops were sweet potato, beans, and peanuts. The Tainos also grew and smoked tobacco in the form of cigars. They hunted small animals and birds, which they grilled on *barbecues* (one of the Taino-Arawak words to have survived into present day usage.

By 1000 CE, a devastating threat to Taino culture emerged from the same South American jungle, which had earlier sheltered the Tainos themselves. The threat came in the shape of the Caribs, another Amazon-originating people who had followed the Tainos into the Orinoco delta and began to pursue them up the island chain. The word Carib was a European invention and quickly became synonymous with savagery and man-eating, the term cannibal being derived from their name. However, these so-called Caribs called themselves Kalinas or Kalinago. The earliest European explorers and colonists learned from the Tainos that fierce tribes of warriors lived on the smaller islands of the Lesser Antilles and they attacked Tainos' communities and allegedly ate their victims. In reality, in the five centuries, which preceded the arrival of Europeans, the Caribs had followed in the tracks of the Tainos from South America into the islands. In the course of this migration, the Caribs raided and pillaged every Tainos settlement that they came across. The Caribs raiding parties, armed with spears and bows and arrows killed all Tiano men and took away all women. Carib society revolved around war and prized feats of heroism above all else. The Caribs did not eat human flesh as food but as a means of taking possession of their dead enemies' qualities. Never the less, the Caribs defeated and replaced the Tainos in every territory from Trinidad to Puerto Rico and were undisputed masters of all the Lesser Antilles and were on the verge of conquering the islands of the Greater Antilles, by the time the Europeans arrived in the Caribbean. The Caribbean bears the name of the Caribs. These people, through their determined resistance to European colonization survived much longer than the other main pre-Columbian population. Yet, the word "*Carib*" became stigmatized with connotations of barbarism, becoming etymologically mixed with the word "cannibal," demonized as a man-eating savage, the prototype for Shakespeare's Caliban, the wretched and subhuman slave of Prospero in *The Tempest*. This was part of the process of European colonization of the indigenous peoples of the Caribbean and justifying the armed seizure of their territories in the name of civilization.

European Expansion and Colonization

Europeans overseas, according to Davies (1996), did not start with Columbus in the Caribbean. One experiment, in the crusader kingdom of the Holy Land, was already ancient history. Another, in the Canaries, had been in progress for seventy years. The Portuguese began buying enslaved Africans from Sierra Leone to work on new sugar plantations on the Cape Verde Islands. Cape Verde was an expensive market for slave merchants, as the alternative was to visit the African coast, where ships were often delayed and payment to tribal leaders complicated. The African coast was rife with disease and rivers and creeks were difficult to navigate. There were other advantages to be gained from buying slaves in Cape Verde. The slaves were healthy and obedient and some had also learned a little Portuguese, so they could understand orders, and they had been baptized. The Church argued that a baptized enslaved African was luckier than a free African, because the former had achieved the chance of a place in heaven. Irwin and Wilson (2003) argue that thousands of those enslaved were Fula, from the Mandingo Empire of Mali. Its people were warriors and their battles generated many of those who were later sold into slavery and were then traded on the African coast. In the Caribbean, the slave economy was in its infancy during the period of Spanish dominance, but even the limited presence of enslaved African labor soon began to create serious problems in the colonies. Governor Ovanddo of Hispaniola asked the Spanish authorities to cease the transportation of enslaved Africans, since many of them fled into the mountains and joined forces with rebel Tainos. The first recorded slave revolt in the Caribbean took place in 1522 on the sugar plantation of Diego Columbus near Santo Domingo. Enslaved Africans also revolted in Puerto Rico in 1527 and in Cuba in 1538.

By the middle of the sixteenth century, enslaved Africans outnumbered Spanish and Creoles by five to one in Hispaniola. A significant number of enslaved Africans successfully escaped and formed free communities and were known as *cimarrones,* a name previously applied to the wild cattle of Hispaniola. The impenetrable mountains of Hispaniola and Jamaica allowed groups of enslaved Africans to escape and live free from fear of recapture and to organize armed bands, which led to colonial authorities in 1545, in Hispaniola, offering to make peace with the *cimarrones*, if they would cease their raids. The Spanish monopoly of the Americas, endorsed by Pope Alexander V1 (1431–1503), born Rodrigo de Borja, was Pope from August 11, 1492 to August 18, 1503, acknowledged fathering several illegitimate children, was an affront to those nations, which were rejecting papal authority and asserting their own identity and economic aspirations, including Henry VIII of England and Francis I of France. Pirates and Privateers became agents of national rival governments determined to challenge Spain's claim to the Americas. England's number one privateer was John Hawkins (1532–95), a smuggler and slave trader who eventually became treasurer to the navy. John Hawkins was the first recorded Englishman to be directly involved in the trafficking of enslaved African, sailing to Guinea in 1562, in defiance of the Portuguese monopoly and delivering 300 enslaved Africans to the north coast of Hispaniola. Receiving payment in silver, sugar and hides, Hawkins return to Plymouth with a healthy profit, which herald the start of the British "triangular trade" (the name given to the trafficking of enslaved Africans from Africa to the Caribbean and commodities from the Caribbean to Europe and manufactured goods to Africa, in exchange for more enslaved Africans). Many investors were encouraged by Hawkins' profitable trafficking in enslaved Africans and were eager to invest in his company. However, Hawkins' fourth trafficking expedition ended in disaster, when bad weather forced him to seek shelter at San Juan de Ulua, close to Vera Cruz, were a Spanish *flota* trapped him in a one-sided battle, from which only him and his cousin Francis Drake (1540–1596) and a handful of others were able to escape.

Once contact had been made with distant islands, Europeans sailed overseas in ever-increasing numbers. They sailed for reason of trade, of loot, of conquest and increasingly of religion. It was acknowledged that inhabitants of these conquered lands were human beings. To confirm the point, Pope Paul III (1468–1549) decreed in 1537 that "all Indians are truly men, not only capable of understanding the Catholic faith but...exceedingly desirous to receive it." The existence of a vast fourth continent in the west was gradually established by trial and errors, sometime in the 20 years after Columbus' first return to Palos. Giovanni Caboto [John Cabot], another Genoese, sailed from Bristol aboard the *Matthew* in May 1497 under license from Henry VII; he landed on Cape Bretou Island, which he took to be part of China. The Florentine Amerigo Vespucci (1451–1512), made three or four transatlantic voyages between 1497 and 1504. He obtained the post of *"piloto mayor"* [Chief Pilot] of Spain. It was this fact which determined that the fourth continent should be named after him. Vasco Nunez de Balbao (1475–1519), walked across the Isthmus of Panama and sighted the Pacific. In 1519–22, a Spanish expedition led by the Portuguese captain Ferdinand Magellan (1480–1521) circumnavigated the world, which proved beyond doubt that the earth was round, that the Pacific and Atlantic were separate oceans and that the Americas lay between them.

The presence of a fifth continent in the antipodes was not suspected for another century. In 1605, a Spanish ship out of Peru and a Dutch ship out of Java both sailed to the Gulf of Carpentaria. The main outlines of the great Zuidland or "Southland" (Australia and New Zealand) were charted by the Dutch navigator Abel Tasman (1603–59) in 1642–3. The Portuguese were quickest to exploit the commercial opportunities of the new lands. They claimed Brazil in 1500, Mauritius in 1505, Sumatra in 1509, Malacca and the "Spice Islands" (Indonesia) in 1511. The Spanish did not hesitate to apply their military might. Lured by the dream of El Dorado the *Conquistadores,* who had so recently subdued Iberia, now turned their energies to the conquest of America. They settled Cuba in 1511 and used it as a base for further campaigns. In 1519–20 Hernando Cortez (1485–1547) seized the Aztec empire in Mexico in a sea of blood. In the 1520s and 1530s, permanent settlements were established in Costa Rica, Honduras, Guatemala, and New Granada (Colombia and Venezuela). From 1532, Francisco Pizarro (1476–1541) seized the empire of the Incas in Peru. European colonization in North America began in 1536, with the founding of Montreal in Canada, by the Breton sailor, Jacques Cartier (1491–1557), and in 1556 of Saint Augustine in Florida by Pedro Menendez (1519–1574), who had just destroyed a nearby Huguenot settlement, in the future South Carolina, where he hanged America's first religious exiles "as Lutherans." Three years later, the Huguenots' compatriot, Dominique de Gourgues (1530–1593), arrived on the same spot and hanged the Spanish garrison "as robbers and murders." The Dutch and English were relative late comers to colonization, but in the late sixteenth century they both strove to reap its benefits.

Having founded Batavia in Java in 1597, the Dutch began to wrest the East Indies from Portuguese. The English colony of Virginia, invaded in 1598, received its first successful settlement at Jamestown in 1607. The Mayflower, carrying 120 puritans and their families, landed in Massachusetts Bay on December 11, 1620. Although refugees from religious persecution in England, they were no more tolerant than their persecutors. The colony of Rhode Island (1636) was founded by dissenters expelled from Massachusetts. By that time the existence of a worldwide network of European colonies and their seaborne lines of communication, was an established fact. Europe's colonies and overseas possessions continued to multiply after 1650, and in some cases reached independent viability. Spain and Portugal had their hands full, exploiting their possessions. In North America, the Spanish pressed inland from New Spain (Mexico) to California, Arizona, and Colorado. In South America, aided by systematic Jesuit settlements, they concentrated their efforts on Venezuela, New Granada (Bogota), Peru, Paraguay, and La Plata (Cordoba). They attempted to keep all trade to their own ships, until forced by the Asiento Treaty of 1713, to admit foreigners. The Portuguese survived a long campaign by the Dutch to take over the Brazilian coast. After the treaty of 1662, they moved south from san Paulo to the River Plate (1680) and westwards into the gold rich interior at Minas Gerais (1693) and the Mato Grosso. Apart from the East Indies, the Dutch were left with colonies in Guyana and Curacao. But, most new colonial enterprises were started by the French and the British. France launched the *Compaignie des Indes* in 1664, establishing stations on the east coast of India at Pondicherry and Karaikal, with staging posts on the islands of Madagascar and Reunion.

In 1682, Louisiana was founded on the Mississippi in honor of Louis XIV (1638–1715), known as Louis the Great or the Sun King, with its capital at New Orleans (1718). England consolidated its American colonies with the foundation of Delaware (1682), the Quaker colony of Pennsylvania (1683), and Georgia (1733). In India, the East India Company, which now held Bombay and Calcutta as well as Madras, was hard-pressed by French competition, as commercial interests went hand in hand with maritime discovery. In 1766–8, the French admiral Louis Antoine de Bougainville (1729–1811) circumnavigated the globe, as did the three expeditions of Captain James Cook (1728–1779), between 1768 and 1779. In these circumstances, Franco-British colonial conflict became almost inevitable. These conflicts were settled by superior British naval power. Britain took Newfoundland in 1713, French India in 1757, and French Canada in 1759–60, thereby confirming its status as the prime colonial power. The German states, Austria, and Italian states did not take part in colonial competition. The German states lagged behind the Polish fief of Courtland, whose duke brought Tobago in 1645 and briefly maintained a trading post in the Gambia or Denmark, whose West India Company obtained both St. Thomas and St. John (1671) and St. Croix (1733). At the start of the seventeenth century, Spanish control of the Caribbean was still intact, although under regular attack by French and English pirates and privateers. In 1595 Sir Walter Raleigh (1552–1618), passing Trinidad on his way to look for El Dorado up the Orinoco river, stopped on the island and destroyed the newly built Spanish settlement of San Jose de Oruna (St. Joseph). Two years later, Sir Anthony Shirley (1565–1635) led an expedition ashore in Jamaica and marched to Spanish Town, which he plundered and burnt. In 1609, an English expedition landed on Bermuda and began the occupation of what would become England's longest-lived colony.

A first attempt to settle in St. Lucia in 1605 ended in disaster when Caribs massacred all the English colonists and a similar venture in Grenada failed in 1609. The Spanish colonists attempted to grow a range of crops in the Caribbean, which they brought over from Europe. Some were unsuccessful: barley, wheat and oats and vines and olives were disappointing. But, citrus fruits prospered and rice became established in wetland areas. Bananas, brought from the Canary Islands, were ideally suited to the climate. Other crops included cassava, indigo, and tobacco. Sugar became the center of the region's agricultural economy and which remains to this day in several Caribbean islands. The Spanish also brought with them institutions, customs and attitudes, which remain part of the cultural landscape of the Caribbean today, especially in Cuba, Puerto Rico, and the Dominican Republic. Language, religion, and architecture were exported from Castile to the islands, as were legal systems and military technology. The early colonists also transported the animals and plants, which have since changed the face of the Caribbean and largely determined its economic development. Mortality and morbidity rates among the first generation of Spanish colonists were high. Exposure to tropical diseases, hunger, and violence took a huge toll in European lives. But, the hardships endured by the European colonizers were insignificant to the suffering they imposed on the region's indigenous peoples and later enslaved Africans. Within half a century of Columbus' first arrival the Tainos were made extinct by Europeans and the Atlantic slave trade began.

Portugal was engaged in the slave trade longer than any other European state and had control over Angola, a major source for enslaved Africans and colonial control over Brazil, the largest market for enslaved Africans. In the sixteenth century, while the leading Lisbon merchants were preoccupied with trading for gold in Africa and spices in Asia, the less glamorous business of buying, transporting, and selling enslaved Africans was left to others, among them Portuguese "New Christians" – Jews who had been forcibly converted in 1497. As with the persecuted Protestants in France, their own experience as victims failed to deter some of them from profitable engagement in the slave trade. Even the development of slave-based sugar production in Brazil was financed by the Dutch, partly through the commercial enterprise of Jewish families with members in both the Netherlands and Brazil. Lisbon trading houses increasingly became agents of British suppliers to the Brazilian market. In 1500 a Portuguese ship was blown off its course and carried to the east coast of South America, on landing they planted their flag and named the place *Brazil*, because of the red wood that they found.

Both France and Spain demonstrated a lack of respect for Portugal's claim to sovereignty over Brazil.

In 1521, the Portuguese established a garrison at Pernambuco and in 1530 dispatched five ships to explore the 3,000 miles' eastern coast. By 1549 Brazil had sixty sugar mills and a population of between 17,000 and 25,000 Portuguese, 18,000 Indians and 14,000 enslaved Africans. In 1630, the Dutch seized Pernambuco and rapidly extend their control northward. Technologically the most advanced people of the time, they introduced new ways of growing and processing sugar and imported substantial number of enslaved Africans to provide the labor. In 1640, a Papal Bull against any traffic in Indians slaves was issued, which resulted in riots in Rio de Janerio, Sao Paula and Santos, but there were never enough Indians to enslave for the plantations and mines. In the sixteenth century, only 50,000 enslaved African had been imported but in the succeeding centuries that followed, Brazil imported over three and half million enslaved Africans. It is estimated that about thirty-eight percent of all enslaved Africans transported to the hemisphere were landed in Brazil (Segal, 1995:72). Labor was not the only use to which slaves were put. They were sexually used on such a scale that Brazilians proclaim miscegenation as having been a major factor in the making of their national identity. Portuguese emigration to the territory during the sixteenth and seventeenth centuries consisted almost entirely of men, who took first Indian and then increasingly enslaved African women as concubines and wives, with the blessing of the authority.

For over fifty years after Christopher Columbus' arrival in the Caribbean the Spanish Crown ruled without serious competition from European rivals. Initially, England, France, and Holland saw little reason to contest Spain's rule in the Caribbean, especially as they were far away and there was little evidence of wealth, which the *conquistadors* had gone to seek. However, has it become clear during the 1540s and 1550s that the Spanish convoys were transporting vast cargoes of precious metals and other commodities into Seville, other European government began to take notice. The steady flow of Mexican gold and Peruvian silver into Spanish coffers seemed to threaten other European nations, especially after the Spanish defeat of the French in 1525 and the marriage of Charles V (1500–1558) to Isabel (1503–1539), the daughter of the King of Portugal. By the middle of the sixteenth century, piracy had become endemic to the Caribbean and the towns and settlements of the Spanish islands were among its targets. *The Mystery, Company, and Fellowship of Merchant Adventurers for the Discovery of regions, Dominions, Islands and Places]*, better known as "The Company of Merchant Adventurers, was founded in London by Richard Chancellor, Sebastian Cabot (1474–1557), and Sir Hugh Willoughby (1495–1554) and received a royal charter from King Edward VI in 1553. Following a disastrous first voyage, the company was re-chartered as the *Mascovy Company,* by Queen Mary I of England in 1555. The company's privileges were confirmed by an Act of Parliament in 1556 as "The Fellowship of English Merchants for the Discovery of New Trades. *The Company of Adventurers of London Trading to the Ports of Africa* (1618), more commonly known as *"The Guinea Company"* was the first joint stock company to trade in Africa for profit. It was a slave trading company. King James I (1556–1625) granted the company a 31-year monopoly on the exploitation of goods from West Africa to be imported into England. The African Company of Merchants was a British chartered company in the Gold Coast area of modern Ghana, in the land of the Fante people. It was founded in 1752 and replaced the Royal African Company, which was dissolved in that year. The company was abolished in 1821, as the slave trade had not been suppressed in these privately held areas. Originally known as the Company of Royal Adventurers Trading to Africa, by its charter of 1660, it was granted a monopoly over English trade with West Africa.

The Gambia Adventurers was granted a ten-year license for African trade north of the Bight of Benin, in January 1669. In 1672: The *Company of Royal Adventurers Trading to Africa* was re-structured and received a new charter from the King, as *"The Royal African Company."* Its new charter included the right to set up forts and factories, maintain troops, and exercise martial law in West Africa, in pursuit of trade in gold, silver, and enslaved Africans. In the 1660s, the company was transporting some 5,000 enslaved Africans a year across the Atlantic. Many were branded with the letters "DY" – Duke of York, who succeeded his brother to the throne in 1685, becoming James II. Other enslaved Africans were branded with the company's initials, "RAC," on their chest. Between 1672 and 1689, the company transported 90,000 to 100,000 enslaved Africans across the Atlantic. Its profits made a major contribution to the increase in the financial power of those who controlled the City of London. The company stopped transporting enslaved Africans in 1731, in favor of ivory and gold dust. The Royal African Company was dissolved in 1752 but was succeeded by the African Company of Merchants. From 1668 to 1722, the Royal African Company provided gold to the English Mint and the coin made with such gold bore an elephant below the sovereign and was called a guinea.

The French lagged behind the English for much of the seventeenth century, in colonizing expeditions to the Caribbean, due mainly to religious conflict at home. In 1553, Francois Le Clerc (d.1563), led a fleet of ten French ships into the Caribbean and began to sack and loot Spanish towns, capturing Santiago in Cuba and forcing its inhabitants to flee inland to Bayamo. French corsairs moved into the Caribbean after France signed a treaty with Portugal in 1536, forbidding its nationals to attack Portuguese shipping off the coast of Africa. Operating from bases in Bahamas and Florida, French pirates became an increasing cause of concern to the Spanish islands. In 1635, France began the task of colonizing

Martinique and Guadeloupe, the two islands, which were to remain at the heart of the French Caribbean. Between the 1630s and 1650s, the French moved into the smaller islands of St. Barthelemy, Les Saintes, and Marie-Galante. In all these islands, they had to contend with fierce resistance from the Caribs, but eventually in 1650, a group of settlers managed to establish a permanent base in St. Lucia, fending off Carib's attacks. In the same year, a French expedition from Martinique landed in Grenada and established a foothold and eventually conquered the Caribs and the last forty Caribs on the island of St. Lucia committed suicide by jumping into the sea from the high cliffs at a place, which is now called Sauteurs (Leapers).

The Dutch, who in 1609 had finally won their independence from Spain and the Hapsburg Holy Roman Empire, after a protracted forty-year struggle, comprised the fourth European group who sought a piece of the Caribbean cake. With a Caribbean trade monopoly and an established toehold on the west coast of Africa, the Dutch West India Company, was granted a charter for a trade monopoly in the West Indies by the Republic of the Seven United Netherlands, and given jurisdiction over the Atlantic slave trade with, Brazil, the Caribbean and North America. Among its founders, in 1621, was Willem Usselincx (1567–1647) a Flemish slave trafficker and diplomat, who was instrumental in drawing both Dutch and Swedish attention to the importance of the New World. The Dutch West India Company was ideally placed to enter the lucrative slave trade, supplanting Portuguese control of the business and supplying the Spanish, French, and English colonies directly. Modelled on the already successful Dutch East India Company, which was originally established as a chartered company in 1602, was proof of an aggressive and plundering class of people. The Dutch in the Caribbean concentrated more on breaching the Spanish monopoly and establishing trading supremacy, rather than on founding agricultural colonies. Yet, the Dutch onslaught on Spanish trade allowed the English and French to establish their territorial presence. However, between 1630 and 1640 the Dutch took control of four small Caribbean islands – Curacao, Saba, St. Eustatius, and St. Maarten – all unsuitable for extensive plantation agriculture. These islands were primarily used as trading depots and directed the flow of goods and commodities between Amsterdam and the New World. In 1648, both French and Dutch colonists agreed to partition St. Maarten decided by a race between a Frenchman and a Dutchman who set off in different directions from the center of the island, walking around the coast until they met. The Treaty of Mount Concordia was signed on March 23, 1648 and holds to this day, dividing the 89 square-kilometer island between the two European nations. By the mid-seventeenth century, England, France, and Holland had all staked rival claims to Spanish supremacy in the Caribbean. The English sought to impose their dominancy in the mid-seventeenth century with the Navigation Acts of 1651, which proclaimed that, all trade with the English colonies was to be the exclusive preserve of English ships, with an English captain and a crew of a least two-thirds Englishmen. The Dutch refused to accept it and war broke out between the English and Dutch in 1652–4 resulting in an English victory. It was the first of many such wars, in which trade and politics were to be mixed in the arena of the Caribbean.

In May 1655, English troops landed at Hunt's Bay, Jamaica and swept aside some token resistance and marched inland to Spanish Town. But their delay in negotiating surrender terms gave some Spanish time to escape to Cuba and others the opportunity to free their enslaved Africans who fled to the mountains and forming Jamaica's first Maroon communities. However, Cromwell was determined to make a success of this first non-Spanish colony in the Greater Antilles and English sovereignty over Jamaica was formally recognized in Treaty of Madrid in 1660. The foundation both of the Dutch East India Company and the world's first stock exchange in Amsterdam in 1602, can be taken to mark a new era in commercial history. As overseas trade expanded, Europe received a wide range of new staple foods, such as pepper, coffee, cocoa, sugar, and tobacco, which was to change European's diet, cuisine, and palate forever. The haricot bean, which was first recorded in France in 1542, the tomato, which spread far and wide via Italy and the capsicum pepper, which was grown throughout the Balkans, were all American in origin.

During the Age of European Discovery in the fifteenth and sixteenth centuries, Portugal and Spain pioneered European exploration of the globe, and in the process established large overseas empires. Envious of the great wealth these empires generated, England, France and the Netherlands began to establish colonies and trade networks of their own in the Americas and Asia. The First British Empire began to take shape during the early seventeenth century, with the English settlement of North America and the smaller islands of the Caribbean, and the establishment of joint-stock companies, most notably the East India Company, to administer colonies and overseas trade. Following a series of wars in the seventeenth and eighteenth centuries, and union between England and Scotland in 1707, Great Britain became the dominant colonial power in North America and the Caribbean. Britain also became the dominant power in the Indian subcontinent after the East India Company's conquest of Mughal Bengal at the Battle of Plassey in 1757. The Ecclesiastical Appeals Act of 1533, was an Act of the English Parliament, which forbade all appeals to the Pope in Rome, on religious or other matters, making the King the final legal authority in all such matters in England and wales, and other English possessions. This was achieved by claiming that England was an Empire and the English crown was an Imperial Crown. A year later, the First Act of Supremacy was enacted, which made Henry VIII the only supreme head in earth of the Church of England. The period between 1583 and

1783, has subsequently been referred to by some historians as the "First British Empire."

The independence of the Thirteen Colonies in North America in 1783, following the European-American War of Independence caused Britain to lose some of its oldest and most populous colonies. Britain's attention soon turned towards Asia, Africa, and the Pacific, and after defeating the French in the Revolutionary and Napoleonic Wars (1792–1815), Britain emerged as the principal naval and imperial power of the nineteenth century. The Revolutionary Wars were divided into two periods; the War of the First Coalition (1792–97) and the War of the Second Coalition (1798–1802). Between 1815 and 1914, the "Second British Empire" became the global hegemon – the political, economic, or military predominance or control of one state over others – and adopted the role of global controller. Alongside the formal control that Britain exerted over its own colonies, its dominance of much of world trade meant that it effectively controlled the economies of many regions, such as Asia and Latin America. But, by the beginning of the twentieth century, Germany and the United States had begun to challenge Britain's economic lead. Subsequent military and economic tensions between Britain and Germany were major causes of the First World War. The transfer of Hong Kong to China in 1997 marked for many the end of the "Second British Empire."

Counting the Cost of Diseases

Italians, Germans, Poles, and English all called it "the French disease." The French called it "the Neapolitan disease." The Neapolitans called it "the Spanish disease." The Portuguese called it "the Castilian disease" and the Turks "the Christian disease." The Spanish doctor, Ruy Diaz de la Isla, who was one of the first to treat it, called it "the Serpent of Hispaniola." Syphilis made its European debut in Barcelona in 1493. Diaz de Isla later claimed to have treated the master of the *Nina,* Vicente Pinzon, and it was assumed to have crossed the Atlantic with Columbus' crew, but there is no evidence that it existed in the New World. It reached Naples in 1494 in time to welcome the invading French army. When the French King's mercenaries dispersed the following year, they took it with them to almost every European country. Of Charles VIII's campaign in Italy, Voltaire later wrote: "France did not lose all she had won. She kept the Pox." For reasons that are unclear, the spirochete microbe, *Treponema pallidum,* which causes syphilis, assumed an especially virulent form in Europe. It bored into the human genitals, exploiting the scabrous fissures that were common in the unwashed crotches of the day, forming highly contagious chancres. Within weeks it covered the body in suppurating pustules, attacked the central nervous system, and destroyed all hair. It killed within months, painfully! Over six or seven decades, the spirochete created its own resistance and calmed down. Henceforth, it would be the cause of a common three-stage venereal disease that left its deformed and sterile hosts a longer life-span. But by then, amongst millions, its victims had included Pope Julius II (1443–1513, Cardinal Thomas Wolsey (1473–1530), Henry VIII, and Ivan IV Vasilyevich, commonly known as Ivan the Terrible (1530–1584). It was not tamed until the advent of penicillin in the 1940s.

The impact of syphilis was far reaching and has been linked to the sexual puritanism which took hold on all classes, short of the aristocracy, to the banishment of hitherto popular and licentious bath houses; to the institution of handshaking in place of public kissing; and from 1570 onwards, to the growing fashion for wigs. In 1530, the Italian poet, Girolamo Fracastoro (c.1476/8–1553), composed a poem about a shepherd boy who insulted the Greek god Apollo and was punished by Apollo with a horrible disease. The shepherd's name was Syphilus (Davies, 1996:512). The New World quickly became a melting pot of diseases especially with the introduction by Europeans carrying small pox and influenza. On the island of Barbados, heat, humidity, insects, and atrocious hygiene had taken a grievous toll and the "Bleeding Fever" or the "Barbados Distemper" was spread by a particular species of mosquito. It was to be 250 years before this was known. The yellow fever virus causes headaches, loss of appetite and muscle pain, followed by high temperatures, a raging thirst and agonizing back pain. Death usually came with sufferer spewing up mouthfuls of dark blood, as the virus caused liver and kidney failure and multi-organ hemorrhage. The chaos caused by the epidemic, together with a severe drought in late 1647, resulted in the deaths of as many as 6,000 out of a population of 25,000, by 1648 (Segal, 1995: 45).

Life expectation at birth during the seventeenth century in England was about thirty-five years, but in the West Indies, it was as low as ten years. In parts of Barbados, like St. Michael parish, which included Bridgetown, the register records four times as many deaths as marriages during the 1650s and three times as many deaths as baptisms (Parker, 2011: 84). On May 31, 1694, the Governor of Jamaica, Sir William Beeston (1636–1702), was informed that the French were planning to attack Jamaica. The French landed unopposed on the easternmost parish of the island, on the morning of June 17, 1694. They marched inland, killing cattle and sheep, burning and plundering all in their path. In July, the French re-embarked and cruised westwards, before landing at Carlisle Bay, with a view of attacking Spanish Town. The English forces were quickly put on the defensive. Slaves, pressed into service, fought for the English and at least 14 were subsequently freed for their bravery. Before leaving Jamaica, however, the French had caused immense damage, destroying more than 50 sugar works and carrying off some 2,000 slaves. When Du Casse and his men gave up their attempt to conquer Jamaica, they left behind a deadly virus. Until the late 1690s, Jamaica had been relatively free of yellow fever. Before the French invasion, early mortality was common in Jamaica, but after the invasion the death rate was at its worst in Jamaica's history. In Kingston, a quarter of the population perished, and it has been estimated that about 200 per thousand of the town's population died every year during the first decades of the eighteenth century. This compared to 25 to 30 per thousand in England. For example, one of the sugar families of Jamaica, Colonel Beckford, lost two wives and two daughters in the space of five years.

The two biggest killers [for Europeans] in Jamaica were malaria and yellow fever, both carried by mosquitoes, which thrived in the wake of forest clearances to grow sugar. Forest clearance also reduced the bird population that ate the insects. Discarded clay pots, needed for the sugar industry, provided an ideal breeding ground for yellow fever-carrying mosquitoes (*Aedes aegypti),* which can spread dengue fever, chikungunya, and yellow fever viruses. Both Port Royal and Kingston had nearby swamps, which provided breeding grounds for the Anopheles, malaria-carrying mosquito (Parker, 2011: 195). As in Barbados, the yellow fever virus thrived in Jamaica because it found a European population with no immunity. In addition, the European population was hemmed in by the effective Maroon control of the island's hinterland. Around 3,000 Europeans died during the epidemic, reducing their presence in Jamaica to 7,000 by 1700, where it remained for the next decade. In contrast the slave population continued to grow sharply, reaching 42,000 by 1700. Ironically, it was only the arrival of enslaved Africans, most of whom had some immunity to yellow fever that eventually checked the disease (Parker, 2011: 196). For the next 150 years, about a third of all Europeans died within three years of arriving in the Caribbean. Only just over a third of marriages left surviving children. With no increase in the profitability of tobacco, cotton, ginger, or any other staples, a great number of smallholders were forced to sell out to the new sugar barons, such as Christopher Cordrington, the Walrouds, and other rich landowners. Richard Ligon (1585–1662) was the first to record the use of the word "Pickanninney" to describe a black child, taken from the Spanish/Portuguese "*piqueno-nino*") commented on how some who had arrived with virtually nothing "are now risen to very great and vast estates" (Parker, 2011: 46). Henry Morgan, who would become one of the richest and most powerful men in the Caribbean, was probably a servant in Barbados in 1650, having contracted himself into indenture to avoid the life of a poor Welsh farmer.

The Seven Years' War and British Dominance in the Caribbean

The Seven Years War, also known in North America as the French and Indian War, was blundered into by France and Britain after skirmishing in North America and at sea. The conflict between 1756 and 1763, saw fighting in Europe, India, North America and the West Indies, where it was at its most severe. The war started with the loss by Britain of Minorca and the execution of Vice Admiral John

Byng (1704–1757), which led to the fall of the government, and a new ministry being formed, led by the aggressive imperialist William Pitt (1708–1778). Under the new leadership of Charles III, Spain joined the Seven Years War in January 1762. Britain responded by attacking Havana, the heart of Spanish power in the Caribbean. But following a siege between June 7 and August 13, 1762, the British force had suffered appallingly from yellow fever, losing 12,000 men from their original force of 15,000 men. At the end of the war, Havana was returned to Spain, but England gained Florida from Spain in return. Martinique was given back to France in exchange for Minorca. The French were also given the choice of retaining Guadeloupe or ceding large parts of Canada, they chose to hand over the under-developed and relatively worthless wasteland of Canada (Parker 2011: 304). Britain added considerable to its Caribbean possessions, by gaining Dominica, Grenada, St. Lucia, St. Vincent and Tobago, all soon producing sugar. In 1797, Trinidad was seized from the Spanish with a slave population of about 10,000. The decade after the Seven Year war, represents the high-water mark of the "First" British Empire.

Trade expanded in tropical and subtropical commodities – sugar, tea, spices from India and China; tobacco, rice, and indigo from the southern mainland colonies of North America; rum, coffee, cotton, and dye wood from the West Indies; raising the standards of material welfare, paid for the reverse flow of British manufactures and employed ships and seamen for the Royal Navy, which provided global security for the system and *underpinning it all was the slave trade*. After the Seven Year War, many Scots and others rushed to plant the newly British and relatively under-developed islands of Dominica, St. Vincent, Grenada, and Tobago with sugar, which led to a wave of speculation in land and an increase demand for slaves. A field hand slave, who cost 25 pound in 1755, went for sixty pounds in 1770. But a sharp fall in the price of sugar led to a credit crisis in 1772–3. Between 1783 and 1789 the progress of the French sugar islands, of Saint Domingue especially, was the most amazing phenomenon in colonial development. The fertility of the French soil was decisive. French sugar cost one-fifth less than British sugar. During the years 1771 to 1781, the plantations of the Long family in Jamaica earned an average profit of nine-and-a-half percent. But, in 1788, the net profit in Jamaica had declined to four percent, as compared with an average of eight to twelve percent in Saint Domingue. In 1775, Jamaica had 775 slave plantations; by 1791, 125 had been sold for debt, 12 were in the hands of receivers, while seven had been abandoned, and the West Indian slave plantation owners indebted to the sum of £20 million. French colonial exports were over £8 million and imports over £4 million, employing 164,000 tons of shipping and 33,000 sailors. British colonial exports were £5 million, with imports less than £2 million and employing 148 tons of shipping and 14,000 sailors. The Caribbean was no longer a British lake.

Company Trading

The geographical discoveries of the fifteenth and sixteenth century were not made by Englishmen. Spain was the foremost colonizing power of the "New World," but English sailors resolved to attack Spanish power in all parts of the world. This according to Southgate (1954) could be regarded as piracy, which was partly inspired by national and religious feelings. In the Channel, in the West Indies, in the Pacific and Indian Ocean, it was English and Protestant, in opposition to Catholic Spain. Out of these adventures, exploration, piracy, and religion, opportunities for commercial intercourse arose and they were seized by English merchants. From the sixteenth to eighteenth century, commerce was carried on by companies, which held charters granted by the Crown. The Government found the company system preferable to that of trade carried on by host of private adventurers. However, individual traders often ventured to parts of the world which were not reached by chartered companies, and trading developed as a result of such enterprise. This sometimes led to the formation of new companies (Southgate, 1954: 75). The business of a merchant required training and in some companies, it was usual to require candidates for admission to have undergone apprenticeship to a merchant already engaged in the trade. The trading companies were of two distinct types, regulated and joint-stock. Regulated companies were associations of merchants, which possessed charters authorizing their members to engage in specific trade. But, the company as a whole did not trade. Each venture was supported by members, singly or in partnership and only those who were concerned in an undertaking shared its profits or bore its loss. Joint-stock companies were organizations where capital is contributed by the members as a whole, carries on its affairs through its paid officials and its members, or shareholders, receive their proper proportion of the profits in the form of dividends on their shares.

Unlike the members of regulated company, all the shareholders of a joint-stock company are financially affected by the success or failure of every transaction in which the company is engaged. In 1580 Portugal passed under the rule of Philip II of Spain and though it was not formally incorporated into Spain, Portuguese possessions became, for all practical purposes, Spanish possessions, and Portuguese trade became Spanish trade. The East India Company received its first charter on December 31, 1660. The trading activity of the East India Company extended as far as China and Japan. From the middle of the eighteenth century the history of the company is bounded up with the extension of British influence in India. It became a governing as well as a trading corporation, though its political activity was controlled by the British Government, under the Regulation Act of 1773 and the India Act of 1784. In 1833, it ceased to trade and was abolished in 1858. Trade with the west coast of Africa was in the hands of the Royal African Company. Several attempts to establish companies for this trade had been made in

Elizabeth and early Stuart times, but it was not until the reign of Charles II that the Royal African Company was founded. This company traded in enslaved Africans, who were transported in terrible condition to the sugar plantations in the West Indies. This company was abolished in 1821. There were a number of other companies formed to trade in enslaved Africans and goods. In 1588 the Guinea Company was formed to trade in ivory and palm oil and in 1618 in enslaved Africans. In 1662 a company was formed to export 3,000 enslaved African per year to British colonies in America. In 1750 a new company was formed to take over the property and liabilities of the Royal African Company. The Hudson Bay Company was formed in 1670, in the reign of Charles II, whose cousin, Prince Rupert, was interested in its formation. Certain additional rights, apart from trading with American natives around the Hudson Bay, were conceded to the Company by the Treaty of Utrecht, in 1773. The right of supplying 4,800 enslaved Africans per year to Spanish colonies was granted to it for thirty years. The company retained its original privileges until 1807.

King Sugar

Matthew Parker (2011) argues that it was in New Guinea that sugar cane, a giant member of the grass family, was first domesticated. From New Guinea, cane cultivation spread westwards, and in around 500 BCE it was in India that the juice obtained from crushing the plant was first processed into sugar, through being boiled in a succession of ever smaller and hotter cauldrons. By the sixth century CE, sugar cultivation and processing had reached Persia, from where it was carried into the Mediterranean by the Arab expansion. It was grown on Crete, Cyprus and Sicily. Spanish and Portuguese expansion in the fifth century carried the cane ever southwestwards, to warmer and wetter climes. In 1425, Henry the Navigator sent cane plants from Sicily to Madeira with the first Portuguese colonists. From the tiny island of Gomera in the Canaries, Christopher Columbus carried cane seedlings to the New World on his second voyage in 1493 (Parker, 2011: 10). Sugar became the center of the region's agricultural economy and which remains to this day in several Caribbean islands. The first plants which arrived with Columbus in 1493, thrived in Hispaniola's rich soil and gradually spreading among Santo Domingo's landowners. Sugar was extremely rare in Europe and was cultivated on a small scale in Southern Spain, the Canary Islands, Madeira, and Crete or imported from North Africa and was so precious that pharmacists sold it by the gram as an exotic luxury item. Columbus had traded sugar between Madeira and Genoa and his wife's family had thrived in the business. Columbus declared that Hispaniola in the West Indies was the finest place in the world to grow the crop and one hundred and fifty years later the western part of Hispaniola became the world's most productive sugar producing hothouse in the world.

In the 1490s, the islands of Sao Tome and Principe in the Gulf of Guinea were colonized by Portugal and put to cane cultivation, which when combined with the supply from Madeira, made Portugal the world's leading sugar producer. In 1500, Portugal claimed Brazil, and within 20 years had created a huge industry in sugar. Numerous sugar factories were established by the 1520s and from the 1530s, the industry expanded rapidly, particularly around Pernambuco, Olinda, and Bahia (Parker, 2011: 11). In 1515 Governors Velazquez sent an expedition to the Bay Islands off the coast of Honduras, which returned to Cuba with several hundred captives. In 1516 the first sugar mills were built in Hispaniola and they were powered by horses, oxen, or men who turned a central crushing wheel – the *trapiche*, which was eventually superseded by the water-powered *ingenio*. By 1523, there were 20 *ingenios* in Hispaniola and soon afterwards these mills were constructed in Jamaica, Cuba, and Puerto Rico. However, for production to increase significantly, one critical problem had to be solved – the shortage of labor to cultivate the fields and operate the mills. Raids on other islands rounded up groups of indigenous prisoners who were treated as slaves. According to Ferguson (1999) between 1515 and 1542 as many as 200,000 Indians are thought to have been seized by slaving parties in Central America and brought to the Greater Antilles. Another attempt to solve the shortage of labor for the sugar cane fields and mills was European forced labor. In February 1519, an expedition, led by Hernan Cortes (1485–1547), of some 600 men sailed from the Cuban port of Havana, bound for the Yucatan Peninsula, marked a turning point in the role of the Spanish Caribbean colonies.

In the wake of Cortes, went thousands of Spanish fortune-seekers, enthused by reports of gold and silver in Mexico and beyond. In the 1520s, the Spanish Empire was extended through the Central America isthmus and down into Venezuela, Ecuador, and Peru. Florida was settled in 1528, and in the following decade, the Spanish built cities in a vast area encompassing modern-day Colombia, Paraguay, Bolivia, and Argentina. The Caribbean colonies, settled between 1493 and 1511, languished despite the attempts of the Spanish Crown to prevent emigration to the mainland. In 1526, King Charles decreed execution for any colonist abandoning the islands and two years later ordered every male settler in Puerto Rico to marry within two years or risk losing his *encomicenda* (plantation). The sugar revolution in Barbados increased production and lowered prices, and consumption rose fourfold in forty years after 1640. This demand was as a direct result of other new tropical products coming onto the English market. London's first coffee house opened in 1652 and tea from China, by the East India Company, started gaining popularity at the same time and for the rich, chocolate became fashionable. By 1770, sugar had achieved a revolution in eating habits in England, along with coffee, tea, cocoa, and jam. Processed foods – chocolate and confectionary – were now being consumed in much greater quantities. Breakfast became sweeter, rather than savory. In Hannah Glasse's famous 1747 book, *The Art of Cooking Made Plain and Easy* her recipe for "Cake in the Spanish Way" required three pounds of "best moist sugar." Marmalade, as invented by Rebecca Price, required a pound of sugar for every four oranges. The tea break had arrived, with even the poorest laborer taking sustenance from the combination of stimulant and calorie hit. It was recommended that 12 to 16 pounds of sugar be used with every pound of tea. It is suggested that by the end of the eighteenth century, a typical poor family in England would spend as much as six percent of its income on sugar.

Alongside sugar, a new product was also being marketed by Barbados – rum. From the Portuguese, the English plantation owners had learnt to take some of the sugar by-products, skimming and molasses, distil them into "a hot hellish and terrible liquor." Eventually called "rumbullion," as reported by Richard Ligon, was "Kill Devil." Rum consumption, like that of sugar, grew almost exponentially and soon invaded almost all areas of English social life (Parker, 2011: 297). From 2,000 gallons, a year in 1700, by 1773 rum imports into England and Wales had risen to two million gallons, further swelling the coffers of the sugar barons. The unloading, storing and selling of all this sugar, which was worth more than half of all imports from the colonies by the end of seventeenth century, was in the hands of a relatively small number of English men. In 1680, 28 London merchants imported nearly half of all products from the West Indies by value. But the benefits from sugar were spread far more widely. The Crown made three hundred thousand annually from sugar duties by the 1670s. Some seven hundred, small-town merchants, by 1686, sent cargoes of foodstuffs to the islands. All the sugar processing machinery was manufactured in England and shipped out in English or colonial ships. Some ten thousand men were directly employed in the transoceanic trade. In London, banks, insurance companies, and brokers all participated in and benefited from the trade in enslaved Africans and sugar. By the end of the seventeenth century, most English inventors, merchants and consumers, were in some way implicated in the economy fueled by enslaved Africans and sugar. While in Europe the power of land still held sway, in England, commerce and industry were becoming of central importance and while trade with continental Europe stagnated, Atlantic commerce flourished.

According to a pamphleteer of 1695, England was becoming "the center of trade...standing like the sun in the midst of its plantations" (Parker, 2011: 127). Britain's wealth from sugar prompted Adam Smith to write in 1776 that: "The profits of sugar plantation in any of our West Indian colonies are generally much greater than those of any other cultivation that is known either in Europe or America" (Adam Smith, *Wealth of Nations,* 1937: 366, in Segal, 1995:41). Although annual returns fell from twenty percent to twelve percent in 1775 and below six percent in 1810, it was almost twice as much when compared with return of 3.5 percent on good English farming land. It is estimated that throughout the period of enslavement of Africans in the Caribbean, European slave owners made an aggregate profit of over £150,000,000 during the eighteenth century (Craton, *Sinews of Empire,* pp.139–40, in Segal, 1995: 41). Sugar was the most valuable import into Britain, worth more than the total exports of all North American mainland colonies combined. Towards the end of the eighteenth century, the younger Pitt estimated that four-fifths of British incomes derived from overseas came from the West Indies. Jamaica was described as a constant mine whence Britain draws prodigious riches and as a necessary appendage to our present refined manner of living. Sugar was a driving force and an important part of Britain's rapidly expanding and now global commerce, along with its sister slave trade. By the 1750s, the English were pre-eminent in the slave trade, shipping some 200,000 during the decade. Both merchants in Britain and planters in the West Indies used the argument that the slave trade and slavery were incredibly important to the British economy. Both groups played the "nationalist" card in arguing that the government had asked them to invest in their property for the expansion of the British state and in return the British state should protect their property.

Each of the ten thousand voyages of British slave traders to the coast of West Africa left its mark on societies of the interior as well as those of the coast. The British slave trade became significant in the 1660s (6,700 per year) and reached its height in the 1770s (42,000 per year), linking London, Bristol and Liverpool merchants with African markets. The slave trade also lined these ports with the West Indies (the "Golden Triangle"). Between 1698 and 1807, about 2,108 slaving ships were fitted out in Bristol, with on average each ship capable of holding 250 enslaved Africans. Between 1668 and 1708, four ships left Bristol to trade in slaves each year, but by 1720, this rose to 25 ships per year and by 1732 the number of ships leaving Bristol's port was 48 each year, which was half the number of ships involved in the slave trade. By 1738, however, Liverpool had overtaken Bristol to become the major port in Britain, trading in enslaved Africans, a position it held until the end of the legal trafficking in 1807. After 1748, the number of ships involved in the slave trade leaving Bristol declined from twenty-five percent in the 1750s to just two percent in 1807.

The British Slave Trade

According to Eric Williams (1943), the British colonial possessions up to 1776 can broadly be divided into two types. The first is the self-sufficient and diversified economy of small farmers, "mere earth scratchers." The second type is the colony which has facilities for the production of staple articles on a large scale for an export market. In the former, fell the northern colonies of the American mainland; in the latter, the mainland tobacco colonies and the sugar islands of the Caribbean (Williams, 1943: 4). But, in the Caribbean land and capital were both useless unless labor could be commanded. For the Caribbean colonies, the solution to the shortage was to be found in slaves' labor. In 1663 the recently restored Charles II founded the Company of Royal Adventurers and in 1672 the Royal African Company, both with a monopoly on "trade" with Africa and the Caribbean colonies. The slave traders welcomed state involvement in the trade, as it provided them with protection from rival nations. Between 1672 and 1713 the Royal African Company built seventeen forts on the West African coast, sent some 500 ships to Africa, and sold approximately 100,000 enslaved Africans to the planters on the English islands. By 1700, some 50 ships from Bristol were actively involved in the trafficking of enslaved Africans. The precise number of enslaved Africans shipped across the Atlantic is not known and figures between twelve and fifteen million have been put forward. It is estimated, that of all the Africans who left their continent in the course of the transatlantic slave trade, between seventy-five and eighty percent arrived alive in the Caribbean and the Americas. Of the missing twenty to twenty-five percent, some went to Europe or the Atlantic islands, but many died during the Middle Passage.

The Royal African Company, for example, recorded a mortality rate of almost twenty-five percent among its enslaved Africans it shipped between 1680 and 1770 and at times individual ships recorded up to fifty percent loss. Between 1701 and 1810, British ships transported an estimated 2,467,000 enslaved Africans from Africa to the Caribbean. The British early trade was conducted by the Royal African Company, invested with a monopoly in 1672. The governor of the Royal African Company was the Duke of York and remained so after becoming King James II, in 1685. Among the many shareholders was John Locke (1632–1704), the most influential of Enlightenment thinkers, and commonly known as the "Father of Liberalism," but, only it seemed if you were white. The Glorious Revolution of 1688, which put an end to the reign of James II, put an end to the company's monopoly and it became the right of every freeborn Englishman to trade in enslaved Africans. In the first nine years after the company's monopoly ended, the port of Bristol alone accounted for the shipment of some 161,000 enslaved Africans. In 1771, no fewer than 190 ships, with accommodation for 47,000 enslaved Africans, left British ports. By 1771, the merchants of Liverpool dominated the African slave trade and by 1795 ships from the port were accounting for over half (five-eighths) of the British slave trade and nearly half (three-sevenths) of the European total. In the 1780s, the slave trade was estimated to be bringing Liverpool alone a clear annual profit of £300,000. Malachi Postlethwayt (1707–1767), an eighteenth-century writer on economic matters, described the slave trade as "the first principle and foundation of all the rest, the mainspring of the machine which sets every wheel in motion. The slave trade contributed greatly to making Britain the leading naval as well as commercial power in the world.

Further, the provision of goods to exchange for captive Africans, promoted the rapid growth of the related industries, especially in the production of cotton cloth, which was concentrated at Manchester. The seventeenth and eighteenth centuries were the centuries of trade, and for Britain, that trade was primarily the triangular trade. In 1718, William Wood (1671–1730), a hardware manufacturer and mint master, stated that the slave trade was "the spring and parent whence the others flow." In this triangular trade, England – France and colonial America equally – supplied the exports and the ships; Africa the human merchandise; the plantations the colonial raw materials (Williams, 1943: 51). By the late eighteenth century, Manchester was exporting goods to Africa worth some £200,000 a year and employing in their manufacture some 180,000 men, women and children. Cotton provided a classic example of the cumulative profits to be made out of the triangular trade – cotton goods were profitably exchanged for captive Africans in Africa; captive Africans were sold profitably in America, partly in profitable exchange for cotton; and in Britain the cotton was profitably manufactured into cloth. The metal industry also thrived on the slave trade – fetters, chain, padlocks, and branding irons – were implements of slavery. Others – copper wire, iron bars, brass pans, and kettles, guns – were trade goods for procuring slaves. The gunsmiths of Birmingham accounted the African market their principal customer, along with their West Indian customers.

The main product of slavery was sugar and Britain secured the profits from the refining process, by prohibiting the colonies which produced the crude sugar from establishing refineries. It was the growing challenge to British colonial sugar from cheaper supplies elsewhere in America that first reinforced the arguments against the slave trade. A fast industrializing Britain had everything to gain from promoting an end to the slave trade. Confirming the argument for free trade, British imports from the United States, mainly of slave-produced cotton, rose in value from $9 million in 1792 to $31 million in 1801. In 1785, exports of British cotton manufactures topped £1 million in value, but in 1830, such exports were worth £31 million. Cuba, faced with a shortage of enslaved Africans, used them side by side, with indentured Chinese coolies and, after emancipation, turned to Haiti and British West Indies for workers. Williams (1943) argues that Negro slavery was only a solution, in certain historical circumstances, of the Caribbean labor problem. Sugar meant labor and at times that labor was Indians, at other times indentured Europeans and at other enslaved Africans. But, without enslaved Africans the great development of the British Caribbean sugar plantation system, between 1650 and 1833, would have been impossible. Enslaved Africans were the backbone of the western world, between 1650 and 1833, and was a matter of very high importance to the British government up to the 1780s. The English involvement in the Atlantic slave trade started with Sir John Hawkins slave-trading expedition in 1562. Like so many Elizabethan ventures, it was a buccaneering expedition, which was an encroachment on the papal arbitration of 1493, which made Africa a Portuguese monopoly. In accordance with the economic policies of the Stuart monarchy, the slave trade was entrusted to a monopolistic company, which in this case was the Company of Royal Adventurers trading to Africa, incorporated in 1663, for a period of one thousand years. But, less than ten years later, in1672, a new company, the Royal African Company was formed. Between 1680 and 1686 the Royal African Company transported an annual average of 5,000 enslaved Africans. But, in 1731, the Royal African Company abandoned the slave trade, due to competition, and confined itself to the trade in ivory and gold.

Of the slave traders listed in 1755, nearly 240 were Bristol based, with 147 listed in London and 89 in Liverpool. In the first nine years of free trade, Bristol alone shipped 160,950 enslaved Africans to sugar plantations in the West Indies. But the slave trade was more than a means to an end, it was also an end in itself. The British slave traders provided the necessary laborers, not only for their own plantations, but for those of their rivals. Spain was always, up to the nineteenth century, dependent on foreigners for her slaves, due either to the papal bull of 1493, or lack of capital and the necessary goods for the slave trade. British merchants defended the trade, legal or illegal, with the Spanish colonies, in enslaved Africans and manufactured goods, especially as the Spanish paid in coins, which increased bullion supply in England. During the nine months of British occupation of Cuba in the Seven Years' War, 10,700 enslaved Africans were imported on that island. The Seven Years' War, fought between 1754 and 1763, but principally in the seven-year period from 1756 to 1763, involved every European great power of the time, except the Ottoman Empire and spanned five continents, affecting Europe, the Americas, West Africa, India and the Philippines. The conflict split Europe into two coalitions, led by the Great Britain on one side and France on the other. The Privy Council Committee of 1788 paid special attention to the fact that of the annual British export of enslaved Africans, two-thirds were disposed of to foreigners. Thus, Britain was not only the foremost slave trading country in the world in the eighteenth century; it furnished the sugar plantations of France and Spain with half a million enslaved Africans.

The story of the British slave trade is the story of Liverpool. Liverpool's first slave ship, a vessel of some 30 tons, sailed for Africa in 1709. By 1730, it had fifteen ships employed in the slave trade and by 1771, it had over a hundred ships employed in the inhumane trade. In 1795, Liverpool handled five-eighths of the British slave trade and three-sevenths of the whole European slave trade. The space allocated in a ship to each enslaved African during the Atlantic Crossing measured five-and-a-half feet (1.27m) in length by sixteen inches (0.4m) in width, each captive African had less room than a man in a coffin. In the 1730s, in Bristol, it was estimated that on a fortunate voyage the profit on a cargo of about 270 slaves reached seven and eight thousand pounds, exclusive of the returns from ivory.

Profits of one hundred percent were not uncommon in Liverpool and one voyage netted a clear profit of at least three hundred percent. Prior to 1783, all classes in English society presented a united front with regards to the trade in captive Africans, including the monarchy, government, church and the general public. In 1773, the Jamaica Assembly imposed a duty on every imported Negro, but merchants of London, Liverpool, and Bristol protested and the Board of Trade condemned the law as unjustifiable, improper, and prejudicial to British commerce. In 1774 the British government disallowed Jamaican Acts restricting the slave trade. The slave trade held high office in England, including royalty, alderman, dukes, earls, lords, countesses, and knights. The slave traders were firmly established in both houses of Parliament. Many earls and lords owed their seats in the Upper House to the slave trade. Some protests were voiced by a few eighteenth-century intellectuals and prelates, such as Daniel Defoe (1660–1731), William Cowper (1731–1800), and Robert Southey (1774–1843) and others, along with two economists, who condemned the expensiveness and inefficiency of slave labor.

British Banking

Money-lending as usury was practiced by the Jews before their expulsion from England in 1190, and in the later Middle Ages, the Crown occasionally negotiated loans from wealthy traders and from such corporations as the Hanse Merchants and Merchant Adventurers. Usury was prohibited by both Civil and Canon Law, but during the Tudor period, opinion in England changed and it was no longer viewed as immoral to accept interest from a merchant, on loan which might be used by the borrower in the course of his business and from which he might make a profit. An Act of 1545 legalized the extraction of interest and although this act was reversed in 1552, it was revived in 1571. Another Act of 1624 permitted a maximum rate of interest of eight percent. With this legislation banking was free to develop. From the time of Henry VIII, goldsmiths had acted as money-changers, dealing for the convenience of other merchants in the currencies of various countries. In the time of Charles I, the goldsmiths began to receive sums of money from their customers for safekeeping, on promise of repayment on demand. Goldsmiths soon realized that it was unlikely that payment of the whole of the money deposited with them would be required at any one time, and they found it possible to lend out part at interest, reserving only sufficient to meet all probable demands. Charles II, in 1672, suspended repayments due from the Exchequer to the goldsmiths, and undertook merely to pay interest on his debts to them. This Royal action placed goldsmiths in difficulties, as they were unable to meet the claims of their depositors, leading to a serious financial crisis.

Criticism was directed against goldsmiths, and it was argued that banking ought to be in the hands of a chartered institution. The Bank of England was founded in 1694, on lines suggested by William Paterson (1658–1719). The company undertook to lend to the Government the sum of £1.2 million, at eight percent interest, along with the sum of £4,000 per annum for management expenses. The charter of the Bank of England was granted for a limited period and it was renewed periodically. In 1708, it was enacted that no other bank with more than six partners should be established with the privilege of issuing notes. For nearly a century and a quarter, after 1708, the only competitors to the Bank of England were private bankers – the goldsmiths and their successors. In 1757, the Bank of England was entrusted with the full management of the National Debt. Banking business was mainly confined to London before 1750, though a few banks had been established. According to Southgate (1954), between 1793 and 1825 several financial crises occurred and each of these occasions was marked by the failure of a number of country banks. In1797, fear of a French invasion brought about a run on the Bank of England. The Government authorized the bank to discontinue payment of its notes. By 1821 the normal honoring of notes in gold was in full working order. In 1823, the Government negotiated with the Bank of England to extend its Charter until 1834, if the Bank would consent to a limitation of its monopoly to London and the surrounding country within a radius of 65 miles, so that joint-stock banks might be established in provincial towns beyond that limit.

Following the financial crisis of 1825, arising in part out of speculative investments in Latin America, which precipitated the closing of six London banks and 60 county banks. The crisis affected markets in Europe, Latin America, and the United States. The Bank of England was offered the choice between the active exercise of its powers, enjoyed under its monopoly, by opening branches all over the country and the surrender of its privileges beyond the 65-mile limit, suggested in 1823. The Bank of England chose to stay within London and its 65-mile limit. In 1833, joint-stock banks were permitted to transact business in London or elsewhere within the 65-mile limit, provided that they did not issue notes. By the same act, the notes of the Bank of England were made legal tender. The passing of this act was followed by the formation of several important banks, including the London and Westminster Bank (1834), the London Joint-Stock Bank (1836), the Union Bank and the London and Country Bank (1839). Due to restriction on their activities, they relied on the deposit side of banking and encouraged their customers to use the check system. The Bank Charter of 1844, limit the issue of notes by banks other than the Bank of England. The Bank of England was to be divided into two departments – the Issue Department and the Banking Department. The Act of 1844 did not prevent the repetition of serious financial crisis, as occurred in 1847, 1857, and 1866, but after 1866 no serious crises arose until 1914. The Bank of England possesses a monopoly of the issuing of notes; it manages the National Debt and is frequently concerned in the stock issues of local authorities and colonial government. It is a bankers' bank and other banks deposit the bulk of their reserves with it.

By the Currency and Bank Notes Act of 1914, Treasury notes, of the face value of one pound and ten shillings, were to be issued and were to be legal tender to any amount. They were not bank notes, but they were convertible into gold at the Bank of England, although the export of gold coin and bullion and the melting down of gold coin, by private individuals was forbidden. By the Gold Standard Act of 1925, the withdrawal of gold for the purposes of export, in exchange for notes, was permitted provided that the maximum quantity taken at any one time was four hundred ounces troy of pure gold. The price per ounce was to correspond to 113 grains of pure gold to one-pound sterling. By the Currency and Banking Notes Act of 1928, it was decided that the issue of currency notes should be discontinued and that bank notes of similar denomination should be substituted for them. In early 1946, the Bank of England was formally "nationalized"; it became a state institution. From 1816 to 1914, the monetary system of Great Britain was based upon gold – the Gold Standard. Eric Williams (1943) has highlighted the link between the great wealth from the triangular trade and banking. The industrial expansion of the eighteenth century required finance, and no groups were better placed to afford the ready capital than West Indian plantation owners, slave traders, and merchants. It was noted the readiness with which absentee plantation owners purchased land in England and were able to use their wealth to finance the great developments associated with the Agricultural Revolution. But profits from the triangular trade were also invested in British Industrial Revolution.

Many of the eighteenth-century banks established in Liverpool and Manchester, the slaving metropolis and the cotton capital respectively, were directly associated with the triangular trade. Large sums were needed for the cotton factories and canals, which improved the means of communication between the two towns. Typical of the eighteenth-century banker is the transition from tradesman to merchant and then to banker. The term "merchant," in the eighteenth-century context, often involved the gradations of slaver captain, privateer captain, privateer owner, before settling down on shore to the respectable business of commerce. The Heywood Bank was founded in Liverpool in 1773 and endured as a private bank until 1883, when it was purchased by the Bank of Liverpool. Its founders were successful merchants and later elected to the Chambers of Commerce. Typical of the commercial interrelationships of the period, the daughter of one of the partners of the Heywood later married Robertson, son of John Gladstone (1764–1851), merchant, slave trader, Member of Parliament and the father of British Prime Minister, William Ewart Gladstone, who obtained a partnership in the bank. Following the 1833 Abolition Act, which abolished slavery in the British Empire, John Gladstone expelled most African workers from his plantations in Jamaica and Guyana and imported large numbers of indebted

Indian indentured servants, through false promises. He received £106,769, the largest of all compensation payment made by the Slave Compensation Commission, for property losses (enslaved Africans), incurred as a result of the 1833 Abolition Act.

In 1788, the firm set up a branch in Manchester, called the "Manchester Bank." Eleven of 14 descendants up to 1815 became merchants or bankers. Thomas Leyland, who was an African slave trader, with his partner, in 1802 became a senior partner in the banking firm of Clarkes and Roscoe. This was a strange coalition, the successful slave trader and the consistent opponent of slavery, William Roscoe. Leyland and Roscoe parted company and in 1807, Leyland joined in partnership with the slave trader Richard Bullins. Leyland and Bullins Bank lasted until 1901, when it was amalgamated with the North and South Wales Bank Limited. The Heywood and Leyland are only the outstanding examples of the general rule in the banking history of eighteenth-century Liverpool. The banker William Gregson and Lord Mayor of Liverpool (1762–4) was also a slave trader, shipowner, privateer, and underwriter. Francis Ingram was a slave trader, with shares in a rope business and was also involved in partnership with Thomas Leyland and the Earles, who amassed a huge fortune in the slave trade. The founder of Hanley's bank, Captain Richard Hanley, was a slave trader, whose sister was married to a slave trader. Hanley was a prominent member of the "Liverpool Fireside," a society composed almost entirely of captains of slave vessels and privateers. Jonas Bold was a sugar refiner, who became a partner in Ingram's bank. Thomas Fletcher began his career as apprentice to a merchant banker who carried on an extensive trade with Jamaica.

Charles Caldwell and Company was a partner in Oldham, whose transactions were principally in sugar. Isaac Hartman, another banker, owned West Indian plantations. What has been said of Liverpool is equally true of Bristol, London, and Glasgow. Among members of an influential committee set up in Bristol in 1780, to oppose abolition, was William Miles, Alderman Daubeny, Richard Bright, Richard Vaughan, John Cave and Philip Protheroe, were all bankers in Bristol. For London, only one name needs to be mentioned, and that name is Barclay. Two members of this Quaker family, David and Alexander, were engaged in the slave trade in 1756. The Barclays married into the banking families of Gumey and Freame, which kept Quaker wealth in Quaker hands. The rise of banking in Glasgow was immediately connected with the triangular trade. The first provincial bank in Glasgow, which began business in 1749, was officially known as Dunlop, Houston and Company, after its principal partners one of whom was Andrew Buchanan (1690–1759), a tobacco merchant of the city. There were others, including William Macdowall, Alexander Houston, one of the leading West Indian houses in Scotland. Other banks, such as the Arms Bank and the Thistle Bank, were to follow.

The South Sea Company, which was formed in 1711, and to which the trading concessions gained by Great Britain in the Treaty of Utrecht had been assigned, proposed to the Government that it should be granted a monopoly of the whole of the foreign trade of this country. In return, it offered to become the sole creditor of the State and to be content with a uniform rate of interest of five percent. It also suggested that the existing creditors of the Government should be offered shares in the South Sea Company to the value of their Government stock and that those who refused the offer should be paid off, the Company offering the Government £7.5 million, for this purpose. Shares in the South Sea Company increased ten-fold, which attracted unscrupulous financiers who took advantage of the public excitement to form fraudulent companies. The shares of these companies were seen as worthless and in the general crash, the South Sea Company itself suffered. Within a short time, its shares fell from over £1,000 to £175, and many people were ruined. The Government reassumed control of and responsibility for the National Debt, and the South Sea Company was limited to its former sphere of activity. Sir Robert Walpole (1676–1745) established a sinking fund of £1 million per annum towards the repayment of the National Debt.

In 1724, Walpole established bonded warehouses for tea and coffee. After the Peace of Aachen, in 1748, the National Debt stood at £78 million and at the beginning of the Seven Years War, in 1756, the amount of the National Debt was £72 million, but at its close it had reached £160 million. 20 years later, at the end of the War of American Independence, it stood at £250 million. To increase the revenue Pitt the Younger devised taxes on servants, racehorses, carriages, hats, paper, gold and silver plates, windows, and other items. In 1797, Pitt increased assessed taxes and in the following year, he levied an income tax, which was payable on incomes of £60 per annum or more. It was a graduated tax, with those earning over £200 paying two shillings in the pound per annum. It was understood strictly as a war tax, which would be removed upon the return of peace. At the close of the French Revolutionary War (1792–1802) the National Debt stood at £530 million. The Napoleonic War (May 18, 1803–November 20, 1815) followed 13 months later, requiring heavy military and naval expenditure, so the scheme of taxation was carried on, as in the French Revolutionary War. In 1815, the funded debt of Great Britain stood at £831 million and the unfunded debt amounted to £47 million. On the return of peace, the income tax was abolished in 1816, although national income still had to be raised. Duties of sever level were levied upon hundreds of articles, which adversely affected the poor. A year after Peel became Prime Minister in 1842 he removed the duties from large numbers of articles of wholly or partly manufactured goods. He also abolished many duties on exports. Russell, who succeeded Peel as Prime Minister in 1846, attacked the sugar duties. The rate levied on British colonial sugar had been 14 shillings per hundredweight, with sugar from other sources prohibitive. Russell reduced the rate on foreign sugar to 14 shillings per hundredweight, thus abolishing the preference to the colonies. Further changes were introduced in 1853 by Gladstone, who was Chancellor of the Exchequer. The duties on 123 articles were removed, with those on 133 articles reduced. To compensate for the loss of revenue, Gladstone returned to the legacy duties.

Upon the outbreak of the Crimean War in 1854, Gladstone doubled the income tax for the year, and placed additional duties on spirits and sugar. His successor at the Exchequer, Sir Georg Lewis, in 1855 increased the duties on sugar, tea, coffee, and spirits. He also added two pence in the pound on income tax, which now stood at one shilling and four pence in the pound. After the return of peace, income tax was reduced and in 1859, it stood at only five pence in the pound. Between 1798, when Pitt levied an income tax, and 1907, when Asquith no longer regarded the income tax as a temporary tax, it became recognized as a permanent feature of national finance. By 1909, the growth of expenditure for national defense and for social reform necessitate the seeking of new sources of income. Prime Minister Asquith (1852–1928) and his Chancellor of the Exchequer, David Lloyd George (1863–1945), established a super-tax on incomes over £5,000 per annum and Death duties were increased. The European War of 1914–18 made demands upon the finances of Great Britain that were greater than anything known before. Taxation, especially the income tax, rose to levels hitherto undreamt of. Towards the close of the war the income tax reached six shillings in the pound and was accompanied by a super-tax of a further six shilling in the pound on every larger income. At the close of the war, the National Debt exceeded eight billion.

The Triangle Trade

In 1640, when a Portuguese King was once again on the throne, he recognized the Dutch claim to part of Brazil, in return for Dutch help against Spain. But, Brazilian settlers rose in rebellion and succeeded in driving the Dutch from most of the territory they held and by 1654 the Dutch withdrew altogether from Brazil. Many of these Dutch, which included Jews, arrived in the Caribbean, where they taught the English settlers how to make marketable sugar. The supply of indentured servants from England was soon inadequate to meet the needs of the sugar industry in Barbados and it was the Dutch who informed the planters of how well African slave labor would serve the purpose. They also proceeded to provide the necessary slaves at a competitive price to them. The growth of sugar consumption and the requirements of the plantation saw a parallel and interrelated industry developed, linking Europe, Africa, Caribbean and the Americas in one of the seventeenth century's largest commercial enterprise, involving the forced migration of people from one continent to another. Another feature of this commercial enterprise was its explicit racialization, creating a whole ideology of racial superiority in order to justify the system of colonial slavery. Most ships departed from European ports between July and September, in order to avoid the rainy season in Africa, which posed health risks to Europeans. The slave trading areas in Africa stretched down from Senegal to Angola, with active markets in what are now Guinea-Bissau, Sierra Leone, the Gold Coast, Benin, and Nigeria. Upon arrival, there were two principal methods of procuring slaves. One was to use the services of an agent who could ensure a readily supply. The other was to sail from district to district, buying enslaved Africans from individual traders and bargaining European manufactures for human cargo.

It could sometimes take up to ten months to fill a ship with 450 enslaved Africans and in the meantime, those who were already brought were kept in *barracoons* or pens, waiting to be put on board the slave ship. The second leg of the voyage across the Atlantic was known as the Middle Passage, which took on average 60 days when the destination was the Caribbean. Rations were limited, water often ran short, and crews were unwilling to allow enslaved Africans to exercise on deck for fear of violent rebellion. Arriving in the Caribbean, those who appeared strongest were usually sold to private buyers and the others were sold at public auction. Slave traders were first paid in sugar or rum, but later they accepted bills of exchange drawn on the accounts of merchants in Europe to whom the planters consigned their sugar. By 1750, there was hardly a trading or manufacturing town in England which was not in some way connected with the triangular trade. Slave ship sailed from England with a cargo of manufactured goods, which were exchanged, at a profit, on the coast of Africa for captives, who were then traded on the plantations, at another profit, in exchange for a cargo of colonial produce to be taken back to England, for another profit. The profits obtained provided one of the main streams of accumulated capital in England, which financed the Industrial Revolution. The West Indian islands became the hub of the British Empire, which was of immense importance to the grandeur and prosperity of England. It was these enslaved Africans who made these sugar colonies the most precious colonies ever recorded in the annuals of imperialism.

The British Empire was a magnificent superstructure of American commerce and naval power on an African foundation. Sir Josiah Child estimated that every Englishman in the West Indies, with ten enslaved Africans that worked for him, would make employment for four men in England. It has been suggested that every family in the West Indies gave employment to five seamen and many more artificers, manufacturers and tradesmen and every white person in the West Indies brought in ten pounds annually clear profit to England, 20 times as much as a similar person in England. According to Sir Dalby Thomas (1650–1711) slave trader and merchant, every person employed on the sugar plantation was 130 times more valuable to England than one at home. It has been estimated that in 1775 British West Indian plantations represented a valuation of 50 million pound sterling. In 1798, Pitt assessed the annual income from West Indian plantations at four million pounds, as compared with one million from the rest of the world (Williams, 1943:53). Records show that for the years 1714–1773, twenty percent of British imports came from the Caribbean, with six percent export going to the same place. Twelve percent of Britain's total foreign commerce was accounted for by the Caribbean. During these years, half percent of British imports came from Africa, with two percent of exports going there. In 1697, little Barbados, with its 166 square miles, was worth more to British capitalism than New England, New York and Pennsylvania combined.

In 1773, British imports from Jamaica were more than five times the combined imports from the bread colonies and exports were one-third larger than those of New York and Pennsylvania combined. For the same years, Jamaica as an export market was as valuable as New England. Sir Dalby Thomas wrote that the pleasure, glory, and grandeur of England had been advanced more by sugar than by any other commodity, wool not excepted. But, colonial trade was a monopoly of the home country and was viewed as a strength to their mother country and must be kept dependent on her. The colonies were obliged to send their valuable products to England only and use English ships. The keystone of this mercantilist arch was the Navigation Laws, which were aimed at Dutch, Scottish, and Irish. Scotland's attempt to set up an independent African Company aroused great fear in England and was largely responsible for the Act of Union in 1707. Enslaved Africans, the most important export of Africa, and sugar the most important export of the West Indies, were the principal commodities enumerated by the Navigation Laws. This external trade naturally drew in its wake a tremendous development of shipbuilding and shipping. The "long voyage" was an admirable nursery for seamen and merchantmen, which was an invaluable aide to the navy in time of war. Advocates of the slave trade argued that its abolition would annihilate the marine by cutting off a great source of seamen. In 1678, the Commission of Custom reported that the plantation trade was one of the great nurseries of the shipping and seamen of England and one of the greatest branches of its trade.

In 1690, the sugar colonies employed 114 ships and 1,203 seamen. The West Indian trade in 1709 employed one-tenth of British shipping engaged in foreign trade. Between 1709 and 1787, British shipping engaged in foreign trade quadrupled and ships clearing for Africa multiplied 12 times and the tonnage 11 times. Shipbuilding in England received a direct stimulus from the triangular trade, and many shipwrights in Liverpool were slave traders, such as Baker and Dawson, John Gorell, and John Okill. The number of ships entering the port of London trebled between 1705 and 1795, and warehouses on the Thames' quays were inadequate to store imports from the West Indies. Sugar was piled six or eight hogs' heads high on the quay, increasing the danger of fire and encouraging thefts. The West Indian merchants lobbied Parliament and eventually secured an act authorizing the construction of the West India Docks. The first stone was laid in

1800 and the docks were publicly opened in 1802, the first ship being named after the then Prime Minister (Henry Addington). The development of the triangular trade and of shipping and shipbuilding led to the growth of the great seaport towns. Bristol, Liverpool, and Glasgow occupied, as seaports and trading centers, the position in the age of trade that Manchester, Birmingham, and Sheffield occupied later in the age of industry.

It was the slave and sugar trades which made Bristol the second city of England during three-quarters of the 18th century. According to Eric Williams (1943), there is not a brick in the city of Bristol that is not cemented with the blood of an enslaved African. When Bristol was outstripped in the slave trade by Liverpool, it turned its attention from the triangular trade to the direct sugar trade. The West Indian trade was worth to Bristol twice as much as all her other overseas commerce combined. As late as 1830, five-eighths of its trade was with the West Indies. It was said, in 1833, that without the West Indies trade Bristol would have remained a fishing port. In 1847, forty percent of Bristol's tonnage was bound for the West Indies, and shipping returning from the West Indies represented a mere eleven percent. In 1871, no ship left Bristol for Jamaica, and imported tonnage from the islands constituted less than two percent. Bristol's trade with the West Indies did not revive until the end of the nineteenth century, with the advent of the banana on the world market. What the West Indian trade did for Bristol the slave trade did for Liverpool. Until the end of the 17 century the only local event of importance was the siege of the town during the English Civil War. In collecting ship money, Strafford assessed Liverpool at £15; but Bristol paid £2,000. The shipping entering Liverpool increased four-and-a-half times between 1709 and 1771; the outward tonnage increased six-and-a-half times. Customs receipts soared from an average of £51,000 for the years 1750 to 1757, to £648,000 in 1785. The population rose from five thousand in 1700 to thirty-four thousand in 1773.

Not until the Act of Union, in 1707, was Scotland allowed to participate in colonial trade. Sugar and tobacco underlay the prosperity of Glasgow in the eighteenth century. In 1760, Bishop Richard Pococke (1704–1765) wrote "the city as above all others felt the advantages of the Union, by the West India trade which they enjoy, which is very great, especially in tobacco, indigoes and sugar" (Williams, 1943: 64). The Royal African Company stated in petition in 1696 that the slave trade should be supported by England, because of the exports it encouraged of woolen and other English manufacturers. The woolen manufacturers of England took prominent part in the long and bitter controversy, waged between the Royal African Company and other traders. Those from whom the company purchases argued that the interlopers caused disturbances and dislocation of the trade and that the trade declined when the company's monopoly was modified. In 1694, Witney's clothiers petitioned Parliament in favor of the company's monopoly. Cloth workers of Shrewsbury and weavers of Kidderminster followed suit in 1696. Weavers of Exeter and woolen tradesmen of London took the company's side. But the weight of the woolen interests was on the whole thrown on the side of free traders. Monopoly meant one buyer and one seller and, according to testimonies of two London merchants in 1693, the monopoly had reduced the exports of wool by nearly one-third. Suffolk exported 25,000 woolen cloths a year, two years after the incorporation of the company, the number declined to 500. In 1690, the clothiers of Suffolk and Essex and manufacturers of Exeter petitioned Parliament against the company's monopoly. Exeter petitioned again in 1694, 1696, 1709, and 1711, in favor of free trade. Similar petitions were presented to Parliament against the monopoly by the woolen traders of London and the woolen merchants of Plymouth in 1710.

The merchants and traders of Liverpool in 1709 contended that the company's monopoly was detrimental to the woolen industry. In 1690, planters of Jamaica protested against the company's monopoly as a discouragement to trade. Petitions from the industrial North in 1735 disclosed that Wakefield, Halifax, Burnley, and Kendal were all interested in the manufacture of woolen goods for Africa and the West Indies. What the building of ships, for the transportation of enslaved Africans, did for eighteenth century Liverpool, the manufacture of cotton goods, for the purchase of Africans, did for eighteenth century Manchester. The growth of Manchester was intimately associated with the growth of Liverpool, its outlet to the sea and the world market. The capital accumulated by Liverpool from the enslavement of Africans, poured into the hinterland to fertilize the energies of Manchester. Lancashire's foreign market meant chiefly the West Indian plantations and Africa. The export trade was worth £14,000 in 1739, but by 1779, it was worth just over £300,000, with one-third going to the slave coast of Africa and one-half to the American and West Indian colonies. It was this dependence on the triangular trade that made Manchester. According to estimate given to the Privy Council in 1788, Manchester exported annually to Africa goods worth £200,000 per annum, of which £80,000 was for enslaved Africans. This export gave employment to 180,000 men, women, and children. In the same year, Manchester furnished for the West Indian trade more than £300,000 annually in manufactured goods, providing additional employment to many thousands. In the early eighteenth century, England depended on the West Indies for between two-thirds and three-quarters of its raw cotton. In 1764, British imports of raw cotton amounted to nearly four million pounds, half of which came from the West Indies.

In 1778, Britain imported over £6.5 million, two-thirds of which came from the West Indies. But this was to change dramatically as the center of gravity shifted from the islands of the West Indies to mainland America. According to Adam Smith (1723–1790), "our tobacco colonies send us home no such wealthy planters as we see frequently arrive from our sugar islands." The sugar planter ranked among the biggest capitalists of the mercantilist epoch. The West Indian planter was a familiar figure in English society in the eighteenth century. The main reason was that once the planter made his fortune in the Caribbean he returned to Britain (Williams, 1943: 85). In 1698, the West Indies were sending back annually to England about three hundred children to be educated. The planter, once returned to Britain, would acquire estates, blend with the aristocracy, and remove the marks of their origin. Absenteeism had serious consequences in the British West Indies. Plantations were left to the mismanagement of overseers and attorneys. The Deficiency Laws failed to restrain the practice of absenteeism. One of the most prominent sugar planters in England was the Beckfords, a Gloucestershire family. In 1670, Alderman Sir Thomas Beckford, one of the first absentee proprietors, was getting £2,000 per annum from his Jamaican property, clear of all charges. Peter Beckford became the most distinguished of the new colonists and at his death in 1710 he was in possession of the largest property in Europe. In 1737, Peter Beckford's grandson, William, inherited the family wealth and became the most powerful West Indian planter in England. He built Fonthill Abbey – also known as Beckford's Folly, a large Gothic revival country house built between 1796 and 1813, at Fonthill Gifford, in Wiltshire. In 1837 Beckford was awarded over £15,000, by way of compensation for 770 enslaved Africans he owned in Jamaica.

The Hibberts were West Indian slave owner as well as merchants, who supplied cotton and linen checks for Africa and West Indian plantations. Robert Hibbert (1769–1849) lived in Bedfordshire off the income from his West Indian property. A relative, George, was partner in an opulent trading firm in London, and for many years was a Jamaica agent in England. George Hibbert (1757–1837) took the lead in the construction of the West India Docks and was elected the first chairman of the board of directors. His portrait hangs in the boardroom of the Port of London Authority. The Hibberts received over £31,000 in compensation for their 1,618 enslaved Africans. Also, connected with Jamaica were the Longs and Charles Long, at his death, left property in Suffolk, a house in Bloomsbury, London and 14,000 acres in Jamaica. A relative, Beeston Long Jr., was chairman of the London Dock Company and a Bank director. Another member of the family, Lord Farnborough, built Bromley Hill Place in Kent, noted for its ornamental gardens. John Gladstone was indirectly connected in the slave trade, as a slave owner in the West Indies. The sugar and other produce which he sold on the Liverpool Exchange were grown on his own plantations and imported in his own ships. The fortune amassed by this means permitted him to open up trade connections with Russia, India, and China. He made large investments in land and houses in Liverpool. The Codringtons were another well-known family which owed its wealth and status to their enslaved Africans and sugar plantations. Colonel Christopher Codrington (1640–1698) was governor of Barbados during the seventeenth century, and his plantations in Barbados and Barbuda was quite valuable.

The Warner family was dispersed over the Leeward Islands, some in Antigua, Dominica, St. Vincent, and Trinidad. Joseph Warner rose to be one of the three leading surgeons of his day, at Guys Hospital, and one of the first members of the College of Surgeons, founded in 1750. In the nineteenth century, another Warner was President of the Council of Antigua, with another, as Attorney-General of Trinidad and was a great advocate of East Indian immigration. Sir Pelham Francis Warner MBE was a famous English Test cricketer, who was born in Port of Spain, Trinidad in 1873, who was educated at Rugby School and Oriel College, Oxford. The public schools of Eton, Westminster, Harrow, and Winchester were full of the sons of West Indians slave and plantation owners. The combination of slave and plantation owners, merchants and colonial agents in England, constituted the powerful West India interest of the eighteenth century. They used their wealth to buy votes and rotten Boroughs and so got into Parliament. The Earl of Chesterfield was laughed to scorn, in 1767, when he offered £2,500 for a seat for which a West Indian would offer double. In the elections of 1830, a West Indian slave owner successfully spent £18,000, getting himself elected in Bristol. The election expenses of an unsuccessful West India candidate in Liverpool in the same year cost nearly £50,000, of which John Bolton, a rich West Indian merchant, slave trader and slave owner contributed £10,000.

West Indian interest was well represented in Parliament, by Gladstone, the Beckfords, Hibbert, and Colston, to name but a few. Ten out of 15 members of one of the most important committees of the Society of Planters and Merchants held seats in the English Parliament. West Indian interest was also entrenched in the House of Lords, especially as peerages were readily conferred in return for political support. Richard Pennant became Lord Penrhyn, of Ireland in 1783 and the Lascelles, an old Barbadian slave owing family, were ennobled in 1812 and Edward Lascelles became the first Baron of Harewood. The Earl of Balcarres, first created in the Peerage of Scotland in 1651, for Alexander Lindsay, owned sugar plantation in Jamaica, and received over £12,000 in compensation for 640 enslaved Africans. The slave traders, owners, and merchants, were all in evidence everywhere, as aldermen, mayors, and councilors. William Beckford was alderman of the City of London and twice Lord Mayor. In the London Guildhall, there stands a splendid monument erected in his honor and his brother Richard was also an alderman. George Hibbert became an alderman of London and William Miles became alderman of the City of Bristol. The agent for Massachusetts reported in 1764 that there were fifty or sixty West Indian voters in the British Parliament who could turn the balance on any side they pleased. But, in the coming century, there appeared another combination of fifty or sixty voters, and they were the Lancashire cotton interest, and its slogan was not monopoly but *laissez faire.*

Laissez-faire

The principles of *laissez-faire* prevailed long before the publication of Adam Smith's "The Wealth of Nations," in 1776. In 1689, the passing of the Toleration Act indicated the abandonment by the State of its policy controlling the religion of the nation and in 1695, the censorship of the press was discontinued. During the period of Whig predominance, from 1689 to 1761, the Statute of Artificers ceased to be generally enforced and the laws relating to colonial trade were not rigidly enforced. The philosophical basis of *laissez-faire* was the assumption that the maximum benefit was to be attained by the individual through the exercise of free, unfettered competition, and that if men were liberated from regulation and restriction in their activities, they would choose such courses of action as would be to their greatest advantage. According to Southgate (1954), it is self-evident that this supposition ignores the fact that what is to the advantage of one is usually to the detriment of another, so that the net gain to the community is much less than might result from their co-operation. During the Industrial Revolution, when factories came into existence no attempt was made to supervise their erection and equipment and conditions of labor in them were entirely unregulated. In course of time, it was recognized that freedom for the employer might mean a condition of slavery for the worker, as an employer and an employee did not stand on equal footing. The housing problem was treated from the same pint of view. The State should leave the provision of houses to be provided by private enterprise (Southgate, 1954: 336).

Laissez faire became a practice in the new industry long before it penetrated the textbooks as orthodox economic theory. The spinning jenny, the water frame and the mule, revolutionized the industry, which, as a result, showed a continuous upward trend. Between 1700 and 1780, imports of raw cotton increased more than three times and exports of cotton goods 15 times. Between 1757 and 1773, the population of Manchester increased by nearly fifty percent and the number of people engaged in the cotton industry quadrupled between 1750 and 1785. The Humanitarians were disposed to challenge the conclusion which was drawn from existing economic views, and they contended that attempts ought to be made to reform social conditions. Between 1833 and 1850 several Factory Acts were passed, the effect of which was to establish a measure of regulation of the conditions of labor in textile factories, and which laid the foundations for its extension to other industries later in the century. In 1833, the State gave its first grant of twenty thousand pounds to assist in the building of schools. In 1848 a Central Board of Health was set up, with particular focus on water supply and drainage. In 1880, an Employers' Liability Act was passed, by which any workman who met with an accident while at work became entitled to compensation from his employer, as long as it was not the workman's fault.

Further acts in 1896 and 1906 directed that compensation should be payable in all cases of accidents arising out of employment. The institution of Old Age Pensions in 1909 and the establishment in 1911 of schemes of National Insurance against sickness and unemployment, contributed further to the protection of workers. A Trade Boards Act of 1918 authorized the establishment of trade boards in any industry in which there appeared to be insufficient organization for the regulation of wages. By the passing of the Elementary Education Act of 1870, an attempt was made to set up a national system of education. In 1891, elementary education was made by and large free. The 1902 Education Act, abolished School Boards and transferred their property and functions to councils of counties, boroughs, non-county boroughs, and urban districts. Further Education Acts of 1918 and 1944 provided for improvements in the system and made school attendance compulsory. Great Britain was only engaged in the Crimean War between 1854 and 1856, while the attention of some of the European nations was mainly directed towards fighting. The Bismarckian Wars occurred between 1864 and 1871. France, under Napoleon III, was involved in a number of military undertakings; Italy was engaged in the struggle of unification. Under Alexander II, the Tsar Liberator, Russia freed her serfs.

Social and Economic Influence of the Triangular Trade

Insurance is based on the principle that the frequency of events which involve loss, damage, or potential liability can be measured. The most important legal limitation on insurance lies in the requirement of insurable interest. For example, the owner of a house has an insurable interest in his property, for he would suffer loss if it was destroyed. In 1575, a Chamber of Assurances was established in the Royal Exchange, by Thomas Gresham (1519–1579), to arbitrate in marine disputes. In 1601, the Chambers' powers were defined by statute and in 1662, they were further strengthened. But at some time in the course of the 18th century, the Court of Commissioners disappeared. The destruction of the Smyrna fleet in 1693, as a result of attacks by the French in the Bay of Lagos, caused loss to underwriters, some of whom were unable to meet their obligations. In 1720, two important companies, the Royal Exchange Assurance with a capital of £1,152,000, and the London Assurance with capital of £2 million were authorized by Act of Parliament. The South Sea Bubble of the same year caused these companies some difficulties and in 1721 both companies obtained supplementary charters which authorized them to transact life assurance and fire insurance business, in addition to marine insurance. Coffee houses were a prominent feature of the social and economic life of London in the eighteenth century, and the business of marine insurance was carried on by underwriters in the coffee house of Edward Lloyd, originally in Tower Street, but later moved to Lombard Street and Abchurch Lane. Lloyd died in 1713, but the coffee house was carried on in his name. In 1734, the publication of *Lloyd's List* was started, it contained notices of arrivals and sailings of ships and other information of use to merchants and underwriters.

The Industrial Revolution involved the establishment of thousands of factories and their equipment with machinery, and the building of warehouses in which vast quantities of raw materials, and manufactured products were stored. The demand for fire insurance was necessarily high, and an elaborate classification of risks was worked out in light of experience. Life insurance differs from marine, fire and accident insurance, in that death is certain to happen; the only uncertain factor in life assurance is the date that death will occur. In the 18 century, full life assurance became general and certain class of the community, merchants and manufacturers, enjoyed a standard of living which their families might not maintain in the event of their death, unless some provision was made. To such people life assurance offered special attraction and several societies were formed. The Amicable Society, which was founded in 1706, had accumulated sufficient reserves to enable it to grantee a fixed minimum payment on the death of a member, in 1757. The Equitable Society, founded in 1756, proposed to insure lives either for a single year or for a number of years. A good deal of life insurance business at the time was purely speculative and policies might even be taken out upon the lives of famous people by people who had no personal interest in their lives. In 1774 the Life Assurance Act prohibited assurances upon any lives except for the advantage of persons who had an interest in the life of the person assured. The nineteenth century witnessed the establishment of many life insurance businesses, with many new and attractive forms of policy on offer.

In the 18th century, the slave trade was the most valuable trade and West Indian property among the most valuable property in the British Empire and occupied an important position in the eyes of the rising insurance companies. The earliest extant advertisement referring to Lloyd's in 1692, deals with the sale of three ships by auction, which were cleared for Barbados and Virginia. Lloyd's, like other insurance companies, insured slaves and slave ships, and was vitally interested in legal decisions to what constituted "natural deaths" and "perils of the sea." One of the most distinguished chairmen of Lloyds was Joseph Marryat (1757–1824), a British member of Parliament for Horsham and later for Sandwich, of Huguenot descent, and a West Indian slave plantation owner, who successfully fought to maintained Lloyd' monopoly of marine insurance against a rival company in the House of Commons in 1810. Marryat was awarded £15,000 compensation in 1837 for 391 enslaved Africans in Trinidad and Jamaica. In 1782, the West Indian sugar interest took the lead in starting another insurance company, the Phoenix, one of the first companies to establish a branch oversea – in the West Indies. The Liverpool Underwriters' Association was formed in 1802, with its chairman John Gladstone, a prominent West Indian slave merchant.

The triangular trade made an enormous contribution to Britain's industrial development, as the profits from this trade fertilized the entire productive system of the country. The state industry of Wales, which provided material for roofing, was one example of this link. Lord Penrhyn revolutionized a new method on his Caernarvonshire estate, he owned slave plantations in Jamaica and was chairman of the West India Committee at the end of the 18th century. Another example was the development of the railways in England. The leading figure in the first great railway project, which linked Liverpool and Manchester, was Joseph Sanders. Three other men had close connections with the triangular trade – General Gascoyne of Liverpool, John Gladstone, and John Moss. The Bristol West Indian interest also played a prominent role in the construction of the Great Western Railway. Improved methods in coal mining, combined with the influence of steam, resulted in a great expansion of the iron industry. Between 1740 and 1788, iron production increased fourfold and the number of furnaces rose by one-half. The iron bridge and the iron railroad had appeared; the Carron Works had been founded; and Wilkinson was already famous as "the father of the iron trade." Cotton, the Queen of the Industrial Revolution, responded readily to new inventions, unhampered by traditions and guild restrictions, which impeded its older rival, wool.

It has been argued, Southgate (1954), that the Industrial Revolution was a change in industrial method, from hand work to work done by machines driven by mechanical or electrical power and in industrial organization, from work at home to work in factories. The term "Industrial Revolution" is often attributed to Arnold Toynbee (1889–1975), in 1884. It was used by a French writer, Louis Auguste Blanqui (1805–1881), as early as 1837, and later by William Stanley Jevons (1835–1882), Friedrich Engels (1820–1895), and Karl Marx (1818–1883). In the mid-18th century, experiments and improvements were being made in textile machinery. The steam engine as a source of power made its appearance early in the eighteenth century but did not entirely displace the water wheel until the middle of the nineteenth century. The change from domestic work to factory was not completed within a short period. Although the term "Industrial Revolution" is challenged, when the state of British industry in 1850 is contrasted with its condition in 1770, the appropriateness of these changes which occurred will be recognized as revolutionary and the driving force was the triangular trade.

Until the middle of the 18th century the textile work was done in the cottages by people who were engaged also in agricultural labor, and it was done by hand or with the help of hand worked implements. In this cottage textile work, men, women, and children were all engaged. Carding was done by children, wool or cotton was spun into yarn by women, and weaving was usually done by men. The industry was under the control of "dealers" or "clothiers," men who possessed capital and lived in market towns, from where they visited neighboring villages in order to give out wool or cotton and collected the cloth made from the material left in previous visit. From his warehouse in the town, the clothier would send the cloth to a port, where it was purchased by merchant for export. English trade was expanding in the eighteenth century and merchants found an ever-increasing demand abroad for English textile goods. This increased demand required improvement in production, which developed into the Industrial Revolution. The textile machinery invented in the eighteenth century was first applied to cotton. Whilst wool had been the more common material, there was opposition to any change to production. Cotton was supplied from the Levant and the West Indies and near the end of the eighteenth century from the U.S.A. The cotton industry forged ahead and took the premier place in British textiles. Machines were at first driven by waterpower, and the early factories were set up by the side of streams in the countrysides. As there was no accommodation for workmen, cottages were erected for them by the factory owners; factory villages thus came into existence.

The invention of the steam engine provided an alternative which possessed advantages over water as a source of power. With its advent, it became convenient to establish factories in regions where coal was found, in places such as Lancashire and Yorkshire. The change from the domestic system of industry to the factory system was an inevitable consequence of the invention of machinery. The separation between the workers on the one hand and the ownership of capital on the other, accounts for the system being styled capitalistic. In course of time, the congregation of men together in the factories made possible their association in trade unions. The social and political value of such associations was not inconsiderable. The demand for iron for machinery and engines led to a revival of the iron industry and the need for coal brought about great advances in mining. Circumstances in Great Britain favored the accumulation of capital, especially capital from the slave trade, a necessity for industrial expansion. The success achieves by trading companies had brought wealth to their members and money was thus available for investment in industry. Apart from agriculture, the most important industry in England before the Industrial Revolution was the manufacture of woolen cloth. There was however a shortage of wool in the eighteenth century. As early as 1660 the export of wool from England had been prohibited, to protect supplies. Merino wool was imported from Spain for the manufacture of fine cloth. Wool was also imported from Ireland and the Irish was forbidden to export it elsewhere. The embargo on export was not removed until 1825.

There was a considerable immigration of Huguenots from France, after the revocation of the Edit of Nantes in 1685, and the silk industry attained a considerable measure of importance in the first half of the eighteenth century. Raw silk was imported from India, where the East India Company encouraged its production, and from Italy. The manufacture of cotton goods was unimportant in the early years of the eighteenth century. East India cotton goods were popular in England, but to protect the woolen and silk industries, cotton goods from the east was prohibited in 1700. For over 50 years after 1720, a fabric, which was a mixture of linen and cotton, was produced in England. In the second half of the eighteenth century, new factors arose which gave greater importance to the cotton industry. Following the death of the Mogul Emperor Aurangzeb (1618–1707), resulted in a struggle between France and England for predominance in India, which interrupted the supply of Indian cotton to England. Steam power was harnessed in 1711, by Thomas Newcomen (1663–1729), to a clumsy great machine for pumping floodwater from a mine in Devon. The steam engine was improved by James Watt (1736–1819), a Scots instrument maker from Glasgow, who in 1763 was called in to repair a model of Newcomen's engine, and perfected the condenser. From then on, the different sorts of machinery to which the motive power of steam could be applied seemed limitless.

The water frame, invented by Richard Arkwright (1732–1792) in 1769, was capable of producing cotton yarn strong enough to serve as warp. In 1774, the prohibition which had been imposed in 1721, on the use of printed cotton goods in England was removed. Another factor was the introduction of cotton from the southern states of the United States of America, and by the end of the century, an unlimited supply of cotton was available from this source, especially as this cotton was produced by enslaved Africans and was therefore much cheaper than otherwise would have been. The chief difficulty of spinning was solved by James Hargreaves (1720–1778), in 1767, a Blackburn weaver, who constructed the spinning jenny, which was capable of turning eleven spindles at once. In 1769, Richard Arkwright invented a spinning machine which was based on an entirely new principle. Arkwright machine (water frame) required waterpower and needed a large space. Special buildings were needed, so that its induction marked the beginning of the factory system. In 1771, Arkwright and Jedediah Strutt (1726–1797) established a factory at Cromford, in Derbyshire, for the production of yarn for stockings. By 1776, Samuel Crompton (1753–1827) had invented his mule, a machine which combined the principles of the jenny and the water frame, which produced a yarn both fine and strong. Mules were constructed that could turn hundreds of spindles. For several reasons, Lancashire proved to be a more suitable area for the cotton manufacture than any other part of England. The heavy rainfall of Lancashire, with its humid atmosphere, along with the Pennine and Rossendale valleys provided waterpower for the early machinery.

After the induction of the steam engine, coal was abundantly available, which drove the machinery. England's cotton industry suffered a serious setback during the American Civil War (1861–1865), with the blockade of southern ports by the federal navy, which cut off supplies. Cotton mills were closed, owners found themselves in financial difficulties and unemployed operatives suffered great hardships. Many cotton mill workers drifted into other occupations, and some emigrated. As a result of cotton famine attention was directed to India and Egypt. Fears of shortage of supplies in the twentieth century led to the formation in 1902 of the British Cotton Growing Association. This body encouraged cotton growing in various tropical areas of the British Empire, especially in India, the West Indies, Nigeria, Uganda, and the Sudan. Steampower and machines could not be put into widespread use unless coal – the most efficient fuel for raising steam – could be mined on a much-expanded scale. This was achieved through a number of innovations, including underground pumps, Humphry Davy's (1778–1829) safety lamp (1816) and the use of gunpowder for blasting. Machines which had to be made of hardened steel, could not be built in quantity unless the production of iron and steel could be expanded. This was achieved through a series of improvements, including those introduced at Carron ironworks in Scotland (1760) and Henry Cort's (1741–1800) patents for the puddling and rolling of steel. The concentration of industrial workers under one roof, in a factory; long preceded the arrival of power-driven machinery – factory is a shortened form of "manufactory"; meaning "production by hand." However, the appearance of factories caused the sudden growth of new urban centers. The archetype lay in Manchester, capital of Lancashire's cotton industry.

The first British census of 1801 showed that Manchester had grown tenfold in a quarter of a century, from the proportions of a single parish to a town of 75,275 registered inhabitants. Inland communications were crucial; they had to be rendered as cheap and as effective as maritime trade. Huge loads of coal, iron, cotton, clay, and wool needed to be moved from mines and ports to factories. Manufactured goods needed to be delivered to distant markets. Rivers, road and rail transport were all involved. In 1760, the duke of Bridgewater's engineer, James Brindley (1716–72), improved the scope of earlier canals, by building a waterway that crossed Lancashire's river Irwell on the Barton Aqueduct. In 1804, at Merthyt Tydfil in South Wales, the Cornish engineer Richard Trevithick (1771–1833) coaxed a high-pressure steam locomotive into pulling coal wagons along a short railway. In 1815, J. L. McAdam (1756–1836) gave his name to a system of road construction using chipped stone base and tar surface. When factories were built, they were designed with a view to securing the maximum profit for their owners and no thought was given to the health, comfort, or safety of their employees. Inadequate ventilation, insanitary and crowded factories exposed workers to serious and even fatal accidents. Factory owners discovered that a good deal of the work in their factories could be performed by women and children, whose labor was cheaper than that of men.

The Poor Law of 1601 had ordered that pauper children should be apprenticed to trade. These children were taken to factories, where they were kept at work for between 12 and 16 hours per day. They were not allowed to rest on Sundays, when it was common practice to clean the machinery. They were fed, clothed, and housed by factory owners. The work of the children was supervised by foremen who did not hesitate to us whip and stick to keep their charges busy. Child labor was nothing new, as under the cottage system of textile work toddlers of three or four were expected to assist in simple processes. Politicians and economists were convinced that it was essential to the prosperity of industry that it should be left alone, as it would be improper for the state to interfere in the "free" contract between employer and employee. But, a workman seeking employment cannot bargain on equal terms with his prospective employer. To the employer, it matters little whether he selects one man or another. If an adult workman is unable to bargain with an employer upon equal terms it is certain that a child will be unable to secure satisfactory terms of employment. Attention as directed to the evils of the factory system and by a resolution of the Magistrates of Manchester in 1784, they decided to refuse their sanction to the indentures of parish apprentices if it appeared that they were expected to work at night, or for more than ten hours per day. The Manchester Board of Health was set up in 1795, for the purpose of investigating the conditions of child labor in factories. The nineteenth century witnessed the enactment of a series of Factory Acts, the aim of which was to protect only those who were in need of assistance and protection in the framing of conditions of employment. It was only in the mid-nineteenth century that it was recognized that men of full age were not in a position to demand equitable terms of employment.

The Acts of 1847 and 1850 were to indirectly restrict the working hours of men. In the last quarter of the nineteenth century, the opposition to the extension of factory legislation, with regards to women, was associated with a movement for the improvement of political, social, and economic status of women. The "Women's Rights" movement thought that trade unions of men supported the exclusion of women from factory employment. The first Factory Act, which was introduced by Sir Robert Peel, himself a factory owner, was passed in 1802, which was called the "Health and Morals of Apprentices Act." It dealt with only apprentices in cotton and woolen factories. But, this act may be appropriately regarded as part of the Poor Law, rather than of the code of Factory Legislation. In 1819, an Act was passed which applied to all children employed in cotton factories. Children under nine years of age were not to be employed and those under 16 were not to work for more than 12 hours per day. Nothing, however, could happen without money. Immense amounts of money were needed from investors willing to take risks to make immense, but uncertain, gains. Such money could only be forthcoming where other forms of pre-industrial enterprise had accumulated a ready store of capital. The processing of colonial raw materials gave rise to new industries in England. The refining process of brown sugar transformed it into white sugar, which was durable and capable of preservation. The earliest reference to sugar refining in England is an order of the Privy Council in 1615. The importance of the refining industry increased in proportion to its production on plantations in the West Indies. As sugar became one of the necessities of life, instead of the luxury of kings, in the middle of the eighteenth century, there were a hundred and twenty refineries in England, employing over a thousand men. In addition, the distribution of the refined sugar called into existence a number of subsidiary trades.

The frequent association of Glasgow with the tobacco industry is only a part of the truth. The prosperity of the city in the eighteenth century was due as much to its sugar refining business. The Wester Sugar House was built in 1667, followed by Easter Sugar House in 1669 and shortly after the South Sugar House and another in 1707, prior to the Act of Union, direct trade relations with the colonies were prohibited. The majority of refineries were located in and around Glasgow – eighty compared with Bristol's twenty. In 1774 there were eight refineries in Liverpool and there were others in Chester, Lancashire, Newcastle, and Southampton. The main reason why sugar was refined in England and not on plantations in the West Indies, was a deliberate policy of the British government. The duty placed on refined sugar was four times that of brown sugar. Under the mercantile system, the sugar planters had a monopoly of the British market, as foreign imports were prohibited. But, while the price of sugar was being forced down in the world market by increases of sugar from French, Spanish, and Portuguese colonies, British planters were intent on maintaining a monopoly price in Britain. Yet another colonial raw material gave birth to yet another English industry. One of the important by-products of sugar is molasses, from which rum may be distilled. But rum never attained the importance of cotton or sugar, as contribution to British industry, because rum was imported directly from the islands in its finish state. However, rum was indispensable in the fisheries and fur trades and as a naval ration. Rum was also an essential part of the cargo of slave ships and no slave trader could afford to dispense with a cargo of rum. African dealers were piled with it and were induced to drink till they lost their reason, and then their deal was struck.

Slave trading demanded manufactured fetters, chains, and padlocks to fastened enslaved Africans securely on slave ships. Iron bars were the trading medium on large parts of the African coast and constituted nearly three-quarters of the value of the cargo of the Swallow in 1679. In 1682, the Royal African Company was exporting about 10,000 bars of iron a year. Guns formed a regular part of every African cargo. Birmingham became the center of the gun trade as Manchester was of the cotton trade. Birmingham guns of the eighteenth century were exchanged for enslaved Africans and the African musket was an important export, reaching a total of about 150,000 annually, making Africa the most important customer of Birmingham gun makers. Exports of wrought iron and nails went to West Indian plantations. Along with iron, went brass, copper and lead. Exports of brass pans and kettles to Africa dated back before 1660 but increased with free trade after 1698. According to tradition, ships sailed to Africa with their holds full of idols, while their cabins were occupied by missionaries. The needs of shipbuilding gave a further stimulus to heavy industry. Iron chain and anchor foundries in Liverpool, lived off the building of ships. Copper sheeting for vessels gave rise to local industries. Between thirty and forty vessels were employed in transporting the copper, smelted in Lancashire and Cheshire, from works at Hollywell to warehouses in Liverpool. When questions of abolition came before Parliament, manufacturers of, and dealers in, iron, copper, brass, and lead, in Liverpool, petitioned against the project, as it would affect employment in the town. Birmingham declared that it was dependent on the slave trade to a considerable extent for a large part of its various manufactures. They also declared that abolition of the slave trade would ruin the town and impoverish many of its inhabitants. In 1710, the British West Indies took over one-fifth of British exports, but in 1735 less than one-sixth. The peak was reached in 1729, when the West Indies took nearly one-quarter of the total exports.

The steamship came into existence many years before the first steam railway was open. As early as 1802 a steamship, the *Charlotte Dundas,* was working on the Forth and Clyde Canal. In 1809, the Atlantic was crossed by a steamship, the *Savannah,* and another, the *Enterprise,* made the voyage to India by way of the Cape in 1825, the year of the completion of the Stockton and Darlington Railway. The opening of the Suez Canal in 1869 was not used by sailing ships. The four-cylinder engine, which was introduced in 1854, produced much higher steam pressure with lower fuel consumption. The compound engine was succeeded by the triple-expansion engine, which further reduced the amount of fuel needed for a given voyage. The invention of the turbine, by Sir Charles Parsons (1854–1931), resulted in further increase in speed and reliability. Since the repeal of the Navigation Acts, British shipping was not subjected to Government control. Ships were subject to no test of seaworthiness and sometimes were heavily insured and sent to sea in hope that they would be lost. Between 1785 and 1800, eighty-two steam engines were constructed for cotton mills, fifty-five of these in Lancashire alone, with the first steam loom factory being built in Manchester in 1806. In 1835, there were 116,800 power looms in Great Britain, all but six percent in the cotton industry. Between 1785 and 1830, British cotton manufacturers rose from one million pounds to thirty-one million pounds and cotton cloth printed in Great Britain increased from twenty million yards in 1796, to three-hundred-and-forty-seven million yards in 1830.

The benefits of British West Indian colonies contributed an increased in the population employed in the cotton industry, which rose from 350,000 in 1788 to 800,000 in 1806. Cotton was "raising men like mushrooms." Oldham in 1760 was a village of 400 inhabitants, but in 1801 it had 20,000. Manchester's population increased six fold between 1773 and 1824. British cotton imports rose from eleven million pounds in 1784 to two-hundred-and-eighty-three million pounds in 1832. The New World had come, not for the last time, to the rescue of the Old. The United States supplied less than one-hundredth of British cotton imports in the years 1786–1790, three-quarters in the years 1826–1830, and four-fifth in the years 1846–1850. The British West Indian slave plantation owners could not keep pace with Manchester's requirements. The sugar islands provided seven-tenth of British cotton imports in the years 1786–1790, one-fifth in the years 1826–1830, but less than one-hundredth in the years 1846–1850. The West Indies had built up Manchester in the eighteenth century, but they became a tiny speck on Manchester's limitless horizon in the year her magnates sent their first delegates to Westminster. In 1817 the production of woolen pieces in West Riding, the chief center of the industry, was six times the figure for 1738. By 1800, the imports of wool were 4000 tons; by the late 1830s, they were five times as large. The value of woolen fabrics exported rose from four million pounds in 1772 to seven million in 1801. In 1802, for the first time, the export of cotton-manufactured goods exceeded wool exports and by 1830 exports of wool were one-sixth of the value of cotton exports.

Britain's mechanized might was making the world her footstool. She was clothing the world, exporting men and machines and had become the world's banker. Between 1815 and 1830, at least fifty-million pound sterling had been invested in the most stable European governments, twenty million in Latin America, and nearly six million in the United States of America. But no one would advance a shilling on West Indian plantations. British purchases of Southern slave produced cotton stimulated the expansion of the cotton kingdom; private and state-owned banks in the south sought loans in London. In 1821, British exports to the world amounted to forty-three-million pound sterling, in 1832 they were sixty-five million. Britain's exports to East Indies and China rose from one-twelfth in 1821 to one-tenth in 1832. In 1821, the British West Indies took one-ninth of total British exports, but only one-seventeenth in 1832. The British West Indies were becoming increasingly insignificant to British capitalism and what were successes in the mid-eighteenth century were a failure eighty years later. In 1871, some powers in connection with the mercantile marine were given to the Board of Trade, which proved to be inadequate. By the Merchant Shipping Acts of 1875 and 1876, penalties were to be imposed on ship-owners who sent vessels to sea in an unseaworthy condition. The Merchant Shipping Act of 1894 extended and codified the law on the subject. For the safety of passengers and crew at sea, the provision of lifebuoys, lifebelts, and lifeboats were required. According to Southgate (1954), before 1890 Great Britain constructed about eighty percent of the world's shipping and owned about sixty percent. During the war of 1914–18, British shipping suffered heavily as a result of the German submarine blockade of Great Britain. The British mercantile marine after the war consisted of fast, well-equipped, and up to date vessels. But for many years after the war in many of the ports of Great Britain merchant ships were laid up because there was no demand for their services.

Slavery and Racism

Diop (1974) argues that during the Middle Ages, the memory of a Negro Egypt that had civilized the world had been blurred by ignorance of the antique tradition hidden in libraries or buried under ruins. It would become more obscured during those four-hundred years of slavery. Inflated by their recent technical superiority, Europeans looked down on the African world and condescended to touch nothing but its riches. Ignorant of the African past, combined with the economic necessity to exploit, the European distort the moral personality of Africans and their intellectual aptitudes. Thereafter, "Negro" became a synonym for primitive being, "inferior" endowed with a pre-logical mentality (Diop, 1974: 24). European desire to legitimize colonization and the slave trade, engendered an entire literature to describe the so-called inferior traits of the African. The minds of several generations of Europeans would be gradually indoctrinated to accept as revealed truth the equation: Negro equal inferior humanity. To crown this cynicism, colonization would be depicted as a duty of humanity. They invoked "the civilizing mission" of the west, charged with the responsibility to raise the African to the level of other men. From then on, capitalism had clear sailing to practice the most ferocious exploitation under the cloak of moral pretexts. As most Europeans recognized that the Negro has artistic gifts, linked to his sensitivity as an inferior animal. Such was the opinion of the Frenchman Joseph de Gobineau (1816–1882 CE), who decrees that the artistic sense is inseparable from Negro blood, in particular, the sense of rhythm is related to the Negro's emotional aptitudes.

Hieroglyphics were allegedly deciphered in 1822 by Champollion the younger, who died in 1832, using the Rosetta Stone. Egyptologists were dumbfounded with admiration for the past grandeur and perfection then discovered. But it became increasingly "inadmissible" to continue to accept the theory – evident until then – of a Negro Egypt. Hence, the birth of Egyptology was marked by the need to destroy the memory of a Negro Egypt at any cost and in all minds. In a letter to his brother, Champollion the Younger made reference to bas-reliefs on the tomb of Sesostris I (r.1971–1926 BCE), dating back to the Eighteenth Dynasty, and representing the races of man known to the Egyptians. This is what he says: "Right in the valley of Biban-el-Moluk, we admired, like all previous visitors, the astonishing freshness of the paintings and the fine sculptures on several tombs... At first I had thought, from copies of those bas-reliefs published in England, that these peoples of different races led by the god Horus holding his

shepherd's staff, were indeed nations subject to the rule of the Pharaohs...
According to legend itself, they wished to represent the inhabitants of Egypt and
those of foreign lands... Men led by Horus, the shepherd of the peoples, belonging
to four distinct families. The first, the one closest to the god, has a dark red color,
a well-proportioned body, kind face, nose slightly aquiline, long braided hair, and
is dressed in white, the race of men par excellence; i.e., the Egyptians. There can
be no uncertainty about the racial identity of the men who come next: he belongs
to the black race, designated under the general term Nahasi. The third presents a
very different aspect; his skin color borders on yellow or tan; he has a strongly
aquiline nose, thick, black pointed beard, and wears a short garment of varied
colors; these are called Namou. Finally, the last one is what we call flesh-colored,
a white skin of the most delicate shade, a nose straight or slightly arched, blue
eyes, blond or reddish beard, tall stature and very slender, clad in a hairy ox-skin,
a veritable savage tattooed on various parts of his body; he is called Tamhou"
(Diop, 1974:46). We find there Egyptians and Africans represented in the same
way, but the Namou (Asians) and the Tamhou (Europeans) present significant and
curious variants. Champollion stated that he did not expect, on arriving at Biban-
el-Moluk, to find sculpture that serve as vignettes for the history of the primitive
Europeans.

As early as the Eighteenth Dynasty (1550–1292 BCE), the Egyptians
habitually represented, in a manner that could not possibly be confused by the
white and yellow races of Europe and Asia, the two groups of their own race:
civilized Blacks of the valley, and Blacks from certain areas in the interior.
According to Diop (1974), the color of the two men closest to the god Horus is
merely the expression of two Negro shades. On numerous bas-reliefs under the
Eighteenth Dynasty, all the specimens of the White race were placed behind the
Blacks; in particular, the "blond beast" of Gobineau and later Nazis, a tattooed
savage, dressed in animal skin, instead of being at the start of all civilization, was
still essentially untouched by it and occupied the last echelon of humanity.
According to Campollion, the first tribes that inhabited Egypt, that is, the Nile
Valley between the Syene cataract and the sea, came from Abyssinia to Sennar.
The Ancient Egyptians belonged to race quite similar to the Kennous or Barabras,
present inhabitants of Nubia. In the Copts of Egypt, we do not find any of the
characteristic features of the ancient Egyptian population. The Copts are the result
of crossbreeding with all the nations that have successively dominated Egypt. It is
therefore wrong to seek in them the principal features of the old race. Despite this
constant and very ancient crossbreeding the Negro characteristics of the early
Egyptian race have not yet disappeared, and in most cases their color does not
differ from that of other Black Africans.

Champollion's opinion on the Egyptian race was recorded in a memoir
prepared for the Pasha of Egypt, to whom he delivered it in 1829. However, for

Champollion-Figeac, the brother of Champollion the Younger and father of Egyptology, black skin and woolly hair "do not suffice to characterize the Negro race." For Figeac, it is no longer enough to be black from head to toe and to have woolly hair to be a Negro. Yet, after arguing that black skin and woolly hair do not suffice to characterize the Negro race, Champollion-Figeac contradicts himself, by stating that "frizzy, woolly hair is the true characteristic of the Negro race" (Diop, 1974: 53). This alteration of the fact was to become the cornerstones on which "Egyptological science" would be built. That is why Egyptologists so carefully avoided discussing the origin of the Egyptian race. Champollion-Figeac's alterations show how hard it is to prove the contrary of reality and still remain intelligible. He argued that the inhabitants of Africa belong to three races, quite distinct from each other for all time – Negroes of Central and West Africa; Kaffirs on the east coast and Moors, similar in stature, physiognomy and hair to the best formed nations of Europe and western Asia, and differing only in skin color which is tanned by the climate. However, the very scientists and philosophers who have transmitted present-day civilization to us, from Herodotus to Diodorus, from Greece to Rome, unanimously recognized that they borrowed that civilization from Blacks on the banks of the Nile: Ethiopians or Egyptians.

Emile Amelineau (1850–1915), after his in-depth study of Egyptian society, states: "From various Egyptian legends, I have been able to conclude that the populations settled in the Nile Valley, were Negroes, since the goddess Isis was said to have been a reddish-black woman." Amelineau designated the first black race to occupy Egypt by the name Anu. He shows that it came slowly down the Nile and founded the cities of Esneh, Erment, Qouch, and Heliopolis, for all those cities have the characteristic symbol which serves to demote the name Anu. If we accept the evidence of their own creations, *The Book of the Dead* among others, these Anu, whom Maspero tried to transform into Arabs…appear essentially as Blacks. It is worth pointing out that, according to Diop, *an* means man, in Diola. Thus, Anu originally may have meant men. According to Amelineau, this black race, the Anu, probably created in prehistoric times all elements of Egyptian civilization, which persist without significant change throughout its long existence. These Blacks were probably the first to practice agriculture, to irrigate the valley of the Nile, build dams, and invent sciences, arts, writing, and the calendar. They created the cosmogony contained in The *Book of the Dead*, texts which leave no doubt about the Negroness of the race that conceived these ideas. To this people, we can attribute without fear of error, the most ancient Egyptian books, The *Book of the Dead and the Texts of the Pyramids*, consequently, all the myths or religious teachings. The people already knew the principal arts; it left proof of this in the architecture of the tombs at Abydos, especially the tomb of Osiris, and in those sepulchers objects have been found bearing the unmistakable stamp of their origin – such as carved ivory, or the little head of a Nubian girl found in a tomb near that of Osiris, or the small wooden or ivory receptacles in the form of a feline head.

It is difficult to say whether or not racism was unusually strong before the sixteenth century, the first in which Northern Europeans came into frequent contact with peoples from other continents. In the early anti-Semitic ballads about the alleged murder of Little Sir Hugh, the evil Jew does not appear to have been seen as particularly dark. It is possible that with the influx of French and Italians after the Norman Conquest, dark skin had high status, as early ballads do sometimes contrast the poor fair girl with the rich brown one. On the other hand, there is no doubt that the "fair maid" is seen as morally superior and the ballads of two sisters, which appear to have very old Norse antecedents, lay emphasis on the wicked dark sister as opposed to the good fair one. By the fifteenth century, clear links were seen between dark skin color and evil and inferiority, when the newly arrived Gypsies were feared and hated for both their darkness and their alleged sexual prowess. It is generally accepted that a more clear-cut racism grew up after 1650 and that this was greatly intensified by the increased colonization of the Caribbean and North America, with its twin policies of extermination of the Native Americans and enslavement of Africans, aided by Jewish finance. Both these presented moral problems to Protestant societies, in which equality of all men before God, and personal liberty, were central values which could be eased only by strong racism. The Classical writer most often appealed to, for the justification of slavery was Aristotle, who linked "racial superiority" to the right to enslave other peoples, especially those of a "slavish disposition."

Similar perceptions of "racial" differences appear to have been central to the thought of John Locke (1632–1704), late seventeenth century Whig. There is no doubt that Locke, who was personally involved with slave-owning American colonies, was what we should now call a racist, as was David Hume (1711–76). Locke's consistent disparagement of Native Americans was essential to his politics, because the land the indigenous population inhabited was needed for English and other European settlers. Locke refused to justify the enslavement of people of the same nationality and called what might appear to be slavery of this kind mere "drudgery." For him and other so-called thinkers of the time, slavery was justified only when it was the result of capture as an alternative to a deserved death in a just war. Christian European attacks on heathen Africans and Native Americans were classed as "just wars" because the latter were not defending their property, but merely "waste land." Locke had the convenient belief that Africans and Native Americans did not practice agriculture and the only entitlement to land came from cultivation. Further, the very existence of large numbers of enslaved African led to belief that they were "natural slaves" in the Aristotelian sense. By the 1680s, there was a widespread opinion that Negroes were only one link above the apes in the "great chain of being." Most eighteenth century English-speaking thinkers like Hume and Benjamin Franklin (1706–90) were racist. In the case of Hume, he was a pioneer of the view that there had been not one creation of man but many different ones (polygenesis), because "such a uniform and constant difference could not happen in so many countries and ages, if nature had not made an original distinction betwixt these breeds of men" (Bernal, 1987: 203).

The centrality of racism to European society after 1700 is shown by the fact that this "polygenetic" view of human origins continued to grow in the early nineteenth century, even after the revival of Christianity. Apart from the extraordinary achievements of natural science during the period of Romantic dominance from 1790 to 1890 there was an enormous interest in history, and in both the chief model used was that of the "tree." However, the image of the tree had disadvantages in the description of European and Greek history. Johann Friedrich Blumenbach (1752–1840), a professor of natural history at Gottingen, was the first to publicize the term "Caucasian," which he used for the first time in the third edition of his great work in 1795. According to him the Caucasian was the first and most beautiful and talented race, from which all the others had degenerated to become Chinese, Negroes, etc. Blumenbach believed the Georgians to be the finest "white race." There was also the religious belief that man usefully be seen as coming after the Flood and, that Noah's Ark had landed on Mount Ararat in Southern Caucasus. Blumenbach included "Semites" and "Egyptians" among his Caucasians. The Caucasus was the traditional site of the imprisonment and cruel punishment of Prometheus, who was considered the epitome of Europe. Not only was he the son of Iapetus, identified as the biblical Japhet, the third son of Noah and the ancestor of the European. His heroic action of stealing fire for mankind soon came to be seen as typically Aryan.

In the 1780s, another Gottingen professor, August Ludwig von Schlozer (1735–1809), tried to set up a "Japhetic" linguistic family which included most of the languages later subsumed under the name Indo-European. Schlozer identified five fundamental factors for development: "The life-style determines, climate and nutrition creates, the sovereign forces, the priest teaches, and example inspires." Gottingen, according to Bernal (1987), in the period from 1775 to 1800, established many of the institutional forms of later universities and much of the intellectual framework within which later research and publication within the new professional disciplines was carried out. After the 1780s, the intensification of racism and the new belief in the central importance of "ethnicity" as a principle of historical explanation became critical for perceptions of Ancient Egypt. The Egyptians were increasingly detached from the noble Caucasians, and their "black" and African nature was more and more emphasized. Thus, the idea that they were the cultural ancestors of the Greeks, the epitome and pure childhood of Europe, became unbearable. According to Romantics, languages are peculiar as they are attached to a particular place, landscape, and climate. They are therefore seen as the individual expression of a specific people. Romantic influence can be seen in the discipline's two chief models – the tree and the family – which became widely popular throughout nineteenth century scholarship and science.

Although he did not spell it out, the concept of an Aryan race can be traced back to Karl Wilhelm Friedrich Schlegel (1772–1829), whose Romantic passion and conviction of the superiority of the Ancient Indian Race were sufficient to surmount the total lack of evidence and provide simple answer to what had now become "the Egyptian problem." Schlegel was one of the main figures of the Jena romantics and inspired Samuel Taylor Coleridge (1772–1834), who helped to introduce German idealist philosophy to English-speaking culture, Adam Mickiewicz (1798–1855), who is a principal figure in Polish Romanticism, and Kazimierz Brodzinski (1791–1835), another influential figure in Polish Romanticism. The question was, how could Africans have produced such a high civilization? For Schlegel, the answer lay in the fact that Egypt had been colonized and civilized by Indians. This notion of Egypt's Indian origin was to remain powerful throughout the nineteenth century. The idea of a Semitic-Hamitic of Afro-Asiatic linguistic 'superfamily,' including Semitic and Egyptian and other African languages, was not generally accepted until after the Second World War. The extraordinary growth of racism in the early nineteenth century included the increasingly pejorative "racial" classification of the Chinese and Egyptians. For the most part, seventeenth- and eighteenth-century writers considered them to belong to a distinct but inferior race. But the period of the Opium Wars (1839–1842 and 1856–1860), in which British forces fought to legalize the Opium Trade and expanded the coolie trade. All of China was open up to British merchants and exempted foreign imports from internal transit duties and all foreign traders gained rights to travel within China. These wars and events weakened the Qing Dynasty (1644–1912) and reduced China's separation from the rest of the world and made the Chinese racially contemptible.

The new anthropologist envisioned the "Yellow" races in the middle, below the white and above the black. For the racist pioneers, Joseph Arthur (1816–1882) and Comte de Gobineau, the yellow tribes have little physical vigor and tend towards apathy…feeble desires, a will that is obstinate rather than extreme… They invent little, but they are capable of appreciating and adopting what they can use. The new racial position of the Chinese was quite sufficient to exclude them from the romantic picture of dynamic world history. The racial position of the Ancient Egyptians was much more precarious than that of the Chinese for two reasons; scholars differed greatly on their "race," and the Egyptian themselves were balanced between the white acme of mankind and its black pit. For Cuvier, the Negro race is marked by black complexion, crisped or woolly hair, compressed cranium and a flat nose. The projection of the lower parts of the face, and thick lips, evidently approximate it to the monkey tribe. Jean Leopold Nicolas Frederic

Cuvier (1769–1832), known as Georges Cuvier, was a French naturalist and Zoologist, who was instrumental in establishing the fields of comparative anatomy and paleontology through his work in comparing living animals with fossils. His name is one of the 72 names inscribed on the Eiffel Tower. For Gobineau, the black variety is the lowest and lies at the bottom of the ladder. The animal character lent to its basic forum imposes its destiny from the moment of conception. It never leaves the most restricted intellectual zones… Many of the senses are developed with vigor unknown in the other two races: principally taste and smell. It is precisely in the greed for sensations that the most striking mark of its inferiority is found.

Hence, if Europeans were treating Blacks as badly as they did throughout the nineteenth century, Blacks had to be turned into animals or, at best, sub-humans. But, if it had been scientifically "proved" that Blacks were biologically incapable of civilization, how could one explain Ancient Egypt, which was inconveniently placed on the African continent? For many, there were three solutions. One, to deny that the Ancient Egyptians were black; the second was to deny that the Ancient Egyptians had created a "true" civilization; the third was to make doubly sure by denying both. The third explanation has been preferred by most nineteenth and twentieth century historians. Although, at least, for the last seven-thousand years, the population of Egypt contained African, Southwest Asian, and Mediterranean types, it is clear that the further south, or up the Nile, one goes, the blacker and more Negroid the population becomes. The Egyptian civilization was fundamentally African and that the African element was stronger in the Old (2686–2181 BCE) and Middle (2000–1700 BCE) Kingdoms, before the Hyksos invasion. Moreover, many of the most powerful Egyptian dynasties which were based in Upper Egypt – the 1st, 11th, 12th, and 18th – were made up of Pharaohs whom one can usefully call black. Herodotus referred to the Egyptians as having "black skins and woolly hair" (Bernal, 1987: 242). Where the racial stereotype of natural European superiority failed, like in Haiti, artificial intervention was necessary to preserve it. It is still remarkable that at precisely the time when Egyptians were controlling large areas of Greece, the invasion of Danaos, the Egyptian should have been denied. The image of Blacks on Greek soil was seen as particularly appalling. It was convenient for historians who were convinced that Africans were racially and categorically inferior to admit that Egyptians could form heroic conquering armies on a par with those of Napoleon, Wellington, or Blucher.

If Egyptian religion was monotheist, it could be seen as the basis or origin of Christianity. But in the late nineteenth century, the racial question was more salient. If Egyptian religion was monotheist, it would impinge on the Aryan-Semitic monopoly of civilization. The denial of Egyptian philosophy and suspicion of Egyptian religion dominated Egyptology until the 1960s. In 1948, Abbe Etienne Drioton (1889–1961), Director General of the Egyptian Antiquities

Services, began to see genuine religion in the Egyptian Wisdom Literature and to consider the possibility of an earlier monotheism. Since the 1960s, this more open attitude has begun to establish itself, especially in France and Germany. Some Egyptologists, like the German Hellmut Brunner, are even calling for a "new picture of Egypt." But there is still a considerable gap between the discipline of Egyptology and its "countercultures." In the United States of America, masonry, Egypt, and hieroglyphics were central to the foundation of Mormonism in the 1820s and had a major influence on middle to late nineteenth-century American writers. Herman Melville's (1819–1891) novels – especially *Moby Dick* – are full of Egyptian symbols and hieroglyphs, while Hawthorne's *The Scarlet Letter* bears the same stamp. However, from the mid-eighteenth century until 1978, The Church of Jesus Christ of Latter-Day Saints (Mormons) had a policy which prevented most black men from being ordained to the church's lay priesthood. Brigham Young (1801–1877) taught that black suffrage went against church doctrine, as God had taken away the rights for blacks to hold public office and that God would curse whites who married blacks. Young was also instrumental in officially legalizing slavery in Utah territory.

In Europe, the Rosicrucian kept Egypt as the center and origin of their beliefs. The mystical Swedenborgians of the eighteenth and nineteenth century and later Theosophists and Anthroposophist also placed Egypt in a central position. The increased evidence of African influence on Pre-Columbian America after 1000 BCE and discoveries of the Meso-American Pyramids, which contain burial space, strengthen the possibility of indirect Egyptian influence on these much later civilizations. In the early nineteenth century, Edme-Francois Jomard (1777–1862), the mathematician and surveyor attached to Napoleon's Expedition, put together the results of his own survey of the Great Pyramid at Giza and its precise geographical position, with ancient descriptions of the mathematical significance of its measurements. He was convinced that the Ancient Egyptians must have had an accurate knowledge of the earth's circumference and based their units of linear measurement upon it. In 1880, Flinders Petrie (1853–1942) went to Egypt to check the accuracy of previous measurements of the pyramids. He concluded that the Great Pyramid had been aligned to the cardinal points of the compass with more accuracy than any later building and that the measurements of the inner chamber demonstrated a knowledge of pi as 22 over 7 and of Pythagorean triangles. He was also astounded by the technical and mathematical skills that had gone into the pyramids' construction.

Throughout Western Europe, the Greek War of Independence was seen as a struggle between European youthful vigor and Asiatic and African decadence, corruption and cruelty. The barbarians of Genghis Khan and Tamerlane were revived in the nineteenth century. War to the death had been declared against European religion and civilization. In the eighteenth century, Turkish rule in

Greece and the Balkans had begun to be seen as unnatural, the result of the conquest of a superior race by an inferior one, as the Turks were placed in the racial hierarchy between the Chinese and the Egyptians. Before 1860, English and North American writers were sympathetic towards the Moors, because Islam was less pernicious to them than Catholicism. By the end of the century, "racial" considerations had transcended the religious ones. Hence, Arab rule of Spain was seen as sterile and "doomed" throughout its eight hundred generally flourishing years. In the arts, Karl Marx (1818–1883) argued that Egyptian mythology could never have been the foundation or womb of Greek art. Hence, Marx was able to deny Egyptian influence on Greece outright. Barthold Georg Niebuhr (1776–1831) has never been compared to Adam Smith (1723–1790), Jeromy Bentham (1748–1832), or James Mill (1773–1836), but there are close parallels between Niebuhr and Edmund Burke (1729–1797). One of Niebuhr's major theories was that the Patricians and the Plebeians were not merely different classes but different races. The idea that class differences originated from race differences had been used earlier in France; there the belief that the nobility were descendants of the Germanic Franks, while the *Third Estate* were native Gallo-Romans, had played a significant role in the development of the revolutions of 1789 and 1830.

Another pattern that is likely to have influenced Niebuhr is the Indian Caste system, which is supposed to have originated from the Aryan conquest and was an attempt to maintain the purity of the conquerors. It was Niebuhr who gave this theory academic cachet. The great Romantic French historian Jules Michelet (1798–1874) saluted Niebuhr for having discovered the ethnic principle of history as early as 1811. This was also the message taken from Niebuhr by his English disciple Dr. Arnold, the headmaster of Rugby School. Niebuhr was even more admired for his introduction of race into history. He was adamant about the desirability of national and racial purity. Niebuhr's preference for physical rather than "linguistic" racism may well have come from his father, and through him from the British in India. Physical racism was essential to Niebuhr's principle of the racial nature of class, given that different classes and even castes speak the same languages. Niebuhr brought together the Romanticism and the racism of the 1790s. In many ways *Rasse* (race) or *Geschlecht* (kind) were merely the "scientific" terms for Romantic Volk (people) or *Gemeinshaft* (community). In 1814, he called for European and Christian unity to fight Islam. The first conception of the superior White Race included Arabs and Jews, and this was the sense in which many English writers took the word Caucasian until the end of the nineteenth century. For instance, in the 1840s, Disraeli described Moses as "in every respect a man of complete Caucasian model," while he wrote that the European Jews could not have borne all their suffering if they had not been "of the unmixed blood of the Caucasians"; later, in the 1870s, George Eliot referred to Jews as "pure Caucasians." Even violent anti-Semitic Christian Lassen (1800–

1876), a professor of Old Indian languages and literature at the University of Bonn, did not refuse the Jews Caucasian status.

Professor Robert Knox (1793–1862), maintained in 1850 that "the race is everything, is simply a fact, the most remarkable, the most comprehensive, which philosophy has ever announced. Race is everything; literature, science, art – in a word, civilization depends on it." Knox gloried in the opportunities for white men to commit genocide: "What a field of extermination lies before the Saxon Celtic and Sarmatian." The Sarmatians were a large confederation of Iranian people during classical antiquity, flourishing from about the fifth century BCE to the fourth century CE. They spoke Scythian, an Indo-European language. However, Knox described the Jews as a "sterile hybrid," accusing them of having always been uncreative parasites. He asked, where are the Jewish farmers, mechanics, and laborers? Why does the Jew dislike handicraft labor? Has he no inventive power, no mechanical or scientific turn of mind? Knox argues that the Jews who follow any calling were not really Hebrews but sprung from a Jewish father and a Saxon or Celtic mother: "the real Jew has no hear for music, no love of science or literature, pursues no enquiry." Knox was not alone in such anti-Semitic thoughts, as thinkers like Charles Darwin (1809–1882) and Herbert Spencer (1820–1903) were working along similar lines. Jews and Phoenicians had long been seen as closely related, as scholars like Samuel Bochart (1599–1667) had been fully aware that Hebrew and Phoenician were dialects of the same language. By the 1780s, the two had been subsumed with Arabic, Aramaic, and Ethiopic under the title "Semitic." Physiological racists perceived the Semites as both "female" and "sterile," incapable of creative thought or action. From the 1880s onwards, the intellectual atmosphere of Europe was transformed by the triumph of anti-Semitism in Germany and Austria, and its sharp rise elsewhere. One of the main causes was the mass migration of east European Jews to Western Europe and America. The surge of racism was linked to imperialism and the sense of national solidarity built up in the metropolitan countries against the barbarous non-European "natives." Paradoxically, the 1880s and 1890s were also the decades in which Europe and North America took complete control of the world. The indigenous peoples of America and Australia had been largely exterminated and those in Africa and Asia were totally subdued and humiliated, and there was no reason why the white "man" should give them any political credit.

Slavery and English Racism

The English entered the slave trade in 1562, with the slave-trading voyages of Captain John Hawkins (1532–1595), who was backed by a host of luminaries, including the Lord Mayor of London. Queen Elizabeth I also enjoyed a proportion of the profits from these voyages. Both James 1 and Charles 1, licensed companies to trade in slaves, and by the 1620s, enslaved Africans were to be seen in ports in

England, especially Bristol and London. Although Dutch factories and forts were established on the West African Coast, the desired goods were gold and ivory, not slaves. But it was a Dutch ship that landed the first slaves in an English colony, at Virginia, in 1619, which was captured from the Portuguese, by Dutch privateers. Then in 1626, the Dutch West India Company abandoned its previous policy and started giving permission for the shipping of slaves from Africa to Dutch settlements in South America. More than anything else it was sugar that led the Dutch to get involved with the slave trade with gusto. In the late 1630s, with huge cane growing areas of Brazil under their control, the Dutch started importing into the New World tens of thousands of enslaved Africans. So, when the Dutch helped transport sugar to Barbados, they were looking for a market for their slaves, as well as new sugar producers for their refineries. It was racial, cultural and religious differences which made it simpler to justify and rationalized the coercion considered to be necessary to get the grueling work done in extreme heat of the factories and fields. But above all, it was the economic imperative.

It was the British who were most seriously engaged in colonizing the Caribbean, and at least 30,000 of them are estimated to have settled on various islands there during the reign of James 1 and Charles 1 in the first half of the seventeenth century (Segal, 1995: 38). The first English settlement to succeed was on the island of St. Christopher, where English and French joined forces in 1624 to massacre the island's Caribs, beat back Spanish attacks, and share the possession uneasily between them for eighty years. The most successful was the settlement in 1627 of Barbados, where the climate and terrain favored agriculture, the absent of hostile Caribs and neither Spanish nor French chose to attack. On Barbados, upon till 1640s, the English settlers used indentured servants to support an agricultural economy of tobacco and a little cotton. On December 26, 1654, for the first time, imperialism was to be directed by Parliament, when a fleet left England. Colonies were to be acquired by order of London, rather than by the actions of merchant syndicates, entrepreneurs, or adventurers. Cromwell decided that the Spanish provided the best target for his desire to fulfil what he saw as England's destiny of leading the opposition to the Church of Rome. Cromwell claimed to be revenging the cruelties of the Spanish in the Americas and releasing the region's indigenous peoples from the "Miserable Thralldom and bondage, both Spiritual and Civil" of the King of Spain: "because the creature itself also shall be delivered from the bondage of corruption into the glorious liberty of the children of God" (Romans 8:21 KJV).

Cromwell saw England's destiny as the head of a navigation and mercantile system and looked to dominate trade in the West Indies. To gain an interest in the West Indies that was in the possession of Spain, Puerto Rico and Hispaniola were suggested as first steps. In addition, the capture of Havana, "the back door of the West Indies" will obstruct the passing of the Spaniards' Plate Fleet into Europe.

Cartagena should be taken as well, as this was where Cromwell wanted to situate the capital of his new empire. On April 9, 1655, Admiral William Penn and General Robert Venables set sail from Barbados to capture Hispaniola. Three days later, the English force entered the eastern end of Hispaniola. On April 14, 1655, the English force headed west of Santo Domingo, but with the wind astern and lacking an experienced pilot, the mariners sailed past the landing point and not making shore until nearly 40 miles from the city. They found the small defenses there unmanned and some 7,000 troops landed unopposed. By May 4, all the surviving men were embarked in a most sad and lamentable condition. On Wednesday morning of May 9, a soldier in Venables' army sighted Jamaica and preparation was made to invade the island the following day. The combined land area of Barbados, St. Kitts, Antigua, Nevis, and Montserrat is less than a tenth of Jamaica's 4,441 square miles.

Columbus called St. Ann's Bay "Santa Gloria," as he found Jamaica "the fairest island that eyes have behold; mountainous and the land seems to touch the sky." In 1494, Jamaica had been populated by Tainos for over 2,500 years and they may have numbered around 50,000. In 1655 when the English arrived in Jamaica the Tainos had been made almost extinct, due to introduced diseases, hunger, enslavement, abortion, and suicide. The remaining population, in 1655, was only 2,500 and was outnumbered nearly three to one by the invading force under Admiral Penn and General Venables. Jamaica, soon to be the prize among England's Caribbean possessions, was seized from the Spanish colonists, in May 1655, when an English fleet bearing 7,000 men sailed into Kingston Harbor and captured Jamaica for Cromwell. Nine years later, systematic English settlement began. From the outset, it was envisioned that sugar was to be the principal crop and a settler with a wife was granted ninety acres, but a capitalist with one hundred slaves was granted three thousand acres. Sugar production accounted for the vast bulk of the labor used in this slave society. For its first adventure in aggressive, state-sponsored imperialism, England had put together a wretched army of the poorest quality soldiers, which were ill equipped and ill led. One English officer called the men of the army the "very scum of scums, and mere dregs of corruption" (Parker, 2011:107). The death of Cromwell in late 1658 left a power vacuum and lack of direction to the colonies from the metropolitan center, so Barbados and other islands went about their business unmolested, according to Parker (2011).

Jamaica in the mid-1670s had only four priests for the entire island, and the 2,000 white children had only one schoolmaster between them. Between 1671 and the 1680s, sugar production had increased tenfold in Jamaica. The number of sugar works had jumped from 57 in 1671 to 246 in 1684. Thirty years after Barbados, the Sugar Revolution had arrived in Jamaica and from the 1680s the profits, political and social power were in the hands of sugar plantation owners, such as Francis Price, Peter Beckford and the Drax family. In 1664, the English launched a broad offensive in the Caribbean, in King Charles II words, "to root the Dutch out of all places in the West Indies." Almost all English islands participated and Sir Thomas Modyford (1620–1679) unleashed his Port Royal buccaneers and within the year, virtually all the Dutch settlements in the West Indies were in English hands, along with valuable booty of slaves, cannon, horses and other merchandise. In January 1666, France entered the grab for the Caribbean, by supporting the Dutch against the English. The development of sugar production in Jamaica was slow, because about half of the white male population was involved in buccaneering, which was encouraged by the governor, Sir Thomas Modyford. A new governor was sent to Jamaica in 1671, Sir Thomas Lynch (1603–1684), to arrest Modyford and suppress the buccaneers. The arrest of Modyford and Henry Morgan (1635–1688) was the beginning of what has become known as "the Golden Age of Piracy." But, in 1676, Henry Morgan was knighted for service to England. Among the first to start making serious money from sugar was Peter Beckford, who in 1676 took over the 1,000 acres in St. Elizabeth, in Jamaica, granted to his kinsman Richard three years earlier. At the age of 33, Peter Beckford had a plantation of 2,238 acres.

During the 1670s, some 700 immigrants from England arrived in Jamaica each year, with a large number coming from Barbados. By 1673, the population of Jamaica consisted of about 4,000 white males, 2,000 white females, 1,700 white children, and about 9,500 enslaved Africans. The main reason for white people emigration to Jamaica was to make money. A report in 1675, boasted that a sugar plantation with 60 slaves in Jamaica could make more profit than one with 100 in "in any of the Caribbean Islands, by reason the soil is new." In 1640, when a Portuguese King was once again on the throne, he recognized the Dutch claim to part of Brazil, in return for Dutch help against Spain. But, Brazilian settlers rose in rebellion and succeeded in driving the Dutch from most of the territory they held and by 1654 the Dutch withdrew altogether from Brazil. Many of these Dutch, which included Jews, arrived in the Caribbean, where they taught the English settlers how to make marketable sugar. The supply of indentured servants from England was soon inadequate to meet the needs of the sugar industry in Barbados and it was the Dutch who informed the planters of how well African slave labor would serve the purpose. They also proceeded to provide the necessary slaves at a competitive price to them. The growth of sugar consumption and the requirements of the plantation saw a parallel and interrelated industry developed, linking Europe, Africa, Caribbean and the Americas in one of the seventeenth century's largest commercial enterprise, involving the forced migration of people from one continent to another. Another feature of this commercial enterprise was its explicit racialization, creating a whole ideology of racial superiority in order to justify the system of colonial slavery

Matthew Parker (2011) has traced the rise of sugar barons in the Caribbean and has shown how the production of sugar changed the demographics of the area. Producing sugar was far more demanding in terms of the amount of labor, capital, and expertise required for success. Planting, weeding and harvesting the cane was much more physically demanding work than producing cotton or tobacco crops. The cane had to be cut during the dry months of January to June and then the juice had to be extracted as fast as possible. This required the sugar planter to have immediate access to a grinding mill. The juice had to be conveyed immediately to a boiling house, where through a succession of operations, ever-greater quantities of liquid were removed from the crystallizing sugar. Within or adjacent to the boiling house, a series of four or five large copper kettles stood over a furnace. The juice went in the largest first and then ladled into the next smaller kettles, becoming hotter until at least the sugar was thick, ropy, and dark brown in color. Quicklime was added to aid granulation and at the right moment the boiler dampened and the sugar ladled into a cooling cistern. If everything went to plan, the planter now had a raw brown sugar called muscovado, combined with a liquid by-product, molasses. To cure the sugar, it was packed into earthenware pots, the molasses drained for up to a month, and the remaining golden-brown sugar spread in the sun to dry before being sent in leather bags to Bridgetown, where it was packed into hogsheads – large barrels that held about 1,500 lbs. of sugar. The hogsheads were then carried away to Amsterdam, Hamburg or London, were the sugar commanded consistently high prices.

The sugar plantation was an integrated combination of agriculture and industry, with every part depending on the others, "as wheels in a clock." Drax was the first to build a "factory in the field" and persuaded a number of smallholders nearby to grow canes for his mill. At the same time, he started rapidly increasing his slave holding. For payment, Drax engaged with three London merchants to ship them sugar or other commodities. By 1645, cane covered forty percent of Barbados' agricultural acreage. In the same year, a war of liberation broke out in Brazil as the Portuguese attempted to expel the Dutch, which stopped Brazil's sugar production, sending the price of sugar soaring, which made Barbadian sugar growers suddenly very rich. It was said that in 1646, some growers were getting about 4,000 weight of sugar, ordinarily 3,000, from an acre of land. In 1640 an acre of land was sold for 10-shilling, but by 1646, it was up to five pounds an acre. All over the island the forests were destroyed with renewed vigor and land previously given over to provisions was now put to growing cane. This benefitted supplier of provisions from Europe and North America, and by 1647, there was regular trade between the northern colonies and Barbados. It has been argued that the process whereby the sugar islands became slave societies was straightforward. A pattern was established of using the profits of servants' labor to invest in enslaving African men, women and children.

The early Christian Church endorsed the institution of slavery, which survived in parts of Europe alongside other forms of coercive labor such as feudalism and serfdom into the fifteenth century. Before slavery was adopted as the preferred solution to the Caribbean's labor shortage, strenuous attempts were made to ensure a steady supply of European workers. From the 1620s onwards, the system of indenture labor was widespread in English and French islands. Planters agreed to pay the passage of poor agricultural laborers, who were contracted to serve terms of between three or five years in return for subsistence and a small wage and a land grant, averaging four acres. During the term of service, the laborer was the legal property of the planter, forbidden to leave the plantation or to sell his services elsewhere. In England, rural poverty, unemployment and under-employment and the effect of the enclosures pushed an estimated 110,000 white servants towards the Caribbean colonies between 1610 and 1660. Some white laborers were kidnapped or press-ganged and others were political or religious dissidents who were transported to the Caribbean islands as virtual slaves. The backers of new colonies in the Caribbean needed able and willing hands – to clear land, build forts and plant crops.

Under the system of indenture, developed by the Virginia Company in the 1620s, young men and women contracted themselves to work for a master, for a period ranging from three to nine years. In return, they were given passage to the colonies and subsistence during their tenure. Some were paid annual wages, but most were promised a one-off payment – usually around ten pounds – or some land (in Barbados, it was ten acres) at the end of their contract. During the reign of Charles 1 (1625–1649), some 30,000 indentured servants went to the Caribbean, with a similar number going to the North American colonies. Although among them there were dissenters and those who were politically disaffected, most were from the rural poor, adversely affected by severe economic and social troubles in England during the 1620s and 1630s, which included depressions and bad harvests. The majority of these servants were from the West Country, East Anglia, or Ireland. There were others who saw emigration as a route to a new freedom, be it religious, political, economic or social (Parker, 2011: 25). In the 1630s, there were ready supplies of willing immigrants, but the following decade witnessed a declining birth rate in England, death from the Civil War and a rise in wages, meant there was a shortage of indentured laborers. At the same time, the switch to sugar increased the demand for labor. The result was that growing numbers of those arriving in Barbados were now unwilling immigrants. Henry Colt (1646–1731) had declared in 1631 that the great hope for Barbados was in cotton, although it was a more difficult crop to grow and more capital intensive than tobacco. Nonetheless, by 1634, there were a number of cotton gins and warehouses in operation, with the value of the crop surpassing tobacco by the late 1630s.

There was growing demand from mill owners in Lancashire, who were all too pleased to be released from their reliance on imports from Cyprus and the Levant. As would be the case with sugar, the leading cotton producers were Hilliard, Holdip, and James Drax. William and James Drax went into partnership with a Thomas Middleton and acquiring land in St. George's parish. By 1641, James Drax had over 400 acres and was the first to have significant number of enslaved Africans. In 1640, the prices for cotton and indigo fell, but here was one commodity which seemed to be on the rise – sugar. The arrival of sugar into the English and French colonies was largely due to events in Brazil, when Dutch settlers were forced out of Brazil from the 1640s onwards, many went to the Caribbean with their knowledge and skills of sugar production. Cromwell found that he could sell his Royalist prisoners of war as servants in Barbados. After Cromwell's victories at Drogheda, Worcester, and Dunbar in 1649–51, there was a large influx of Irish and Scots to the colony. After 1655, Cromwell issued pardons to criminals, on the condition that they go overseas. In a fit of Puritan zeal 400 women from brothels of London were shipped to Barbados in 1656. These political prisoners were treated with great cruelty (Parker, 2011:48). Studies of ships' rosters from the 1630s have shown that emigrants were overwhelmingly male – over ninety percent, with seventy percent aged between 15 and 24.

Ten years later, a visitor to Barbados complained of the incest, sodomy, and bestiality prevalent on the island. The Earl of Carlisle had instructed that leases on land be granted – seven years to life – on the basis of ten acres per white servant in each household. However, by the end of the seventeenth century, white indentured servant was effectively finished, superseded by enslaved African. The Civil War in England in 1641 ushered in a decade of benign neglect of the Caribbean by England. Into the vacuum stepped the Dutch, who had established trading stations on islands all over the West Indies. They furnished the island with enslaved African, copper, stills and all other things appertaining to the making of sugar. The stage was set for the triumph of sugar and everything that would go with it. With the vital help of the Dutch and the leadership of James Drax and others, a new and radically different society was about to be created and one that would result in the enslavement and death of millions of Africans (Parker, 2011: 31). Slavery and slave trading were already widespread in West Africa at the time of the first contact with Europeans. But, in African societies, unlike European slave traders, such slaves had rights and were not treated as mere chattels. Most European slave traders, preferred to conduct their business through African agents, who were usually paid a year in advance and African rulers benefited from this arrangement.

Haywood, (2009) argues that the steady growth of European demand for enslaved Africans had a huge impact on West Africa, as many of the kingdoms on the coast, such as Asante and Benin, were enriched by the slave trade with

Europeans. But, others became victims of raids by stronger kingdoms to take prisoners who could be sold into slavery. This massive loss of healthy strong young people held back economic growth in Africa (Haywood, 2009: 185). Slaves were cheaper than indentured servants and a Barbadian planter could buy an enslaved African male for about 20 pound – less for a woman and a child – which was in the region of twice the price of a five-year contracted indentured servant. Slaves were owned for life and the slave-owner also owned any offspring the slave might have. The plantation owners decided that the black man was the better worker. Although the Dutch were the main suppliers of enslaved Africans, English traders who had thrived in the servant trade, like William Vassall, Martin Noell, simply switched their operations to dealing in the slave trade. Just as Bristol had been the center of the servant trade, so now the city became the center of the slave trade (Parker, 2011:57). At the Restoration of Charles II (1660) Noell was one of four eminent merchants – the others being Thomas Povey, Sir Nicholas Crispe, and Sir Andrew Riccard – who took their seats among the courtier on the Council for Plantations. Certain generalization can be stated about the institution of slavery in the English Caribbean. An enslaved African was defined as *"chattel,"* a word derived from the Latin for livestock. Enslaved Africans were alienated from their families and cultures, with no legitimate rights, as it was a state of total degradation and were property and an instrument of his or her master's will. The institution of slavery, whenever or wherever it was found, relied on violent coercion to function and on the continuing degradation of its victims.

The shortage of indenture servants to replace those who had served their term and experience gained with the indentured system would prove invaluable when applied to the trade in enslaved Africans. Kidnaping in Africa encountered no such difficulties as were encountered in England. Captains and ships had the experience of the indentured trade to guide them in the African slave trade. Capital accumulated from the indentured trade financed the African slave trade. The felon drivers on the plantations became without effort slave drivers. It is self-evident that enslaved Africans fitted into a system already well developed. Hence, as Williams (1943) argues, the origin of the English slave trade was economic, not the color of the labor, but the cheapness of the labor. Further, when compared with Indian and white labor, enslaved Africans were eminently superior (Williams, 1943: 19). Both Indian slaves and white servants were to go down before the black man's superior endurance, docility, and labor capacity. The physical features of the African were only later racialized to justify a simple economic fact: that the colonies needed labor and African labor was the cheapest and best. This white servitude is of cardinal importance for an understanding of the development of the New World and the African's place in that development. Sugar, tobacco, and cotton required hordes of cheap labor, which the small farms of the ex-indentured white servants could not afford, as the small tobacco farms of Barbados were displaced by the large sugar plantations. In 1645, Barbados had 11,200 white small farmers and 5,680 enslaved Africans, but by 1667 there were 745 large plantation owners and 82,023 enslaved Africans. In 1645, the island had 18,300 whites fit to bear arms, but by 1667 there were only 8,300.

The white small farmers were squeezed out as land became scarce. The poor whites began to disperse all over the Caribbean from Barbados to Nevis, to Antigua, and thence to Guiana and Trinidad and later Carolina and Jamaica. Everywhere they were pursued and dispossessed by the same inexorable economic force, sugar. Between 1672 and 1708 the white men in Nevis decreased by more than three-fifths, with the population of enslaved Africans doubling. Between 1672 and 1727 white males of Montserrat declined by more than two-thirds and in the same time enslaved Africans increased more than eleven times. Williams (1943) argues, that King sugar had begun to change flourishing commonwealths of small farmers into vast sugar factories, owned by a camarilla of absentee capitalist magnates, worked by a mass of alien proletarians. Laws were introduced to compel absentee owners to keep white servants on their plantations. The increase of wealth for the few whites was as phenomenal as the increase of misery for the many enslaved Africans. In 1666, Barbados was computed to be seventeen times as rich as it had been before the planting of sugar. The price of land rocketed and a plantation of five hundred acres which sold for £400 in 1640 fetched £7,000 for a half-share in 1648. Where the plantation system did not develop, as in Cuba, enslaved Africans' labor was rare and white labor predominated. No sugar, no enslaved Africans. The blood of the enslaved Africans reddened the Atlantic and both its shores. It is ironic that a product, so sweet and necessary to human existence, should have occasioned so much crimes, bloodshed, and suffering.

According to Williams (1943), the British Empire center of gravity shifted from the Caribbean Sea to the Indian Ocean and from the West Indies to India. In 1783, the British Prime Minister, Pitt, began to take an abnormally great interest in British dominions in the east. In 1787, Wilberforce was encouraged, by Pitt, to sponsor the proposal for the abolition of the slave trade. In the same year, the East India Company turned its attention to the cultivation of sugar in India. Prior to 1783 the British government was uniformly consistent in its policy towards the slave trade. The greatest disaster, however, for the British sugar slave plantation owners was that the revolt of America left them face to face with their French rivals. The withdrawal of the 13 colonies considerably diminished the number of enslaved Africans in the British Empire and made abolition much easier than it would have been had the 13 colonies been English when the cotton gin revivified the moribund slave economy in the southern former colonies. In July 1783, an Order in Council decreed free trade between Britain and the United States, following which British imports from her former colonies increased fifty percent between 1784 and 1790. When the invention of the cotton gin entered the picture,

British imports increased from $9 million in 1792 to nearly $31 million in 1801. In June 1783, the British Prime Minister, Lord North, complimented the Quaker opponents of the slave trade on their humanity, but regretted that abolition was an impossibility, as the trade had become necessary to almost every nation in Europe. The West Indian colonies were still the darlings of the empire, the most precious jewels in the British diadem (Williams, 1944: 126).

Britain's acquisitions, after the defeat of the French at Trafalgar in 1805, was dramatically increased in the Caribbean, with the Guianese colonies adding some extra 200,000 square kilometer to the empire and expanded the potential for sugar and cotton production. During the 1790s British slave traders controlled more than half of the transatlantic trade and had the capacity to introduce thousands of new enslaved Africans into the newly acquired British territories. This prospect horrified the planters of Jamaica and Barbados, because of increased competition from Trinidad, Cuba and Brazil and if the new British territories were also to produce sugar their own industries were doomed. The only solution was to cut off the supply of slaves to their competitors. The British government also viewed the likelihood of massive over-production with alarm. Thus, an unlikely alliance of abolitionists and representatives from the traditional West Indian interest took the first step in banning the slave trade in May 1806. By cutting off slave supplies to competitors such as Cuba, Brazil and any remaining French colonies, Britain was supporting its own colonial sugar industry and protecting national interests, when it passed the Abolition Bill into law on May 1, 1807. Having unilaterally outlawed the trade, the British government had to close the legal loopholes, which allowed the continued traffic in enslaved Africans within its own colonies. One such clause was that which allowed a slave-owner to travel within the colonies accompanied by two domestic servants. This clause allowed nearly 10,000 so-called "domestics" to be imported into Guiana between 1808 and 1825 and a further 4,000 into Trinidad. An Act of Parliament in 1811 made slave trading a felony, punishable by transportation to the penal colonies and in 1827 another Act ruled it to be piracy and hence a capital offence. The British aim was to totally abolish the slave trade, because the government feared that other European colonies, notably the French and Spanish, would profit from a continuing flow of enslaved Africans.

In 1815, the Congress of Vienna ended 12 years of Anglo-French conflict an offered an opportunity for Britain to push France towards abolishing the slave trade. The Congress also marked the final settlement of inter-European rivalry in the Caribbean and in a spirit of reconciliation Britain restored Martinique and Guadeloupe to France, but held on to St. Lucia, Tobago and (from Spain) Trinidad. As a result of the Congress of Vienna, Britain controlled almost the whole of the Lesser Antilles as well as Jamaica and the Bahamas. Spain maintained its hold on Cuba, Puerto Rico, and Santo Domingo. Holland kept its handful of small trading posts and the mainland colony of Suriname, while Demark held the three Virgin

Islands of St. Thomas, St. John, and St. Croix. A hundred and fifty years of territorial competition, in which an island like St. Lucia had changed hands fourteen times between 1660 and 1814, was over. St. Lucia had become an emblem of British imperial ambition. In 1817, Spain agreed to abolish the slave trade by May 1820 along with Portugal and France. However, the slave trade continued despite the formal signing of treaties, especially by France and Spain. It is argued that Britain's campaign to abolish the slave trade was a remarkable failure and both Cuba and Brazil imported greater numbers of enslaved Africans after 1808 than they did during the earlier period.

When the general enslavement of Caucasians and mulattoes ended and slavery was confined to those with African skins, color itself became the trademark of slavery and, therefore, anathema, evil, and the worst that could happen to a human being was to be born black. Hence, one can readily understand why those Negroes who wish to escape Black or African identity are pushing for an identity of color with their kind in those countries where they are seen as "white" – Egypt, Algeria, Tunis, Morocco, Syria, Jordan, Iraq and Saudi Arabia – and therefore, in a class distinctly superior to the still enslaved or subordinated Blacks still living there. The confusion about "Black Jews" derives from the same historic developments which have been explained about white and black Arabs. Jews were in Africa from the earliest times and that Africans were in Palestine from the earliest times. Just as the Jews ruled in African Egypt for several centuries, so also the Africans ruled over Palestine for several centuries. In cases of warfare, both Jews and Africans might capture segments of the population to be marched off to work in the victorious nation, a notable instance being the Jewish captivity in Egypt and their later emancipation and return under the leadership of Moses. Many African Jews cross the Red Sea with Moses, such as the wife of the lawgiver himself. The people we call "Jews" indiscriminately are Hebrews by race and Jews by religion. Hence, anyone can be a Jew, but not a Hebrew. The Hebrews and Arabs are both Semitic peoples.

During the colonial era, white racism, faced with the consequences of their sexual conquest of enslaved African females, distinguished four degrees of color for blacks, negro (wholly); mulatto (half); quadroon (quarter – one black and three white grandparents); and mustee (eighth), but a law of 1781 classified all blacks "three degrees removed from the Negro ancestor exclusive" as whites and accordingly free. At the height of the British slave trade, between 1793 and 1800, the tonnage of shipping leaving British ports for Africa and the triangular trade route doubled. For example, in 1798 Liverpool sent 155 ships and transported an estimated 57,000 slaves from Africa. It is estimated that between 1700 and 1786, about 610,000 slaves were imported from Africa to Jamaica alone and by 1778, slaves outnumbered whites by eleven to one on the island. Most had been sold to European slave traders operating from slaving ports of the modern West African coast of Ghana and Nigeria. These slaves came from various tribes, including Yoruba, Fula, Ibo, Coromantee, and Mandingo. Sugar farming required a significant labor force and it was this that led to the large-scale importation of African slaves. Thus, a sugar industry based on slave labor and dominated by a few plantation magnates and Jewish middlemen was soon flourishing. Once again, the development of Jamaica into Britain's prime sugar producer made a few white slaver owners hugely rich, but at the price of killing hundreds of thousands of enslaved Africans

Anti-Slavery Campaigns

In 1825 the Navigation Laws had been modified, allowing the colonies to trade directly with any part of the world. The first nail in the monopolistic coffin had been driven. Another was driven, in the same year, when sugar from Mauritius, an eastern possession acquired in 1815, was admitted on the same footing as British West Indian sugar. The British West Indies in 1832 were, socially, an inferno; and economically an anachronism. Mercantilism had run its course and in this new political landscape West Indian slave owners were facing their end and in the new Parliament of 1832 colonial trade meant very little. The attack on West Indian slave owners was more than an attack on slavery, it was an attack on monopoly and their opponents were humanitarians and capitalists. It was deemed that the West Indian economic system was vicious and unprofitable and as such its destruction was inevitable. If West Indian slavery was detestable, West Indian monopoly was unpopular and the united odium of both was more than the colonies could bear. The slave trade was abolished in1807, slavery in 1833 and sugar preference in 1846, and the very vested interests which had been built up by the slave system now turned and destroyed that very system. Humanitarians spoke the language that the masses could understand, while capitalists defected from the ranks of slave owners and traders. When, to their surprise, the "invisible hand" of Adam Smith turned against them, they could only turn to the invisible hand of God.

The rise and fall of mercantilism, was the rise and fall of slavery. If corn was the King of monopolies, sugar was his Queen. The attack on the preferential sugar duties of the West Indies was part of a general philosophy, which in 1812 destroyed the East India Company's monopoly and in 1846 the Corn Laws of England. The Anti-Corn Law League said its treasurer was "established on the same righteous principle as the Anti-Slavery Society. The object of that society was to obtain the free right for Negroes to possess their own flesh and blood – the object of this was to obtain the free right of the people to exchange their labor for as much food as could be got for it" (Williams, 1944: 137). The protectionists were on the side of the West Indian slave owners, and the landed aristocracy of the corn bushels joined hands with the landed aristocracy of the sugar hogsheads. Peel, a free trader in cotton and silk, was a protectionist in corn and sugar. The West Indian cause was ably championed by Bentinck, Stanley, and Disraeli, but after 1846 Disraeli turned against them. The colonial system was the spinal cord of the mercantile epoch. In the age of free trade, industrial capitalists wanted no colonies, least of all the West Indies.

From the standpoint of the British Prime Minister, William Pitt the Younger (1759–1806), the age of the British sugar islands was over, and he now turned his attention to India. Pitt's plan was two-fold: to recapture the European market with the aid of sugar from India, and to secure an international abolition of the slave trade, which would ruin Saint Domingue. The French was very dependent on British slave traders that even a unilateral abolition by England would seriously dislocate the economy of the French colonies. Pitt's plan failed, because imports of East India sugar, on the scale planned, was impossible owing to high duties imposed on all sugar into England not produced in the British West Indies. Further, the French, Dutch, and Spanish refused to abolish the slave trade. Behind Pitt' cloak of humanitarianism concealed his political motives. At this juncture, the French Revolution came to Pitt's aid. Fearful that the idealism of the revolutionary movement would destroy the slave trade and slavery, the French slave owners of Saint Domingue offered the island to England in1791, and were soon followed by those of the Windward Islands. Pitt accepted these offers, when war broke out with France in 1793. Expedition after expedition was sent unsuccessfully to capture the precious colony, first from the French, then from the emancipated Negroes. Britain lost thousands of men and spent thousands of pounds sterling, in attempts to capture Saint Domingue. England failed, but the world's sugar bowl was destroyed in the process and French colonial superiority smashed forever.

Pitt could not have had Saint Domingue and abolition as well. Without its 40,000 enslaved African imports, each year, Saint Domingue might as well have been at the bottom of the sea. The very acceptance of the island meant, logically, the end of Pitt's interest in abolition. Under Pitt's administration, the British slave trade alone more than doubled, and Britain captured two more sugar colonies, Trinidad and British Guiana. The destruction of Saint Domingue meant the end of the French sugar trade. But the ruin of Saint Domingue did not mean the salvation of the British West Indies. Two new enemies appeared on the scene – Cuba and beet sugar. Under the American flag, Cuban sugar still fond a market in Europe, British West Indian surpluses piled up in England and bankruptcies were the order of the day. Between 1799 and 1807, 65 slave plantations in Jamaica were abandoned, 32 were sold for debts and in 1807, and suits were pending against 115 others. A parliamentary committee set up in 1807 discovered that British West Indian slave owners were producing at a loss. In 1800 their profit was 2.5 percent, in 1807 nothing. In 1806 the surplus of sugar in England amounted to 6,000 tons. Production had to be curtailed, but to restrict production the slave trade had to be stopped. The "saturated" colonies needed only 7,000 slaves per year. It was the new colonies that had to be restrained, and they were permanently crippled by abolition. This explains the support of the Abolition Bill by so many West Indian slave owners.

The British West Indies had lost their monopoly of sugar cultivation and by 1789 they could not compete with Saint Domingue; or in 1820 with Mauritius, neither in 1830 with Brazil, nor in 1840 with Cuba. Cuba could contain the British islands in the Caribbean and one of Brazil's mighty rivers could hold all the West Indian islands without its navigation being obstructed. India could produce enough rum to drown the West Indies. The West Indian situation was aggravated by the fact that production was in excess of the home consumption, by an estimate twenty-five percent. This surplus had to be sold in European markets, in competition with cheaper Brazilian and Cuban sugar. Overproduction in 1807 demanded abolition; and overproduction in 1833 demanded emancipation. Whilst Liverpool still carried on the slave trade in 1807, the trade had become less vital to the port's existence. In 1792, one out of every 12 ships belonging to the port was engaged in the slave trade, but in 1807 it was one in 24. In 1779, eleven ships sailed from Liverpool to Africa, the dock duties were £4,957, but in 1824 they were £130,000. If Liverpool turned against the slave trade, it still retained its interest in slavery. It was no longer West Indian slavery but American, no longer sugar but cotton. In 1802 half of Britain's cotton imports came through Liverpool, in 1812 two-thirds and nine-tenths in 1833. In the age of mercantilism, Manchester was Liverpool's hinterland, in the age of *laissez-faire* Liverpool was Manchester's suburb. Capitalists had first encouraged West Indian slavery and then helped to destroy it. When British capitalism depended on the West Indies, they ignored slavery or defended it. When British capitalism found the West Indian monopoly a nuisance, they destroyed West Indian slavery, as the first step in the destruction of West Indian monopoly.

Before and after 1815 the British government tried to bribe Spanish and Portuguese governments to abolish the slave trade. In 1818 Spain was given £400,000, in return for a promise to do so, but all to no avail, as abolition would have ruined Cuba and Brazil. Thereafter, the British government urged on by the West Indian slave owners, decided to adopt more drastic measures. Wellington was sent to the international conference at Verona to propose that continental powers boycott the produce of countries still involved in the slave trade; but his proposal was rejected. After 1833 British capitalists were still involved in the slave trade itself. British goods from Manchester and Liverpool, cotton, fetters and shackles, were sent directly to the coast of Africa or indirectly to Rio de Janeiro and Havana, where they were used by the Cuban and Brazilian consignees for the purpose of purchasing enslaved Africans. In 1845 Peel refused to deny the fact that British subjects were engaged in the slave trade. British banking firms in

Brazil financed the slave traders and insured their cargoes, thereby earning the goodwill of their hosts. British mining companies owned and purchased slaves to work in their enterprises. Benjamin Disraeli (1804–1881), Prime Minister of the United Kingdom (1868–1868 and 1874–1880) also condemned the suppression of the slave trade on grounds of economy and Arthur Wellesley (1769–1852), First Duke of Wellington, called it criminal – a breach of the law of nations – a breach of treaties. Even W. E. Gladstone (1809–1898) served as Prime Minister of the United Kingdom on four separate occasions (1868–74, 1880–1885, 1886–1886 and 1892–94), was forced to choose between the needs of British capitalists and the needs of West Indian slave owners. In 1841 he was all for suppression, but in 1850 he condemned the policy of suppression as anomalous and preposterous. Ironically it was the former slave owners of the West Indies who now held the humanitarian torch. Those who in 1807 were protecting the slave trade were after 1807 protesting against a system of man stealing against a poor and inoffensive people. A great mass movement for abolition of the slave trade developed in Jamaica in 1849. All classes, colors, parties, and sects were united on the question of justice to Africa. British capitalism had destroyed West Indian slavery, but it continued to thrive on Brazilian, Cuban and American slavery.

Much has been said about the contribution of those humanitarians who spearheaded the onslaught which destroyed the West Indian slave system and feed the Negro. However, according to Williams (1943) their importance has been seriously misunderstood and grossly exaggerated, especially by those who placed reason before evidence (Williams, 1943: 178). British humanitarians were a brilliant band; Clarkson personifies all the best in humanitarianism of the age. In 1793 Clarkson wrote a letter to Josiah Wedgwood which contains some of the finest sentiments that motivated his humanitarian peers. There were James Stephen senior and James Stephen junior. Stephen Sr. had been a lawyer in the West Indies and knew the conditions that enslaved Africans were living in at first hand. Stephen Jr. became the first outstanding permanent Under-secretary of the Colonial Office. He was constantly spurring on Wilberforce to greater and more public efforts, instead of the policy of memorials and interviews with ministers. Stephen Sr. drafted the Emancipation Bill, which included concessions he was loth to make to West Indian slave owners. Stephen Jr. wrote in 1841, "Popular franchises in the hands of the masters of a great body of slaves, were the worst instrument of tyranny which were ever yet forged for the oppression of mankind" (ibid 180). One of the earliest and most diligent of abolitionists was James Ramsay, who, as a rector in the West Indies, had had some 20 years' experience of slavery. In 1787 he informed Wilberforce, "The only use I can be of in the business is as a pioneer to remove obstacles; use me in this way and I shall be happy." West Indian slave owners pursued Ramsay with relentlessness reserved for him alone. Beside these men, the effeminate Wilberforce appears small in stature.

As a leader, Wilberforce was inept, addicted to moderation, compromise, and delay. He relied for success upon aristocratic patronage, parliamentary diplomacy, and private influence with men in office. He was a lobbyist, and it was common saying that his vote could safely be predicted, for it was certain to be opposed to his speech. But he was a persuasive and eloquent speaker, which earned him the sobriquet of "the nightingale of the House." These were the men the West Indian slave owners called visionaries and fanatics and likened to hyenas and tigers. With the aid of men like Macaulay, Wesley, Thornton and Brougham, they were successful in raising anti-slavery sentiments almost to the status of a religion in England, and these religious reformers who made Clapham into more than a railway junction were not inappropriately nicknamed "the saints." The abolitionists were not radicals and in their attitude to domestic problems they were reactionary. The Methodists offered the English workers bibles instead of bread and Wesleyan capitalists exhibited open contempt for the working class. Wilberforce supported the Corn Laws, repressed working class discontent in 1817, opposed feminine anti-slavery associations and thought the First Reform Bill too radical. Abolitionists, for a long time, eschewed and repeatedly disowned any idea of emancipation. Their interest was solely in the slave trade, whose abolition, they thought, would eventually lead, without legislative interference, into freedom. Wilberforce in 1807 publicly disowned such intentions. It was not until 1823 that emancipation became the avowed aim of abolitionists. The chief reason was the persecution of missionaries in Guiana, Barbados and Jamaica. Even then emancipation was to be gradual, "Nothing rash," warned Buxton. As in the United States, slavery was to wither away. This was the situation in 1830, when the July Revolution broke out in France and fanned the flames of parliamentary reform in England.

Conservatives and radicals clashed in a great anti-slavery meeting in May 1830. Buxton had proposed the usual resolutions, but Thomas Pownall rose to put his amendment – immediate abolition. The effect on delegates was electric. Buxton depreciated, Brougham interposed and Wilberforce waved his hands for silence, but the amendment was eventually put and carried with a burst of exulting triumph. These abolitionists inaugurated a sort of pious and silly crusade and urged their sympathizers to boycott slave-grown produce in favor of the free grown produce of India. The act of emancipating enslaved Africans in the British West Indies passed its Third reading on August 7, 1833. Forty-eight hours earlier, the East India Company's Charter had come up for renewal in the House of Lords. The Bill included a clause which declared that slavery "should be abolished" in India. Repeated declarations were made in Parliament on behalf of the government that the East India Company was preparing legislation with a view to the "amelioration" of slavery. As late as 1841 none of these rules and regulations for the mitigation of slavery had been produced. In defense of the East India Company it was pleaded in 1842, that they had prohibited the selling of children into slavery in periods of scarcity. Yet this was the tropical produce that abolitionists were recommending to the people of England. As an apology for the East India Company, Zachary Macaulay urged that "they had obtained dominion over countries which had been previously under Hindu and Mogul government." In 1837, Buxton expressed the fear that sugar would produce a system of slavery in the east as disgraceful as it had produced in the west. In 1843, Brougham was still looking forward with sanguine hope to the abolition of slavery in India. But some of the Clapham Sect, had East Indian interests and perhaps their detestation of West Indian slavery was sharpened by a sense of the unfair discrimination against the growing sugar plantations of India.

The Thorntons owned East India stock, as well as Zachary Macaulay, who had shares in East India Company. More important than Thornton or Macaulay was James Cropper, a prominent abolitionist. Cropper was the greatest importer of East India sugar into Liverpool and was the founder and head of the independent East India House, Cropper, Benson and Company of Liverpool, with a trade of a thousand pound a day. The real significance of abolitionists' support of East India and later Brazilian sugar is that there was more than the inhumanity of West Indian slavery involved. If these abolitionists had recommended Indian sugar, on humanitarian principle, it was their duty to their principle and their religion to boycott the enslaved African grown sugar of Brazil and Cuba. According to Williams (1943), in failing to do this it is not to be inferred that they were wrong, but it is undeniable that their failure to adopt such a course completely destroyed their humanitarian argument. Before 1833, abolitionists boycotted the British slave owners and after 1833, they continued to oppose West Indian plantation owners, who now employed free labor. But after 1833, these abolitionists espoused the cause of Brazilian slave owners. Abolitionists were boycotting enslaved Africans grown produce of British West Indies, dyed with the blood of enslaved Africans, while British capitalism depended upon enslaved Africans grown cotton of the United States. These boycotters of West Indian sugar sat upon chairs of Cuban mahogany, before desks of Brazilian rosewood and used inkstands of slave cut ebony; but it would do no good to go around and inquire into the pedigree of every chair and table. Abolitionists took the side of capitalists.

The Emancipation Act marked the end of these abolitionists' efforts. It never dawned upon them that the enslaved Africans' freedom could only be nominal if sugar plantations were allowed to endure. It never occurred to them that enslaved Africans might want access to or control of the land. For Buxton, freed Africans are blessed with a particular aptitude for the reception of moral and religious instruction and they should be supplied with missionaries, to institute schools and bibles. It is the only compensation in our power. In 1840 Gurney wrote that the ultimate and only radical cure of the vices and miseries of Africa is Christianity. The barbarous removal of enslaved Africans from Africa continued for at least 25 years after 1833, to sugar plantations of Brazil and Cuba. The desire for cheap sugar after 1833 overcame all abhorrence of slavery. The Cuban slave driver, armed with whip, cutlass, dagger, and pistol, and followed by bloodhounds, aroused not even a comment from these abolitionists. Brougham's philanthropy was excited only by sugar and not by cotton, only by the slave trade and not by slavery, only by the slave trade between Africa and Brazil and not by the slave trade between Virginia and Texas. In 1841 Thomas Babington Macaulay, later Lord Macaulay, argued that "My especial obligations in respect to Negro slavery ceased when slavery itself ceased in that part of the world for the welfare of which I, as a member of this House, was accountable" (Williams, 1943: 193). This left him free to import Brazilian sugar for refining. These great abolitionists – Wilberforce, Buxton, Macaulay, and Brougham – all now regarded slavery in a new light. Disraeli, like many in Britain and the United States, condemned emancipation as the greatest blunder ever committed by the English people.

The history of the abolition of slavery by the English is a story of ignorance, injustice, blundering, waste, and havoc. Even intellectuals were engulfed. Coleridge had been awarded the Browne Gold Medal at Cambridge for an Ode on slavery and had abstained from sugar. But in 1811 he sneered at the philanthropy trade, accused Wilberforce of caring only for his own soul, and criticized Clarkson, as a man, made vain by benevolence. In 1833 he was strongly opposed to frequent discussions of the "rights" of Negroes who should be "taught to be thankful for the providence which has placed them within the reach of the means of grace." Wordsworth, in 1833, argued that slavery was in principle monstrous but was not the worst thing in human nature, and in 1840 he refused to be publicly associated with the abolitionist's movement. Southey favored compulsory manumission by which slavery would, with reasonable hope, be extinguished in the course of a generation. Carlyle wrote an essay on "The Negro Question," sneering at the "Exeter-Gallery and other tragic Tomfoolery" which, proceeding on the false principle that all men were equal, had made of the West Indies a Black Ireland. The slave plantation owners had to deal not only with the British Parliament but with enslaved Africans and freed Africans. In 1823 the British Government adopted a new policy of reform towards West Indian slavery. The reform included abolition of the whip, enslaved Africans to have a day for religious instruction, prohibition of the flogging of enslaved African female, compulsory manumission, and freedom of female children. It was not emancipation but amelioration, not revolution but evolution. Slavery would be killed by kindness. But not one of these recommendations received unanimous approval by West Indian slave owners. Not only did they question these specific proposals of the British Government, they also challenged the right of the imperial parliament to legislate on their internal affairs.

West Indians in Parliament reminded the British people that by persisting in the question of right we lost America. Contrary to popular and even learned belief, the most dynamic and powerful social force in the colonies was the slaves themselves. The owners of enslaved Africans looked upon slavery as eternal, ordained by God, and went to great lengths to justify it by scriptural quotations. Slaves took the same scriptures and adopted them to their own purposes. To coercion and punishment, they responded with indolence, sabotage, and revolt. The docility of the enslaved African is a myth. Maroons of Jamaica and Bush Negroes of British Guiana testify to this myth. The successful slave uprising in Saint Domingue was a landmark in the history of slavery in the New World, and after 1804, when the independent republic of Haiti was established, every white slave-owner in Jamaica, Cuba, or Texas, lived in dread of another Toussaint L'Ouverture. Pressure on West Indian slave owners from capitalists in Britain was aggravated by pressure from enslaved Negroes in the West Indian colonies. All over the West Indies slaves were asking, "Why Bacchra no do that King bid him?" (Williams, 1943: 203). Enslaved Africans were not prepared to wait for freedom to come to them as a dispensation from above, as witnessed by the frequency and intensity of uprisings of enslaved Africans after 1800. Tension was rapidly mounting, British Guiana (1808), Barbados (1816), and in 1823, British Guiana went up in flames for the second time. Enslaved Africans from fifty plantations revolted, embracing a population of 12,000, demanding unconditional emancipation. Although these revolts were severely quilled, the spirit of discontent is anything but extinct, wrote the governor of British Guiana.

In 1831, enslaved Africans took matters into their own hands. An insurrectionary movement developed in Antigua and Barbados, with the prevailing idea that the King had granted emancipation. The climax came with an uprising in Jamaica during the Christmas holidays. With Jamaica on fire, nothing could stop the flames from spreading. The question, wrote a Jamaican to the governor, will not be left to the arbitration of a long angry discussion between the Government and slave owners. Enslaved Africans themselves have been taught that there is a third party, and that party is themselves. They know their strength and will assert their claim to freedom. In 1833 the alternatives were clear; emancipation from above, or emancipation from below. Economic change, the decline of the monopoly, the development of capitalism, humanitarian agitation in Britain and the determination of enslaved Africans to be free, was to destroyed plantation system of the West Indies. What was characteristic of British capitalism was typical also of capitalism in France. There was not a single great ship-owner at Nantes who, between 1714 and 1789, that did not buy and sell enslaved Africans. In this lies the essential importance of the slave trade; on its success or failure depended the progress or ruin of all other trades. Britain, far ahead of other European countries, and France were the two countries which ushered in the modern industrial world development and parliamentary democracy. The other foreign stream which fed the accumulation of capital in Britain, the trade with India, was secondary in the period up to 1783. It was only with the loss of the American colonies, which began in 1776 and continued through the French Revolution and the Napoleonic Wars to the Reform Bill of 1832, which was in many respects a world crisis that Britain turned to the serious exploitation of her Indian possessions.

Freedom Fighters

"Everywhere in every age the chain of slavery has been fashioned by the hands of liberty" [Rev. James Ramsay, 1733–1789).

Slave uprisings have occurred in nearly all societies that practice slavery and are amongst the most feared events for slave owners. The poet-prophet Ali bin Muhammad led imported enslaved East Africans in Iraq during the Zani Uprising against the Abbasid Caliphate in the ninth century. There were many enslaved Zanj uprisings against their Arab enslavers in Iraq. It was in early Iraq, where the largest enslaved African uprising occurred, when tens of thousands of enslaved East African laborers called Zanj, which was the name used by medieval Muslim explorers to refer to both a certain portion of Southeast Africa, and to the area of Bantu inhabitants. Zanj is also the origin of the place name Zanzibar. These Africans from Kenya, Tanzania, Ethiopia, Malawi and Zanzibar and other parts of East Africa, worked in the humid salt marshes of Southern Iraq in conditions of extreme misery. Fed scant portions of flour, semolina, and dates, they were constantly in conflict with the Iraqi slave system. The Zanj rebelled on at least three occasions between the seventh and ninth centuries. The largest of these rebellions lasted 15 years, from 868 to 883 CE, during which time these enslaved Africans inflicted defeat after defeat upon the Arab armies sent to suppress their uprising. The slave Spartacus led an uprising against the Romans. The English peasants uprising of 1381, led to calls for reform of feudalism in England. In Russia, the enslaved people were usually called Kholops and slavery remained a major institution in Russia until 1723, when Peter the Great (1672–1725) converted the enslaved household into house serfs. Sixteenth and seventeenth centuries' runaway serfs and Kholops, known as Cossacks (outlaws), formed autonomous communities in the Southern Steppes. In the Caribbean, there was resistant to the economic and political domination of Portuguese, Spanish, British, Dutch, and French, by enslaved Africans, especially against these Europeans' attempts at destroying the African's cultural personality, by the imposition of European ideas and values.

The first uprising by enslaved Africans in Spain's New World was on the island of Hispaniola, on December 27, 1522. The uprising started when 20 enslaved Africans on the estate of Don Diego, son of Christopher Columbus, joined with a similar number on a nearby estate to attack and kill a few Spaniards. Many of the freedom fighters were later hunted down and hanged. The impenetrable mountains of Hispaniola and Jamaica allowed groups of enslaved Africans to escape, to live free from fear of recapture and to organize armed bands, which led to colonial authorities, in 1545, in Hispaniola, offering to make peace with the *cimarrones*, a name previously applied to the wild cattle of Hispaniola, if they would cease their raids. The history of enslaved Africans' resistance runs parallel to that of slavery itself and the brutality of the plantation system never succeeded in crushing the spirit of the millions of enslaved Africans who were transported to the Americas and the Caribbean and their struggle to escape from enslavement took many forms. In May 1655, English troops landed at Hunt's Bay, Jamaica and swept aside some token Spanish resistance and marched inland to Spanish Town, the capital. But their delay in negotiating surrender terms gave some Spanish time to escape to Cuba and others the opportunity to free their enslaved Africans who fled to the mountains. These escapees formed Jamaica's first Maroon communities. In 1656, a year after the British replaced the Spanish rulers in Jamaica, English military commanders reported that the Negroes live by themselves in several parties and do very often, as our men go into the woods destroy and kill them with their launces, our English seldom killing any of them. Reward was offered in 1670 for one Juan de Serras, leader of one of the free settlements on the island.

In 1673, rebellion in the Parish of St. Ann, resulted in about 200 enslaved Africans escaping to the mountains and was never recaptured. Two years later, in 1678, martial law was declared in connection with uprisings at Caymanas in St. Catherine. As a result of uprisings on four plantations at Guanaboa Vale, in 1685, seven enslaved African freedom fighters are killed and fifty captured, with sixty-three escaping. In 1686 a guerrilla band numbering forty to a hundred enslaved Africans, whose ship had been wrecked off the island, were reported to be operating in St. Mary, St. George and St. Thomas ye Vale. Between1685 to 1688, fifty-two enslaved Africans were executed for rebellious behavior. In 1690, some five-hundred enslaved Africans rebelled at Suttons in Clarendon, with some hundred and fifty-armed enslaved African freedom fighters establishing a strong settlement in the central mountains. At the start of the eighteenth century, in Jamaica, there was an insurrection involving thirty enslaved Africans, twelve of whom were killed. The Governor of Jamaica, Thomas Handasyde (1702–1711), reported that the ringleaders were taken and executed and the rest sent off the island. In 1718 there were reports of freedom fighters freeing enslaved Africans from plantations. Between 1728 and 1729 troops were sent from Britain to assist the local militia, which caused enslaved African escapees to come together in two main groupings, which was the start of the Maroon Wars. The two Maroon groupings consisted of the Windwood Maroons, led by Nanny and the Leeward Maroons, led by Cudjoe, were the leaders of the First Maroon War, between 1730 and 1740. Nanny was born around 1686 in Ghana, West Africa, into the Ashanti tribe and was brought to Jamaica as a captive slave. Along with her brothers Accompong, Cudjoe, Johnny, and Quao, they escaped from their plantation and hid in the Blue Mountains area of northern St. Thomas.

While in hiding, they split up, in order to organize more Maroon communities across Jamaica. Cudjoe went to St. James, Accompong settled in St. Elizabeth, in a community called Accompong Town, Nanny and Quao founded communities in Portland. Nanny was married to a Maroon named Adou, but never had any children. By 1720, Nanny and Quao controlled an area in Blue Mountain – Nanny Town – consisting of 2.4 square kilometers, overlooking Stony River, via a 270-metre ridge, making a surprise attack by the British practically impossible. Lookouts were organized and warriors designated who could be summoned by the sound of a horn, called an Abeng. Maroons at Nanny Town and similar communities survived by sending traders to market towns to exchange food for weapons and cloth. The community raised animals, hunted, and grew crops and was organized like a typical Ashanti tribe in Africa. The Maroons were also known for raiding plantations for weapons and food, burning plantations, and leading enslaved Africans back to their communities. Nanny was responsible for freeing about eight-hundred enslaved Africans. Many in her community attributed Nanny's leadership skills to her obeah power, an African derived religion that is still widely practice in the West Indies and part of South America, including Jamaica, Barbados, Trinidad, and Tobago and Guyana. It is also known that Nanny possessed wide knowledge of herbs and other traditional healing methods. In the *Journal of the Assembly of Jamaica,* March 29–30, 1733, reference is made to a "resolution, bravery and fidelity" awarded to "loyal slaves…under the command of Captain Sambo," namely William Cuffee, who was rewarded for having fought the Maroons in the First Maroon War and who is called "a very good party Negro, having killed Nanny, the rebel (sic) old obeah woman" (Campbell, 1990: 177).

Campbell (1990) refers to these hired Maroon soldiers as "Black Shots" (Parker, 2011: 37). In 1738, Governor Edward Trelawny (1699–1754) commissioned Colonel John Guthrie either to destroy Maroon leader Kojo's main settlement or to seek peace. Guthrie chose the latter. Thus, the First Maroon War ended with Captain Cudjoe signing a peace treaty with the British in 1739, with the Maroons promised ten square kilometers in two locations. They were to remain in their five towns – Accompong; Trelawny Town; Mountain Top, Scots Hall and Nanny Town, established in honor of Nanny – living under their own chief with a

British supervisor. In exchange, the Maroons agreed not to harbor new escaped enslaved Africans, but rather to help catch them. The Maroons were paid to return captured enslaved Africans and fight for the British in the case of attack from either the French or the Spanish. The author views this so-called peace treaty a sell-out of their fellow enslaved Africans by the Maroons. Although many enslaved Africans aspired to escape, it was hard to achieve this on the smaller, flatter and more densely populated islands like Barbados or Antigua and punishment was also a real deterrent. Yet, in the larger, more mountainous islands, runaways did manage to evade recapture and form Maroon communities.

By the middle of the eighteenth century, British Jamaica and French Saint-Domingue had become the largest and most brutal slave societies of the region, rivalling Brazil as a destination for enslaved Africans. Death rates was three to four percent higher than birth rates on these slave islands, due to overwork and malnutrition, as enslaved Africans worked from sun up to sun down in very harsh conditions. These enslaved Africans also had poor living conditions and consequently they contracted many diseases. Coromantins were involved in many uprisings in the Caribbean and especially Jamaica. The Coromantins and other Akans had the single largest African cultural influence on Jamaica. For example, Maroons culture and language was seen as a derivation of Akan. Names of some notable Coromantins' leaders such as Cudjoe, Quamin, Cuffy, and Quamina, correspond to Akan day names Kojo, Kwame (Kwamina), Kofi, and Kwabena. In 1645 there were fewer than 6,000 enslaved Africans in the Caribbean, compared with 20,000 Europeans, but forty years later there were some 50,000 enslaved Africans on the islands. In 1760, there was another uprising in Jamaica, known as "Tacky's Revolt," starting in the Parish of St. Mary, in the early morning of Easter Monday. Tacky was an overseer on the Frontier plantation and was therefore in a position to organize other enslaved Africans on neighboring plantations. Tacky killed the owners of these plantations, before going on to attack Fort Haldane, where the munitions to defend the town of Port Maria were kept. After killing the storekeeper, Tacky and his fellow freedom fighters took four barrels of gunpowder and forty firearms with shots, before marching on to take the plantations at Heywood Hall and Esher. They stopped at Ballard's Valley to rejoice in their success, but an enslaved African from Esher plantation slipped away unnoticed and raised the alarm. Soon some eighty local mounted militias and the use of marines from a British warship, along with some Maroons mercenaries, were mobilized.

Many of these enslaved Africans decided to return to their plantation, but Tacky and about 25 of his men decided to fight on. Tacky was eventually killed by a Maroon "Black Shot," named Davy, who cut off his head. Those freedom fighters, who decided to fight on, later committed suicide, rather than surrendered to their enemies. A number of other uprisings broke out that same year, on other plantations, which may have been influenced by the "Tacky Revolt." In Westmoreland, it took three army companies, the militia from three western parishes and a hundred marines, to quell some six-hundred enslaved Africans, who rose up and rebelled against their enslavers. At the end of these uprisings, over four-hundred enslaved Africans were killed during fighting or were later executed, including two ringleaders who were burned alive and two other who were hung in iron cages at Kingston Parade, until they starved to death and over six hundred were transported to the Bay of Honduras in Central America. In the year 1795, enslaved Africans, right across the Caribbean, rose up in revolt, from St. Lucia in the east to Jamaica in the west. 1795 was also the year of the Second Maroon War in Jamaica, which led to the eviction of more than five hundred Maroons from Jamaica to Nova Scotia (Canada). In Nova Scotia, the Maroons kept up their resistance and they were eventually shipped to Sierra Leone. The primary cause of the trouble was said to be the fact that a Negro work house driver had wielded the whip that flogged a Maroon, who was accused of stealing a pig, and that many of the other prisoners who had been allowed to look on and mock were runaway slaves who had been caught by the Maroons and handed over to the authorities for punishment.

After four-and-half months of fighting the British, once again, signed a peace treaty with the Maroons. In accordance with the peace treaty, the Maroons involved gave up their arms. The island's Assembly deported those involved to Nova Scotia, but they were later sent to Sierra Leone. The needless escalation of the trouble was due to the action of the newly arrived Governor, who believed in strong measures to deal with unrest. In the year 1795, one of the bloodiest uprising took place in Grenada. The "Fedon Rebellion" in Grenada, which started with a coordinated attack on the towns of Grenville, La Bayle, and Charlotte Town (Gouyave) on March 2, 1795. Julien Fedon (?–1796) was the owner of the Belvedere estate in St. Johns and his main Franco-Grenadians co-conspirators, principally Jean-Pierre la Vallette, Charles Nognes, Stanislaus Besson, Etienne Ventour, and Joachim Phillip, were inspired by the French Revolution and its message of *liberty, equality* and *fraternity.* The 1789 Declaration of the Right of Man and the Citizen had been elaborated upon by decrees between 1791 and 1794, which granted full citizenship to free colored (mulatto) and emancipation to enslaved Africans in France's Caribbean territories. It is, however, worth noting that Grenada was under the control of France from 1664 to 1763 and from 1779 to 1783. Fedon, a free colored planter and slave owner and his compatriots were struggling against discrimination by the British, on account of their color and French nationality, and against restrictions on their political and social rights. The free colored freedom fighters were joined by many enslaved Africans, who saw the free colored as allies in fighting against the system of slavery. Fedon led about one hundred free coloreds and enslaved Africans in an uprising and killing a number of English settlers at the town of Grenville, in the northern section of the island. Simultaneously, another group of free coloreds and enslaved Africans under the leadership of Etienne Ventour and Joachim Phillip, both free mulattoes, seized the English inhabitants at Charlotte Town on the northwest. The insurrection ended on June 19, 1796, causing extensive damage in its wake and about 7,000 dead enslaved Africans, from a total slave population of 28,000.

The Black Carib War of 1795, in St. Vincent, was led by Chatoyer (Chatawae) against the British. Chief Chatoyer was killed on March 14, 1795, but his heroism inspired the first full-length play written and performed by black people in the U.S.A., "The Drama of King Shotoway" in 1823. In 1795 there was also the "Guerre des Bois" (Bush War) in St. Lucia. Curacao witnessed a major rebellion by enslaved Africans, which was led by Tula, Mercier, and Karpata. In Demerara (Guyana) there was an insurrection by enslaved Africans. In 1798, nineteen escaped slaves moved to the area formally occupied by the Maroons in the Second Maroon War. Troops were sent after them, killing some, but others survived. In 1816, enslaved Africans rose up in the largest major rebellion in Barbados history, when 20,000 of them from over 70 plantations rebelled. They drove whites off the plantations, but wide spread killing did not take place. The uprising was later called the "Bussa's Rebellion" after the slave ranger Bussa. Bussa's Rebellion failed and 120 enslaved Africans were killed in combat or were immediately executed and another 144 were brought to trial and executed. The Baptist War, also known as the Christmas Uprising and the Great Jamaican Slave Revolt of 1831–32, was a 10-day rebellion that mobilized as many as 60,000 of Jamaica's 300,000 enslaved Africans, led by enslaved African Baptist preacher, Samuel Sharpe (1801–1832). Sharpe was the enslaved person of a Montego Bay solicitor, and the instigator of the week-long Christmas Rebellion, that began on Kensington Estate on the December 27, 1831.

Samuel Sharpe was one of the few semi-literate enslaved Africans and acted as a deacon of Montego Bay's Burchell Baptist Church, and as religious meetings were the only legal gatherings for enslaved Africans, Sharpe used this forum to encourage peaceful protest. However, the peaceful protest turned into a violent conflict, when the Kensington Estate was set on fire. Enslaved Africans demanded emancipation and a working wage of half the going rate. Upon refusal of their demands, the strike escalated into full uprising. The uprising was suppressed by militia, belonging to Jamaican plantocracy. It is thought that the militia killed more than 1,000 enslaved Africans, during and after the uprising. Only 14 whites were killed by armed freedom fighters during the uprising, but property damage was estimated to be £1,154,589 (over £52,000 000, in today currency). Groups of white colonials destroyed chapels that housed enslaved African congregations. Its impact and the public outcry over the terrible retribution that followed were catalysts for the British Parliament passing the Abolition Bill in August 1834. Sam

Sharpe was executed in Montego Bay on May 23, 1832, a true freedom fighter. His last words were:

I would rather die upon yonder gallows than live in slavery.

Enslaved African females were active contributors in the struggle to weaken the slave system and to its eventual collapse. Many enslaved African females often feigned illness, malingered, committed arson, stole, and self-mutilated. More drastic measures included running away, poisoning their masters, self-manumission, and armed uprising. Women also took specific action in the form of infanticide and abortion. Through these measures, they sought to bring a speedier end to slavery. Suicide was also a means of rebelling against slavery. In the heyday of slavery, the British slave owners valued women as work units more than as breeding units. In the wake of the abolition of the slave trade, slave owners sought to implement ameliorative measures, in order to enhance population growth. But, in spite of all their efforts to encourage reproduction the slave population on all the sugar islands declined until Emancipation in 1834, with the exception of Barbados. It was the ending of slavery that influenced women's fertility rate, with their improved health. During slavery, women were seen as a prime worker and a breeder, a twofold responsibility that did not extend to the men. Like her male counterpart, enslaved female had a natural right to freedom and by any means necessary they sought to attain it. Enslaved women in the Caribbean also played a large role in religion and religious practices, such as "Shango" in Trinidad, "Ju-Ju" in the Bahamas and "Obeah" in Jamaica. Indeed, Obeah women played an important role in the resistance to their colonial masters and also worked as community leaders and teachers of cultural heritage. Women were often persecuted by colonialists if they were involved in these religious practices, as slave owners viewed them as evil witchcraft.

Shango (god of Thunder) worshippers in Yorubaland in Nigeria do not eat cowpea, because they believe that the wrath of the god of iron would descend on them. The Sango god necklaces are composed in varying patterns of red and white beads; usually in groupings of four and six, which are his "sacred numbers." Ceremonies for Sango devotees in the New World are focused on achieving power and control over their lives. Juju is a spiritual belief system incorporating objects, such as amulets, and spells used in religious practice, as part of witchcraft in West Africa. Obeah is a term used by the Igbo tribe in Nigeria to refer to sorcery, and religious practices developed among enslaved West Africans, specifically those of Igbo origin. The term *"Obeah"* is first found in documents from the early eighteenth century, as in its connection to Nanny of the Maroons, but discussion of it becomes more frequent when it was made illegal in Jamaica after the Tacky's War, between May and July 1760, in which an Obeahman provided advice to the rebels. It was said that Obeahmen were skilled in using poisons, and an anti-Obeah law passed in Barbados in 1818, specifically forbade the possession of "any poison, or any noxious or destructive substance." Enslaved women used oral tradition to keep past traditions and histories alive. Dance became an integral part of enslaved Africans' culture and it was a way for both men and women to offer up prayers to their gods as well as release emotion. Enslaved Africans would often engage in dancing ceremonies in their free time, freely expressing themselves and their cultural heritage against the order of their colonial masters.

Enslaved women provided the dominant agricultural labor input on British Caribbean sugar plantations from at least the end of the eighteenth century. There was also an increased dependence upon women for the reproduction of plantation labor. This dual role placed women at the center of planters' strategies designed to ensure the survival of the slave system. Girls as young as four years old were put to work on plantations and those between 12 and 19 worked mainly as field hands and domestic laborer. Other forms of work for matured women included midwives, housekeepers, digging holes, weeding and hoeing. But the vast majority of women between the ages of 19 and 54 were field hands. By the late eighteenth and early nineteenth century, there were more women working as field hands than men, mainly due to their lower mortality rates. Between 1790 and 1838 the price for a "new" female slave was approximately £50–£60, compared for a "new" male slave of £50–£70. Slave women were confined to fighting for lower positions in the socio-economic hierarchy and were always excluded from the more prestigious and skilled jobs, such as carpentry. The most prestigious job for women slaves was nursing. But, one way in which women slaves could occasionally amass income and resources for themselves was through prostitution. In Jamaica, the vast majority of enslaved domestic women in towns were expected to support themselves through prostitution.

Martial law was declared in the Parish of St. Mary, in 1675, after a conspiracy was discovered, resulting in the execution of 35 enslaved Africans, including their leaders Peter, Scanenburg and Doctor. In 1683 an alleged conspiracy involving about 180 slaves is betrayed in Vere. In 1769 an alleged conspiracy for a rebellion was betrayed and many enslaved Africans were put to a "painful" death. In 1799 French slave owners brought their slaves to Jamaica, to escape the Haiti Revolution, but a conspiracy was discovered and around a thousand of them were deported. In 1803 an alleged conspiracy was discovered in Kingston, resulting in the execution of two enslaved Africans. An alleged conspiracy was discovered in St. George, which is now part of Saint Mary and Portland, one enslaved African was executed and five others deported. In 1809, there was another alleged conspiracy discovered in Kingston, which resulted in the execution of a number of enslaved Africans by hanging and a number of others deported. One of the largest alleged conspiracy involving two-hundred-and-fifty enslaved Ibos was discovered in 1815 and the ringleaders were executed by hanging. In 1823 an alleged conspiracy was discovered and its leaders executed. The following year an alleged conspiracy in Hanover was suppressed by a large militia force, resulting in the hanging of eleven enslaved Africans and the deportation of many others.

The Problem of Emancipation

In May 1833, the Emancipation Bill was introduced into the House of Commons, by Lord Derby, the Secretary of State for the colonies. It ruled that all slaves under the age of six years old would be unconditionally freed on August 1, 1834, and that all others would be freed after a period of 12 years "apprenticeship," during which they would work for their former owners in exchange for allowances. In the face of fierce opposition from slave owners, Parliament agreed to offer £20 million as compensation to the slave owners and amend the period of apprenticeship from 12 years to six in the case of fieldworkers and four years in the case of others. Of the 667,925 enslaved Africans in the British West Indies in 1833, there were 311,070 on the island of Jamaica. Whilst the average value placed on a slave on the islands controlled by Britain was £24.80, in Jamaica, £6,149, 955 was paid out to planters in compensation, at an average of £19.75, but the British government paid out £4,295,989 in British Guiana for 82,824 slaves, at an average of £51.86. This meant that the price of slaves in British Guiana had the second highest monetary value in the British West Indies, only superseded by slaves on the island of British Honduras at £53.35. The cheapest slaves could be found in Bermuda and the Bahamas, where they were valued between £12.50 and £12.70. Of the £20m offered to the planters £16.6m was eventually paid out to planters on 17 Caribbean islands.

Apprenticeship was intended as a transitory measure towards waged labor and a means of preventing the freed slaves from deserting the plantation *en masse.* Under the apprenticeship system former slaves were forced to work for forty hours every week without wages, only receiving lodging, clothing, medical care, and food. For the remaining part of the week the apprentices were allowed to hire themselves out for pay or work on their own allotted grounds. From the outset, it was clear that the apprenticeship system was a failure, as the former slaves wanted their "full free," as they called it, because they saw little material improvement in their lives under this system. The planters were also opposed to the apprenticeship system and tried to extract as much labor as possible from their workforce, often in contravention of agreed legislation. Another problem was the children freed by the Emancipation Act were, in many cases, made destitute by former slave owners who saw no reason to continue supporting them. As the date for full freedom for some workers, August 1, 1838, approached, Parliament recognized that many owners of enslaved Africans were making a mockery of the Emancipation Act and fearing that there was a risk of revolt by former slaves, Parliament ordered the full freedom of all apprentices on August 1, 1838. If the former slaves of the Caribbean were free men and women, it was largely in name alone. Island legislatures introduced measures aimed at limiting former slaves' freedom of movement and ability to buy or rent land. On some islands, so-called "contract laws" were passed, which forced laborers into agreements with individual plantation owners, which could lead to eviction. With a monopoly of land and political power the European plantation owners were able to continue much as before slavery. On other islands, land was more freely available to former slaves. In Jamaica, for example, where Maroon communities had existed in the rugged interior since the seventeenth century, families and larger groups were able to establish free villages away from European plantations.

The emancipation of enslaved Africans and the inadequacy of white indentured worker put the sugar plantation owners back to where they had been in the seventeenth century. Then they had moved from Indians to European indentured labor to enslaved Africans. Now, deprived of their enslaved Africans, they turned once again to Europeans and then to Indians, but this time the Indians were from the east. India replaced Africa and between 1833 and 1917, Trinidad imported 145,000 East Indians, with British Guiana importing 238,000, with smaller number distributed to other British West Indian colonies. By 1845, it is reckoned that there were almost 20,000 peasant freeholders in Jamaica and 50,000 by 1859, producing a range of agricultural commodities both for the local and export markets. Following the abolition of the slave trade and slavery, the plantation owners believed that with full freedom the apprentices would all quit the estates and settled on inland areas or in the mountains. Apart from East Indians, there was also effort to import European labor from abroad to replace the emancipated Africans. The first of these immigrants – 63 Germans from Bremen – arrived as early as 1834. There were other importations of Germans, as well as Scots and Irish people to Jamaica, but by and large the experiment was a failure. The majority died, a number left the estates to do domestic work or take jobs in the police force and elsewhere, while a great many left the island on their own or asked to be sent back home. German migrants to Jamaica were baptized with names such as Hanover or Berlin and to this day, the presence in Seaford Town of white-skinned "Germanics" with names like Wedermeyer recalls the plantation owners and colonial authority's unsuccessful attempt to solve Jamaica's labor problems.

Slaves intercepted by the British Navy, *en route* to Brazil or Cuba, were freed but encouraged to work as contract laborers in British colonies. By 1861, the racial and cultural diversity of the islands was widened in the decades following emancipation. European, African and Chinese migration was dwarfed by the arrival in the Caribbean, between 1838 and 1917, of almost half a million Indian indentured laborers, which changed demography and culture of British Guiana (now Guyana) and Trinidad in particular, while also affecting most of the other sugar producing islands. Of these new arrivals 240,000 arrived in British Guiana, 135,000 in Trinidad and 33,000 in Jamaica. Promoted as a solution to the Caribbean's labor crisis since the abolition of the slave trade and slavery, Indian labor was first recruited on five-year contracts during the late 1830s in British Guiana. But, the high death rates among the Indian laborers, prompted Prime Minister Lord John Russell (1792–1878) to ban further Indian migration in 1840. Due to pressure from plantation owners and the Colonial Office, the embargo was lifted between 1845 and 1846 and improved migration support from the 1850s, such as improved housing and health facilities reduced the mortality rates. The indentured Indian laborers, mainly male and aged between ten and thirty, were hired at recruiting terminals at Calcutta or Madras before embarking on the ten to 18-week crossing over the "black waters" between India and the Caribbean. Indian indentured laborers were contracted to work for five years with the promise of a free passage back to India at the end of that period. Most of those who survived opted to return and to prevent such departures, the colonial authorities offered grants of land to those who would stay. The influx of Indian indentured laborers, alongside black wage labor, increased sugar production on islands such as British Guiana and Trinidad. However, a series of droughts combined with the closure of many sugar estates created high levels of rural unemployment.

Two plants of great economic value were introduced to Jamaica in 1778 (ackee) and 1789 (mango) from West Africa. The first ackee slips were purchased from the captain of a slaver, while the first mango seedlings to reach Jamaica were part of a collection sent to the French West Indian islands from Mauritius at the command of the French government. The ship carrying the plants was captured by one of Lord Rodney's ships and was sent to Jamaica where they were successfully grown at the botanical garden at Gordon Town. In 1791 the Jamaica Assembly resolved to give every encouragement to the cultivation of yam, Cocos, maize, plantains, and such products as the nutmeg, cloves, cinnamon, and coffee, since it believed that the cultivation of these crops would be of benefit to the island in many ways, while making it less dependent on America for food and other supplies. The breadfruit was first brought to Jamaica by Captain William Bligh in 1793 from the Pacific island of Tahiti. The breadfruit tree, as well as the Otaheite apple (Spondias dulcis), or June plum and jackfruit, were planted in the Botanical Gardens at Bath (St. Thomas in the east) and from there distributed over the island. But, the slaves refused to eat the breadfruit, because it did not resemble any food plan to which they had been accustomed to in Africa or the West Indies so, for fifty years, breadfruit was fed to pigs. In Jamaica, people turned increasingly to subsistence farming as a survival strategy, but the plantation owners, absentee for the most part, and island Assembly were unwilling to sell or let land to poor peasants. Squatting became more commonplace, as did violent evictions and in

1865 a group of Jamaican laborers petitioned Queen Victoria directly, asking to rent vacant Crown Lands.

The Queen's response was negative and urged them to work harder on plantation owners' estates. The Queen recommended to the laboring classes, hard work as the solution to their difficulties, pointing out that it was from their own efforts and wisdom that they must look for an improvement in their conditions. Governor Edward John Eyre (1815–1901) had fifty thousand copies of the letter printed in poster form and distributed throughout the island. To the masses this was a cruel blow, it made many felt that their last hope had died and that "Missis Queen" who set them free had now deserted them. Some even feared that slavery may be reintroduced. Rural hardship was exacerbated by an utter absence of democracy and local accountability. In 1864, from a population of 450,000, Jamaica had 1,903 registered voters, of which 1,457 voted. This could not in no way be described as a democracy, with only 0.32% of the total population voting. The rising colored middle class was pressing to exert political power but was often excluded by vested interests. Conditions on the island of Jamaica had reached a very bad state by the beginning of 1865. There were problems of small planters in getting land to cultivate; there was unemployment and low wages, with the rate for men being between nine and 12 pence per day. In addition, a series of droughts had ruined most of the food crops, while the price of imported food, especially of salted fish and grain had risen steeply, because of the civil war then raging in the United States. This led to the calling of protest meetings in various parts of the island, later known as "Underhill Meetings."

In 1865, Dr. Edward Underhill, Secretary of the Baptist Missionary of Great Britain, wrote a letter to the Colonial Office describing Jamaica's poor state of affairs for the mass of the people. Black Jamaicans learned of the letter and began organizing in Underhill Meetings. Black formers in St. Ann parish sent a petition to Queen Victoria, asking for Crown lands to cultivate. The Queen's reply was made known, and she encouraged the poor to work harder, even though they had no access to lands on which to work. George William Gordon (1820–1865), a wealthy mulatto politician, who was one of two representatives from St. Thomas in the east, began encouraging the people in his parish to find ways to make their grievances known. One of his followers was a black Baptist deacon named Paul Bogle (1822–1865). In 1865, Bogle led a deputation of black people from St. Thomas in the east to the capital, Spanish Town, hoping to meet with the governor to discuss their concerns, but the governor refused to receive them. On October 7, 1865, a black man was put on trial, convicted, and imprisoned for trespassing on a long-abandoned sugar plantation, a charge and sentence that angered many black Jamaicans. During the proceedings, James Geoghegon disrupted the trial in Morant Bay. When police tried to remove him from the courthouse, a fight broke out between the police and some spectators. In the following pursuit to arrest

Geoghegon, two policemen were beaten and stoned. On the following Monday, the court issued arrest warrants for several men for rioting, resisting arrest, and assaulting the police. Warrant was also issued for the arrest of Paul Bogle.

Most Jamaicans were prevented from voting by the leveling of high poll taxes, and their living conditions had worsened following crop damage by floods, cholera, and smallpox epidemics and a long drought. In the election of 1864, out of a total population of 436,000, in which blacks outnumbered whites by a ratio of 32:1, less than 2,000 black Jamaican men were eligible to vote and women could not vote at the time. On October 11, 1865, hundreds of black people, led by Paul Bogle, marched to the courthouse in Morant Bay, protesting injustice and widespread poverty. After seven men were shot dead by the volunteer militia, the protesters retaliated by burning down the courthouse and nearby buildings. Black people rose up across St. Thomas in the east parish and controlled most of the area. Governor Edward John Eyre (1815–1901) declared martial law and sent government troops, under Brigadier-General Alexander Nelson (1814–1893), to hunt down the protestors and bring Bogle back to Morant Bay for trial. Although the troops met with no organized resistance, they killed blacks indiscriminately, most of whom had not been involved in either the protest at the courthouse or the later uprising. According to one soldier "we slaughtered all before us…man or woman or child." In the end, soldiers slaughtered 439 mostly innocent black people and arrested 354 more, including Paul Bogle, who was later murdered, after a sham trial. Other punishments included flogging of more than 600 men and women, including pregnant women, and long prison sentences. Soldiers burned thousands of homes belonging to black people, without any justifiable reason, leaving impoverished families homeless.

Opponents of Governor Eyre established the Jamaica Committee in the same year, shortly after the massacre in Jamaica, calling for Eyre to be tried for mass murder. Some members of the Committee wanted Eyre to be tried for the murder of British subject, such as George William Gordon, who was a member of the Jamaican Assembly, claiming that Eyre's actions were illegal. The Committee included many liberals such as the radical John Bright, the naturalist Charles Robert Darwin, the philosopher and economist John Stuart Mill, the biologist Thomas Henry Huxley, judge, politician, and author Thomas Hughes and the philosopher and sociologist Herbert Spencer, among others. However, there were those who applauded Eyre and a Governor Eyre Defense and Aid Committee was set up by among others, the philosopher, satirical writer and historian Thomas Carlyle, Poet Laureate Alfred Lord Tennyson, professor Charles Kingsley, the writer and social critic Charles John Huffam Dickens, one of the leading art critic of the Victorian era John Ruskin and the physicist John Tyndall. Eyre was twice charged with murder, but the cases never proceeded to trial.

Black People in Britain

Black people in Britain, according to Peter Fryer (1992), can be traced back to the court of Mary I, in 1555, before there were potatoes, tobacco, or tea and nine years before Shakespeare was born, a group of five Africans were brought to Britain (Fryer, 1992: 4–5). In the same year, John Lok returned to England with: "certain black slaves, where of some were tall and strong men, and could well agree with our meates and drinkes" (Walvin 1984: 33). As the slave empires prospered, ever more Africans – often enslaved – found their way to England. Some came directly from Africa, but the vast majority came via the New World. Many were resold or bartered in England, often through the columns of London newspapers, as English law allowed black slavery in England. The Royal Proclamation issued by Elizabeth I, in 1603 states:

> Whereas the Queen's majesty, tendering the good and welfare of her own natural subjects, greatly distressed in these hard times of dearth, is highly discontented to understand the great number of Negroes and blackamoors which (as she is informed) are crept into this realm…who are fostered and relieved here, to the great annoyance of her own liege people who want the relief which these people consume…hath given especial commandment that the said kind of people shall be with all aped avoided and discharged out of this her majesty's dominions (Majors 2001: 13).

This proclamation testified to the growing presence of black people in Britain, as early as the beginning of the seventeenth century, before England had an empire in the Caribbean. By 1764 *The Gentleman's Magazine* thought there were 20,000 black people in London alone. Although some black people became quite prominent – for instance Equiano, Francis Barber, Sancho, Richmond, and Molineaux, the majority were poor. The majority of black people in late eighteenth century England were male and a large number of them formed liaisons with, or even marry, poor white women. However, these liaisons were denounced and as early as 1710, one man spoke of the "little race of mulattos" to be found in England (Walvin 1984: 34). There were expressions of outrage about miscegenation and racist writers of the late eighteenth century, writing in support of plantation owners and slave traders, denounced miscegenation in the most rabid terms. In the years of slavery and the slave trade, all sorts of conclusions were drawn to justify the enslavement of Africans. A mix of biblical and pseudo-scientific arguments was produced to justify the enslavement of Africans. In 1753, the empiricist (a person relying on observation or scientific methods) David Hume (1711–1776) argued that Negroes and all other species of men to be naturally inferior to the whites. He maintained that there was no civilized nation of any complexion other than white, or even any individual eminent either in action or speculations. There was no ingenious manufacture amongst them, arts, or sciences, even though there was evidence to the contrary. Mythologies, including the biblical theme of the curse of Ham, served as evidence of black inferiority, while pro-slavery ideologies stressed that only a debased people could sell one another into captivity, conveniently overlooking the role of European slave-traders in creating the demand for slaves, also reinforced by widespread conviction that Africans were happier in slavery than subject to endemic violence and starvation in their native Africa, ignoring the fact that Africa was the continent of plenty.

In London, black people were a common sight in the late eighteenth century, on the streets as sweepers and beggars; in private homes as servants in pubs and at the periodic fairs as entertainers. It was a widely held view that black people were especially musical, and many were employed as musicians. It was customary for white employers to baptize and convert their black servants and many became devout Christians and frequent worshippers. In addition to the many black people who resided in England in the late eighteenth century, and largely in London, there was a regular stream of black visitors in Britain, especially those engaged in education or training. African children attended schools in London, Liverpool, and Lancaster and there was a constant flow of black sailors in an out of British ports. Although black people in London organized themselves into formal and informal social and political groups, which sought to free local black slaves and provide them with help, they also joined with white working class in their struggle for social and economic improvements. Two black radicals who suffered for their beliefs and activities were William Davidson (1781–1820) – hanged and then beheaded, and Robert Wedderburn (1762–1835), the son of an enslaved African, who was jailed for two years and both were born in Jamaica. William Davidson was born in Kingston in 1786, the son of the island's attorney-general and his mother an enslaved African. At the age of 14 and against his mother's wishes, he was sent to Edinburgh to complete his education. He was later apprenticed to a Liverpool lawyer, but after three years ran away to sea with the navy. After leaving the navy, Davidson studied mathematics in Aberdeen, but was soon apprenticed to a Lichfield cabinet-maker.

Davidson moved to London and later joined the Marylebone Union Reading Society, which was formed in 1819, in response to the Peterloo massacre on August 16 that year in St. Peter's Field, Manchester, when cavalry charged into a crowd of over 60,000, who had gathered to demand the reform of parliamentary representation. Eleven unarmed demonstrators were killed and five-hundred injured. Before long Davidson had become secretary of the newly formed shoemakers' trade union and was chairing meetings of the "Committee of Thirteen" and "Executive of Five." Davidson defended the English tradition of resistance to tyranny. It was, he declared, an ancient custom: "with arms to stand and claim their rights as Englishmen; and if every Englishman felt as I do, they would always do that…" And our history goes on further to say, that when another of their Majesties the King of England tried to infringe upon those rights, the people armed, and told him that if he did not give them the privileges of Englishmen, they would compel him by the point of the sword… Would you not rather govern a country of spirited men, than cowards? (Fryer, 1984: 219). Freedom of the press was fought for and won by the working-class radicals of the early nineteenth century, many of whom served prison sentences for publishing opinions on religious and other matters, which challenged the ideas and interests of the ruling class.

One of those imprisoned for freedom of speech was a black radical tailor named Robert Wedderburn, who was born in Jamaica. His mother, Rosanna, was an enslaved African on the estate of Lady Douglass, and his father, James Wedderburn, came from Inveresk, near Edinburgh, who owned large sugar plantations on the island. When Robert was about eleven years old, he witnessed the flogging of his grandmother and also saw his mother flogged, while pregnant. Forty years later, Robert expressed anger when he recalled these scenes. In 1778, Robert came to England, and later went to sea on a warship. At some time, he was licensed as a Unitarian preacher, which entitled him to put "Reverend" before his name, but he rejected the doctrine of the Trinity. In Mach 1817 an Act of Parliament was passed with the aim of suppressing the Spenceans, of which Robert was an active member. Thomas Spence (1750–1814) was a radical English man who advocated for the common ownership of land. Robert was often in the company of other radicals, such as William Cobbett (1763–1835), W. T. Sherwin and Thomas Jonathan Wooler (1786–1853). Robert opened a meetinghouse in the shape of a Unitarian chapel in Hopkins Street, Soho, where he and a Spencean shoemaker-poet, Allen Davenport, were reported to be making "very violent, seditious, and bitterly anti-Christian Spencean speeches." By the autumn of 1819, it is said that up to 200 people were paying six-pence to attend debates on Monday and Wednesday evenings, besides "Lectures every Sabbath day on Theology, Morality, Natural Philosophy, and Politics, by a Self-Taught West Indian" (Fryer, 1984: 223). Robert Wedderburn was prosecuted for sedition and blasphemy and was locked up briefly in Newgate jail, until £200 bail was raised for him by sections of the public. Robert also campaigned against colonial slavery and saw Wesleyans and missionaries as "vipers" and "church robbers," whose role was to try to make slaves submit instead of rebelling at the same time taking money from them. He was also able to get copies of his writing to Jamaica, which was the first revolutionary propaganda sent to the West Indies from Britain. He advised against petitions for emancipation, "for it is degrading to human nature to petition your oppressors" (Fryer 1984: 225). Robert was found guilty of blasphemy and sent to Dorchester jail for two years, merely because he differed in opinion from the State religion and had too much honesty. He was again jailed in 1831 at the age of 68 for an affray outside a brothel, after which little is known.

A tailor called William Cuffay (1788–1870) was one of the leaders and martyrs of the Chartist movement, the first mass political movement of the British working class. His father was an enslaved African on the island of St. Kitts. Like Davidson and Wedderburn before him, Cuffay was made to suffer for his political beliefs and activities. William Cuffay was born in Chatham, Kent, in 1788, his spine and shinbones were deformed. He became a journeyman tailor in his late teens and stayed in that trade all his life. He was married three times but had no children. In 1834, he took part in a strike that lost him his job, which he had held for many years and found it hard to get work afterwards, which is how he became actively involved in politics. In 1839, he joined the great movement in support of the People's Charter, drawn up by the cabinet-maker William Lovett (1800–1877), with the help of Francis Place (1771–1854), demanding universal male suffrage, annual parliament, vote by secret ballot, payment for MPs, abolition of property qualifications for MPs, and equal electoral districts. Before long Cuffay, 4ft 11in. tall, had emerged as one of the dozen or so most prominent leaders of the Chartist movement and was in favor of heckling at meetings of the middle-class Complete Suffrage Movement and Anti-Corn Law League. *Punch* lampooned him savagely and *The Time* referred to London's Chartists as "the Black man and his Party" (Fryer 1984: 239).

Cuffay was a strong supporter of (Red) Fergus O'Connor's (1794–1855) Chartist land scheme – to take unemployed people out of the slums and give each family two acres of good arable land. In 1846, Cuffay was one of London's three delegates to the Birmingham land conference. He was also a supporter of the Irish struggle. In 1848, Cuffay was put on trial for levying war against Queen Victoria and was among the first victims of the Act of Parliament making the new political crime of "felony" punishable by transportation, for the term of his natural life. After a voyage lasting 130 days on the prison ship *Adelaide,* Cuffay landed in Van Diemen's Land (present day Tasmania) on November 1849, aged 61. He was permitted to work at his trade for wages – which he did until the last year of his life. After much delay his wife was allowed to join him in April 1853 and in 1856, Cuffay was pardoned. At one of his last public appearances he called his working-class audience "Fellow slaves" and told them: "I'm old, I'm poor, I'm out of work, and I'm in debt, and therefore I have cause to complain" (Fryer 1984: 245). In October 1869, Cuffay was admitted to Tasmania's workhouse, the Brickfields invalid depot, in whose sick ward he died in July 1870, aged 82.

Samuel Taylor Coleridge (1875–1912) was born at 15, Theobalds Road, Holborn, on August 15, 1875. His father, David Peter Hughes Taylor, came to Britain from Sierra Leone in the late 1860s, studied medicine, qualified as a member of the Royal College of Surgeons, practiced in Croydon, went back to

271

Africa, was appointed coroner of the Gambia in 1894 and died there in 1904. Samuel's mother, Alice Holmans, an Englishwoman married Daniel Taylor and brought up his son, who was named after the poet. In 1890, at the age of 15, Samuel entered the Royal College of Music as a violin student. In 1896 Samuel met with the American poet Paul Lawrence Dunbar (1872–1906), the son of a former enslaved African, who was visiting London to give public readings of his works. Samuel set some of Dunbar's poems to music and in 1897 both men gave joint public performances in London. By 1898 Elgar, then Britain's leading composer was describing Samuel Taylor Coleridge as "far and away the cleverest fellow amongst the young men" (Fryer, 1984: 27–8). In 1904, Samuel visited America and thousands of black people turned out to greet their hero, and pay their respect in Washington. The critics praised both his music and his skill as a conductor. He met Booker Taliaferro Washington (1856–1915), the black educator, who both Samuel and William Edward Burghardt Du Bois agreed was not radical enough. In 1906, Samuel repeated his success with concerts in New York, Boston and other cities.

In 1910, he conducted his own works at a musical festival in Norfolk, Connecticut and received what he called "royal reception" (Fryer, 1984: 259). Samuel was a strong supporter of the Pan-African movement and took charge of the musical side of the program at the Pan-African Conference, held at Westminster Town Hall in July 1900, and was elected to the executive committee of the Pan-African Association. Samuel Taylor Coleridge died in1912 of a double dose of pneumonia, at the early age of 37. He left two children – Hiawatha (born 1900) and Avril (1903). According to Fryer (1984) black people in Britain between 1830 and 1918 came from Africa, America, and the West Indies, with some making a permanent home here, whilst other stayed for months or years. They were active in politics, medicine, law, business, the theatre, music and dance, sport, journalism and local affairs. Others were writers, and men of God, orators and entertainers, two editors, a nurse and a photographer (Fryer 1984: 237). All of them, in one way or another, challenged racism and by the turn of the twentieth century, Africans and person of African descent living in Britain had done much to create the political tradition known as Pan-Africanism, whose challenge to imperialism would later inspire freedom movement all over Africa and the West Indies, of which more will be said.

The West India Regiment (WIR)

Black people have made contribution in other areas of the British Empire, especially in expanding and defending it. Between April 24 and September 1, 1795, eight West India Regiments were commissioned, which also incorporated the Carolina Corps that had been in existence since 1779. In 1807 all serving black soldiers, recruited as enslaved Africans, in the West India Regiments of the British army were free under the Mutiny Act, passed by the British Parliament that same year. In 1812, a West African recruiting depot was established on Blanche Island in Sierra Leone to train West African volunteers for the West India Regiments. By 1816 the end of the Napoleonic Wars and the reduction of the West India Regiments to six enabled this depot to be closed. Thereafter all recruitment for the various West India Regiments that fought in WWI and II, were West Indian volunteers, with officers and some senior NCOs coming from Britain. The West India Regiments became a valued part of the British forces garrisoning the West Indies, where losses from disease and climate were heavy amongst white troops. The black Caribbean soldiers by contrast proved better adapted to tropical service. Free black Caribbean soldiers played a prominent and often distinguished role in the military history of Latin America and the Caribbean. The West India Regiments saw considerable service during the period of the Napoleonic Wars, including participation by the First West India Regiment in the occupation of the French island of Marie-Galante in 1808. The Regiments were also involved in the war of 1812, both on the Atlantic coast and in the Gulf of Mexico, taking part in the British attack on New Orleans.

In 1800 there were 12 battalion-sized regiments, which were seen as valuable in dealing with slave revolt in the West Indies colonies. The West India Regiments were infantry units of the British army, recruited from and normally stationed in the British colonies of the Caribbean, between 1795 and 1927 (132 years). In 1888 the two West India Regiments were reduced to a single unit of two battalions. A third battalion was raised in 1897 but was disbanded in 1904. A battalion generally consists of between 300 and 800 soldiers. This regiment differed from similar forces raised in other parts of the British Empire, in that it formed an integral part of the regular British army. Throughout their history, the West India Regiments were involved in numerous campaigns in the West Indies and Africa. They also served in World War One, in the Middle East and East Africa. The First West India Regiment from Jamaica went to the Gold Coast of Africa to fight in the Ashanti War of 1873–4. The regiment served in West Africa throughout the nineteenth century. In the early part of the twentieth century, one battalion was stationed in Sierra Leone and the other was stationed in Jamaica recruiting and training, with these battalions exchanging every three years (Brian Dyde, 1998: 250).

The Anglo-Ashanti Wars were five wars between the Ashanti Empire, in the Akan interior of the Gold Coast, now Ghana, and the British Empire in the nineteenth century, between 1824 and 1901. The ruler of the Ashanti (or Asante) was the Asatehene. The Ashanti Royal House traces its line to the Oyoko, Abohyen Dynasty of Nana Twum and the Beretuo Dynasty of Osei Tutu Opemsoo, who formed the Empire of Ashanti in 1701 and was Crowned Ashantehene (King of all Ashanti). He was killed in battle in 1717. These wars were mainly over the Ashanti establishing strong control over the coastal areas of what is now Ghana.

Coastal peoples, such as the Fante and the inhabitants of Accra, who were chiefly Ga, came to rely on British protection against Ashanti incursions. The First Anglo-Ashanti War took place between 1823 and 1831. In 1823 Sir Charles MacCarthy (1764–1824) led an invading force from the Cape Coast against the Ashanti. MacCarthy was defeated and killed by the Ashanti, and his head, along with Ensign Wetherall, were kept as trophies, at the Battle of Nsamankow. The Second Anglo-Ashanti War took place in 1863, when a large Ashanti delegation crossed the river pursuing a fugitive, Kwesi Gyana, which led to fighting between the British and the Ashanti. There were casualties on both sides, but the British governor's request for additional troops from England was refused and sickness forced the withdrawal of his remaining troops. The Third Anglo-Ashanti War lasted five days from January 31 to February 5, 1874. In 1869, a German missionary family and a Swiss missionary had been taken to Kumasi and a ransom was demanded for their return.

In 1871, Britain purchased the Dutch Gold Coast from the Dutch, including Elmina which was claimed by the Ashanti. The Ashanti invaded the new British protectorate. General Garnet Wolseley with several thousand West Indian and African troops, including some Fante and 2,500 white troops, was sent against the Ashanti. Wolseley went to the Gold Coast in 1873 and made plans before the arrival of his troops in January 1874. He fought the Battle of Amoaful on January 31 and five days later fighting ended with the Battle of Ordashu. The British were impressed by the size of the Ashanti's palace and scope of its contents, including "rows of books" in many languages. The Ashantehene signed a harsh British treaty, the Treaty of Fomena in July 1874, to end the war. The Treaty, signed by Kofi Karikari, included payment to the British 50,000 ounces of gold. The Fourth Anglo-Ashanti War was brief, which took place between December 1895 and February 1896. The Ashanti turned down an unofficial offer to become a British protectorate in 1891, extending to 1894. Wanting to keep the French and German forces out of Ashanti territory, and its gold, the British were anxious to conquer the Ashanti once and for all. The fighting started on the pretext of failure of the Ashanti to pay the fines levied on them by the Treaty of Fomena, after the 1874 war. Sir Francis Scott (1824–1863) left Cape Coast with the main expeditionary force of British troops, including soldiers from the West India Regiments, in December 1895 and arrived in Kumasi in January 1896.

The Ashantehene directed the Ashanti not to resist, but casualties from sickness among British troops were high. Among the dead was Queen Victoria's son-in-law, Prince Henry of Battenberg. Robert Baden-Powell led a naïve levy of several local tribes in the campaign. In the War of the Golden Stool (1900), the remaining Ashanti Court, not exiled to the Seychelles mounted an offensive against the British and Fanti troops, resident at the Kumasi Fort, but they were defeated. The Ashanti impressively withstood the British in some of these wars but, in the end, the Ashanti Empire became a British protectorate, as part of the Gold Coast colony, on January 1, 1902. In the early part of the twentieth century, one battalion of the West India Regiment was stationed in Sierra Leone and the other was stationed in Jamaica, recruiting and training. The battalions exchanged duties every three years. On the outbreak of war in August 1914, the 1 Battalion of the West India Regiment was stationed in Freetown, where it had been based for two-and-a-half-years. A detachment of the Regiment's signalers saw active service in the German Cameroons, where Private L. Jordon earned a Distinguish Combat Medal (DCM) and several other men were mentioned in dispatches. The 1 Battalion returned to the West Indies in 1916. The 2 Battalion was sent from Kingston to West Africa in the second half of 1915. They took part in the capture of Yaounde in January 1916. In April 1916, the 2 Battalion was sent from Freetown, Sierra Leone, to Mombasa in Kenya, to take part in the East Africa Campaign against German colonial forces based in German East Africa. The East African Campaign was a series of battles and guerrilla actions, which started in German East Africa and spread to parts of Mozambique, Northern Rhodesia, British East Africa, Uganda, and Belgian Congo. The Campaign was effectively ended in November 1917.

German East Africa became mandates of Britain, Belgium, and Portugal. The five hundred and fifteen officers and men of the 2 Battalion formed part of a column that took Dares Salaam on November 4, 1916. They also took part in the Battle of Nyango in October 1917. For their service in East Africa the West India Regiment earned eight Distinguished Conduct Medals (DCM), as well as the Battle Honor "East Africa 1914–18." After the war, the 1 and 2 Battalions of the West India Regiment were amalgamated into a single Battalion in 1920, which was disbanded in 1927. In 1915 a second West Indies Regiment was formed from Caribbean volunteers, who had made their way to Britain. Initially, these volunteers were drafted into a variety of units within the British army, but in 1915 it was decided to group them into a single regiment, named the British West Indies Regiment. The 1 Battalion was formed in September 1915, at Seaford, Essex, England, which was made up of men from British Guiana (A Company), Trinidad (B Company), Trinidad and St. Vincent (C Company), Grenada and Barbados (D Company). In total 15,600 men served in the British West Indies Regiment, with two-thirds coming from Jamaica and others coming from the Bahamas, British Honduras, Tobago, the Leeward Islands, and Saint Lucia. The British West Indies Regiment played a significant role in the First World War, especially in Palestine and Jordan, where they were employed in military operations against the Turkish army. General Allenby regarded the 1 British West Indies Regiment highly and while the 1 and 2 Battalions served mainly in Egypt and Palestine, the 3, 4, 6 and 7 Battalions served in France and Flanders, with the 5 Battalion acting as reserve draft unit. The 8 and 9 Battalions also served in France and Flanders, before being transferred to Italy in 1918, while the 10th and 11th Battalions served in France and Italy.

Following the Armistice in November 1918, the battalions of the British West Indies Regiment were concentrated at Taranto, Italy, to prepare for demobilization. But they were still required to work; loading and unloading ships, building and cleaning latrines for white soldiers which caused resentment, especially when they discovered that white soldiers had been awarded a pay rise which they were not. On December 6, 1918, the soldiers of the 9 Battalion refused to obey orders, and 180 sergeants signed a petition complaining about poor pay, allowances, and promotions. On December 9, 1918, the 10th Battalion also refused to work. Over a period of four days a black non-commissioned officer (NCO) was killed and a Lieutenant Colonel assaulted. In response soldiers of the Worcestershire Regiment were sent to restore order. The 9 Battalion was disbanded, and soldiers redistributed to other battalions, which were disarmed. Some sixty soldiers were tried for mutiny, and given sentences ranging between three and five years, with one soldier getting 20 years and one executed by firing squad. Bitterness persisted after the munity was suppressed and on December 17, 1918, about sixty NCOs of the British West Indies Regiment met to form the Caribbean League, calling for equal rights, self-determination, and closer union in the West Indies. During the First World War the British West Indies Regiment was awarded 81 medals for bravery and 49 soldiers were mentioned in dispatches. After the war soldiers of the British West Indies Regiment were demobilized and sent back to the West Indies. The high rates of unemployment in the West Indies created serious unrest, culminating in riots and strikes. In a desperate attempt to restore order, local authorities introduced a scheme of financially assisted relocation for workers, particularly for veterans who were considered a threat. One-third of those veterans were relocated to Cuba.

Members of the British West India Regiment distinguished themselves in action, including Private Samuel Hodge VC (1840–1868), the first soldier of the British West India Regiment to be awarded the Victoria Cross, and the second black service man. William Edward "Nelson" Hall VC (April 28, 1827–August 27, 1904) was the first black serviceman and the third Canadian to receive the Victoria Cross, for his actions at the Siege of Lucknow, in India, during the Indian Rebellion of 1857. On October 28, 1859, Hall was presented with the Victoria Cross by Rear Admiral Charles Talbot. William Hall remained with the Royal Navy and rose to the rank of Petty Officer First Class. He retired from the Royal Navy in 1876. Private Hodge was promoted to the rank of Lance Corporal and was presented with the Victoria Cross on June 24, 1867. He was a soldier in the 4 British West India Regiment. Sergeant William James Gordon VC (November 19, 1864–August 15, 1922) of the 1 Battalion of the British West India Regiment, was awarded the Victoria Cross for an act of heroic devotion to duty, at the battle of

Toniataba, in the 2 Gambia Campaign (on display at the Jamaica Defense Force Museum). The British West Indies Regiment was awarded a Battle Honor, for their role in the Battle of Messines (June 7–14, 1917), under the command of General Sir Herbert Plumer (1857–1932), near the village of Messines in Belgium, West Flanders.

European Scramble for Africa

According to Norman Davies (1996), European Imperialism in the late nineteenth century differed from earlier form of the phenomenon in several important ways. It was part of a worldwide scramble for control of the last remaining countries suitable for exploitation. The "Scramble for Africa" was the invasion, division, colonization, and annexation of African states, countries, and kingdoms by Europeans, between 1881 and 1914. The scramble for Africa involved Great Britain, France, Spain, Germany, Portugal, Belgium, and Italy. In 1870, only ten percent of Africa was under European control; by 1914 it had increased to ninety percent of the continent, with only Ethiopia, the Dervish state, and Liberia independent. The Dervish were an early twentieth-century Somali Sunni Kingdom, that was established by Mohammed Abdullah Hassan (1856–1920), a religious leader who gathered Somali soldiers from across the Horn of Africa and united them into a loyal army known as the Dervishes. This Dervish army enabled Hassan to carve out a powerful state through conquest of lands claimed by the Somali Sultans, the Ethiopians and the European powers. The Dervish State acquired renowned courage in the Islamic and western worlds, due to its resistance against the European empires of Britain and Italy. The Dervish forces successfully repulsed the British Empire in four military expeditions and forced it to retreat to the coastal region. As a result of its fame in the Middle East and Europe, the Dervish State was recognized as an ally of the Ottoman Empire and the German Empire. It also succeeded at outliving the Scramble for Africa, and remained throughout World War I, the only independent Muslim power on the continent. After a quarter of a century of holding the British at bay, the Dervishes were finally defeated in 1920.

In the two decades starting in 1875, over one quarter of the land surface of the globe was seized by six European powers. Colonies were viewed as an integral part of the advanced industrial economies. The Berlin Agreement of February 26, 1885 allowed the colonial powers to establish protectorates in Africa by diplomatic notification, even without actual possession on the ground. In practice, a protectorate often has direct foreign relations only with the protecting power. Similarly, the protectorate rarely takes military action on its own, but relies on the protector for its defense. A protectorate is a territory which is not formally annexed, but which, by treaty, grant or other "lawful" means; the Crown has ultimate power and jurisdiction. Some British colonies were ruled directly by the

Colonial Office in London, while others were ruled indirectly through local rulers who were supervised behind the scenes by British advisors. In 1890 Zanzibar became a protectorate of Britain. Prime Minister Salisbury explained his position thus:

> The condition of a protected dependency is more acceptable to the half-civilized races, and more suitable for them than direct dominion. It is cheaper, simpler, less wounding to their self-esteem, gives them more career as public officials, and spares of unnecessary contact with white men (Andrew Roberts: Victorian Titan, 2000: 529).

British law makes a distinction between a protectorate and a protected state. Constitutionally the two are of similar status, where Britain provides controlled defense and external relations. But, a protectorate has an internal government established, while a protected state establishes a form of local internal self-government based on the already existing one. The supply of raw materials, cheap labor, and semi-furnished products was planned to maximize the benefit to the "mother country." There was a qualitative as well as quantitative leap in the intensity of exploitation. This growing competition for colonial resources was one of the main causes for international conflicts. Political and economic imperialism was attended by a conscious cultural mission to "Europeanize" the colonies in the image of the mother countries. In this, Christian missionaries formed an important element, through their relationship to the political authorities and to the commercial companies was rarely a direct one. The imperial powers sought to exploit the military potential of the colonies. As the map of the globe rapidly filled up, the European imperialists were obliged to focus their attention on a shrinking range of targets. The Americans had already emerged from the colonial experience. Most of Asia had been subdued at an earlier stage. By the 1880s, only Africa, Indo-China, China, and the Pacific Islands remained. Britain held the largest of empires with a minimum of military force, relying heavily on native princes and local troops. All the larger territories settled by British immigrants were given self-governing dominion status – Canada in 1867, Australia in 1901, New Zealand and Newfoundland in 1907, and South Africa in 1910. Contrary to European belief, Africa was devoid neither of organized government nor of ordered religion; and a huge variety of languages and cultures belied the idea that all Africans were Stone Age savages. But the "Scramble for Africa" took place on the assumption that the land and the peoples were there for the taking.

Abyssinia was the only native empire to maintain its independence, perhaps because it adhered to Coptic Christianity. As predicted by some, colonial conflicts began to occur at the turn of the century. In 1898 Britain and France almost came to blows after their expeditionary forces came face-to-face at Fashoda in Sudan.

In 1899–1902 Britain's war against the two Boer Republics in South Africa was complicated by Germany's support for the Boers. In 1906 and again in 1911, French moves to gain control of Morocco fired active German protest. Naval power was the key to imperial success. Battleships were related to the control of worldwide commercial interests in a way that land armies could never be. The issue was brought very much to the fore in 1898, during the Spanish-American War. The U.S. Navy stripped Spain of a string of its remaining colonies from Cuba to the Philippines. At the same time the German War Minister, Von Tirpitz, took the strategic decision to launch a program of shipbuilding and to challenge Britain's fleet of Dreadnoughts. The European arms race was on. Germany's mighty industrialization had occurred later than that of Britain and France and political unification had only come after 1871. As a result, the German colonial empire had not assumed the proportions which Germany's pride and prowess seemed to deserve. The brilliant and unstable German, Friedrich Wilhelm Nietzsche (1844–1900), Professor at Basle, articulated many of the era's most shocking thoughts. Nietzsche railed against Christianity, democracy and the accepted norms of morality. Morality he explained, is the herd instinct in the individual and religion is a world of pure fiction. "The blond beast, hungry for plunder and victory, is not to be mistaken." Nietzsche called for "a declaration of war by higher men on the masses...the great majority of men have no right to existence." (Davies, 1996: 860).

In no direction was the abandonment of *laissez-faire* principles more remarkable than in the attitude of Great Britain towards the British Empire. The Old Colonial System had been discredited by the loss of the American Colonies and throughout the greater part of the nineteenth century the colonial empire was looked upon as a burden. But, attitude changed after 1870, as the improvements in railways and steamships facilitated better communication between different parts of the Empire. The territories which were included in the British Empire fell, for the most part, into two groups, self-governing Dominions, inhabited and ruled mainly by white men and many other regions inhabited by indigenous people, ruled by English governors and officials. The four "white" Dominions were for a time under the supervision and control of the British Government, but they were later entrusted with power and self-government. Before 1875, government had been established in Canada (occupied by Europeans since July 1867) and Newfoundland, the British Cape Colony, in present-day South Africa and Namibia, named after the Cape of Good Hope, was preceded by an earlier Dutch colony, the Kaap de Goede Hoop, established in 1652 by the Dutch East India Company. The Dutch lost the colony to Britain following the 1795 Battle of Muizenberg. It was, however, returned following the 1802 Peace of Amiens. It was re-occupied by the British following the Battle of Blaauwberg (also known as the Battle of Cape Town) in 1806 and British possession affirmed with the Anglo-Dutch Treaty of 1814.

Australia (occupied by European since January 26, 1788) and New Zealand (occupied by Europeans since September 26, 1907). Six separate colonies were linked together as the Commonwealth of Australia in 1900. In 1887, the Jubilee of Queen Victoria was celebrated in London, which was attended by the prime ministers of most of the colonies. The Diamond Jubilee of 1897 was again attended by prime ministers of these colonies. The Coronation of King Edward in 1902 afforded a third opportunity for these colonies' prime ministers to meet. The tropical provinces of the British Empire, unlike those Dominions in the temperate zones, were not settled in great numbers by British people. These tropical possessions were very valuable to Britain, since they supply her with many commodities, such as raw materials for British industries, including cotton, jute, hemp, and rubber. These tropical colonies offer markets for British manufactured goods. During the "Scramble" for Africa a policy which was prevalent in the sixteenth and seventeenth centuries was revived. Companies received Charters from the Crown, by which privileges were conferred upon them, and these companies took possession of extensive regions in Africa and elsewhere. The British North Borneo Company (1881), the Royal Niger Company (1886), the British East Africa Company (1888) and the British South Africa Company (1889) were among those companies which came into existence at the time. These companies established claims over territories, which were later annexed by the Crown.

Europe continued to be dominated by the Five Great Powers that had organized the Congress of Vienna; and no general conflict had occurred either inwards, to the tasks of internal change, or outwards to fresh imperialist conquests across the globe. Only two intractable problems possessed the capacity to upset the international order. One of them was the accelerating rivalry between France and Germany. The other was the so-called "Eastern Question." For several decades after 1815 a defeated France and a divided Germany were indisposed to brawl. Yet there were old animosities seething just beneath the surface. In 1848 France was seen, once again, as the source of Germany's internal unrest. By the 1860s, when France was launched into the self-confident adventures of the Second Empire and Prussia was asserting itself in Germany, both powers were frightened by the other's aggressive posture. The Franco-Germany War of 1870–1, the third of Bismarck's lighting wars, caused an even bigger sensation than Sadova. During the War of the Bavarian Succession (July 1778–May 1779), Prussian troops occupied the territory between Sadova and Nachod. In early July 1866, the area around Sadova became the scene of the sanguinary Battle of Koniggaratz, the decisive combat of the Austro-Prussian War. Despite France being neutral in that war, the French public resented the Prussian victory and demanded "Revenge for

Sadova" (*Revanche pour Sadova*), which was one factor leading to the Franco-Prussian war of 1870. It was actively sought by the French, who were itching to teach the Prussian a lesson. But, they found themselves facing a coalition of all the German states, whose forces were better armed, better organized, and better led. France's military supremacy, which had lasted since Rocroi in 1643, was annulled in less than two months.

The first cannon-shot was ceremoniously fired on August 1, 1870 by the Emperor Napoleon's son, to cries of "*A' Berlin.*" France fought for eight months; but with Paris besieged, starving and crumbling from Prussian artillery, the government of the Third Republic was forced to sue for a humiliating peace. In May 1871, it submitted, consenting to cede Alsace-Lorraine, to pay huge reparations, and to accept German occupation for two years. Prussia's crowning victory had several long-term consequences. It facilitated the declaration of a united German Empire, whose first Emperor, William I (r.1871–88), King of Prussia, was acclaimed by the princes of Germany assembled at Versailles. In France, it provoked the desperate events of Paris Commune, and it fueled the passions of anti-German hatred that were to call ever more insistently for revenge. The "Eastern Question," grew from two related and apparently unstoppable processes – the continuing expansion of the Russian Empire and the steady retreat of the Ottomans. It gave rise to the independence of the Balkan nations, to the Crimean war (1854–6) and to a chain of complications which eventually sparked the fatal crisis of 1914. The prospect of Ottoman collapse loomed ever more starkly throughout the century. For the Russians, this was entirely desirable, as possession of the Bosporus Straits would fulfil Russia's dream of unrestricted access to warm water. For the other Powers, the demise of the "Sick Man of Europe" held a host of dangers. Britain feared for its lines of communications to India. Austria felt threatened by the emergence of a gaggle of Russian-sponsored states on her southeastern border. Germany military capacity might someday overtake her own. Russia's involvement in the Greek War of Independence sounded the alarm bells and her gains at the Treaty of Adrianople (1829) were restricted to a small corner on the Danube delta.

In both 1831 and 1863, Russian violation of Poland's nominal independence evoked vigorous protests from Britain and France. But it was not unwelcomed to Berlin and Vienna, which had Polish territories of their own to hold down. Russia's advance into Danubian principalities in 1853 provoked an immediate military response from Austria and the onset of the Crimean War. Russia decided to withdraw from North America; and in 1867 Alaska was sold to the U.S.A. for eight million dollars. In 1859, after half a century of brutality and devastation the conquest of the mountain tribes of the Caucasus was completed, and their Chechen hero, Shamil, captured. In 1860, the Amur and Maritime provinces were acquired from China, in 1864 Turkestan from Persia, in 1875 Sakhalim and the Kuriles from

Japan. In 1900, the Russian occupation of Manchuria provoked conflict and defeat in the Russo-Japanese War 1904–5. The Crimean War (1853–6) took place when Britain and France decided to assist the Porte in efforts to defend the Danube principalities and to resist Russian claims of protection over the Ottomans' Christian subjects. Austria immediately occupied the principalities and the Western Powers, aided by Sardinia, sent a punitive expedition to the Crimea. Despite nasty trench warfare, cholera, and appalling losses, the Allied siege of Sebastopol finally succeeded. The Peace of Paris (1856) neutralized the Black Sea, imposed a joint European protectorate over the Ottoman Christians and guaranteed the integrity of both the Ottoman Empire and the principalities. But 20 years later, military intervention by Serbia and Montenegro, diplomatic meddling by Austria and the murder of 136 Turkish officials in Bulgaria elicited a ferocious Ottoman response.

In May 1876, over twenty thousand peasants were slaughtered in the notorious Bulgarian Horrors. Two international conferences were convened to impose conditions on the new Sultan, Abdul Hamid II the Damned (r.1876–1909). The Congress of Berlin (June 13–July 13, 1878) was convened to satisfy British and Austrian demands for the revision of the San Stefano Treaty and the curtailment of Russian ambitions. In many respects the Congress exemplified the most cynical aspects of the European power game. None of the Balkan peoples were effectively represented. None was treated with consideration: Bosnia and Herzegovina were handed over to Austria occupation; Bulgaria was split in two, and excluded from the Aegean; Serbia, Montenegro, and Romania were all refused the piece of territory which they thought most important. The Powers, in contrast, simply helped themselves; Russia, denied the Straits, took Bessarabia from her Romanian ally; Britain took Cyprus from her Ottoman client; Austria took Sanjak of Novi Bazar. The brakes were removed from the pursuit of national interest at all levels. The formation of two opposing diplomatic and military blocs took place over three decades. At first, Britain and France were kept apart by colonial rivalry, Britain and Russia by mutual suspicions over Central Asia, Russia, and France by tsarist-republican animosities. So, for a time, Bismarck was free to construct a system that would protect Germany from French revenge. In 1879, he forged the Dual Alliance with Austria, from 1882 the Triple Alliance of Germany, Austria, and Italy, in 1884–7 and 1887–90 the two reinsurance treaties with Russia. In 1893, the Dual Entente was signed between Paris and St. Petersburg, which at a stroke, released France from isolation, regained her confidence, and threatened Germany from both sides. In 1903 France settled her differences with Britain and entered the *Entente Cordiale*. In 1907, after the Anglo-Russian agreement over Persia, the way was finally opened for the *Triple Entente* of France, Britain, and Russia.

It has been argued (Davies 1996) that Europe was now divided into two massive armed camps, and there was no "honest broker" left. In the first decade of the twentieth century, the long European peace still held. But fears began to be expressed about its fragility. Franco-German rivalry, recurrent Balkan crises, antagonistic diplomatic blocks, imperialist frictions, and the naval arm race all combined to raise the temperature of international relations. Whilst all the Powers professed a desire for continued peace, they were all preparing for war. Austria-Hungary annexed Bosnia in 1908 without a shred of legal justification and without any intervention from any Powers. In 1912–13, three regional wars were fought in the Balkans. In May 1912, Italy attacked the Ottoman Empire, seizing Rhodes, Tripoli, and Cyrenaica. In October 1912, with the Porte diverted by a rising in Albania, the Balkan League of Montenegro, Serbia, Bulgaria, and Greece took the offensive against the Ottomans in Macedonia. In June 1913, Bulgaria attacked Serbia to start the Balkan War of Partition. On each occasion, international conferences were held and treaties were signed. Four weeks, following the assassination of Archduke Francis Ferdinand of Austria-Este (1863–1914), heir to the throne of Austria-Hungary, on June 28, 1914, by a 19-year-old consumptive student, Gavrilo Princip (1894–1918), at Sarajevo, brought Europe's military restraints crashing to the ground. On July 23, 1914, an ultimatum was delivered to Belgrade, demanding Austrian participation in the pursuit of the assassins. On July 28, 1914, Austria-Hungary officially declared war on Serbia. Russia immediately mobilized, prompting Germany to issue ultimata first to Russia and then to France. On August 1, 1914 Germany declared war on Russia and, on August 3, on France. The British government sent an ultimatum to Berlin on August 3, 1914. The Five European Powers were embarking on the general war which they had studiously avoided for 29 years.

In the interminable debates about the causes of the Great War, the diplomatic system of the early twentieth century has often been made a prime culprit. Vast political and economic forces had supposedly created a "geopolitical consensus" in which both sides agreed about the necessity of supporting their allies and the dire consequences of inaction. The Central Powers were bound in advance by the Triple Alliance and Germany was obliged to assist its Austrian ally, if Austria had been attacked. But Austria had not been attacked and Vienna was not in a position to invoke the terms of the existing treaties. In the case of the *Triple Entente*, the chain of obligations was still looser, as the *Entente* was not an Alliance. Russia and France were obliged by treaty to assist each other if attacked; but the third member of the *Entente*, Great Britain, was not formally obliged to take up arms in their defense. Moreover, since none of the *Entente* Powers was formally allied to Belgrade, an Austrian attack on Serbia could not be construed as a *casus belli*. In particular, there was no Russo-Serbian treaty in force. By the Treaty of 1839, Britain was committed to uphold the independence of Belgium. But that was an old obligation which long preceded the undertakings of the *Entente*. Therefore, the diplomatic system of 1914 left governments with considerable room for maneuver.

It did not obliged Germany to support Austria in all circumstances, or Russia to support Serbia, or Britain to support Russia and France. Britain's declaration of war put the final seal on the biggest diplomatic disaster of modern times. It was the fourth such declaration in line – the first by Austria, the second and third by Germany. Britain was the only *Entente* Power to take the initiative in going to war. Britain could have remained neutral, leaving Germany and Austria to fight it out with Russia and France. Vienna was the key to a local war, Berlin to the continental war, London to a global conflict.

From an economic point of view, the British Empire in 1914, was still the capital of world finance, and a war against Britain was a bid for world supremacy. Through her technical and industrial strength was no longer the equivalent of Germany's, Great Britain could mobilize colossal resources. The British Government enjoyed the exceptional luxury of a position where sudden defeat did not come into reckoning and where a protracted war would see British military capacity steadily rising over a period of two to three years. These facts had clear consequences. If the Continental campaigns went well for France and Russia in the early stages, Britain's participation might well tip the balance in favor of a decisive victory. If things went for the Central Powers, Berlin and Vienna could not count on any such favorable outcome. Even if the French and Russian armies were defeated in the first shock, the Central Powers would still be left facing a defiant and impregnable Britain, which would use all its wiles to mount new coalitions against them. In short, whatever happened, Britain had the capacity for ruining the prospects for the quick limited war of which German generals dreamed. In 1914, Europe, through their colonial empires and trading companies, European powers dominated the globe, but by 1945 almost all had been lost: Europeans had fought each other to the point of utter exhaustion. Europe's military and economic power was overtaken and their colonial power was no longer sustainable. When the wartime dust finally settled, European ruins were controlled by two extra-European powers, the U.S.A. and the U.S.S.R., neither of which had even been present at the start.

Although the Wilsonian ideal of national self-determination was widely endorsed, the victorious Allies saw no reason to discuss the aspirations of their own subjected nationalities, such as the Irish, still less the wishes of colonial peoples. The Western Powers showed little sense of solidarity among themselves, and the Americans suspected the British and French of imperialist designs. Both the British and the French suspected the strength of America's commitment. Five major treaties were put into effect and a dozen states were given international recognition. A score of territorial awards were made and a batch of Plebiscites were organized and administered. In the inter-war period, between Armistice Day (11/11/1918) and 1/9/1939, Europe never escaped the shadow of war. Allied intervention in Russia had shown that the west possessed neither the will nor the resources to control the Bolsheviks and French occupation of the Ruhr was to show that Germany could not be coerced. What is more, if Russia and Germany could not be restrained separately, there was no chance of restraining them if they chose to work together. The Western Powers had hoped that their victory would usher in an era modelled in their own image. After all, at the start of the Great War the European Continent contained 19 monarchies and three republics; at the end, it consisted of 14 monarchies and 16 republics. But hardly a year passed when one country or another did not see its democratic constitution violated by one or another brand of dictator. Dictators came in all shapes and sizes – communists, fascists, radicals and reactionaries, left-wing authoritarians, right-wing militarists, monarchs, anti-monarchists, and even a cleric like Father Jozef Tiso in Slovakia (1887–1947). The only thing they shared was the conviction that western democracy was not for them. Of the two new states to come into existence between the wars, Ireland, was a national republic, and the Vatican state, an apostolic dictatorship.

In Ireland the dominant personality, and many times Premier, Eamon de Valera (1882–1975), was a half-Cuban Catholic born of an Irish mother in New York. The Free State declared itself the republic of Eire in 1937, severing all formal ties with Great Britain in 1949. The Vatican State was created in 1929 in pursuance of the Lateran Treaty signed by Benito Mussolini's (1883–1945) Italy and Pope Pius XI (1857–1939). It covered 44 hectares on the right bank of the Tiber in Central Rome. Its population of about a thousand residents was to be ruled by the absolute authority of the Pope. Its creation ended sixty years of the Pope's captivity since the suppression of the Papal States in 1870. After the suppression of Soviet Hungary, Soviet Russia (1917–22) and its successor, the U.S.S.R. (1923–89), long remained the sole communist state. The main fascist regimes emerged in Italy (1922), Germany (1933), and Spain (1936). In any number of European history books, 1939 is the year when "the world went again to war." This only proves how self-centered Europeans can be. War had been on the march in the world for the previous eight years. The Japanese had invaded Manchuria in 1931 and had been warring in central China since 1937. From August 1938, they were embroiled in fighting on the Mongolian frontier against the Soviet Red army. As part of this conflict, Japan had joined Germany and Italy as one of the Axis Powers. What happened in 1939 was simply the addition of Europe to the existing theatres of war. The invasion of Poland which began on September 1, 1939 did not mark the start of fighting in Europe. It had been preceded by the German attack on Lithuania in March 1939 and by the Italian invasion of Albania in April. But, by involving the U.S.S.R., which was already engaged against the Japanese in Mongolia, it established the link between the European and the Asian theatres of operations. Hence, the fact that Japan, the U.S.S.R., Poland, Germany, and the

Western Powers were all enmeshed in the web of conflict makes the best argument for contending that a Second World War had really begun.

At the end of the Second World War, the International Military Tribunal was created in consequence of the Potsdam Agreement. Its Charter was published on August 8, 1945, two days after the bombing of Hiroshima. The opening of the Nuremberg Trials was set for November 20, 1945. From then, the Trials proceeded through 403 open sessions in the main courtroom of the Palace of Justice until the final sentences of the judgment were read more than ten months later, on October 1, 1946. The four Allied judges heard the "not guilty" pleas of 21 defendants. The four Allied prosecutors – an American, a Britain, a French, and a Soviet – with their deputies and assistants, shared the room with German counsel, clerks, translators, and interpreters. In all, the prosecution produced over 4,000 documents, 1,809 affidavits, and 33 live witnesses. They also showed films, exhibits, including heads of men mounted on wooded stands. The defense produced 143 witnesses, together with hundreds of thousands of affidavits. The corpus of the Trial, published in 1946, ran to 43 volumes. The defense could not make direct comparisons with Allied conduct – the failings of the Versailles settlement or of the Allied bombing offensive, nor the subject of Soviet atrocities. Attempts to discuss conditions in Allied internment camps or the forcible expulsion of Germans, which was in progress at the time, were cut short. One of the main criticisms against the trials, was the lack of independence, in view of the fact that the Allied Powers supply both the judges and prosecutors on terms and in an arena dictated by themselves, made for bad legal practice and for poor publicity. Most seriously of all, was the fact that the Nuremberg trials were limited to offences committed by the defeated enemy erected an insuperable obstruction to any general and impartial investigation into War Crimes or crimes against humanity. It created the lasting impression in public opinion that such crimes could not by definition be committed by agents of the Allied Powers. Unlike 1918, there were no urgent demands for a general Peace Conference, as there was no German government with whom a new Treaty might be signed. The only Peace Conference to be held was the one which met at Paris from July to October, 1946, to settle the affairs of five lesser-defeated states – Italy, Romania, Bulgaria, Hungary, and Finland. All the defeated states were obliged to cede territory.

In 1493, the map of Europe from Portugal to the Khanate of Astrakhan contained at least thirty sovereign states. Five-hundred years later, if one discounts Andorra and Monaco, the Union of Colmar and the Swiss Federation, no single one of those thirty states had maintained its separate sovereign existence. Of the sovereign states on the map of Europe in 1993, four had been formed in the sixteenth century, four in the seventeenth century, two in the eighteenth century, seven in the nineteenth century, and no fewer than thirty-six in the twentieth century. The rise and fall of states represent one of the most important phenomena of modern Europe. The traditional approach of analyzing state formation was based on constitutional and international law. The aim was to describe the legal framework within which empires, monarchies, and republics organized their government, control their dependencies and gain recognition. More recently, greater emphasis has fallen on long-term considerations. According to one historian, Norbert Elias, state formation is part of a civilizational process operating since the period of feudal fragmentation through the steady accretion of princely power. Others have looked more at the interplay of internal structures and external relations. Three types of state have prevailed – tribute-raising empires, systems of fragmented sovereignty and national states. Their internal life-force has been dominated either by the concentration of coercion, or by varying concentrations of the two. Money and violence were the prime movers and in the last resort, everything turned on power – "might is right" (Davies, 1996: 456).

The Nation-State

State nationalism is well illustrated in the case of Great Britain. In 1707, when the United Kingdom came into existence, there was no British nation. The people of the British Isles thought of themselves as English, Welsh, Scots, or Irish. But, over the years, the propagation of the dominant English culture and the promotion of its loyal Protestant and English-speaking servants, gradually consolidated a strong sense of overlying British identity. Moreover, in the nineteenth century, when the liberal establishment came to favor mass education, non-English cultures were actively suffocated. All "Britons," were expected to show loyalty to the symbols of a new British nationality – to speak standard English, to stand up and sing the royal anthem and to respect the Union Jack (1801). In this way, the new British nation was successfully forged. Its older component nations were relegated to the status of junior and subordinate partners. According to Davies (1996), most European governments strove to strengthen the national cohesion of their subjects by ceremonies, by symbolic art, by interpretations of history and by education and the promotion of common culture. Popular nationalism was planted under the dynastic states and multinational empire of the era. Firmly grounded in Rousseau's doctrine of popular sovereignty it assumed that the proper forum for the exercise of the general will was provided by the national or ethnic community, not by the artificial frontiers of existing states. Much of the nineteenth century debate on nationality was dominated by the conviction that the peoples of Europe could be divided into "historic" and "unhistorical" nations. The idea first appeared in Hegel and was adopted by social Darwinists, who looked on the competition between nations as an evolutionary process, with some fitted for independent survival and others destined for extinction.

It was largely due to the established Powers – France, Britain, Prussia, Austria, and Russia – possessed a historic destiny, as do the states whom the Powers already recognized – Spain, Portugal, Belgium, the Netherlands, Sweden, Demark and Greece – and the leading national contenders – Italians, the Germans, and the Poles. In reality, the concept of historicity was entirely subjective, not to say spurious. Many of the nations who felt that they had an iron-clad case for self-determination were due to be disillusioned. Politics alone decided that Greeks, Belgians, Romanians, and Norwegians might succeed, where for the time the Irish, the Czechs, or Poles could not. The nationalities of the Tsarist and Habsburg empires, which were to produce the largest number of nation-states, did not come to the fore until the turn of the twentieth century. Throughout the nineteenth century, committed national activists, scholars, and politicians appealed to six main sources of information to construct the image of reality that was to inspire the faithful. History was raked to furnish proof of the nation's age-long struggle for its rights and its land. Prehistory was a favorite subject, since it could be used to substantiate claims to aboriginal settlement. Where facts could not be found, recourse had to be made to myths or to downright inventions. National heroes and heroines, and distant national victories were unearthed to be praised. Anything that reflected discredit on the nation, or credit on its foes, was passed over.

Language was reformed and standardized as proof of the nation's separate and unique identity. Dictionaries and grammars were compiled and libraries collected, where none had existed before. Textbooks were prepared for national schools and universities. Folklore was mined for all its worth, as it was thought to join the modern nation to its most ancient cultural roots. Religion was mobilized to sanctify national sentiment and in many instances to erect barriers between ethnic groups. Racial theories exerted powerful attractions. For example, the notion of a Caucasian race was invented in the late eighteenth century. The allied notion of the "Aryan race" was first uttered in 1848 by a German professor at Oxford, Max Muller. Every nationality in Europe was tempted to conceive of itself as a unique racial kinship group, whose blood formed a distinct and separate stream. In London, the Royal Historical Society sponsored a series of experiments on its fellows showing that the brainpans of those with Celtic names were inferior to those of Anglo-Saxon origin. In Germany, the science of eugenics came up with similar results. In Russia, the panslave movement was loaded with racial overtones. Arguing for unification of all Slav peoples under the aegis of the Tsar, assuming that political solidarity would emerge from the (non-existent) racial affinity of the Slav. All over Europe, every branch of art and literature was mobilized to illustrate and to embroider national themes. Poets and novelists wrote pseudo-historical romances about national heroes and national customs. Musicians recruited the harmonies and rhythms of their native folk dance and folksong to elaborate distinctive national styles that became the hallmark of numerous "national schools."

Nationalism underlined an important distinction between "civilization" and "culture." Civilization was the sum total of ideas and traditions which had been inherited from the ancient world and from Christianity; it was grafted onto the native cultures of all the peoples of Europe from the outside, to form the common legacy. The passions of nationalism inevitably fueled conflict. Almost all parts contained ethnic minorities whose popular nationalism was bound to clash with the state-led nationalism of the authorities. In Britain, there were three potential separatist movements. The Irish participated in a "western democracy," from 1801, when the Union of Ireland and Great Britain was enacted, over fifty Irish MPs sat in the British Parliament at Westminster. It gave them all sorts of benefits except the one they most desired – control over their own affairs. The Catholic Association of Daniel O'Connell (1775–1847) achieved religious toleration in 1829. But discontent was kept on the boil by the sufferings of the famine, by injustices of successive Land Acts and by the lack of political progress. The complacency of English Conservatives, the tenacious resistance of the Ulster Protestants and the violent exploits of the Irish radical wing, which was represented by the Fenians (Irish Republican Brotherhood) from 1859 and by Sinn Fein from 1905, made for political deadlock. In the Irish countryside, the long running war between government-backed landlords and the rebellious tenants of the Land League (1879) created a pervasive climate of fear. In the late nineteenth century, three successive bills for Irish Home Rule were blocked in the House of Lords. It was also a time when the Irish Literary Theatre, the Gaelic Athletic Association, and the Gaelic League were all founded, "on the necessity for de-anglicizing the Irish People." In 1922, when a fourth Home Rule Bill was prepared, both the Ulster Volunteers in Belfast and the National Volunteers in Dublin raised formidable armies. As Europe approached the Second World War, Ireland stood on the brink of civil war.

The British Caribbean Legacy

British-owned Caribbean colonies were severely affected by the 1930s' economic depression, with widespread unemployment as well as falling wages and increased food prices. Large number of unemployed laborers drifted to the islands' main towns in search of work, where they were forced to live in the growing slum communities. Wage levels for unskilled sugar workers were as low as 28 cents per day in St. Vincent and 32 cents in St. Kitts. In Jamaica, it was estimated that nearly half the workforce received only part-time employment. In rural areas, the majority of housing had not significantly changed since the days of slavery and indentured laborers and plantation workers and their families still lived in squalid "barracks," where hundreds of people shared primitive latrines. It was not uncommon for a family of ten to share a single room. The huts constructed of bamboo, coconut palm leaves and wooden planks were little better. Surveys conducted by colonial commissions revealed a dispiriting panorama of deprivation. Inspections of schoolchildren in Jamaica showed extremely high incidences of anemia, malnutrition, and internal parasites and infant mortality rates were extremely high. In 1930s Britain, the average was 58 per 1,000 live births, but in St. Kitts the figure reached 187 per 1,000 live births and 217 per 1,000 live births in Barbados. Children in the British Caribbean colonies were further disadvantaged by an under-funded and anachronistic education system. In 1932 the annual budget per student in Trinidad was £2.15s and in Grenada £1. 5s. 8d compared to £10.7s 9d per child in British boroughs. What the children learned was often useless and inappropriate, an imported curriculum which ignored local history and culture and put the emphasis on "rote" learning and British history.

The hardships experienced by the majority of Caribbean people in the 1930s were a primary factor in the explosion of social unrest, which began in 1935. There were also other political developments, which fueled the movement towards revolt. The experience of the First World War, in which thousands of men from British and French islands had enlisted, had increased expectations of a better life during peacetime. The British West Indies Regiment, totaling 400 officers and 15,000 men, had formed 13 battalions of which two served with distinction in Egypt and the Palestine campaign. The others were used as labor battalions in France, incurring 1,256 fatal casualties. Hence, those who returned to the islands were highly receptive to the message of reform and social justice. Further, the political turmoil of 1930s Europe, with the rise of fascism and the polarization of ideologies, did not go unnoticed in the Caribbean. A particular point of controversy was the invasion of independent Abyssinia (Ethiopia) by Benito Mussolini in 1935 and what many saw as Britain's compliance with the occupation, was evidence that Britain and other European powers were indifferent to the fate of an independent black nation. A prominent figure in the inter-war years and a leading advocate of racial politics was Marcus Garvey (1887–1940), whose blend of "black nationalism" and "pan-Africanism" won him many supporters in the Caribbean.

Between 1935 and 1938 there were a number of disturbances by unemployed workers in many Caribbean islands. The first of these disturbances began in St. Kitts in January 1935 and spread to St. Vincent, Jamaica, St. Lucia, Barbados, and Trinidad, with the loss of many lives, with thousands wounded and arrested, which was to have lasting effects. Before 1935 the trade union movement in the Caribbean was very weak, due to hostility from the colonial authorities and employers. Legislations banned a range of legitimate union activities. But, a new generation of trade union organizers emerged to articulate the needs of the low-paid and unemployed and between 1939 and 1945 an estimated sixty-five trade unions were formed across the Caribbean. The rise of trade unionism was directly connected to the rise of new political leaders. For example, William Alexander

Bustamante (1884–1977) joined the People's National Party (PNP) in 1938, until he left the PNP to set up his own Jamaica Labor Party (JLP) in 1943. The Barbados Labor Party (BLP) has its roots in trade unionism and was led by the lawyer Grantley Adams (1898–1971). Other parties appeared in most of the islands, committed to political and economic change, led by leaders with their roots in union activism, such as Vere Bird (1910–1999) in Antigua and Robert Llewellyn Bradshaw (1916–1978) in St. Kitts. Most of these political leaders were influenced by the British Labor Party and were in favor of gradual and moderate action to improve social conditions.

Across the Caribbean Black Nationalist teachings of thinkers such as Marcus Garvey gained widespread support. As a result, the British government set up the Moyne Commission in 1938 to investigate social and economic conditions in the British territories of the Caribbean. Chaired by Walter Edward Guinness (Lord Moyne, b.1880–1944), the Commission spent fourteen months visiting urban rural communities and interviewing about four hundred witnesses. The Commission concluded that the disturbances could be linked directly to unemployment, poor education and health provision, low wages and unsatisfactory working conditions. In December 1939, the Commission's report was submitted to the British Parliament, but the report was not published until 1945. The report was a damning account of neglect and deprivation in the British Caribbean. Everywhere the report concluded housing was squalid and unhealthy. The report proposed an annual grant of £1 million for twenty years to fund infrastructural schemes and further investment in education, health, and housing. Trade unions, it suggested, should be allowed to operate legally and freely, while the school curriculum should be reformed to include hygiene and agricultural training.

Although no land fighting took place in the Caribbean, the Second World War affected the Caribbean islands in many different ways, further deprivation to unexpected economic fortunes. In 1942 over 300 ships, with a combined tonnage of more than 1.5 million tons, were sunk in the Caribbean region, including oil tankers and ships transporting bauxite. The British colonial authorities imprisoned some trade union and political activists, whom they suspected of potential disloyalty, including Buzz Butler (1897–1977) in Trinidad for four years and Alexander Bustamante, future Jamaican Prime Minister. Thousands of men from the British colonies volunteered to serve in the British armed forces and over 5,000 men from the British colonies volunteered to join the RAF. Others joined the Caribbean Regiment consisting of recruits from almost every island, who were eventually sent to Egypt but never saw action. A shortage of labor in the U.S.A. reversed their anti-immigrant trends of the depression years and in 1943, an agreement with Barbados and Jamaica resulted in more than 100,000 workers going on contract to agricultural and industrial jobs in the U.S.A. The election of reforming governments in Europe encouraged many in the British, French, and

Dutch colonies to believe that they would share in the "peace dividend." A growing mood of anti-colonialism, in Europe as well as in the Caribbean, seemed to hold out the promise of reform. The post-war period witnessed a massive increase in migration from the Caribbean.

The Rise of Pan-Africanism

Before the First World War, black students and Pan-African activists had been a relatively fortunate minority, within the community. The majority of black people in Britain in the late nineteenth and early twentieth centuries lived very hard lives (Fryer 1984: 294). The largest group, in terms of occupation, were seamen, who were dumped from steamers or attracted by work, especially in Cardiff, which was second only to London. Laid off in Cardiff, Newport, Barry, London, Liverpool, Hull, Tyneside, or Glasgow, black seamen found it hard to get another ship and harder still to find work ashore. Their quest was endless and almost hopeless and they often went hungry. Although the Colonial Office would repatriate unemployed seamen, in case of West Indians, the authorities in the islands they came from often refused to let them return. But, the outbreak of the war in 1914 brought dramatic changes for black workers in Britain, with well-paid work for them to do. Black workers were made welcome in the munitions and chemical factories and black seamen, replacing men needed by the navy, were made welcome in the merchant service and by the end of the war, there were about 20,000 black people in Britain. In February 1919, the first of the so-called race riots in British ports took place on Tyneside, when an official of the stewards' and cooks' union, J. B. Fye, incited a crowd of foreign white seamen against Arab seamen, all of whom were British subjects, after refusing them work.

Demobilization had significantly increased Liverpool's black population to an estimated 5,000, a large proportion of whom was out of work. In one week alone, in spring of 1919, about 120 black workers employed for years in the big Liverpool sugar refineries and oilcake mills were sacked because white workers now refused to work with them (Fryer 1984: 299). Unemployed black workers were being turned out of their lodgings and on May 13, 1919, the Secretary of the Liverpool Ethiopian Association went to see the Lord Mayor to inform him that between 500 and 600 black seamen, mostly discharged British soldiers and sailors, were out of work and stranded in the area and anxious to go home. Some, he informed the mayor, were "particularly starving, work having been refused to them on account of their color" (Fryer, 1984: 300). The racism that poisoned the everyday lives of black people in Britain between the end of the First World War and the end of the Second World War did so in the form of what was called "color bar" (Fryer 1984: 356). In industry, the color bar was virtually total and only in the early 1940s, when their labor was needed for the war effort, could black workers get jobs in British factories; and even then, there was often resistance from employers and white employees alike. The color bar also meant "the refusal of lodgings, refusal of service in cafes, refusal of admittance to dance hall."

By 1935, there were an estimated 2,000 Africans or persons of African descent seamen in Cardiff. The local police, quite illegally, placed their own interpretation on the 1920 Aliens Order and the 1925 Special Restriction (Colored Alien Seamen) Order. In the eyes of the police in Cardiff, every black seaman was an alien, regardless of any documentary evidence a black man may produce to prove that he was a British citizen. When a black seaman produced a British passport, the police would confiscate it without giving a receipt. The shipping companies, in cahoots with the police, often refused to give black seamen the pay due to them at the end of a voyage until they presented an alien's certificate of registration. In 1935 two investigations from the League of Colored People (George W. Brown and P. Cecil Lewis) established that in Cardiff, all black men were classified as aliens in spite of indisputable evidence of British nationality. This included men with honorable records of military service. But, "a studied and deliberate policy had been instituted to deprive them of their nationality and the privileges attached thereto" (Fryer 1984: 357). In a country where even stray dogs are "looked after" by special societies a citizen of the world, who is fighting the world's battle for freedom and equality, should have found it necessary to place himself in this humiliating position. It was generally agreed by Ministers that, "it was desirable that the people of this country should avoid becoming too friendly with colored troops."

By the end of 1942, there were about 8,000 West Indian troops in Britain and they were falling foul of white American racists. Before 1944 it was common for London's West End hotels to refuse accommodation to black people. In the summer of 1943, Learie Nicholas Constantine (1901–1971), a black civil servant and a British subject, was refused accommodation at the Imperial Hotel, in Russell Square, London. Constantine brought a case against the Imperial Hotel and won token damages of £5. In 1944, it was suggested that most white British people would be quite unwilling for a black man to enter their homes, nor would they wish to work with one as a colleague, nor to stand shoulder to shoulder with one at a factory bench. By 1948 there were about 8,000 black people in Liverpool; most of them had come to Britain during the war to help with the war effort. About thirty percent of the adults were seafarer, another ten percent had shore jobs, and the rest were chronically unemployed as a result of the color bar. At the 1948 annual conference of the National Union of Seamen, its assistant general secretary made it clear that Liverpool and other British ports were to be "no go" areas for black seafarers (Fryer 1984: 367).

Pan-Africanism, according to Fryer (1984), was one of the major political traditions of the twentieth century, which was largely created by black people living in Britain. In 1787 Ottobah Cugoano (1757–1791), also known as John

Stuart, published in London his "Thoughts and sentiments on the evil and wicked traffic of the slavery and commerce of the human species"; forecasting "universal calamity" for the "criminal nations" that profited from their enslavement. Two years later, Cugoano's friend Olaudah Equiano (1745–1797) published in London his "Interesting Narrative." These two writers anticipated many of the leading ideas of Pan-Africanism; racial solidarity and self-awareness; Africa for Africans; opposition to racial discrimination; emancipation from white supremacy and domination. According to Fryer (1984), London was the capital of a fast-expanding empire and it was in London that Africans, West Indians, African-Americans, Indians, and Anglo-Africans could most conveniently meet, exchange ideas and create networks of contacts. Britain had, from 1938 onward, a Pan-Africanist center linked by a thousand threads to the anti-imperialist mass movement in Africa and the West Indies. What was important among these activists is that none of them allowed themselves to be used by white politicians in Britain. Even when they joined a white political organization, they did so to further the cause of black freedom.

Although black activists found allies in Britain, they took care to keep control of their own organizations. These activists began to formulate a new ideology of colonial liberation designed to challenge existing ideological systems, including communism. The chief stimulus was the Italian invasion of Ethiopia, which touched a highly sensitive nerve, as Ethiopia and Liberia were, in the whole of Africa in 1936, the only territories not under European control. Britain and France failed to respond to Ethiopia's appeal to the League of Nations, as both were selling oil to the fascist dictator whose troops were gassing defenseless Ethiopians. In 1936 the International African Friends of Abyssinia (IAFA), whose main purpose was to arouse the British public's sympathy and support for the victims of fascist aggression and to assist by all means in their power in the maintenance of the Territorial integrity and political independence of Abyssinia. In March 1937, the IAFA was replaced by the International African Service Bureau, with Isaac Theophilus Akunna Wallace-Johnson (1894–1965) as general secretary, Cyril Lionel Robert James (1901–1989) as editorial director, Malcolm Ivan Meredith (1903–1959), known as, George Padmore in the chair and Ras Makonnen, born George Thomas N. Griffiths (1900–1983), as treasurer and fundraiser. Its members saw Pan-Africanism as "an independent political expression of Negro aspirations for complete national independence from white domination – Capitalist or Communist" (Fryer 1984: 345).

Towards the end of 1944 the International African Service Bureau joined with a number of other black organizations in Britain and representatives in Britain of various colonial organizations, to form a "loose umbrella association" called the Pan-African Federation. The new grouping had four objects:

1. To promote the well-being and unity of African peoples and peoples of African descent throughout the world
2. To demand self-determination and independence of African peoples, and other subject races from domination of powers claiming sovereignty and trusteeship over them
3. To secure equality of civil rights for African peoples and the total abolition of all forms of racial discrimination
4. To strive to co-operate between African peoples and others who share our aspirations (Fryer, 1984: 347).

Among the large number of resolutions carried, at the 1945 Pan-African Congress in Manchester, was one on "Colored Seamen in Great Britain" and one of the "Color Bar Problem in Great Britain," demanding that discrimination on account of race, creed, or color be made a criminal offence. The 1945 Pan-African Congress declared that: "We are determined to be free... We are unwilling to starve any longer while doing the world's drudgery, in order to support by our poverty and ignorance a false aristocracy and a discredited imperialism. We condemn the monopoly of capital and the rule of private wealth and industry for private profit alone... We will fight in every way we can for freedom, democracy and social betterment" (ibid: 350).

Sir Learie Nicholas Constantine (1901–1971) mirrors many of the struggles, tensions, and aspirations that black Caribbean people experienced during the twentieth century, from initial rejection, gradual acceptance and, in some areas, final acclaim. His life also spanned and symbolized the wider black struggle from colonial dependency to independence – including the difficulties and unfulfilled expectations that followed. But Constantine was not just an important figure in the Caribbean and its diaspora; he was an immensely impressive human being; many dimensional, widely loved, honest, controversial, proud, and always engaging. In 1947, Learie became chairman of the League of Colored Peoples, following the death of Dr. Harold Arundel Moody (1882–1947), and sat on the organization's executive committee with Hastings Banda (1898–1997), a U.K.-based GP who was later to become the first President of Malawi. But Dr. Moody was the driving force behind the League and without him its influence began to wane and despite Constantine's best efforts the League folded in 1951. Constantine was elected president of the London branch of the Caribbean Labor Congress, a trade union body, in 1948, hosting meetings and talks on politics and labor problems in the Caribbean. He also served as a Colonial Social Welfare Advisory Committee between 1947 and 1950. Throughout his eclectic life as sportsman, welfare worker, broadcaster, politician, author, diplomat, barrister, and race relations pioneer, Constantine consistently pushed back many boundaries, arguing for change in whatever environment he functioned.

As one of the highest paid sportsmen in the world during the inter-war years, he raised cricket to new heights of excitement and prestige, while simultaneously agitating for an end to the "color bar" and class divisions in the game – both in the West Indies and elsewhere. In his role as a welfare officer in Britain during the Second World War, he played a vitally important part in championing the interest of black immigrants and easing racial tensions. Constantine was disappointed with Attlee's Labor government on the issue of race, especially over their collusion with the racist South African authorities in dismissing Seretse Goitsebeng Maphiri Kharma (1921–1980), an English educated Chieftain of the Barmangwato people in the Bechuanaland Protectorate of South Africa, who had upset the South Africans by marrying a white English woman, Ruth William. Under pressure from South African officials, the British government summoned Kharma to London on false pretenses. On arrival he was told that he would no longer be recognized as chief and was barred from returning. Although Kharma became the first President of Botswana, Constantine felt that Kharma should have stood by his rights. Constantine felt that Attlee was a white supremacist.

After many years of toil, Constantine was called to the bar by the Middle Temple in late 1954, at the age of 53. With this achievement, Constantine felt he was ready to return to his native Trinidad. Constantine left Britain with a distinctly thorny going-away present. It was a fifth book; *Color Bar* (1954), a parting shot that left no one in any doubt as to the strength of his feelings on race relations in Britain and the world beyond. The United Kingdom he wrote was "only a little less intolerant" than segregated America or South Africa. Hardly any Englishwoman, he wrote, would sit at a restaurant table with a colored man or woman and inter-racial marriage was considered almost universally to be out of the question. Britain's willful neglect of the human rights of its black subject abroad costs first fortunes of taxpayers' money, then the lives of colored "natives" and white conscripts, and finally the loss of the colony. The excuse is always: "The African is not ready for responsibility." But nothing is done to make him ready; everything is done to prevent the majority of Africans from making themselves ready. A bright boy here and there is picked out and part educated – but only if he is docile and obedient to white control. On September 24, 1956, Constantine won a seat in the general election for the People's National Movement (PNM) led by Dr. Eric Eustace Williams (1911–1981). Trinidad and Tobago had grown to 70,000 people, of whom around forty-seven percent were of African origin, thirty-five percent Indian, and fourteen percent mixed. The PNM party won 13 of the 24 seats it contested in the election, making it the largest party in the Legislative Council ahead of the PDP on five, Trinidad Labor Party (2), The Butler Party (2) and two Independents. Governor Sir Edward Beetham called on Dr. Williams to form a government, in which Constantine was given the role of minister of communications, works, and public utilities, in an eight-strong cabinet. However, in politics Constantine was often caricatured as an "Englishman."

In 1959, Britain had agreed to give Trinidad and Tobago internal self-government with Dr. Williams as prime minister, and Constantine had played a role in the gestation of British backed "nation" of West Indies states – the West Indies Federation, but when this failed in May 1962, Constantine played a prominent part in successful negotiations for Trinidad's independence at Marlborough House in London, on August 31, 1962. Constantine was offered the new post of Trinidad and Tobago's High Commissioner in London, after Constantine had decided not to stand for re-election. The post of High Commissioner officially came into being on June 14, 1961 in a ceremony at Guildhall in London, before Trinidad had gained full independence and while the West Indies Federation was still limping along. Constantine was honored in the New Year's list of January 1962. In April 1963, he appeared on the highly popular *This is your life* TV program, an honor reserved only for the most well-known of public figures, honoring his sportsmanship, statesmanship, and zest for life. In the same year, he also appeared on BBC Radio's *Desert Island Discs* program, choosing among the records "Old Man River," sung by his friend Paul Robeson (1898–1976), "Softly Awakes My Heart" and the calypso "Australia Versus West Indies" by Egbert Moore, known as Lord Beginner. Later the National Portrait Gallery commissioned a bronze bust of Sir Constantine by the sculptor Karin Jonzen. Throughout his unstinting support for the often-controversial causes of Pan Africanism and racial equality, Constantine did as much as any individual to try to improve racial harmony in Britain and to bring about the Race Relations Act of 1965.

In July 1968, Sir Constantine became one of the 12 governors of the BBC appointed by the Prime Minister. In the Queen's New Year Honors List of January 1969, he was awarded a peerage – making him the first black man, though not the first non-white, to sit in the House of Lords and took the title of Baron Constantine of Maraval in Trinidad and Nelson in the County Palatine of Lancaster. His investiture at the House of Lords on March 26, 1969, attracted a full house. He died July 1, 1971, at Brondesbury, Hampstead London. Learie Constantine was a man of many firsts:

- First black Lord
- First black sportsman of any real standing in Britain
- First black governor of the BBC.

As a man of firsts, many of his groundbreaking achievements will, by definition, never be repeated and his achievements will stand the test of time.

Post-1945 Settlers

The post-war period witnessed a massive increase in migration from the Caribbean. The ban on migration into the U.S.A. was partly relaxed and greater opportunities appeared in Canada, but it was to Britain that people from the English-speaking Caribbean turned. Although it is widely accepted that black people have had a continuous presence in Britain, dating back over 500 years, it is also accepted that on May 24, 1948, when 482 Caribbean, many of whom were ex-service men, boarded the former troop ship Windrush at Kingston, Jamaica (the fare was £28. 10s), as a response to the British Government's post-war campaign to recruit workers from the Caribbean, with the slogan "the mother country needs you," has resulted in tens of thousands of black Caribbean migrating to Britain. The British government openly welcomed unskilled labor with recruitment campaigns in the islands. Workers from the Caribbean arrived in England with their British passports, so their arrival was not fully documented, but it estimated that between 230,000 and 280,000 people left the English-speaking Caribbean islands on steamships and charter flights between 1951 and 1961, creating a serious drain of talent and experience from the islands. In some islands such as Montserrat, the impact of the exodus was enormous, as almost a third of the population left the island in the 1950s. The new arrivals usually settled in the major cities such as London, Birmingham, and Manchester, but their arrival in the "mother country" was not always an enjoyable one. Coal dust, snow, and cold-water flats provided an inhospitable environment for Britain's newest residents.

Racism was commonplace, signs in boarding houses saying "No Blacks" was commonplace. Yet, for many, the exodus to Britain was a success and jobs in nursing, transport, and construction were plentiful and relatively well paid. While some people, in due course, returned to the Caribbean, others stayed to bring up a new generation in Britain. Hence, issues relating to race and ethnicity are now recognized to be central to an understanding of contemporary British society. Like other European societies, British society has been, and continues to be, historically diverse in terms of language, religion, territoriality, class, and "race." Although English is the official language of Britain, Gaelic, and Welsh languages are still used. Britain also has a long history of multi-faiths, as evidenced by Pagans, Catholics, Anglican, Fundamentalist, Methodist, Baptist, Congregationalist, and Jewish faiths, with contemporary Muslims, Sikhs, Hindus, and Rastafarians extending this diversity. Although there had been measures to control immigration through the 1905 and 1914 Alien Acts, followed by the 1925 Special Restriction Order, there had traditionally been powerful political pressures inhibiting the restriction of Commonwealth immigrants. However, as Paul Rich (1994) suggests, the 1962 Immigration Act overrode these pressures and marked an important shift away from notions of benign "civilizing" mission behind the Commonwealth ideal (Rich, 1994: 162–3). Further, as Miles (1993) reminds us, by removing the right of entry to, and settlement in, the U.K. from certain categories of British subject, the British state established new (racist) criteria, by which to determine membership of the "imagined community" of nations (Miles 1993: 74). Most Black-Caribbean people in the U.K. are Jamaicans followed by Barbadians, Trinidadians, Grenadians, and Dominicans. However, as Segal (1995) suggests, it must be recognized that all the islands differ from each other, in varying degrees, historically, geographically, religiously, socially, and economically. Indeed, like any other group, the African-Caribbean label masks a complex ethnic diversity.

In 1969, the Select Committee on Race Relations and Immigration (SCRRI) warned of the danger of denying West Indian (sic) youngsters' equality of opportunity in education (SCRRI 1969: 6–7). Eight years later, they once again warned that "the relative underachievement of West Indian pupils seriously affects their future employment prospects and is a matter of major importance both in education terms and in the context of race relations" (SCRRI 1977). In 1979, the Department for Education and Science initiated the Rampton Committee of Inquiry, into the *Education of Children from Ethnic Minority Groups*, which, amid a series of resignations, Lord Swann replaced Lord Rampton. Under Swann, the committee broadened its scope to consider the creation of an education system appropriate to a multi-ethnic society. The Swann Report has precipitated few, if any, discernible changes to the ideological terrain on which central and local governments premise their policies on "race" and education. Gurnah (1987) suggests that, "we should see committees, such as the Swann Committee, as state gatekeepers and caretakers…defending the system, its root as well as its future" (Gurnah 1987: 24). The concept of institutional racism was developed in the continuing political struggles of "black" Americans in the post-war period. During the 1950s and 1960s, the Civil Rights Movement had gained several victories, such as the 1965 Civil Rights Act and the 1965 Voting Act, which effectively ended the legal basis of discrimination against "black" Americans. However, the lives of many "black" people changed little: poor housing, high unemployment, crime, high infant mortality rates, and poor education all marked the experiences of "black" Americans.

Black radical leaders began to argue that the lack of any significant change reflected the fact that racism was entrenched within the structures, organizations, and power relations of American society (Marlow and Loveday, 2000: 29). For Carmichael and Hamilton (1967) racism exists at two closely related levels. Firstly, there is overt, explicit racism that is articulated by individuals. Secondly, at the level of the social formation, there is institutional racism – anti-black attitudes and practices, which are woven throughout all of the major institutions of society, that have the effect of maintaining "black" disadvantage. Carmichael and Hamilton used the term institutional racism in parallel with internal colonialism, arguing that "black" people stood as "colonial subjects in relation to white society"

(Carmichael and Hamilton 1967: 5–6). Their work provided an important tool for challenging existing theories on racism. The use of the term institutional racism demonstrated a break with previous paradigms. The emphasis was now on the organization of society and power relations as opposed to individual prejudices and quirky personalities. Lord MacPherson's, *Inquiry* Report (1999) into the death of the black teenager, Stephen Lawrence (13/09/1974–22/04/1993), defined institutional racism as:

> The collective failure of an organization to provide an appropriate and professional service to people because of their color, culture, or ethnic origin. It can be seen or detected in processes, attitudes, and behavior which amount to discrimination through unwitting prejudice, ignorance, thoughtlessness and racist stereotyping which disadvantage minority ethnic people (cited Marlow and Loveday, 2000: 33).

Further, the Office for Standards in Education, (1999), report also warned that Britain's schools suffered from institutional racism.

De-Colonization

In 1945, Western Europe was still the home base of the world's colonial empires. Although Germany had been stripped of its overseas colonies in 1919 and Italy in 1946, the British, the Dutch, the French, the Belgian, and the Portuguese Empires were largely intact. Many European imperialists had hoped that they would be able to keep, or to reconstitute, their empires. "I did not become His Majesty's PM," said Churchill, "in order to preside over the liquidation of the British Empire" (Davies, 1996: 1068). There were many reasons why, in 1945, the maintenance of Europe's empires had become virtually impossible. Firstly, the elites of the colonial peoples, many of whom were educated in Europe, had learned the nationalism and democracy of their rulers and were now vociferously demanding independence. Secondly, the United States was opposed to old-style colonialism; and so was the United Nation. Except for Britain and Portugal, all the imperial powers had been defeated and occupied during the war, and started from a position of weakness, in the process of decolonization. The British Empire which occupied an area roughly 125 times the size of Great Britain, was already in an advanced state of transformation. All of the "white dominions" had been fully independent since 1931; and many other Crown possessions were being prepared for self-rule or native administration. Of 250,000 employees of the British Colonial Office in 1945, only 66,000 were from Britain. On August 15, 1947, the last Viceroy took the salute in Delhi as the Raj saw the British flag lowered for the last time. India, Pakistan, Burma, and Ceylon; all arose as independent states. In May 1948, Britain returned the mandate of Palestine to the UN after years of violence, both Zionist terrorists and Arab rebels. In Malaya, the communist insurgency lasted from 1948–1957; in Cyprus, the war against Eoka from 1950 to 1960; in Kenya, the Mau-Mau campaign from 1952 to 1957; in Egypt, the struggle culminating in the Suez Crisis from 1952 to 1956; in Southern Rhodesia the emergency over white UDI from 1967 to 1980. Elsewhere in Africa, a procession of peaceful acts of independence started with that of Nigeria in 1951. At the end of the process, almost all of Britain's former colonies had joined the British Commonwealth, a voluntary association originally founded for the self-governing dominions. South Africa left in 1961, Pakistan in 1973. Preferential Commonwealth tariffs were terminated in 1973. The dissolution of the world's largest empire was essentially completed within 25 years. The Dutch Empire, 55 times the size of the Netherlands, was closed down at one blow, as they did not recover the Dutch East Indies after the Japanese occupation between 1941–5.

The French Empire, 19 times larger than France, expired in agony. Many inhabitants of the colonies possessed full French citizenship; and several North African departments, with large French populations, formed an integral part of metropolitan France. Humiliated during the war, French governments felt obliged to assert their authority and wielded enough military power to make their ultimate defeat very costly. Tunisia and Morocco were safely disentangled by 1951, as were the Levantine mandates in Syria and Lebanon. But in Indo-China an eight-year war was fought against the Viet-Cong, until the disaster of Dien Bien Phu, in May 1954, forced Paris to hand over to an incautious Washington. In Algeria, another vicious eight-year war against the FLN, which destroyed the 4 Republic on the way, ended with General de Gaulle's dramatic concession of Algerian independence in May 1962. Preoccupied by the Algerian war, France had already set its other African colonies free. The Belgian Empire, 78 times the size of Belgium, collapsed in 1960, when the Congo sought to follow the example of its ex-French neighbors.

The secession of Katanga caused a civil war which claimed the lives of thousands, including those of Patrice Lumumba and UN Secretary-General Dag Hammarskjold. The Portuguese Empire survived the longest. Angola, which itself was 23 times larger than Portugal, broke away in 1975, together with Mozambique and Goa. All the ex-colonies in Europe but one was set free. Malta was given independence from Britain in 1964. Only a clutch of small colonial dependencies clung on, including Gibraltar and the Falkland Islands (British), the source of the Anglo-Argentine war of 1983. Hong Kong reverted to China in 1997, Macao (Portuguese) in 1999. The effects of decolonization were almost as profound on the ex-imperialists as on the ex-colonies. The former imperial powers lost many traditional economic benefits, especially cheap raw materials and captive colonial markets. But all these ex-imperial powers kept strong cultural and economic links with Asian, African and Caribbean ex-colonies. Ex-imperialist Europe attracted cheap labor from their ex-colonies, to join the "Mother Country" labor force. In the post-imperial decades, far more people from the Caribbean or the Indian sub-continent came to Britain and Muslims to France, than ever came previously, as post-war Europe struggled to rebuild its damaged infrastructure. As the Empire sank from view Britain's principal dilemma lay in the prospect of closer link with her European neighbors. The globalization of the Cold war took place in the course of the 1950s, when many ex-colonial countries were viewed as open to wars by proxy and where, as in the oil-rich Middle East, valuable resources presented irresistible temptations.

African Suffering

A study of the general history of mankind reveals no people have suffered so much in every area of life and survived. The transatlantic trade in enslaved Africans stands historically and conceptually as the most heinous crime against humanity. However, when the British Parliament and the U.S. Congress both voted to abolish this heinous trade, it did not end the trade. In May 1772, Lord Mansfield's judgment in the Somersett's case emancipated an enslaved African in England, which, it is said, helped launched the movement to abolish slavery. By 1783, an anti-slavery movement, to abolish the trade in enslaved Africans throughout the British Empire, had begun among the British public. In 1793, Lieutenant-Governor of Upper Canada, between 1791 and 1796, John Graves Simcoe (1752–1806) signed the Act Against Slavery, passed by the local Legislative Assembly. It was the first legislation to outlaw the trade in enslaved Africans in any part of the British Empire. In 1808, the British Parliament passed the Slave Trade Act of 1807, which outlawed the trade in enslaved Africans, but not slavery. The Royal Navy suppressed the Atlantic trade in human beings, but it did not stop it entirely. Between 1808 and 1860, the Royal Navy's West Africa Squadron captured 1,600 ships, trafficking enslaved Africans and freed 150,000, many of whom they resettled in Jamaica and the Bahamas. In 1823, the Anti-Slavery Society was founded in London, whose members included Joseph Sturge, Thomas Clarkson, William Wilberforce, Henry Brougham, Thomas Fowell Buxton, Elizabeth Heyrick, Mary Lloyd, Jane Smeal, Elizabeth Pease, and Anne Knight.

Following a large-scale revolt by enslaved Africans, in Jamaica, led by the Baptist minister Samuel Sharpe, the British Parliament held two inquiries. The results of these inquiries contributed greatly to the abolition of slavery with the Slavery Abolition Act of 1833, which came into force on August 1, 1834. In practice, only enslaved Africans below the age of six were freed in the colonies. Enslaved Africans over the age of six were re-designated as "apprentices," and their servitude was abolished in two stages: the first set of apprenticeships came to an end on August 1, 1838, while the final apprenticeships were scheduled to cease on August 1, 1840. The Act specifically excluded "the Territories in the Possession of the East India Company, or to the Island of Ceylon, or Saint Helena." The exceptions were eliminated in 1843. The 1833 Act, provided for the compensation for the owners of enslaved Africans, in the sum of £20,000,000. For one reason or another, on the August 1, 1838, full emancipation was legally granted ahead of schedule. However, with no acknowledgement of the economic needs of former enslaved Africans, their economic condition changed little. In 1839, the British and Foreign Anti-Slavery Society was formed, which worked to outlaw slavery worldwide, making it the world's first international human rights organization, and continues today as the Anti-Slavery International. Slavery was abolished in India by the Indian Slavery Act of 1843.

The American Emancipation Bill of 1863, limited emancipation to the "states or parts of states" still in rebellion and did not include a number of loyal states where slavery was legal, such as Delaware, Maryland, Kentucky and Missouri, or large parts of Confederacy in Virginia and Louisiana, occupied by federal troops. As the London *Times* reported, "Where he has no power, Mr. Lincoln will set the Negroes free; where he retains power, he will consider them as slaves." It is argued that Lincoln's only real concern in waging the Civil War was the restoration of the Union and making the American economy safe for whites, not freedom and equality for blacks. Hence, Lincoln's Proclamation did nothing, and was intended to do nothing for black America. In Brazil and Cuba, the last American nations to enact abolition, slavery survived until the 1880s. At the Berlin Conference of 1885 and again at the Brussels Conference of 1889, delegates from 14 nations – all the major European powers, plus the United States – solemnly pledged to use their offices to halt the trafficking of enslaved Africans, whether over land or water, anywhere in the world. But the rhetoric was deceptive. Alleviating the plight of enslaved Africans served as the chief rationalization for partitioning Africa into formal European colonies. Britain and France came away with the greatest number of colonies, but the single largest territory – the Congo Free State, an area equivalent in size to all of western Europe – was given as a protectorate to one man, King Leopold of Belgium. By the time, Leopold was finally compelled to relinquish control of the territory in 1907, an estimated ten million people – about half of the population had died, mainly from the direct brutal rule of Leopold. It took another two decades, for the League of Nations to commit themselves formally to "the complete abolition of slavery in all its form in 1926. In Australia, "blackbirding" and the holding of indigenous workers' pay "in trust" continued into the 1970s. The Slavery Abolition Act of 1833 was repealed in its entirety by the Statute Law (Repeals) Act 1998, as part of a wider rationalization of British statute law. In its place the Human Rights Act 1998 incorporates into British Law Article 4 of the European Convention on Human Rights, which prohibits the holding of persons as slaves.

The Jews, being mostly white, were able to find escape routes, not opened to Africans anywhere in business, finance, and science. They were free to study. They had seen that two certain ways to overcome their oppression were the mastery of wealth and intellectual excellence. Meanwhile Africans were still being hunted down and enslaved and when freed, they were kept as close to the status of slaves as such efforts could achieve. But, Africans have dared to go beyond the limits and guidelines set for them by the czars of history and geography to discover that Ancient Ethiopia covered North Africa to the Mediterranean Sea, that Egypt was the northeastern division of that empire, and that even as late as 3100 BCE, when Asians held Lower Egypt, Ethiopians still held most of their homeland in Upper Egypt. Even when Herodotus arrived, African civilization was known to be ancient, that is its beginning was lost in a distant past beyond memory. But, when he arrived, he found a very mixed Egyptian population of Asians, Caucasians, Afro-Asians, Afro-Caucasians, and Africans. The Greeks were among the first Europeans to recognize the most advanced civilization of the ancient world was in Africa and to proclaim it to the world without reservations. It is from Greek history that we get some of the best insights into the early history of the Africans. They drew upon the land of the Africans for architectural designs, city planning, sculpture, science, and even religion, these they reshaped and made theirs. For the Africans of the world, there is no bright tomorrow, although they may continue to live in their dream world of singing, dancing, marching, praying and hoping, because of the deluding signs of what looks like victories – still trusting in the ultimate justice of their masters – but a thousand years hence, their descendants will be substantially still where they were a thousand years before.

Caucasians, in general, have never changed their real attitude toward Africans, during all the passing centuries, and there is absolutely nothing upon which to base the belief that they will change in the centuries to come. Caucasians control all the African leaders, directly or indirectly, through government and foundation grants. Africans are naive to think that Caucasians intend to include them in the doctrine of human equality, or anything else that means real equality. The African drive to be with Caucasians in every situation is equaled by Caucasian determination to prevent it. African states today are not even half-free and independent, for colonialism was from the beginning exactly what it is today – an economic system for the control and exploitation of the wealth of non-Caucasian peoples. It was and it is a private enterprise system, as initially colonial government was company government. When the political task got too big, because of increased rivalries between the great powers, the "mother" countries would appoint colonial governors and other administrators. This system of economic control still prevails all over Africa today, under the beautiful and high-flying flags of "independent" African nations. The necessary re-education of Africans can only begin when they fully realize this central fact in their lives. African people of the world have come at last to destiny's crossroads but, sadly, there is a terrible crisis of leadership, and there is no real effort to create one.

The great difficulty is that African leaders, unlike the Jews, do not know their own heritage and many do not want to know it. They desire to identify with Caucasian heritage, even though they are totally rejected by them. Some African leaders, equally ignorant of their heritage, simply do not know which way to lead, as they feel compelled to adopt and follow Caucasian ideologies. Many do not feel free, equal, and competent enough to develop an ideology of their own – an African oriented ideology. Hence, many are jumping out of Caucasian capitalistic democracy's frying pan straight into Caucasian communism's fire. Both of which have ruling elites that suppress and exploit the people. The masses are fed and filled with the "ideas and principles" of both systems, and for which they fight and die, screaming these ideals as though they were drugged. Voting creates an illusion of power that does not exist, but only serve the interest of the elites. To gain any semblance of equality, Africans will have to stand on their own two feet. But, because Africans have been made to believe that they are dependent on Caucasians for so many generations, they have become mentally lazy. This illusion of dependency has freed them from initiative, responsibility and strategy required of independent free people. African students are as separate from Caucasian students as they are in society at large. There are different sets of laws, just as there are different career prospects for Africans and Caucasian students. Yet, African students' loyalty and devotion to Caucasians, in spite of all their negative experiences, must mystifies Caucasians and confirms anew their belief that such humble attitudes indicate inferiority independently of anything else. Africans are faced with increased levels of crime, mostly from other Africans, notwithstanding structural violence from states' apparatus. African offenders do not realize that they are enlisted in Caucasian's army to slowly destroy his people, which take many unsuspecting forms, including the increasingly widespread use of drugs among Africans.

The unequal justice system encourages African-on-African crimes and even rewards them with lighter sentences if convicted. African life is cheap and African womanhood is not honored. Both may be destroyed with both ease and relative protection. It is therefore senseless to talk of rehabilitating those who have never been habilitated in the first place. One cannot re-form those who have never been allowed to be formed. To the average African, another African is not as important as someone else of another race. This attitude serves white supremacy position very well, as Africans remain voluntarily mentally enslaved, even after their physical emancipation. Caucasianization of African people was so well done over so many centuries that it is doubtful if real liberation of our minds will be achieved in this generation. "Religion – any kind of religion – has been the means by which hope was maintained by a people without any basis for hope" (C. Williams, 1974:

347). The doctrine of human equality has never meant the triumph of ignorance and incompetence over intelligence and industry. It never meant forcing those at the bottom to the top, regardless of inability or lack of will. It means that the ladder of opportunity should always be there for everyone to rise as high as he or she is able to climb and willing to go. The main thrust of civilization, like religion itself, was toward a more humane society, piloted and guided by the upward march of the human spirit as mankind slowly advanced from savagery to a higher level of humanity.

The present-day confused outlook of the African people is the result of centuries of Caucasian acculturation – a quite natural process wherever one group of people come under the economic, political, and social domination of another group of people. The ideologies and value system of the dominant group quite unconsciously become those of the subjugated group – even when the result is demonstratively self-effacing. The most tragic and formidable mental blockage to African people achieving liberation, is the way religion has been used to capture, enslaved and exploit them, all over the world for over a thousand years. For although Africans are, and always have been, a very religious and highly spiritual people, they have been religiously gullible, believing that the religion of the Caucasians and Asians were the same as their own. For example, while both Christianity and Islam are in themselves great and acceptable faiths, they were used by men whose main purposes were conquests and enslavement, in pursuit of economic and political power. The whole continent of Africa was taken over, its wealth exploited, and its people de-humanized, all in the names of Jesus Christ, Allah and civilization. Thus, the religions of both Christianity and Islam have been disgraced by evil men with bloodcurdling cries of "Holy Wars," or "Jihad" against African non-believers (pagans), or the Christian missions of civilization that rationalized Caucasian conquests.

There are shades of barbarism in twentieth century Europe which would once have amazed the most barbarous of barbarians. The two World Wars of 1914–18 and 1939–45, in particular, were destructive beyond measure; and they spread right across the globe. But their main focus lay unquestionably in Europe. In 1914, Europeans, through their colonial empires and trading companies, dominated the globe, but by 1945 almost all had been lost: Europeans had fought each other to the point of utter exhaustion. Europe's military and economic power was overtaken and their colonial power was no longer sustainable. When the wartime dust finally settled, European ruins were controlled by two extra-European powers, the U.S.A. and the U.S.S.R., neither of which had even been present at the start. The Peace Conference, which deliberated in Paris throughout 1919, was organized as a congress of victors and neither Soviet Russia nor the German Republic was represented. Although the Wilsonian ideal of national self-determination was widely endorsed, the victorious Allies saw no reason to discuss the aspirations of their own subjected nationalities, such as the Irish, still less the wishes of colonial peoples. The Western Powers showed little sense of solidarity among themselves, and the Americans suspected the British and French of imperialist designs. Both the British and the French suspected the strength of America's commitment.

Five major treaties were put into effect and a dozen states were given international recognition. A score of territorial awards were made and a batch of Plebiscites were organized and administered. In the inter-war period, between Armistice Day (11/11/1918) and 1/9/1939, Europe never escaped the shadow of war. Allied intervention in Russia had shown that the west possessed neither the will nor the resources to control the Bolsheviks, and French occupation of the Ruhr was to show that Germany could not be coerced. What is more, if Russia and Germany could not be restrained separately, there was no chance of restraining them if they chose to work together. The limitation of the Western Powers was also made apparent in the wider world beyond Europe. Major problems of the Pacific, of China and of global maritime power had to be settled at the Washington Conference of 1921–2, not at the Peace Conference in Paris. In the Gondra Treaty of 1923, to avoid or prevent conflicts between America's states, the U.S.A. made its dispositions in Latin America without involving its European partners. The center of gravity of world power was shifting and Europe was no longer the sole master of its fate.

In the realm of international finance, confusion reigned for years, due mainly to the arrangements of the wartime *Entente*. Britain and France were owed colossal sums, principally by Russia, whilst they themselves owed still greater sums, principally to the U.S.A. The reparation plan incorporated into the Treaty of Versailles sought to make Germany pay the entire costs of the war, so that Allied governments could then pay off their war debts. But the plan proved unworkable, as Germany refused full payment and the Soviet Government refused to consider re-scheduling. The Western Powers had hoped that their victory would usher in an era modelled in their own image. After all, at the start of the Great War the European Continent contained 19 monarchies and three republics; at the end, it consisted of 14 monarchies and 16 republics. But hardly a year passed when one country or another did not see its democratic constitution violated by one or another brand of dictator. Dictators came in all shapes and sizes – communists, fascists, radicals and reactionaries, left-wing authoritarians, right-wing militarists, monarchs, anti-monarchists, and even a cleric like Father Tiso in Slovakia. The only thing they shared was the conviction that western democracy was not for them. Of the two new states to come into existence between the wars, one, Ireland, was a national republic, the other, the Vatican state, an apostolic dictatorship.

In Ireland, the dominant personality, and many times Premier, Eamon de Valera (1882–1975), was a half-Cuban Catholic born of an Irish mother in New York. The Free State declared itself the republic of Eire in 1937, severing all formal ties with Great Britain in 1949. The Vatican State was created in 1929 in pursuance of the Lateran Treaty of that year, signed by Benito Mussolini's Italy and Pope Pius XI. It covered 44 hectares on the right bank of the Tiber in Central Rome. Its population of about a thousand residents was to be ruled by the absolute authority of the Pope. It creation ended sixty years of the Pope's captivity since the suppression of the Papal States in 1870. After the suppression of Soviet Hungary, Soviet Russia (1917–22) and its successor, the U.S.S.R. (1923–89), long remained the sole communist state. The main fascist regimes emerged in Italy (1922), Germany (1933), and Spain (1936). Nationalist Socialist ideology, both communism and fascism were radical movements which developed ideologies professing a blend of nationalist and socialist elements. Under Stalin, the ideological mix was classified as "National Bolshevism." The German Nazis modified the socialist elements of their ideology over the same period, in 1934. Both communists and fascists claimed to base their ideologies on fundamental scientific laws which supposedly determined the development of human society. Communists appealed to Marxism or historical materialism, the Nazis to eugenics and racial science. All totalitarians cherished the vision of a New Man who was to create a New Order cleansed of all present impurities. It could be the final classless stage of pure communism as preached by Marxist-Leninists; the racist pure Aryan race of the Nazis, or the restoration of a pseudo-historical Roman empire in Italy. From a historical perspective, before 1914, the main ingredients of socialism, nationalism, racism, and autocracy were washing around Europe in various combinations. The struggle for women's right was barely started, let alone won. In Great Britain, for example, Constance Gore-Booth (Countess Markiewicz 1868–1927), who had once been condemned to death for her part in the Easter Rising in April 1916, had the distinction of being both the first female British Member of Parliament and the first female Irish Cabinet Minister. The movement for women's suffrage did not achieve success in Britain until the year of the death of Emmeline Pankhurst (1858–1928).

There are broadly speaking two approaches that have been accepted in efforts to restrain and redress the effects of gross human injustice. The first approach revolves around efforts to define and enforce international norms of humanitarian conduct in regard to three scourges: slavery and the slave trade, offence committed during times of war and genocide. The second approach redress – focus on repairing the injuries that great crimes leave. At the basic level, this entails making provisions for the victims of atrocities and their survivors, and the broader processes of social rehabilitation, aimed at rebuilding political communities that have been shattered. Both these approaches rest on the belief that some crimes are so heinous that the damage they do extends beyond the immediate victims and perpetrators to encompass entire societies. The most common label for such offences is "crimes against humanity." Crimes against humanity are not simply random acts of carnage. Rather, they are directed at particular groups of people, who have been so degraded and dehumanized that they no longer appear to be fully human or to merit the basic respect and concern that other humans command. By implication, all human beings have a right, or an obligation, to respond – to try to prevent such horrors from occurring and to redress their effects when they do occur. At the most basic level, this means trying to prevent further atrocities. But it also means confronting the legacies of bitterness, contempt, sorrow, and shame that great crimes often leave behind – legacies that can divide and debilitate societies long after the original victims and perpetrators have passed away. Human Rights include both negative (from) and positive (to) rights:

- Right to life
- Freedom from torture and inhuman or degrading treatment
- Freedom from slavery and forced labor
- Right to liberty and security
- Right to a fair trial
- Right to respect for private and family life and the home
- Freedom of thought, belief and religion
- Freedom of expression
- Freedom of assembly and association
- Protection from discrimination in the enjoyment of these rights and freedom

Of the estimated ten million people who crossed the Atlantic before 1800, about eight-and-half million were enslaved Africans. The vast majority of whom were imported into the sugar colonies of the Caribbean and South America. Sugar farming required a significant labor force and it was this that led to the large-scale importation of enslaved Africans. As a result of the Treaty of Utrecht in 1713, Jamaica became the distribution center for enslaved Africans for the entire New World. The first enslaved Africans shipped to the Caribbean had been prisoners of war or criminals, purchased from African chiefs in exchange for European goods, and were later auctioned in the Caribbean for about £50. The average life expectancy of an enslaved African on a Caribbean sugarcane plantation was less than seven years. The intellectual justification for slavery was that black people were racially inferior. But, such an idea could only be admitted by those who are prompted by avarice to encroach upon the "sacred rights" of their fellow human. The idea that certain actions were inherently unjust and should be universally prohibited emerged in the eighteenth century. At the root of this belief was the idea of a shared humanity. This conviction received its classic expression in the preamble to the American Declaration of Independence, with its invocation of "self-evident" truths about equality and inalienable rights to life, liberty, and the pursuit of happiness. But, the idea of race, which was also a product of the eighteenth century, has played a particularly important role in blunting the claims of certain groups of people to full equality.

There is a direct connection between resistance and the concept of the human beings' natural right to be free. This universal condition of the human being includes both men and women of all colors and ethnicities, it follows, therefore, that enslaved Africans had a natural right to be free, but which was being withheld from them. The fact that this "natural right" to their freedom that was taken from them, meant that they had a "natural right" to reclaim that freedom. Hence, the uprisings of enslaved Africans could be viewed as part of the struggle for human "natural right" by freedom fighters. The sugar plantation owners treated the colonies much the same as they treated their enslaved Africans, with an interest only in extracting as much from them as possible and the rich in Jamaica sent their progenies to Britain for schooling or simply departed with their families to live in Britain themselves leaving white attorneys, overseers and bookkeepers to manage their estates and dispatch the revenues to them. By the middle of the eighteenth century, absentee ownership had become the rule rather than the exception. In relation to the care and welfare of their enslaved Africans, there was a presumption of innate white superiority, which promoted solidarity in domination and submerged any differences on other issues between leading plantation owners and other whites. Colonial codes were based on the contention that blacks were not British citizens entitled to the rights guaranteed by British law, but constituted property purchased from among prisoner-of-war and other prisoners in Africa. Enslaved Africans, therefore, in the British Caribbean had little hope of legal escape from their condition.

In addressing the issue of immigration in 1987, the then Prime Minister, Margaret Thatcher (1925–2013, identified the fear of native Britons being swamped by people from the New Commonwealth and Pakistan with a different culture. Here race is coded as culture, a kind of historical specific form of connectedness and solidarity. For many writers, the term racism has become a source of considerable confusion, covering belief, ideology, attitude, feeling, sentiments, and behavior. It is therefore important to understand the dynamic nature of racism and the power of racial ideas to mobilize mass movements. It is not simply a set of abstract ideas and doctrines that function at the level of ideology, it is also a means of mobilizing and engendering social action and political identities. Hence, race can here be understood to mean either socio-economic status or relation to the mode of production. As status, race can be viewed as an index of social standing or rank, in terms of criteria like wealth, education, style of life, linguistic capacity, residential location, and consumptive capacity, and so on. Status has to do with one's ranking in a social system relative to the position of others, where the ranking involves a critical complex of self-conception and devaluations by others. However, this is not to equate race with class. For we are thus encouraged to identify race misleadingly as class, as class under another name, leaving unexplained those *cultural* relations that race is so often taken to express or it wrongly reduces them to more or less veiled institutions of class formation.

A plethora of recent studies have demonstrated that there are significant differences in both the socio-economic position and identities of different minority ethnic groups in Britain. Castles and Miller (1993), argue that from the sixteenth to the nineteenth century most migration was directly or indirectly related to colonialism. Like other European societies, British society has been, and continues to be, historically diverse in terms of language, religion, territoriality, class, and "race." Although English is the official language of Britain, Gaelic and Welsh languages are still used. Britain also has a long history of multi-faiths, as evidenced by paganist, Roman Catholic, Anglican, Fundamentalist, Methodist, Baptist, Congregationalist and Jewish faiths, the contemporary presence of Muslims, Sikhs, Hindus and Rastafarians simply extends this diversity. Parekh (1990) suggests that although the nature of this historic diversity differs in both degree and nature from Britain's present plural society, it provides an important backcloth to twentieth century developments and undermines the myths that issues of race and culture have only arisen because of post-war immigration. However, as May reminds us:

> In every country of the world, cultural and linguistic diversity is emerging as one of the great political issues of this century. We live in a time of both increasing globalization and increasing localization. Human movement on a massive scale will be a defining feature of this century, which will produce increased diversity at a local level. This is a globalization that simultaneously means localization (May 1999: 247).

Sports and Music

In spite of the difficulties attached to everyday life, Jamaican people revel in a rich and inventive cultural life that helps to compensate for at least some of the hardships. The people's travails have helped to fuel tremendous creativity in the arts and sport, where success offers one of the few ways out of ghetto life. In a society where the poor have few formal means of expression or opportunity, cricket and reggae music have given millions of Jamaicans the freedom to shape something in their own image. If one sport could define Jamaica and the West Indies, that sport would be cricket. Jamaica is the biggest and most populated of the cricket-playing islands in the Caribbean and Kingston Cricket Club, which was formed in 1863 and moved to Sabina Park in 1880, has witnessed some great cricketing feats. From the 1920s Jamaica began to establish herself as a force in the region. It was during the 1920s and 1930s that many distinguished touring teams from England visited Jamaica. Jamaican Test ground have witnessed many splendid individual performances, especially by Jamaica's all-time hero, George Headley, who scored an unbeaten 270 against England in 1935, to secure the West Indies first ever rubber. But, until the 1930s black players were by and large excluded from the national team, and it was cricketers like George Headley (1909–1983) who made the case for equality by becoming one of the acknowledged all-time greats of the sport.

Headley's unsuccessful campaign to become the first black captain of the West Indies became intertwined with the independence movements and helped turn cricket into a political and cultural arena of great importance in Jamaica. However, it was not until the 1960 game between West Indies and Australia, that Frank Worrell (1924–1967), of Jamaica, became the first black cricketer to captain the West Indies cricket team. Other Jamaican cricket legends include Gerry Alexander (1928–2011), Collie Smith (1933–1959), Allan Rae (1922–2005), Alf Valentine (1930–2004) and Jackie Kendriks (1933–), Michael Holding (1954–), Jeff Dujon (1956–), and Courtney Walsh (1962–) and the prodigious Lawrence Rowe (1949–) who scored 214 and 100 not out on his test debut, at Sabina Park, against England in 1972. The sight of Roy Gilchrist (1934–2001) and Michael Holding, thundering in overwhelming visiting batsmen, especially in the 1976 Test match against India, when five Indian batsmen declared themselves "absent hurt," was enough to strike fear in many visiting batsmen. Jamaicans support their local players passionately, but their love for cricket is even stronger.

The development of reggae music and its circulation was part of a deliberate effort by Rastafarians to present their message to the wider Jamaican community and to the black world. Prior to the British-owned Radio Jamaica Rediffusion (RJR), there was only one radio broadcast, which was set up in the 1930s. ZQ1 was operated by civil servants between four in the afternoon and nine at night, which played American and British popular hits. When RJR was licensed in 1950, it was permitted to broadcast for longer, but with more or less the same format as QZ1. The first Jamaican Top 30 was made up of entirely of American records. Things were to radically change when the band leader Sonny Bradshaw introduced Teenage Dance Party and Jamaican Hit Parade. These two programs brought a distinct flavor of downtown Kingston to the rest of the country. By 1960 about ninety percent of households had a working radio and most people could listen to R and B, Ska, and Jamaica boogie. As radio began to play Jamaican music a greater audience emerged from all over the island, bringing with them differing ideas. However, an alternative to these radios, were the sound systems. At the start of the 1960s the sound systems became central to the music business. Artists and producers presented a wide spectrum of styles, from groups like the Techniques, Alton Ellis, and the Flames to the Wailing Wailers. In 1963, Coxsone Dodd, the

Jamaican Recording and Publishing Studio Ltd, also known as Studio One, at 13 Brentford Road, installed a one-track board. Before Jamaica had a record industry, the only way to make money from music was to run a sound system.

Dobb became the first black man in Jamaica to own a recording studio, which marked the coming of age of Jamaican producers. One of the early groups of musicians to come out of Studio One was the Skatalites, which consisted of Lloyd Brevette (1931–2012), Lloyd Knibbs (1931–2011), Jackie Mitto (1948–1990), Tommy McCook (1927–), Roland Alphonso (1931–1998) and Lester Sterling (1936–), Don Drummond (1932–1969), Johnny Moore and Joseph Abraham Gordon (aka Lord Tanamo, 1934–2016), Ba Brooks (1935–), Jerome "Jah Jerry" Haynes (1921–?), Harold Moore DaCosta. The leader of this collective was Don Drummond who had learned music at Alpha Boys School, an establishment that was run by nuns for wayward youth on South Camp Road. Don Drummond was a black nationalist and a devout Rastafarian, whose music connected with both the soul of Africa and the black diaspora. Sadly, in the early hours of New Year's Day 1965, Drummond stabbed to death his common law wife before giving himself up at Rockfort police station and was later committed to Bellevue mental asylum, where he died in 1969. It was to be people like Chris Blackwell (1937–), Leslie Kong (1933–1971) the first Chinese-Jamaican to come into the music business, who opened up the selling of records in Jamaica. Ironically, it was these producers that had the reputation of paying musicians the going rates, compared with black producers, which was a damning indictment of slavery and colonialism's aftermath.

This tendency of black people to cheat their own, whilst being willing to roll over and allowed themselves to be cheated by others remain an issue within the diaspora and the music business. Reggae opened possibilities at the cultural, political, and technological level, which enabled reggae artists to enter the international arena and force onto the world an expression of oppression and in doing so were able to withstand the pressures of poverty, unemployment, gun, and marijuana enforcers. By the end of the 1960s, the influence of the Rastafarian movement on the development of the popular culture was evident by the fact that most serious reggae artists adhered to some of the principles of the Rastafarian movement, including Toots and the Maytals, Bob Marley and the Wailers, Dennis Brown, Burning Spear, Mighty Diamonds, Third World and many others embraced Rastafari, and through their songs helped many other Jamaicans to discover their roots and the richness of their history.

Appendices

Caribbean Independent Leaders

Date of Independence	Island	First Head of State	From	To
1981	Antiguan and Barbuda	Sir Vere Cornwall Bird	1976	1994
1973	The Bahamas	Sir Lynden Pindling	1967	1992
1966	Barbados	Earl Barrow	1961	1976
1902	Cuba	Tomas Estrada Palma	1902	1906
1978	Dominica	Patrick John	1976	1980
1844	Dominican Republic	Pedro Santana	1844	1848
1974	Grenada	Eric Gairy	1967	1979
1804	Haiti	Jean-Jacques Dessalines	1804	1806
1962	Jamaica	Sir Alexander Bustamante	1962	1967
1983	St. Kitts and Nevis	Sir Kennedy Simmonds	1980	1995
1979	St. Lucia	Sir John Compton	1964	1979
1979	St. Vincent and the Grenadines	Milton Cato	1974	1984
1962	Trinidad and Tobago	Eric Williams	1956	1981

Famous Caribbean

Samuel Sharpe (1801–1832) was the slave of a Montego Bay solicitor, and the instigator of the weeklong Christmas Rebellion, that began on Kensington Estate on December 27, 1831. Its impact and the public outcry over the terrible retribution that followed were catalysts for the British Parliament passing the Abolition Bill in August 1834. Sharpe was one of the few literate slaves and acted as a deacon of Montego Bay's Burchell Baptist Church, and as religious meetings were the only legal gatherings for slaves, Sharpe used his forum to encourage passive rebellion. However, the passive rebellion turned into a violent conflict, when the Kensington Estate was set on fire. 14 colonialists were murdered, swift and cruel retribution followed and it is thought that the militia killed more than 1,000 slaves during and after the conflict, including Samuel Sharpe. His last words were:

I would rather die upon yonder gallows than live in slavery

Sam Sharpe (executed in Montego Bay on May 23, 1832)

George William Gordon (1820–1865), a "free colored" (mulatto) son of a Scottish plantation owner. Gordon became wealthy and as a member of the Jamaican Assembly championed the right of the poor and oppressed. Gordon took part in the Morant Bay Rebellion of October 11, 1865 but fled to Kingston where he was arrested and ferried to Morant Bay, condemned by a kangaroo court and hanged.

Paul Bogle, a black Baptist deacon in the hamlet of Stony Gut, organized passive resistance against the oppression and injustice of the local authorities and planters in St. Thomas. On October 11, 1865, Bogle and 400 supporters marched to the Morant Bay courthouse to protest the severe punishment meted out to a destitute who had been arrested on a petty charge. An armed militia shot into the crowd and a riot ensued in which 28 people were killed, and the courthouse and much of the town center were burned to the ground. Bogle fled with a £2,000 bounty on his head, but he was soon captured by Maroons and hanged the same day from the center arch of the burned-out courthouse.

Sir William Alexander Clarke Bustamante was born on February 24, 1884, on the Blenheim Estate, near Lucea Hanover, where his father, Robert Constantine Clarke, was an impoverished overseer. He claimed that he took the name Bustamante to honor an Iberian captain who befriended him in his youth. His mother Mary nee Wilson was of mixed race. He left Jamaica with limited education in 1903, worked in several countries, including Cuba and Panama, before returning in 1932, with the surname Bustamante. In 1937, he became treasurer of the Jamaica Workers' Union, which was founded by labor activist

Allan G. S. Coombs, a former police Constable and Lance Corporal of The West India Regiment. Bustamante began speaking out against the appalling social and political conditions in Jamaica and during the 1938 labor rebellion he became the spokesman for striking workers. Coombs Jamaica Workers' Union became the Bustamante Industrial Trade Union (BITU) after the revolt. The BITU (allied to the JLP) and the Trade Union Congress TUC (allied to the PNP party) went into cane fields, bauxite plants and shipping facilities to fight for supremacy and violence became the norm in unionism and politics alike, which was also the beginning of gang violence in Jamaica.

In 1940, Bustamante was imprisoned for subversive activities but was released in 1943 and founded the Jamaica Labor Party (JLP), although he was previously a member of the People's National Party (PNP) which was founded by his cousin Norman Manley. In 1944, his Jamaica Labor Party contest the island's first general election, held under universal adult suffrage, and won 22 of the 32 and thus became Jamaica's first unofficial government leader, as Minister of Communications. He also served as mayor of Kingston in 1947 and 1948. In 1954, he was knighted (Grand Cross of the Order of the British Empire, GBE) by Queen Elizabeth II. He steered the nation to independence, following a special referendum in which Jamaicans voted to secede from the West Indies Federation, in 1962 and led the JLP to victory in the general election later that year, thereby becoming the first Prime Minister of an independent Jamaica. Although he officially retired in 1967, he had withdrawn from active participation in public life in 1965 and real power was held by his deputy Donald Sangster. He was named a national hero prior to his death in 1977.

Marcus Garvey was born in St. Ann's Bay on August 17, 1887. As a young man he traveled extensively throughout Costa Rica, Panama, and England. Inspired to raise the consciousness and well-being of black people, he founded the United Negro Improvement Association (UNIA) in 1914, with the aim of uniting all the Negro peoples of the world. In 1916 he traveled to the U.S., were he formed a branch of UNIA in New York and where he also established a weekly newspaper, the *Negro World*. Garvey was influenced by the prominent Black Nationalist Booker T. Washington and built an enormous following under the slogan: "One God! One Aim! One Destiny!" The U.N.I.A. became the largest mass movement among black people in the last century, 996 branches in 43 countries and over five million members. There were U.N.I.A. branches in thirty-eight states in the U.S., fifty-two branches in Cuba and there were branches in the Caribbean, North and South America, Europe, Australia and South Africa. These U.N.I.A. branches were kept together by the ideas expounded in the *Negro World* newspaper. Garvey also fostered black enterprises and set up the Black Star Line, a steamship company that aimed to repatriate black people to Africa. At the 1920 U.N.I.A. Convention the Red, Black, and Green flag was adopted as the official color of the

Black race – Red for the blood which must be shed for the redemption and liberty of the people; Black for the color of the noble and distinguished race to which we belong; and Green for the luxuriant vegetation of the Motherland. At the same historic Convention of 1920, the anthem "Ethiopia, Thou Land of Our Fathers" was accepted:

> *Ethiopia, thou land of our fathers,*
> *Thou land where the gods love to be*
> *As storm clouds at night suddenly gather*
> *Our armies come rushing to thee.*
> *We must in the fight be victorious*
> *When swords are thrust outward to gleam;*
> *For us will the vict'ry be glorious*
> *When led by the red, black and green.*
> Chorus:
> *Advance, advance to victory*
> *Let Africa be free;*
> *Advance to meet the foe*
> *With the might of the red, black and green*

Garvey maintained that:

> *If the white man has the idea of a white God, let him worship his God as he desires. If the yellow man's God is of his race let him worship his God has he sees fit. We, as Negroes, have found a new ideal. Whist our God has no color, yet it is human to see everything through one's own spectacles, and since the white people have seen their God through white spectacles, we have only now started out (late though it may be) to see our God through our own spectacles. The God of Isaac and the God of Jacob let him exist for the race that believes in the God of Isaac and the God of Jacob. We Negroes believe in the God of Ethiopia, the everlasting God – God the Father, God the Son and God the Holy Ghost, the one God of all ages. That is the God in whom we believe, but we shall worship him through the spectacles of Ethiopia.*

However, the U.S. and U.K. colonial governments regarded Garvey as a dangerous agitator and so conspired against him, and he was arrested on trumped-up charges of mail fraud in 1922. He spent two years in Atlanta Federal Prison before being deported to Jamaica. Back in Jamaica he founded the reformist People Political Party but failed to gather enough support at the polls.

According to Garvey:

> *I know of no national boundary where the Negro is concerned. The whole world is my province until Africa is free.*

In 1935 he departed for England, where he died in poverty in 1940. However, his remains were repatriated to Jamaica in 1984 and reinterred with state honors in National Heroes Park.

Sir Norman Washington Manley, born July 4, 1893, at Roxborough, in Manchester Parish, the son of Thomas Albert Samuel Manley, who was an illegitimate son of an English trader from Yorkshire and a former slave. Norman's mother, Margaret Shearer, was the daughter of a pen keeper of Irish descent and his mulatto wife. He enlisted and fought in the First World War, in the Royal Field Artillery and was awarded the Military Medal (MM). Norman studied law at Jesus College Oxford, as a Rhodes Scholar and was a QC. He became a leading lawyer in the 1920s and founded the left-wing People's National Party, six months into the 1938 labor rebellion, with a platform of Fabian (using delaying tactics and avoiding direct confrontation) socialism and a call for gradual de-colonialism. The PNP was tied to the Trade Union Congress and the National Workers Union in 1938. He married Edna Swithenbank, the English-born daughter of a Methodist missionary and his Jamaican wife, and brought her home to Jamaica after the war. He served as the colony's Chief Minister from 1955 to 1959 and was a proponent of Jamaica's participation in the Federation of the West Indies but bowed to pressure to hold a referendum in 1961, which resulted in Jamaica withdrawing from the Federation. Norman was a member of Alpha Phi Alpha fraternity, the first intercollegiate Greek-letter organization established by African American students, on December 4, 1906, at Cornell University in Ithaca, New York. The fraternity's aims are: "*Manly deeds, Scholarship, and the love for all mankind.*" Its motto is: "*First of All, Servants of All, We shall transcend All.*"

Sir Grantley Herbert Adams CMG, QC, was born on April 28, 1898, at Colliston, St. Michael, Barbados. In 1918, he won the Barbados Scholarship and departed the following year for his under-graduate studies at Oxford University. Adams founded the Barbados Labor Party (BLP) in 1938 and became president of the Barbados Workers' Union from 1941 to 1954. While being a staunch supporter of the monarchy, Adams and his party also demanded more rights for the poor and other people of Barbados. Progress toward a more democratic government was made in 1942, when the exclusive income qualification was lowered and women were given the right to vote, and by 1949 governmental power was wrested from the planters. Adams became the first Premier of Barbados in 1958, and as the island proceeded towards self-governance. He was also the first and only Prime Minister of the West Indies Federation. From 1958 to 1962, Barbados was one of the ten members of the West Indies Federation. Adams continued defense of the monarchy was used by his opponents against him. Errol Barrow had left the BLP and formed the Democratic Labor Party, a liberal alternative to Adams' conservative government, and became the new people's advocate. Adams is honored as one of Barbados heroes. For a more details read F. A. Hoyes (1963) The Rise of West Indian Democracy, *The Life and Times of Sir Grantley Adams.*

Sir Vere Cornwall Bird was born on the Island of Antigua, on December 9, 1910 and became the first Prime Minister of Antigua and Barbuda. He had no formal education, beyond primary schooling. He was an officer in the Salvation Army for two years but gave up the Salvation Army for politics. In 1943, he became the president of the Antigua Trades and Labor Union and was also elected to the colonial legislature in 1945. He formed the Antigua Labor Party (ALP) and was elected as Antigua and Barbuda first Prime Minister, on November 1, 1981. Vere Cornwall Bird was a member of an elite group of militant trade unionists who blazed the trail through colonial times up to or near political independence of the Caribbean Islands. The group included Bustamante and Norman Manley of Jamaica, Robert Bradshaw of St. Kitts and Nevis, Grantley Adams of Barbados, Cheddi Jagan of Guyana, Ebenezer Joshua of St. Vincent and the Grenadines and Eric Gairy of Grenada. Birds achievements, included:

- Better wages and conditions for workers in the sugar industry
- In 1965, along with Errol Brown of Barbados and Burnham of Guyana, he brought the Caribbean Free Trade Association into being
- Fought for change to election qualification
- Was the first PM of Antigua and Barbuda.

Dame Eugenia Charles was born on May 15, 1919 in Dominica, she attended the University of Toronto, Canada and the London School of Economic. She helped to form the Dominica Freedom Party (DFP) and was its leader from the early 1970s to 1995. The DFP swept to power in the 1980 election, and she became Prime Minister. She was the third longest serving female Prime Minister, behind Indira Gandhi of India and Sirimavo Bandaranaike of Sri Lanka. But she was the world's longest, continuously serving female PM, from 1980 to 1995. Dame Eugenia Charles was very involve in the U.S. led invasion of Grenada, following the execution of Maurice Bishop, the PM, and appealed to Jamaica and Barbados to support the U.S. led invasion.

Errol Walton Barrow, Privy Council, QC was born on January 21, 1920. On December 31, 1940, Barrow enlisted in the Royal Air Force during WWII. He flew some 45 operational bombing missions over the European Theatre, and by 1945 he had risen to the rank of Flying Officer. He was also appointed personal navigator to the Commander-in-Chief of the British Zone of occupied Germany,

Sir William Sholto Douglas. After the war he studied law at the Inns of Court and economics at the London School of Economics, concurrently, awarded degrees in 1949 and 1950 respectively. He also chaired the Council of Colonial Students, where is contemporaries included Forbes Burnham, Michael Manley, Pierre Trudeau and Lee Kwan Yew, all destined to become political leaders in their home countries. Barrow returned to Barbados in 1950 and was elected to the Barbados Parliament in 1951, as a member of the Barbados Labor Party (BLP). In 1955 he founded the Democratic Labor Party (DLP), as a progressive alternative to the Barbados Labor Party and became its leader in 1958. Barrow served as Premier of Barbados from 1961 until 1966, when after leading the island to independence from Britain, he became Prime Minister. During his ten years tenure the DLP accelerated industrial development, expanded the tourist industry, introduced National Health Insurance and Social Security and expanded free education to all levels. Regionally, Barrow was a dedicated proponent of closer integration with other islands in the region and spearheaded the formation of the Caribbean Free Trade Association in 1965. In opposition, he spoke out against the U.S. invasion of Grenada in 1983 and was critical of Caribbean leaders who kowtowed to the U.S., in the hope of getting economic handouts. In 1986 Barrow and the DLP was re-elected to power and as Prime Minister, he continued to be critical of the U.S. President, Ronald Ragan, and in his first press conference after re-election he referred to Ragan as "that cowboy in the White House." Just over a year after Barrow's re-election as Barbados Prime Minister, on June 1, 1987, he collapsed and died at his home and becoming the second Barbadian Prime Minister to die in office.

Linden Frobes Sampson Burnham, born 20/02/1923, died 06/08/1985 (aged 62), was the political leader of Guyana from 1964 to 1985 – Premier from 1964–1966, then Prime Minister from 1966 to 1980 and finally President from 1980 to 85. In 1942, Burnham won the Guyana Scholarship as the country's top student and went on to study law at the University of London, where he graduated in 1948 with an honors degree. Burnham was one of the principal founders of the People's Progressive Party (PPP), which was launched on 01/01/1950. In 1953, the PPP won 18 of 24 seats in the first election permitted by the British colonial government. In 1955, there was a split in the PPP, between Burnham and Jagan and as a result Burnham went on to form the People's National Congress (PNC) in 1958. The PNC entered its first election in 1961. On May 26, 1966, British Guiana became an independent country and was re-named Guyana. In 1970, Burnham established strong ties with Cuba and the former Soviet Union. On February 23, 1970, Burnham declared Guyana a "Co-operate Republic." He was a strong believer in self-help and self-development.

Edward Seaga, the son of a Syrian-Lebanese family from Kingston, was born in Boston and educated at Harvard. In 1954 he went home to Jamaica and carved out a place for himself. At Harvard he achieved a BA degree in sociology; with a focus on Afro-Jamaican revivalist cults and their music. He wrote a pamphlet about revivalist religion and opened a little recording studio in West Kingston where he started producing mento, ska, and some early reggae music. Despite Seaga's white skin, his friendship with members of the Pocomania church leader, Kapo Reynolds, sent a crucial message through West Kingston. Seaga joined the JLP, after it was mooted that he wanted to join the PNP but was refused entry by Norman Manley and was appointed to the Legislative Council in 1959 by Alexander Bustamante. Seaga won the West Kingston seat in Parliament in 1962 and was named Minister of Welfare and Development. In 1966 he embarked on slum clearance in the West Kingston shantytown called Back O Wall. The neighborhood was inhabited mainly by PNP supporters and Rastafarians squatters. After the squatter were removed and their shanties levelled, work began on a housing project called Tivoli Gardens, where Seaga rewarded his supporters with houses. His supporters became his people for life. As members of Parliament from both sides consolidated power by building housing projects for their supporters, a Mafia-style link was quickly formed between the construction industry and the gangs.

Sir Lynden Oscar Pindling, Privy Council, KCMG, OM, JP was born on March 22, 1930, whose father was a native of Jamaica, who had earlier immigrated to The Bahamas to join the Royal Bahamas Police Force, as a constable. Lynden attended the elite Government High School from 1943 to 1946. Following his graduation, he took a job as a junior clerk in the Post Office Saving Bank before traveling to London to study law. He graduated from the King's College, University of London in 1952, with a Bachelor of Law (LLB) degree and was called to the English Bar at the Middle Temple in February 1953 and to the Bahamas Bar later that same year. By the end of 1953, Pindling had joined the newly formed Progressive Liberal Party (PLP) as its legal advisor. In 1956, he became Parliamentary leader, when the PLP chairman, Henry Taylor, was defeated in the general election that year. Pindling was elected the party's leader over Randol Fowkes and went on to win successive elections to the House of Assembly from 1962 to 1997. On January 10, 1967, Pindling formed the first black government in Bahamian history and went on to lead Bahamians to independence from Britain on July 10, 1973.

In music a footnote must go to Nesta Robert Marley, born February 6, 1945, at Nine Mile, in the Parish of St. Ann and from immensely humble beginning he applied himself with unstinting perseverance to spreading his prophetic musical message. He died on the May 11, 1981, in the Cedars of Lebanon hospital in Miami, U.S.A.

Conclusion

I have tried to address the issue of stolen inheritance, with regards to the peoples of both African and those in the African diaspora. I have also endeavored to identify by who, when, and how it was stolen. I have, with relevant evidence, charted the decline of African power and influence from 3,000 BCE to the present day, which spanned over 5,000 years of recorded evidence. This is indeed an expansive historical era, which this research can, by no means, capture nothing but a glimpse of that rich tapestry of human socio-economic, political, and geographical experiences. I can only present, what I considered to be my truth, in terms of my reality. The truth is most often used to mean being in accord with fact or reality – the state of things as they actually exist, rather than as they may appear or might be imagined. A fact is something that is postulated to have occurred or to be correct. The usual test for a statement of fact is verifiability – that is, whether it can be demonstrated to correspond to experience. The word fact derives from the Latin *factum* and was first used in English with the same meaning: *a thing done or performed*. The common usage of "something that has really occurred or is the case." Fact is sometimes used synonymously with *truth,* as distinct from opinions, falsehood, or matter of taste. Fact may derive through a process of evaluation, including review of statements. Reality includes everything that is and has been, whether or not it is observable or comprehensible. Reality is often contrasted with what is imaginary, illusory, fictional, abstract, or false. Hence, the truth refers to what is real. But, the concept – the fundamental building blocks of our thoughts and beliefs – of truth is discussed and debated in several contexts, including philosophy, art, and religion. Many human activities depend upon the concept, which include the sciences, law, and everyday life.

Truth has been viewed as the correspondence of language or thought to an independent reality, in what is sometimes called the correspondence theory of truth, which states that truth or falsity of a statement is determined only by how it relates to the world and whether it accurately describes that world. According to the German philosopher, Martin Heidegger (1889–1976), the original meaning and essence of truth in Ancient Greece was un-concealment, or the revealing or bringing of what was previously hidden into the open, as indicated by the original Greek term for truth, *aletheia.* One theory of truth (social constructivism) holds that truth is constructed by social processes, which is historically and culturally specific, and that it is in part shaped through the power struggles within a community. Hence, all of our knowledge is "constructed," because it does not reflect any external "transcendent" realities. In the words of one of their advocates, Giambattista Vico (1668–1744), "*Verum esse ipsum factum*" (What is true is precisely what is made). Another theory of truth (consensus theory) holds that truth is whatever is agreed upon, or in some versions, might come to be agreed upon, by some specific group. Whilst determinists, generally agree that human actions affect the future, but that human actions itself is determined by a causal chain of prior events.

In philosophy, the concept fact is considered in epistemology and ontology – how do we know what we know. Moral philosophers have debated whether values are objective, and thus factual. In David Hume's "A Treatise of Human Nature," he pointed out that there is no obvious way for a series of statements about what *ought* to be the case to be derived from a series of statements of what *is* the case, and it's, therefore, fallacious to attempt to derive values from facts. According to Friedrich Nietzsche (1844–1900) modern Europe and Christianity exist in a hypocritical state, due to a tension between master and slave morality. Both values, he argues, contradictorily determining, to varying degrees, the values of most Europeans. Nietzsche claimed that the Christian faith, as practiced, was not a proper representation of Jesus' teachings, as it forced people merely to believe in the way of Jesus but not to act as Jesus did. In science, a fact is a repeatable careful observation or measurement, also called empirical evidence – knowledge received by means of the senses; particularly by observation and experimentation. From this empiricist's view, one can claim to have knowledge only when based on empirical evidence. However, according to Thomas Kuhn (1970), the role of observation as a theory neutral arbiter may not be possible, as observers may disagree on the nature of empirical data. Kuhn's point is, that knowing what facts to measure, and how to measure them, requires the use of other theories.

In mathematics there are two main approaches to truth, which are the *model theory* and the *proof theory*. The model theory is the study of classes of mathematical structures (e.g. groups, fields, graphs) from the perspective of mathematical logic. Proof theory is a major branch of mathematical logic that represents proofs as formal mathematical objects, facilitating their analysis by mathematical techniques. It can be described as the study of the general structure of mathematical proofs and arguments with demonstrative force as encountered in logic. However, according to Edward Hallett Carr (1892–1982), history is written by the winners. In his 1961 volume *What is History?* Carr argues that the inherent biases from the gathering of facts makes the objective truth of any historical perspective idealistic and impossible. He stated that, facts are like fish in the ocean, of which we may only happen to catch a few, which is only an indication of what is below the surface. The composition of history is inevitably made up by the compilation of many different biases of fact-finding – all compounded over time. Carr concludes that for a historian to attempt a more objective method, one must accept that history can only aspire to a conversation of the present with the past and that one's methods of fact gathering should be openly examined.

Historical truth and facts, which is my focus here, changes over time, and reflect only the present consensus, if that. In law, a question of fact is a question that must be answered by reference to facts and evidence as well as inferences arising from those facts. The theory of justification is a part of epistemology that attempts to understand the justification of propositions and beliefs. For me, one fact is clear, it is difficult to examine any aspects of racism without encountering Asians and Caucasians' original practice of patriarchy, and by default sexism and female oppression. The history of patriarchy is closely linked to the concept of gender roles, which is often grafted onto a social hierarchy, in which males' freedom to venture outside of the domicile and thereby control the public space. It has been suggested that patriarchy began in the Neolithic Era, from about 10,200 BCE to about 2,000 BCE, when men became hunters and women became gatherers. During this time, the realization occurred that it took a male and female to produce offspring. It is theorized that with this realization, these Neolithic men first became aware of their role in paternity. These same men began to take private ownership over their individual herds. With this new concept of ownership came the desire to have private herds left to the descendants of the owner. It became necessary therefore for women to be virgins before mirage and for them to abstain from adultery after marriage, which is nothing more than a claim to ownership, so that a man could have the reassurance that his offspring was his own. Patriarchy was furthered at the end of the Neolithic Era when women began to be traded as commodities, especially between families or villages, long before men traded other men. Women were also used to have sex with visitors, as deed of hospitality by tribal chiefs, and the ritual rapes during festivals. Children became an economic asset, and if a woman was unable to produce them, she was seen as all but worthless. As culture evolved, patriarchy grew increasingly misogynistic. Initially, the family had been a biological unit, but in some places, especially in western Asia, it took on the form of a political and economic unit. Wives and mothers became obligatory, and women who did not follow the traditional functions faced legal consequences. Women became the legal wards of their fathers, brothers, or husbands and had no rights of their own.

Unlike in many African communities, matriarchy was viewed as an integral aspect of African lives. In Egypt, for example, the principle of gods and goddesses was exemplified by Isis and Osiris, representing opposite and equal. The record shows that women were heads of states in Africa, especially in Egypt, where the names of great African queens have withstood the test of time. Queen Sobekneferu – "the beauty of Sobek" – was associated with the Nile crocodile and first female pharaoh. Queen Hatshepsut was the fifth pharaoh of the Eighteenth Dynasty. Queen Tiy became the Great Royal Wife of pharaoh Amenhotep III and mother of Akhenaten and grandmother of Tutankhamun. Queen Twosret (r.1191–1189 BCE), was the last pharaoh of the Nineteenth Dynasty. Queen Candace was a formidable African Queen, world famous military tactician, and field commander and Empress of Ethiopia 332 BCE. When Alexander reached her border, he refused to engage her in battle, as he was afraid of being defeated by a woman. Queen Amanitore (died c.20 CE) was a Nubian Queen of the Ancient Kushite Kingdom of Meroe. She is often mentioned as co-regent with Natakamani. Her Royal Palace was at Gebel Barkal, in modern-day Sudan, which is now a UNESCO heritage site.

Before the nineteenth century, there was a search for biological explanation of gender roles. According to some sociologists, patriarchy arises more as a result of inherent biology than social conditioning. In 1973, Goldberg published *The Inevitability of Patriarchy,* which advanced a biological interpretation of male dominance. He argues that one important female preference in selecting a mate is which males control more resources to assist her and her offspring. This, in turn, causes a selection pressure on men to be competitive and succeed in gaining resources, in order to compete with other men. However, expressing such opinions does not make it a fact and Goldberg's interpretation of the male dominance, is more a justification for patriarchy and the perpetuation of women's oppression. Patriarchy has become a global socio-economic and political system, which has disadvantaged both women and men globally. In the context of patriarchal society, discrimination against women is evident in a number of different spheres, such as political, legal, economic, or familial. But, it must be noted that there are a variety of differing classes, ethnicities and nationalities, and some groups of women may enjoy a higher status and more power, relative to select groups of men.

Hence, gender discrimination is tied in with ethnicities and class discrimination – a concept known as "intersectionality," first named by feminist sociologist Kimberle Williams Crenshaw, in her insightful 1989 essay, "Demarginalizing the Intersection of Race and Sex: A Black Feminist Critique of Antidiscrimination Doctrine, Feminist Theory and Antiracists Politics" (see the case of DeGraffenreid v. General Motors 1976). The three main domains on which intersectionality can be observed are wages, discrimination, and domestic labor. Before the Second World War, there were few international mechanisms to protect fundamental rights, or even vehicles through which concerns about them could be raised. The 1919 Covenant of the League of Nations made no reference to human rights. Attempts to include some obligations concerning religious freedom were made, but British and American delegates objected to a proposal to add prohibitions on discrimination against foreign nationals on the basis of race or nationality. The fact that one country ran a racially segregated Empire and the other legally discriminated against its own population on the grounds of race may have had something to do with their objections.

The history of rights was authoritarian and hierarchical, with different people being granted different rights, and some having more rights than others. In contrast, modern conceptions of rights often emphasize liberty and equality as among the most important aspects of rights, though conceptions of liberty (e.g. positive or negative) and equality (e.g. of opportunity or of outcome) frequently differ.

- 622 CE: the constitution of Medina – instituted a number of rights and responsibilities for the Muslim, Jewish, and Pagan communities of Medina.
- 1215 CE: it required the King of England to renounce certain rights and respect certain legal procedures and to accept that the will of the King could be bound by law.
- 1573: The Henrician Articles were a permanent contract that stated the fundamental principles of governance and constitutional law in Polish-Lithuanian Commonwealth, including the right to rebel in case the King transgressed against the laws of the republic or the right of the nobility.
- 1689: The Bill of Rights declared that Englishmen as embodied by Parliament possessed certain civil and political rights.
- 1789: The Declaration of the Rights of Man and of the Citizen was one of the fundamental documents of the French Revolution, defining a set of individual right and collective rights of the people.
- 1789–1791: The United States Bill of Rights, with the first ten amendments of the constitution specified rights of individuals in which government could not interfere, including the rights of free assembly, freedom of religion, trial by jury, etc.
- 1948: The Universal Declaration of Human Rights is an overarching set of standards by which government organizations and individuals would measure their behavior towards each other. The preamble declares that the:
- Recognition of the inherent dignity and of the equal and inalienable rights of all members of the human family is the foundation of freedom, justice, and peace in the world.
- 1950: The European Convention on Human Rights was adopted under the auspices of the Council of Europe to protect human rights and fundamental freedom.
- 1966: The International Covenant on Civil and Political Rights is a follow-up to the Universal Declaration of Human Rights, concerning civil and political rights.

- 1982: The Canadian Charter of Rights and Freedoms to protect the rights of Canadian citizens from actions and policies of all level of government.
- 2000: The Charter of Fundamental Rights of the European Union is one of the most recent proposed legal instruments concerning human rights.

Crimes Against Humanity are particularly odious offences, in that they constitute a serious attack on human dignity or grave humiliation or a degradation of one or more human beings. They are part either of government policy or of a wide practice of atrocities tolerated or condoned by a government or a *de facto* authority. Chattel slavery was by any standard, stands at the apex of a crime against humanity, as human beings were denied their human status. Murder, extermination, torture; rape; political; racial; or religious persecution are also crimes against humanity. However, isolated inhumane acts of these nature may constitute grave infringements of human rights, or depending on the circumstances, war crimes. On October 2, 2000 the British government formally adapted the Human Rights Act, which was authorized by an Act of Parliament in 1998. Going forward, there is a need for an open and honest debate about the effects of the crime, of chattel slavery, committed by Europeans and their descendants in the Americas. The peoples of these countries need to recognize the social, political, and economic advantages they have derived from the enslavement of Africans for centuries. The descendants of those enslaved in the Americas, including the Caribbean, deserved to be heard, in order that their contributions to our present social, political, and economic systems can be better understood. The roles of Africans in the Atlantic slave trade must be acknowledged, so that a better understanding can be developed between Africans and those in the diaspora.

No society can claim to be civilized if the contributions and participation of women are marginalized. For Engels, the historical origin of the modern monogamous family, in which the woman has only one husband, is also linked to the origin of private property and class. A major study by Harbury and Hitchens (1979) suggests that between two-thirds and four-fifths of those who died rich in the 1970s owed their wealth to inheritance. Increasingly, the family is viewed as a site of conflict. Women of all ethnic groups are increasingly in full-time and part-time employment, which have implications for the future structuring of the family. The future role of black men within the family is ambiguous, to say the least. The low rate of educational achievements of young black men, plus the high level of knowledge and skills demanded by industry and commerce will undermine black men's ability to provide emotional, social, or economic support to their families. Hence African-Caribbean families experience will be shaped by disadvantages that accrue from their class position. Similarly, "black" women face the "triple oppression" of class, gender, and racism (intersectionality). Feminist writers have also demonstrated how experiences of many "black" women differ to those of "black" men and "white" people because of the intricate relationships between class, gender, sexuality, and racism.

Hence, from a critical perspective, the family embodies the essence of patriarchy and capitalism. All victims of oppression must, as a minimum, work together to challenge all forms of oppression at the personal, cultural, or structural levels simultaneously. It is not enough for a person to be against one form of oppression and yet collude with the oppression of others. Human rights must be upheld in all places and with all people, and no oppressor should be immune from accountability for oppressive acts. In this globalized world, in which time and space has become compressed, we are all affected by what happens around the globe, whether it be environmental, political, social or economic. In the era of mass media, we cannot ignore the imposition of selective nature of an alienating knowledge that is destroying the aspirations of women, by confining them to the sphere of domestic servitude. Women and black people have been socialized to see themselves through the lenses of racism and sexism and view themselves as an insignificant part of world history. Hence, the inheritance of both enslaved Africans and their descendants, which have been scattered across Eurasia and the Americas, and women in general, have been stolen by elite Eurasian men. The result of this historical theft has impoverished both Africans and women in general. It is therefore important to recognize the need for change. According to Dalrymple and Burke (1995), change involves reflecting, challenging and rethinking our taken for granted views of the structures within which we operate.

It is my honest belief that there is a need for sustaining conditions for new and emergent relationships and also for greater confidence in changes, which reinforce social values. It is also of utmost importance to understand how class and gender oppressions are implicit in the way that knowledge, values, and identities are constructed in a variety of social settings. Powerlessness involves structures of social, political, and economic division, and often entails issues of status. In the context of British society, the struggles for justice by excluded and oppressed groups, within common and shared value system, or public and civic culture, have still not taken place. Nor are they reflected in curricula, which would integrate the diverse life experiences into one nation and many misconceptions, fed mainly by politicians and the media, still exist concerning the size, growth, and composition of ethnic minority groups living in the U.K. *McCarthy and Crichlow* (1993), argues that as an important agent of modernization, schooling proved to be an important agent of colonization, designed to teach colonial subjects their place in the great chain of being, which was associated with several defining characteristics, such as the imposition of a Euro-centric curriculum that effectively erased the culture and language of the colonized. Colonial education was aimed at assimilating the colonial subject and other racial groups into the lower rungs of the colonial labor force. Colonial education was also associated with disciplining power, in order to produce docile subjects. All young people have a right to a curriculum that develops their critical thinking capacities and expands rather than limits their potentials. For an educational system to be democratic, Gutmann (1988), suggests that all children must be educated to participate intelligently in the politics that shape their society.

Further, an educational experience based on critical reflection, reinterpretation, and self-conscious efforts are needed to develop a political life that, suggests Outlaw (1998), allows for democratic inclusiveness, yet critical recognition and appreciation of cultural legacies of persons and people who together comprise our body politic. The omissions and distortions of the past need to be corrected – and a transformation of the curricula is another essential part of this change. This implies moving decisively beyond the discourse of basic skills mastery and proficiency testing. Joe Kincheloe (1995) suggests that vocationalism be replaced with a critical work education the purpose of which would be to restore the knowledge of the work process and the overview of the relation of the job to the larger economic processes. Racial legacy and cultural traditions can provide a ready-made answer to the critical question of identity, which can also play the role of a symbolic and selective resource to answer the challenges of identity in a complex society. However, the expression of differences must be intrinsically connected with the need for communication and solidarity, for we cannot communicate or relate to differences by simply staying ourselves. The possibility of interaction and intersection between young people from different cultural backgrounds could enhance the construction of a more accurate understanding of the locality's past and present and may, in turn, enable them to construct a less biased and more meaningful respect for a multi-cultural future. Young people should be supported, through intercultural activities – such as music, arts, drama, and literature, to engage in a process of shared experiences. Historically, the perceptions and understanding of non-European arts and cultures have been channeled through the perceptions and value judgments of colonial administrators.

Author's Final Note

Both Herodotus and Diodorus were outstanding in setting forth for posterity the attitude of the Eurasian world, of their day, towards the African world. The reason is plain: the early Africans were the most advanced of all the peoples known to them. They did not hesitate to declare and to acknowledge the debt their own "European" civilization owed to the civilization of Africa. For this, later western historians have never forgiven them. Pliny the Elder, *Historia Natural*, is a fair example of writers on Africa, where it is possible to find bits and pieces of important data scattered throughout large volumes. Among other writers who made noteworthy contribution in varying degrees was Strabo (d.24 CE), whose *Geographica* included history along with its main subject matter. Plato and Plutarch are reference sources, the latter's *De Iside et Osiride* being more directly relevant. Many historians and geographers drew heavily on the works of such early writers as Hecataeus, Argatharchides, Herodotus, and Menetho. The numerous discoveries of relatively recent archaeology have substantially confirmed their work, such as inscription on palettes, stelae, the walls of tombs and temples, and the Palermo and Rossetta stones. Petrie (1853–1942), early pioneer of systematic methodology in archaeology, Breasted (1865–1935) archaeologist and historian, Budge (1857–1934) who published numerous books on the ancient Near East (Western Asia). Arkell (1898–1980) archaeologist and colonial administrator, noted for his work in Sudan. Leo Africanus (1494–1554) wrote a book on the geography of the Maghreb and Nile Valley, which was regarded among his scholarly peers in Europe as the most authoritative treatise on the subject, at the time. Baikie (1866–1931), author of *A Century of Excavation in the Land of the Pharaohs*. Boas (1858–1942), anthropologist, and Delafosse (1870–1926), ethnographer and colonial official who worked in the field of the languages of Africa. Garstang (1876–1956), archaeologist, F. L. Griffith (1862–1934), archaeologist, and Nims (1906–1988). With the spread of Islam in Africa and the entrance of France, Arab and French writers dominated the scene upto and through the nineteenth century and their sources became indispensable in African research.

Bibliography

Anthias, F. and Yuval-Davis, N. (1993). *Racialized boundaries*: *Race, Nation, Gender, Colour and Class and the Anti-Racist Struggle.* London: Routledge.

Molefi Kete Asante and Ama Mazama (2009) *Encyclopedia of African Religion.* Sage.

William Russell Bascom (1980). *Sixteen Cowries: Yoruba Divination from Africa to the New World.* Indiana University Press.

Martin Bernal (1987). *Black Athena: The Afroasiatic Roots of Classical Civilization.* London: Vintage.

Charles Julian Bishko. *The Spanish and Portuguese Reconquest, 1095–1492,* in *A History of the Crusades,* vol. 3: *The Fourteenth and Fifteenth Centuries,* Harry W. Hazard (1975) (ed.). Madison.

Black, Clinton V. (1991). *History of Jamaica.* Longman Group U.K. Ltd.

Lloyd Bradley (2000). *Bass Culture: When Reggae Was King.* London: Penguin Books.

Bridge, F. R. and Roger Bullen (1980). *The Great Powers and the European States System 1814–1914.* Harlow: Pearson Education Ltd.

James William Brodman (1974). *The Trinitarian and Mercedarian Orders: A Study of Religious Redemptionism in the Thirteenth Century.* U.S.A.: University of Virginia.

James William Brodman (1986). *Ransoming Captives in Crusader Spain: The Order of Mercedon the Christian – Islamic Frontier.* Pennsylvania: University of Pennsylvania Press.

Barbara Bush (1990). *Slave Women in Caribbean Society, 1650–1838.* Bloomington University Press.

Barbara Bush (1996). *Hard Labor: Women, Childbirth and Resistance in British Caribbean Slave Society*, in David Barry Gaspar and Darlene Clarke Hine, (eds.). *More Than Chattel: Black Women and Slavery in the Americas.* Bloomington: Indiana University Press.

Carmichael, S. and Hamilton, C. (1968). *Black Power: The Politics of Black Liberation in America.* London: Jonathan Cape.

Castles, S. and Miller, M. J. (1993). *The Age of Migration.* London: MacMillan.

Hugh Chisholm (ed.) (1911). *"Psammetichus" Encyclopedia Britannica*, 11th ed. Cambridge University Press.

Peter Clayton (1994). *Chronicle of the Pharaohs: The Reign-by-Reign Record of the Rulers and Dynasties of Ancient Egypt*. London: Thames and Hudson.

Michael Craton (1982). *Testing the Chains: Resistance to Slavery in the British West Indies*. NewYork: Ithaca.

Jane Dalrymple and Beverley Burke (1995). *Anti-Oppressive Practice*. Buckingham: Open University Press.

Norman Davies (1996). *Europe, A History*. BCA: OUP.

Robert Davis (2003*). Christian Slaves, Muslim Masters: White Slavery in the Mediterranean, the Barbary Coast and Italy, 1500–1800*. London: Palgrave.

Cheikh Anta Diop (1974). *The African Origin of Civilization, Myth or Reality*. Lawrence Hill Books, Chicago Review Press.

Richard Dunn (1973). *Sugar and Slaves: The Rise of the Plantations in the English West Indies 1624–1713*. New York: W. W. Norton.

Brian Dyde (1998). *The Empty Sleeve: The Story of the West India Regiments of the British Army*. Caribbean: Hansib Publishing Ltd.

Edwards, I. E. S. (1971). *The Cambridge Ancient History: The Early Dynastic Period in Egypt*, Cambridge University Press, Cambridge.

Sidney Zdeneck Ehler and Morrall, John B. (1967) (eds.). *Church and State Through the Centuries: A Collection of Historic Document with Commentaries*. Congress Library.

Charles Freeman (1996). *Egypt Greece and Rome, Civilizations of the Ancient Mediterranean*. Oxford University Press.

James Ferguson (1999). *The Story of the Caribbean People*. Kingston, Jamaica: Ian Randle Publishers Ltd.

Peter Fryer (1984). *Staying Power, The History of Black People in Britain*. Pluto Press.

Roy Arthur Glasgow (1971). *Queen Nzinga and the Mbundu Resistance to the Portuguese Slave Trade*. OUP.

Peter Benjamin Golden (2011). *Central Asia in World History, New Oxford World History*. Oxford: Oxford University Press.

Gozzoli, Reberto B. (2006). *The Writing of History in Ancient Egypt During the First Millennium BCE (ca. 1070–180 BCE)*. London: Trends and Perspectives.

George Granville Monah James (1954). *Stolen Legacy*. www.ICGtesting.com.

Gurnah, A. (1987). *Gatekeepers and Caretakers: Swann, Scarman and the Social Policy of Containment*, in B. Troyna (ed.) *Racial Inequality in Education*. London: Tavistock. pp.11–28.

Gutmann, A. (1988). "Democratic Theory and the Role of Teachers in Democratic Education," *Journal of Education Policy,* 3 (5): 183–99.

Abdelmajid Hannoum (2003). *Translation and the Colonial Imaginary: Ibn Khaldun Orientalist. History and Theory.* Wesleyan University, U.S.A.

Harbury, C. D. and Hitchens, David M. W. N (1979). *Inheritance and Wealth Inequality in Britain.* Hemel Hempstead: Allen and Unwin.

George Hart (2005). *The Routledge Dictionary of Egyptian Gods and Goddess,* 2nd edition. Psychology Press, Oxford.

John Haywood (2008). *The Great Migrations, From the Earliest Human to the Age of Globalization.* London: Ouercus.

Gad Heuman (1994). *The Killing Time. The Morant Bay Rebellion in Jamaica.* Knoxville, Tennessee: University of Tennessee Press.

John Hunwick (2003). *Timbuktu and the Songhay Empire.* Brill, Leiden.

Robert Hutchinson (2013). *The Spanish Armada.* London: Weidenfeld and Nicolson.

Aisling Irwin and Colum Wilson (2009). *Cape Verde Islands.* England: Brandt Travel Guides Ltd.

History of Jamaica. Wikipedia https://en.wikipedia.org/wiki/History_of Jamaica

Malek Jaromir (2003). *The Old Kingdom (2686–2160 BCE), in The Oxford History of Ancient Egypt* (ed.). Ian Shaw: OUP

Richard Ladd Kirkham (1992). *Theories of Truth: A Critical Induction.* Cambridge, MA: MIT Press.

Kitchen, Kenneth A. (1986). *The Third Intermediate Period in Egypt (1100–650 BC),* 3rd edition. Warminster: Aris and Phillips Ltd.

Kitchen, K. A. (1991). *The Chronology of Ancient Egypt World Archaeology.* 23 (2)

Kuhn, Thomas S. (1970). *The Structure of Scientific Revolution,* 2nd edition. Chicago: University of Chicago Press.

Nehemia Levtzion (1981); John F. P. Hopkins (ed.) (2000). *Corpus of Early Arabic Sources for West Africa.* NY: Marcus Weiner.

Bernard Lewis (2002). *Race and Slavery in the Middle East.* Oxford University Press, Oxford.

Joseph C. Miller (1975). "Nzinga of Matamba in a New Perspective," *Journal of African History*, 16 Edition.

Marlow, A. and Loveday, B. (eds.) (2000). *After Macpherson Policing After the Stephen Lawrence Inquiry.* London: Russell House Publishing.

May, S. (ed.) (1999). *Critical Multiculturalism, Rethinking Multicultural and Antiracist Education.* London: Falmer Press.

McCarthy, C. and Crichlow, W. (1993). *Race, Identity, and Representation in Education.* New York: Routledge.

Joseph Miller (1988). *West Central Africa. The Way of Death.* University of Wisconsin.

Richard Benjamin Moore (1960). *The Name "Negro," Its Origin, and Evil Use*. Baltimore: Black Classic Press.

Kenneth Morgan (2007). *Slavery and the British Empire*. Oxford.

George P. Murdock (1959). *Africa: Its Peoples and Their Culture*. New York.

R. Miles (1993). *Racism After Race Relation*. London: Routledge.

Gottfried Nebe (2002). *Creation in Paul's Theology*, in Hoffman, Yair, Reventlow, Henning Graf. (ed.) *Creation in Jewish and Christian Tradition*. Sheffield Academic Press

M. D. D. Newitt (2010). *The Portuguese in West Africa 1415–1670: A Documentary*. Cambridge: Cambridge University Press.

Roland Oliver and Anthony Atmore (1975). *Medieval Africa 1250–1800*. Cambridge: Cambridge University Press.

L. Outlaw (1998). *Multiculturalism, Citizenship, Education and American Liberal Democracy*, in Willett, C. (ed.) *Theorizing Multiculturalism: A Guide to Current Debate*. Oxford: Blackwell

B. Parekh (1998). *Cultural Diversity and Liberal Democracy*, in G. Mahajan (ed.) *Democracy, Difference and Social Justice*. Delhi: Oxford; OUP.

Matthew Parker (2011). *The Sugar Barons. Family, Corruption, Empire and War*. London: Hutchinson.

The Plowden Report (1967). *Children and Their Primary Schools*. HMSO 1967. London

George Rawlinson (1928). *The History of Herodotus*. Tudor, New York

Andrew Roberts (2000). *Victorian Titan*. London: Phoenix Press.

Don Robotham (1981). *The Notorious Riot. The Socio-Economic and Political Bases of Paul Bogle's Revolt*. Institute of Social and Economic Research: University of the West Indies, Jamaica.

Rich, P. (1994). *Prospero's Return*. London: Hansib.

Bertrand Russell (1912). *The Problems of Philosophy*. Oxford University Press, Oxford.

Ronald Segal (1995). *The Black Diaspora*. London: Faber and Faber.

Peter Lewis Shinnie (1978). *"Christian Nubia" The Cambridge History of Africa: Volume 2, c.500 B.C.–A.D. 1050.* edited by J. D. Fage. Cambridge: Cambridge University Press.

Hugh Thomas (2003). *Rivers of Gold: The Rise of the Spanish Empire*. London: Penguin Books.

Alan Villiers (1956). *Pioneers of the Seven Seas*. London: Routledge and Paul.

James Walvin (1984). *Passage to Britain*. Middlesex: Penguin Books Ltd.

Toby Wilkinson (2001). *Early Dynastic Egypt*. London: Routledge.

Eric Williams (1943). *Capitalism and Slavery*. Chapel Hill: The University of North Carolina Press

Chancellor James Williams (1974). *The Destruction of Black Civilization, Great Issues of a Race From 4500 BC to 2000 A.D*. Chicago, Illinois: Third World Press.

https://en.wikipedia.org/wiki/Kimberle_Williams_Crenshaw